The International
Book of
Family
Therapy

CONTRIBUTING JOURNALS*

American Journal of Family
  Therapy (U.S.A.)
Australian Journal of Family
  Therapy (Australia)
Cahiers Critiques de Thérapie
  Familiale et de Pratiques de
  Reseaux (Belgium)
Family Relations (U.S.A.)
Fokus pä Familien (Norway)
International Journal of Family
  Psychiatry (England)

Journal of Marital and Family
  Therapy (U.S.A.)
Journal of Sex and Marital
  Therapy (U.S.A.)
Marriage and Family Review
  (U.S.A.)
Psychotherapeia (South Africa)
Terapia Familiar (Argentina)
Terapia Familiare (Italy)

---

*Some selections came from books rather than journals; others were written originally for this volume. These are acknowledged accordingly with each chapter.

The International Book of Family Therapy

Edited by

Florence W. Kaslow, Ph.D.

BRUNNER/MAZEL *Publishers* • New York

Library of Congress Cataloging in Publication Data
Main entry under title:

The International book of family therapy.

 Includes bibliographies and index.
 1. Family psychotherapy—Addresses, essays,
lectures. 2. Psychiatry, Transcultural—Addresses,
essays, lectures. I. Kaslow, Florence Whiteman.
RC488.5.I53   1982   616.89′156   82-45472
ISBN 0-87630-316-5

Copyright © 1982 by Florence W. Kaslow

Published by
BRUNNER/MAZEL, INC.
19 Union Square West
New York, New York 10003

To my own parents, Rose and Irving Whiteman, my husband, Sol, and our children—Nadine Joy and Howard Ian—my thanks and love for making family life interesting, rich, lively and fulfilling—most of the time—and for teaching me most of what I know about families.

Foreword

Florence Kaslow's foresight and hard work have produced a multi-faceted, thought-provoking book, based on the recommendation she made to the first international conference of editors of marital and family journals and newsletters. The purpose was to make available to an international readership the best from marriage and family professional journals throughout the world. The articles were selected by the various editors from their own journals, with the addition of a few invited papers to round out those areas not sufficiently covered by the individual selections. Dr. Kaslow has successfully edited and written a commentary of each article, placing it in perspective within the field. This is a unique effort in the family therapy field, which is known for its openness of communication and willingness to have its work observed directly by peers.

The international mental health profession has had an increasing flow of information and international meetings over the past 50 years. Various aspects of exchange and rich cross-fertilization have existed—first in psychoanalysis, child development and treatment, more recently in group therapy, and now, in the past several years, in marital and family therapy. Rapid transportation, the flood of publications, copy machines, and personal communications have instantly spread the number and quality of contributions to the practice, theory and research (in that order) to an international group of colleagues.

The articles reproduced here reflect a common technical language allowing for an exchange of ideas with an ease of understanding that permits each contributor to reflect the cultural differences and problems encountered in family work in his/her country, as well as among differing classes or ethnic groups. Similarities far outweigh differences, although differences are understood and respected, not ignored.

Our armamentarium of theory and practice is used to help people. It is interesting to reflect on how a "supremacy" of weaponry in the practice and conceptualization of family therapy developed in the United States, after having been fed first by Austrian psychodynamics and English object relations theory and marital interaction (Fairbairn, Dicks). This was followed by Canadian transcultural studies, added to by contributions from other countries around the world—Japan, Israel, Kenya, Greece and many others. Studies on the progressive changes from extended families to nuclear families (and now to remarried families) may well follow "universal natural laws," as pointed out by Landau-Stanton, Griffiths and Mason in their article in this book. Internationally, the family remains the major social institution for coupling, procreation and nurturing of the young.

Now, for the moment at least, the new powerful development in therapeutic weaponry has arisen in Italy, where Mara Selvini Palazzoli and her colleagues have developed methods of intervention that appear to be helpful in the most difficult cases. In a field freed of nationalistic chauvinism, the contribution has been welcomed, studied and tested simultaneously in several countries within a few years after the Milan group began to publish. This is an astonishing phenomenon that speaks of a true international pride. Even within one country, as in the United States, the originators of different therapeutic techniques, each supported by its own theory, talk with each other, appear on the same programs, and belong to the same organizations. This spirit has now been broadened to the international scene, where nationalism is put aside for open exchange to help the entire family of man.

But we still have much further to go. Primarily we are healers and helpers. Our colleagues in socialist and third-world countries are not yet participating in the consortium of family therapists. Family life is strong in these countries too, as is each country's culture and family style. It is important to reach out to our colleagues in these countries. Many of them have advanced medical and psychiatric care delivery systems and deal with problems similar to our own; some have problems that differ markedly and delivery systems are not so well developed. We have much to learn, as well as to offer, in such exchanges.

These remarks do not lessen the significance of this first volume but indicate that we still have much room for further growth. Perhaps, through our interest in the family and its component individuals, we can, in collegial exchange, and through the sharing of our knowledge and the use of our "weaponry" for mental health purposes, contribute to lessening the alienation produced by the manipulation of patriotism by national leaders—a patriotism that is endangering the continued existence of the family of man.

Clifford J. Sager, M.D.

Preface

Dateline—July 1979, Tel Aviv, Israel. Attending my first international family therapy conference in Israel left an indelible impression. How exhilarating and stimulating to meet with therapists from many lands and to exchange ideas on the theory and practice of family therapy; to become more keenly aware of the culturally specific kinds of problems, as well as of the universal desires and manifestations of well-being and dysfunction; and to hear about the developments of this relatively new field in such countries as Norway, Sweden, and South Africa. What a privilege it was to deliver one of the keynote addresses on "Profile of the Healthy Family" and to hear assent and see nods of agreement as the profile apparently had multi-cultural dimensions. How strange to be asked what the profile of a healthy family would look like in a family with several wives; how challenging to begin to think about this. A highlight for many who attended was the evening panel on Family Therapy Around the World with presentations from people representing such countries as England, Germany, Australia, Italy, Norway, Sweden, South Africa, and Israel. Representing the United States was both overwhelming and thrilling for me. We all departed with a very special glow.

Dateline—July 1979, On an airplane from Israel to Austria. Thinking back over this monumental experience, it seemed important to try to stimulate an international conference hosted in the United States. If small countries like Israel and Italy could successfully run such spectacular events, certainly we could. Quickly I sent a letter to Ray Fowler, then Executive Director of AAMFT, and Don Williamson, then President of AAMFT, recommending such a Congress under AAMFT auspices.

ix

Dateline—October 1980, Toronto. AAMFT ran its first international conference. Response was excellent, with people coming from near and far. In conjunction with the conference, and in my capacity as editor of the *Journal of Marital and Family Therapy*, I called the first International Editors Meeting of editors of all of the journals in the field. Countries without journals but with newsletters also sent representatives and the meeting was extremely well attended. It was a special treat for each of us to become acquainted with those with whom we had been corresponding, whose works we had read, and who shared similar editorial problems.

Out of the discussion came the idea of more sharing and reciprocity and the idea of a book of contributions selected by the various journals in whatever way each deemed advisable. My editor colleagues asked if I would undertake the project and I was intrigued with the challenge. I was already collaborating with Maurizio Andolfi, Editor of *Terapia Familiare*, on simultaneously bringing out the summer 1981 issues of the journals he and I edited in English and Italian and all was proceeding smoothly, so this endeavor seemed worthwhile and feasible.

Dateline—November 1980, Miami. A call to Brunner/Mazel about the project to see if they would be interested in publishing it. A rapid affirmative response from Bernie Mazel meant that contracts went out to each of the potentially participating journal editors and we were under way. Most of the editors agreed to serve on an International Editorial Advisory Board and to review the manuscripts, which, although previously published, were all to go through the review process again to be certain they fit in an international collection.

Dateline—December 1980 through February 1982. Florida, New York and many countries. Manuscripts quickly began to arrive and be reviewed. Some had to be rejected; most had to be at least partially revised and updated. Several additional papers were requested to round out the collection. Our goal was to include manuscripts reflecting what is happening now in as many countries as possible—so that we cut across space and also placed developments in an historical context.

Some of the first papers to arrive were those by Hilde Bruch and Jay Haley. They represented people who were in the vanguard of the first generation of therapists concerned with family issues and treatment. Then came manuscripts from Hans Jørgen Holm, Ingerid S.

Ravnsborg and Israel Charny and others who seem to be part of the second generation of family therapists. Another batch from individuals like Maurizio Andolfi and Claudio Angelo marked inclusion of the third generation (see Chapter 1 on History of Family Therapy in the United States for time frames on the family therapy genogram), but here we seemed a little sparse, so I requested papers from some of the leading people in this age group, including Paul Dell and Karl Tomm. And then it seemed fitting to try to have at least one chapter representing the just emerging fourth generation. Since the person I know best in this group is my own daughter, and she is doing what from my biased position as her real family-of-origin mom is important work in the area of family therapy with depressed families, I invited her to contribute. With proper respect for her professional family mentors, she asked one of her supervisors, Stephen Pollack, and one of her colleagues, David Harvey, a postdoctoral fellow, to be her co-authors. Thus, for me this became a volume that incorporates many of the people who constitute my extended professional family as well as a significant member of my own personal family.

Because this was conceived primarily as a compilation of existing, albeit revised, articles which other journals had the opportunity to pre-select, it could not be organized as rationally at the beginning as it could have been starting afresh. Instead, the ordering and grouping of chapters came after the manuscripts arrived—with every attempt made to provide some logical flow and to highlight current controversies and key issues in this burgeoning, multifaceted field.

In order to enrich and enliven the collection with some totally new material, not only were a few original papers added, but it was also decided that a commentary on each chapter should be written to enhance the dialogue that might be stimulated in the reader's mind and to weave a thread of continuity, comparison and contrast. Major points have been underscored, divergent viewpoints have been highlighted, and similar trends in different countries have been elucidated.

Part I commences with History and Philosophy and sets the stage for what follows with the articulation of the major assumptions, underlying hypothesis, and epistemology from which clinical practice emanates. Part II then moves into the day-by-day theoretical underpinnings of process and technique—the substantive, scientific body of knowledge and artistry believed to facilitate the occurrence of change. In this section a panoply of models, paradigms, and metaphors for assessment and intervention are presented. Given that a major concern is how to treat in the most efficient and efficacious manner, the process and technique section has received the most emphasis. Part III looks at the larger institutional and societal context in which families exist and with which they come in contact as they pass through transition stages and crises such as relocations, injuries sustained at work, and mental illness. These reflect the growing concern of theoreticians and practitioners with the broader ecological and sociopolitical universe, the impact on the family, and the creative and judicious use of resources and assistance. Part IV shifts from the macro level of analysis and speculation to the micro level of the marital dyad, an important sybsystem of both the nuclear and the extended family. The four chapters in this section span a wide range of problems brought by couples who are experiencing distress to therapists; one sounds a shrill though tongue-in-cheek warning about the glibness of the charlatan as marital therapist. Part V on training contains only one chapter on this subject despite the centrality of training issues; fortunately, this article not only presents a useful technique, but also displays the openness and flexibility required for training family therapists. The final chapter briefly presents the editor's unscientific efforts at being a Crystal Ball Gazer—a look into the future of the field as it appears in 1982.

Dateline—February 1982, West Palm Beach, Florida. As the book is being readied to go to the publishers, in less than a year and a half from its conception, these reflections evoke much nostalgia and appreciation to all of those who have participated in bringing it to fruition. I'd like to thank all of the editors of journals that submitted papers for this volume, all of my colleague-friends who so generously gave of their time to serve on the editorial advisory board, each of the authors who wrote and rewrote papers striving for excellence, Bernie Mazel for his confidence in this undertaking even before he saw a proposed table of contents or one word in writing, and Susan Barrows for her patience, counsel, and encouragement.

Florence W. Kaslow, Ph.D.

Contents

Contributors

MAURIZIO ANDOLFI, M.D.
Director, Family Therapy Institute of Rome; President, Italian Society for Family Therapy, Rome, Italy.

CLAUDIO ANGELO, M.D.
Assistant, Mental Health Services of Bolzano; Teacher, Family Therapy Institute of Rome, Rome, Italy.

DANIEL L. ARAOZ, Ed.D.
Professor of Community Mental Health Counseling, C.W. Post Center of Long Island University, New York, U.S.A.

JORGE E. GARCÍA BADARACCO, M.D.
Associate Professor of Psychiatry, National University of Buenos Aires; Psychiatrist, Clinica Psiquiatrica, Buenos Aires, Argentina.

ARNON BENTOVIM, M.D.
Consultant Psychiatrist, Department of Psychological Medicine, The Hospital for Sick Children, and The Tavistock Clinic, London, England.

LUIGI BOSCOLO, M.D.
Co-director of Training, Centro per lo Studio della Famiglia, Milan, Italy.

HILDE BRUCH, M.D.
Professor Emeritus of Psychiatry, Baylor College of Medicine, Houston, Texas, U.S.A.

CHARLOTTE BURCK, M.S.W.
Social Worker, formerly of the Department of Psychological Medicine, The Hospital for Sick Children, London, England.

GIANFRANCO CECCHIN, M.D.
Co-director of Training, Centro per lo Studio della Famiglia, Milan, Italy.

ISRAEL W. CHARNY, Ph.D.
Associate Professor of Psychiatry, School of Social Work, Tel Aviv University, Tel Aviv, Israel.

RICHARD CHASIN, M.D.
Assistant Clinical Professor of Psychiatry, Boston University School of Medicine, and Harvard Medical School, Boston, Massachusetts, U.S.A.

THEO COMPERNOLLE, M.D.
Director, Child and Youth Psychiatric Outpatient Departments, Catholic University, Louvain, Belgium.

PAUL F. DELL, Ph.D.
Director of Clinical and Theoretical Studies, Colonial Institute, Newport News, Virginia, U.S.A.

MONY ELKAIM, M.D.
President, Institute for Family and Human Systems Studies, Brussels, Belgium.

JOHN GRIFFITHS, M.Sc.
Clinical Psychologist and Senior Lecturer, Department of Psychiatry, University of Zimbabwe, Salisbury, Zimbabwe.

HENRY GRUNEBAUM, M.D.
Director, Group and Family Psychotherapy Training, Department of Psychiatry, Cambridge Hospital, and Associate Clinical Professor of Psychiatry, Harvard Medical School, Boston, Massachusetts, U.S.A.

R. JULIAN HAFNER, M.D. (Lond.), M. Phil., F.R.A.N.Z.C.P.
Senior Lecturer in Psychiatry, Flinders Medical Centre, Bedford Park, South Australia.

JAY HALEY, M.A.
Director, Family Therapy Institute, Chevy Chase, Maryland, U.S.A.

DAVID M. HARVEY, Ph.D.
Associate Professor, Counseling Psychology Program, University of Texas, Austin, Texas, U.S.A.

HANS JØRGEN HOLM, M.D.
Psychiatrist and Clinical Director, Modum Bads Nervesanatorium, Vikersund, Norway.

FLORENCE W. KASLOW, Ph.D.
Director, Florida Couples and Family Institute; Private practice, West Palm Beach, Florida, U.S.A.

NADINE J. KASLOW, M.A.
Doctoral Candidate in Clinical Psychology, University of Houston, Houston, Texas, U.S.A.

WARREN KINSTON, M.D.
Honorary Senior Lecturer, Academic Department of Child Psychiatry, Institute of Child Health, London; Senior Research Fellow, Brunel Institute of Organisation and Social Studies, Brunel University, Uxbridge, Middlesex, England.

JUDITH LANDAU-STANTON, M.G., Ch.B., D.P.M.
Private practice, Philadelphia, U.S.A.; formerly Senior Lecturer, University of Durban-Westville, Durban, South Africa.

MOSHE LANG, M.A.
Director, Williams Road Family Therapy Centre, Windsor, Victoria, Australia.

PETER LOADER, M.D.
Research Fellow, The Department of Psychological Medicine, The Hospital for Sick Children, London, England.

JEAN MASON, M.Soc.Sc.
Senior Lecturer, Department of Social Work and Department of Mental Health and Medical School Work, University of Durban-Westville, Durban, South Africa.

MARY ELLEN OLIVERI, Ph.D.
Investigator, Center for Family Research; Assistant Research Professor, Department of Psychiatry and Behavioral Sciences, The George Washington University School of Medicine, Washington, D.C., U.S.A.

MARA SELVINI PALAZZOLI, M.D.
Research Director, Centro per lo Studio della Famiglia, Milan, Italy.

GIULIANA PRATA, M.D.
Member of the Research Team, Centro per lo Studio della Famiglia, Milan, Italy.

STEPHEN L. POLLACK, Ph.D.
Senior Faculty Member, Houston-Galveston Family Institute, Houston, Texas, U.S.A.

INGERID S. RAVNSBORG, M.D.
Clinical Director, Family Deparment, Modum Bads Nervesanatorium, Vikersund, Norway.

DAVID REISS, M.D.
Director, Center for Family Research; Professor, Department of Psychiatry and Behavioral Sciences, The George Washington University School of Medicine, Washington, D.C., U.S.A.

LILA RUSSELL, M.S.W.
Coordinator, Human Sexuality Clinic, Department of Psychiatry, Victoria Hospital, London, Ontario, Canada.

BRIAN STAGOLL, MB.BS., D.P.M., F.R.A.N.Z.C.P.
Psychiatrist, Williams Road Family Therapy Centre, Windsor, Victoria, Australia.
KARL TOMM, M.D., F.R.C.P. (C)
Associate Professor, Department of Psychiatry, and Director, Family Therapy Program, Faculty of Medicine, University of Calgary, Calgary, Alberta, Canada.
BRUCE J. TONGE, M.B.B.S., D.P.M., M.R.C.Psych., F.R.A.N.Z.C.P.
Director, Department of Child and Adolescent Psychiatry, Austin Hospital, Heidelberg, Victoria, Australia.
E.M. WARING, M.D., D.Psych., F.R.C.P.(C), F.A.B.P.N.
Associate Professor of Psychiatry, Assistant Dean, Continuing Medical Education, and Director of Psychiatric Education, University of Western Ontario; Consultant Psychiatrist, Victoria Hospital, London, Ontario, Canada.

The International
Book of
Family
Therapy

Part I

History and Philosophy

Chapter 1

History of Family Therapy in the United States: A Kaleidoscopic Overview

By Florence W. Kaslow

The field of family therapy has burgeoned during the past three decades. Its inception was spontaneous, happening almost simultaneously in several locales as small groups of researchers began to investigate family phenomena and a few clinicians tried to improve the effectiveness of their therapeutic endeavors. Its dramatic and unique qualities intrigued adventuresome therapists who came to watch the pioneers do family therapy. After a slow start in the 1950s, the rapidity of its growth since 1960 is obvious in the number of conference presentations, journals, workshops, and institutes which are devoted to this topic. This article attempts to encapsulate the history and essence of family therapy.

The history of family therapy is a saga of colorful personalities interacting in a vibrant and dynamic way, generating the sparks that would ignite the theoretical conceptualizations and therapeutic approaches of an emerging mental health speciality. Originally, some saw their practice as a radical departure from the one-to-one model of psychotherapy, but

This is a slightly revised version of an article originally published in *Marriage and Family Review,* Spring/Summer 1980, 3, (1/2), 77-111.

Florence W. Kaslow, Ph.D., is in private practice in West Palm Beach, Fla., and Director of the Florida Couples & Family Institute. She is former editor of the *Journal of Marital and Family Therapy* and serves on numerous editorial boards and as a consultant and workshop leader for various family therapy training programs.

still part of their original discipline. Whether family therapy is a separate specialization or an approach utilized within the traditional disciplines of psychiatry, clinical psychology, social work, and counseling and guidance is a current controversy. In 1978, the Department of Health, Education and Welfare recognized the American Association for Marriage and Family Therapy as the official accrediting agency for marital and family therapy training programs. In January 1981 there were five accredited agency-based training programs and seven accredited university-based graduate programs—many of which lead to specific degrees in marriage and/or family counseling or therapy (Journal of Marital and Family Therapy, January 1981, pp. 112-113).

How did this come about? Given the space restrictions, I will highlight rather than provide an in-depth study of this historic development. The review of the literature is selective rather than exhaustive because, in the slightly over three decades since the infant field made its debut and began to articulate itself in journals and books, the amount of published material has grown at an exponential rate, particularly during the 1970s and 1980s.

This article covers 1) the history of the field; 2) the family of family therapists; 3) the training of therapists; 4) the major schools of thought; 5) research; and 6) a glimpse at future developments. Who the practitioners of family therapy are and why they chose to become family therapists have been discussed sufficiently in the literature so as not to warrant further description here (Committee on the Family, 1970, pp. 536-539; Ferber, et al., 1972).

HISTORY

A Confluence of Forces

One of the first articles which chronicles psychiatric developments in family diagnosis and family therapy was written by two of the field's esteemed pioneers, Don D. Jackson and Virginia Satir (1961, pp. 31-37). They discuss numerous factors as being influential in contributing to the "development of family oriented rather than individually oriented psychological observation and treatment." Their ideas are elaborated upon and recast with additional details supplied by the current author.

Since the end of the 19th century, there has been a gradual movement of psychiatry away from a strictly medical specialty toward being closer to psychology, sociology, and anthropology. The trend has been toward a more psychosocial and less biological interpretation of data on the etiology of emotional illness. The family as a basic primary system became a unit for analysis and treatment.

Another family therapy root was the evolution of the child guidance movement. It began in 1909 with the creation of the juvenile court to treat delinquent children who were considered disturbed. Clinic staffs gradually realized that treating the child alone was insufficient since much of the pathology had to do with faulty child rearing and conflicted family relationships. Treatment initially included the mother, and subsequently the father, if he was willing and available. The usual model had the psychiatrist treating the child while a social worker saw the parent(s). Suggestions as to how to understand and manage the child were given without actually treating family pathology. This model was a forerunner of family treatment utilizing two different therapists.

It rapidly became apparent that if one were to include working parents in treatment, clinics would have to offer hours beyond the usual nine to five workday. The unwillingness of parents to take time off from work or take children out of school was all too often interpreted as "resistance" to therapy. Actually, this was sometimes good reality testing but such families were too quickly labeled "unreachable" or "untreatable." Unfortunately, this problem of inadequate service delivery on evenings and weekends still plagues many clinics and social agencies; yet offering family therapy necessitates flexibility in appointment scheduling. Being located in "dangerous" neighborhoods makes holding evening hours a problem.

A third historic force was and remains the psychoanalytic movement from which came pressure for family diagnoses. As early as 1921, Flugel wrote, "it is probable that the chief practical gain that may result from the study of the psychology of the family will ensue . . . from the mere increase in understanding the nature of, and interactions between, the mental processes that are involved in family relationships" (Flugel, 1921, p. 217).

Numerous concepts have been derived from the psychoanalysts, even though their primary concern has traditionally been the individual patient. For instance, in Freud's classic case of Little Hans (1909), he makes frequent reference to the boy's family and how their anxieties and admonitions affected their son. The Oedipal complex, "originally an intrapsychic construct" (Jackson & Satir, 1961, p. 38), has been increasingly recognized as an interpersonal and transactional phenomenon with fuller comprehension of the pregenital influence of parents. In addition, object relations theory and the concept of object constancy (Fairbairn,

1952) are interactive in nature and these have been incorporated by the psychoanalytically oriented wing of family therapy. Sullivan's material on the mothering person and significant others (1953) has been adapted as have other concepts on the interpersonal aspects of anxiety from Horney (1937), and the ego and its mechanism of defense from Anna Freud (1946). Much of Mahler's work on symbiosis and separation-individuation (1958; 1965) appears particularly pertinent to the work of Murray Bowen and his associates to be discussed later. Clearly then, the ego psychologists and neo-Freudians are also part of the family therapists' ancestry.

Conversely, it was disenchantment with the slow and often ineffective results of psychoanalysis and psychoanalytically oriented individual therapy that led some of the more adventuresome and less hidebound therapists to experiment with new approaches (Kaslow, 1973, p. 196). Their numbers included some classically trained child therapists who had become discouraged by the realization that two to five hours of analysis per week and protection from the parents, who had perhaps caused the malady, was not sufficient to offset the continuing impact of all the other hours their child patients spent under family influence. They found Sigmund Freud's basic stance that relatives of a patient should be excluded from the treatment relationship on the basis of confidentiality and potential interference with the transference and the therapeutic alliance an unnecessarily extreme position.

Some reasoned that a call from relatives could be perceived as positive concern, not as negative manipulation, and decided to invite family members to participate in therapy sessions. This approach, when various members and significant non-relatives are treated along with the patient, has been labeled "conjoint family therapy," a designation most often attributed to the early Palo Alto group. With the introduction and increased utilization of conjoint treatment, a shift occurred away from the analytic emphasis on unconscious, intrapsychic processes and the symptomatology of these hidden forces. The shift was to concern for communication and the interpersonal dynamics in the here and now, or to a conceptualization encompassing treatment of both intrapsychic and interpersonal difficulties.

No historical description would be complete without reference to the work in understanding and treating schizophrenia. Much attention was riveted on this syndrome during the 1930s and 1940s. Several seminal thinkers moved beyond the theory that it was purely an intrapsychic and/or biochemical disease. Sullivan (1953) pointed to the importance of focusing on real life experiences and the patient's present situation. He stressed that within the patient's delusional thought system reality elements are contained. The logical extension of Sullivan's ideas was greater therapist contact with the patient's experience within his family constellation. Similar ideas were articulated elegantly by Fromm-Reichmann (1959).

Numerous staff members of inpatient psychiatric facilities observed that on visiting day the relatives of schizophrenic patients also appeared troubled, dysfunctional, or disturbed. They realized that the previously garbled conversation of some of their charges seemed much more meaningful in the context of the family's mixed-up communication pattern. It was also observed that when many patients were discharged they seemed quite well, but that within 90 days of being released, having returned to live with their parents, they were brought back to the hospital exhibiting the same "crazy" thought and behavior patterns. This led some clinicians to postulate that there must be noxious factors in the family system that reactivated the illness. This was later substantiated in the work of Brown (1959). Interestingly, "if a married patient was able to return to his spouse and remain outside of the hospital over three months, he achieved a higher level of social adjustment than any of the other schizophrenics studied," particularly those who returned to their parents' homes (Jackson & Satir, 1961, p. 35).

Clearly, then, the accruing evidence indicated that to "treat" schizophrenics with the possibility of an effective outcome, one must be willing to deal with family factors and perhaps even see the family together as a unit. The intent was to gain a better diagnostic understanding of the communication network and context, interpersonal relationships, why one particular person became the identified patient, and intervention strategies to improve the functioning of the entire group. The need to include relations as part of the therapeutic process and to solicit their assistance became acceptable.

The work of the communication theorists and social scientists had also begun to be published (Ruesch & Bateson 1951; Parsons, 1951) at the time psychiatrists such as Sullivan and Fromm-Reichman were processing their ideas on family communication patterns. Some cross-pollination occurred. One of Parson's most provocative contributions to the structural-functional analysis of the social system is his description of five pattern variables (or dichotomies) that represent the predisposition of any specific social system toward certain basic choices. In brief, these pattern variables are:

1. affectivity vs. affective neutrality
2. specificity vs. diffuseness
3. universalism vs. particularism
4. quality vs. performance
5. self-orientation vs. collectivity orientation

Parsons utilized these pattern variables in his theory of socialization and his analysis of interpersonal relations within the family social system. Increasingly, catalyzed by Parsons' seminal thinking and the endeavors of the Palo Alto group,[1] therapists began to view the family unit in terms of such social systems concepts as structure and function, closed versus open, and permeable versus impermeable boundaries.

I have found few references in the literature to family service agencies, yet my own clinical experience with several during the early 1950s attests that families were already being seen conjointly at some of the more progressive clinics. There were mergers of family and children's agencies as practitioners recognized that if the goal of such federal programs as Aid to Dependent Children was to keep families together, offering services in separate agencies was likely to further fragment rather than to unify.

Since family service agencies were mostly staffed by social workers grounded in the tradition of Mary Richmond (1917), they saw the efficacy of home visits as a way of acquiring a fuller picture of the family in its own environment. Through such visits, they conveyed a real concern and willingness to do some reaching out to troubled, multi-problem families often deemed inaccessible by therapists who insisted they could only treat those who came voluntarily to their offices.

Thus, in the early 1950s an important confluence of forces occurred. Those working in child guidance clinics with juvenile delinquents had realized that to make any long-lasting progress, the child's parents also had to be involved in order to create a more nurturing emotional climate for the child. A similar realization evolved in the thinking of psychiatrists in inpatient settings when they saw schizophrenic patients in the company of their often strange families. Family service agency staff members noted and recounted that the way spouses and parents described how they related to each other and to their children was quite different than what the therapist actually observed.

Some therapists trained to do individual psychotherapy were discouraged with the slowness of their method and often frustrated by having their strides sabotaged by other family members who did not like the changes that were occurring due to the therapy. The ideas

coming from the communication and systems theorists provided the foundation for reconceptualizing psychopathology in terms of understanding the family unit, the interactional nature of dysfunction, and the idea of the identified patient as the symptom-bearer for the entire family. These were provocative and disquieting ideas and became the springboard for the emergence of family therapy.

THE FAMILY OF FAMILY THERAPISTS—A GENEALOGY

The date usually given as the beginning of family therapy is 1950. That is the year Ackerman and Sobel's "Family Diagnosis: An Approach to the Pre-School Child" appeared in the *American Journal of Orthopsychiatry*. Their insistence that understanding of family processes is critical to understanding the child was antithetical to the typical child guidance approach. Ruesch and Bateson were nearing completion of their seminal *Communication, The Social Matrix of Psychiatry* (1951) which was to infuse the therapeutic professions with a new language, that of senders and receivers of messages, feedback loops, and communication networks. Thus, the efforts of Ackerman and his co-workers on the east coast in New York and Bateson and his colleagues on the west coast in California were all part of a quest for a fuller understanding of intimate interpersonal relationships, the communication patterns through which thoughts and feelings are conveyed, and the means by which these elements converge to cause personality disturbances and psychopathology.

In Guerin's informative chapter, *Family Therapy: The First Twenty-Five Years* (1976, pp. 2-22), he chronicles the history of the field mainly by observing who was working together in various geographic locales. He indicates that most of the data he presents is someone's particular version of factual events, and should not be construed to represent the absolute truth. My own investigative work on the pioneers of family therapy substantiates his rendition (Kaslow, 1977, pp. 204-208). Some of the first generation are alive and well, and gladly retell tales about the heady days that marked the field's inception. Given that the majority of them are strong-willed, innovative, charismatic, and brilliant, each elaborates his own role as central—several even alluding to themselves as the real father of family therapy analogous to Freud's pivotal position as the father of psychoanalysis. This hearty breed, who bucked the therapeutic establishment, were not renowned for their modesty.

Here the history will be sketched by utilizing the treasured ideal of the "family of family therapists," which is now spawning the fourth generation of practitioners, as the vehicle. The periods subdivide roughly from 1950 to 1960; 1960 to 1970; 1970 to 1980; and 1980 to the present. Since 1980, practitioners from all three generations are active. Some recent graduates of family institute, university, medical school and agency-based training and education programs are now only in their late twenties and those in the grandparent generation are in their sixties, seventies and nearing eighty.

After making a laborious effort to employ a genogram format—an extensive family tree (Guerin & Fogarty, 1972, pp. 445-467)—I had to abandon it as too cumbersome. This favorite tool for helping family therapy trainees and patients explore their families of origin seemed uniquely suitable for depicting the genealogy of the field. This professional family, like most healthy families that thrive on an infusion of new blood and controversy, has grown too large. Also, in typical American style, it is a highly mobile family and it is not feasible to show the relocations, unions and mergers. Nor is it possible to include everyone who has made a significant contribution, and so the following criteria for selection were devised; that the person:

1. is often referred to in the literature;
2. has published books and/or articles on family therapy topics;
3. is a frequent presenter at professional conferences as a keynote speaker, workshop leader and guest lecturer;
4. is a member of one or more editorial boards of journals devoted to marital and family therapy.

The key people in the first generation are easiest to identify since the early books in the field were, for the most part, edited collections to which they asked one another to contribute (see for example Ackerman, Beatman and Sherman, 1961; Boszormenyi-Nagy and Framo, 1965). Guerin's (1976) history of the early period is adequate. Therefore, I will summarize his material briefly, elaborate new points, and concentrate most on the activities of the 1970s and early 1980s.

In the early 1950s, Bateson, Jackson, Weakland, and Haley joined together in California to do research on the families of schizophrenics. They were interested in communication patterns and introduced anthropological methods and social systems theory to their work. Jackson founded the Mental Research Institute in 1959, and Haley joined him in 1962 when the Bateson project folded.

Satir, a social worker, came to Mental Research Institute in 1959 and quickly moved into the center of the family therapy movement. In 1964 she popularized their brand of family therapy in her easy-to-read book,

Conjoint Family Therapy. Many therapists were magnetized by her vitality, charisma, and creative therapeutic methodology, which included family sculpting. Some clinicians decided to become family therapists because here was an approach that was engaging, exciting, practical, efficient, and rewarding. To this group is attributed the founding of one wing, the communications school of family therapy.

One of the ideas formulated from their research was the concept of the double bind. Their original paper, *Toward a Theory of Schizophrenia* (1956), is a classic and was the focal point of a recent (1977) conference entitled *Beyond the Double Bind*. The 1977 conference reevaluated the earlier work and all major subsequent contributions to double bind theory (Berger, 1978). B. Ackerman (1979, pp. 29-38), in a critique of the conference deliberations, elucidates the theory of logical types which forms the cornerstone of the double bind hypothesis. He clarifies the distinction between single sentence double binds and those which evolve from continuous interaction. Ackerman redefines metacommunication consistent with logical type theory. He shifts the focus of meta-level communication, "from the messages of the sender to the arena of the communicant's interaction" (1979, p. 29). In brief, the double bind situation in which those who develop schizophrenia have often been placed contains the following necessary ingredients: 1) two or more persons; 2) contradictory messages such as "I insist you make your own decisions" as a repeated happening in the experience of the victim; 3) a primary negative injunction such as "do not do so, or I will punish you" or "if you do not do so, I will punish you"; 4) a secondary injunction conflicting with the first at a more abstract level, and like the first, enforced by punishments or signals which threaten survival. This injunction is usually communicated non-verbally through gesture, posture or facial expression and its implications are concealed in the verbal message; and 5) a tertiary negative injunction forbidding the victim (recipient of the message) from escaping the field. For example, the mother who envelops her son in an all-consuming relationship communicates "you cannot go away to college because I will not be able to survive if you leave." This entire set of ingredients is no longer necessary when the victim has learned to perceive his world in double bind patterns; any part of the sequence is sufficient to trigger rage or panic (Bateson et al., 1956).

Bateson divided the credit for the concept of the double bind (1972) between Haley and himself. He credited Haley with recognizing that the symptoms of schizophrenia suggest an inability to discriminate the logical types. He credited himself with determining that etiology and symptoms could be formally described in terms of continuously receiving confusing, contradictory messages: the double bind hypothesis.

Jackson meanwhile was developing his ideas on family homeostasis based on the premise that the family system seeks to maintain its equilibrium and is resistant to change (1959). Because of this patterned and entrenched behavior, the therapist must comprehend the complex family dynamics and penetrate the family system if desired change is to occur. Jackson was undisputedly one of the leaders of family therapy as his numerous writings on family homeostasis and conjoint therapy (1959; 1961a; 1961b) attest. Along with Nathan Ackerman, he co-founded the field's first journal, *Family Process*, in 1962. His colleague, Jay Haley, was the first editor.

Haley departed from Palo Alto for the Philadelphia Child Guidance Clinic in the early 1960s. Jackson's death in 1969 caused much grief to the extended family network and left the staff at Mental Research Institute depleted. From the original group, Weakland is still active. Other notables at Mental Research Institute are Fisch, Watzlawick, and Bodin (1972) and current director, Carlos Sluzki.

Satir left MRI in the mid 1960s to become the first Director of Esalen. She later became reengaged in family therapy and has continued to write and hold workshops on this topic throughout the 1970s and into the 1980s (1972; 1975). She has been influential in the careers of some of her former trainees; most notably, Luthman and Kirschenbaum (1974), now at the Marin County Family Institute, and Grinder and Bandler, whose *Structure of Magic I and II* (1975; 1976) appeal to those who like to use graphic representations to explain communications and transactions.

Another branch of the family therapy movement developed at the Menninger Clinic in Topeka. From 1949 to 1954 Murray Bowen participated in a five-year study in which various schizophrenic patients and family members were treated. Once family members were included, the relationship system assumed new prominence, and attention became riveted on the symbiotic mother/child attachment. The clinicians were fascinated by the cyclical nature of the symbiotic relationship in which each pair of mothers and patients could at times be so close that they were emotional Siamese twins, or, at other times, so distant and hostile they repelled each other (Bowen, 1965, p. 214). These data on symbiotic entwinement were gradually incorporated into formulations on the etiology of schizophrenia.

Bowen left Topeka to continue his studies in Bethesda, Maryland under NIMH auspices from 1954 to 1959. Bowen believes (1965; p. 215) that the most important steps in the development of family theory were made during this family research study when schizophrenic patients and their families lived in residence on a psychiatric ward. Initially, observation focused on the mother-child relationship exclusively. It soon became evident that the entire family played a part in the illness (Bowen et al., 1959). A study of 250 outpatient families, some judged normal and others neurotic, revealed similar family dynamics.

Bowen continues to be a leading family therapy theorist and practitioner. He has formulated such concepts as "emotional oneness" or fusion of family members, and the idea of an "undifferentiated family ego mass" (1965, p. 219) from which all members have tremendous difficulty individuating. In fact, the schizophrenic is one who can never adequately tear himself away. Another of Bowen's salient contributions was on the "family projection process in schizophrenia" (1965, pp. 223-224). This is the major mechanism by which a parental problem is transmitted to the child. In some way the child serves as a stabilizer for the marriage when it becomes a triangulated relationship. The unstable mother-father dyad becomes dependent on the child, who must become enmeshed in order to maintain the family equilibrium. Thus, for Bowen, treatment involves helping family members differentiate from the family ego mass (1965, p. 237).

Bowen's own journey to revisit members of his family of origin (1971) has been emulated by many other family therapists. From this is derived the concept of the visit home as part of understanding one's history and patterns in the multigenerational family, and reworking unfinished business from the past. The idea of the genogram is also derived from this creative man's work. The evolution and progression of his work is presented in his latest book, *Family Therapy in Clinical Practice* (1978).

Bowen has taught for many years at Georgetown University School of Medicine where he heads the Family Center and conducts an annual Georgetown Family Conference. One of his best known disciples is Philip Guerin, who is now at the Center for Family Learning in New Rochelle, New York.

When Bowen left NIMH, he was replaced by Lyman Wynne, another psychiatrist with a deep interest in schizophrenia. Among conceptual contributions which Wynne has made are his ideas on pseudo-mutuality, that is, the false appearance of family harmony and reciprocity (Wynne, et al., 1958). The "rubber fence" is another Wynne notion. A family may seem to be flexible and to condone individuation, but really maintains an impermeable fence, a boundary that extends only so far and then bounces back before anyone can truly depart from the tight-knit system. Wynne remained at NIMH until the early 1970s when he moved to New

York to assume the chair of the Department of Psychiatry at the University of Rochester. He and several colleagues recently published a new book on schizophrenia (Wynne et al., 1978).

In the 1950s another family therapy stream began in Atlanta. Whitaker, Warkentin, and Malone, who were treating psychiatric inpatients, started experimenting with seeing patients with their families and also with doing co-therapy (1956) as a way to increase therapeutic comprehension and impact. In the 1960s Whitaker left the south for a professorship in psychiatry at the University of Wisconsin. Whitaker's work is an interesting blend of warm responsiveness, candid questioning, tuning in to one's own and the patient's "craziness" with a sense of fun as well as pathos, and a framing of pertinent paradoxes. He entitles it "Psychotherapy of the Absurd" (1975); I think of it as "experiential family therapy." A well-known second-generation Whitaker protege, Augustus Napier, has recently left Wisconsin for Atlanta. Before departing, he co-authored *The Family Crucible* with Whitaker in 1978. In this touching book, one finds a sensitive amalgamation of many families into one. They are followed from the inception of therapy, through the tumultuous and unpredictable course of the treatment process, to termination. Gus and Carl, as the patients call them, emerge as an excellent co-therapy team, each of whom knows intuitively and intellectually when to play melody and when to play harmony, when to respond cognitively and when to interact emotionally. The therapy chapters are interspersed with theory which provides the reader with a solid foundation for understanding what is transpiring and why. This excellent book is evidence that family therapy as a field now has a much better sense of its identity and direction.

Another significant early contributor to family therapy was Nathan Ackerman, a psychoanalyst and child psychiatrist whose interest in the family unit was expressed as early as 1938 in "The Unity of the Family." He was then on the staff of the children's unit of the Menninger Clinic. Ackerman later worked at Jewish Family Service in New York and taught at Columbia University. He was respected for his compassion, wisdom, intuitiveness, and his understanding of the ambiguity which colors intimate relationships. He credited the child guidance movement with providing the "real" beginning of family theory and therapy (Guerin, 1976, p. 4).

In 1965 Ackerman established the Family Institute of New York as a place to treat families and to train clinicians in family therapy. His work, predicated on psychoanalytic foundations, has been labeled psychoanalytic family therapy. It was concerned simultaneously with intrapsychic and interpersonal processes; the impact of the past on the present; and the complex web of relationships and feelings that characterize family units.

As indicated earlier, Ackerman and Jackson joined in 1962 to found *Family Process*. Jackson's choice for first editor, Jay Haley, served for eight years. As legend has it, Ackerman chose Haley's successor, Donald Bloch, who served as editor from 1970-1982. He has been succeeded by Carlos Sluzki, current Director of the Mental Research Institute in Palo Alto, which Jackson founded, probably in accordance with the original blueprint for the Journal's editorship as well as in recognition of Sluzki's stature and skills. Bloch also replaced Ackerman as Director of the New York Family Institute, renamed the Ackerman Institute after the death of its founder in 1971. Under Bloch's leadership the Institute has become a major training center which provides internships and externships and sends faculty members to lead workshops throughout the world.

Israel Zwerling, a psychiatrist greatly influenced by Ackerman, and Marilyn Mendelsohn, who had been analyzed by Jackson, organized the Family Studies Section at Albert Einstein College of Medicine and Bronx State Hospital. Andrew Ferber was named Director of the section in 1964. Guerin left Washington and Bowen to join the Bronx State unit and became director of training in 1970. For a few years this core group, joined by Chris Beels, Betty Carter, Monica Orfanidis, Peggy Papp, and Tom Fogarty, ran a strong extramural training program in addition to making a major contribution to the psychiatry residency training program (Guerin, 1976, pp. 13-14).

Philadelphia has been another hub of family therapy activity. As chairman of Temple University's Department of Psychiatry in the 1950s, O. Spurgeon English encouraged the work of John Rosen in direct analysis and the work of Al Scheflen in communications and the structure of family therapy. In 1960, when the Eastern Pennsylvania Psychiatric Institute (EPPI) was flourishing, Scheflen joined Ray Birdwhistle who was analyzing body language. By then, Boszormenyi-Nagy had organized a research project on schizophrenic families at EPPI (1958). His staff included Jim Framo, one of the few psychologists in the early family therapy leadership; David Rubinstein, a psychiatrist who has remained at the Temple unit at EPPI and conducts a separate family therapy training program; Gerald Zuk, a psychologist and theoretician (1971); and Geraldine Spark (MSW).[2] Boszormenyi-Nagy and Spark were co-directors of the unit for many years, worked as a co-therapy team, and co-authored the provocative book *Invisible Loyalties* (1973). They focus on intergenerational ledgers of balances and entitlements, and stress that there are strong, although often hidden, loyalties and obligations to one's biological relatives.

Ross Speck, who did his residency training at EPPI, along with Carolyn Attneave, later forged the way for network family therapy (Speck & Attneave, 1972, pp. 637-665). This is an approach utilized most often with schizophrenogenic families where everyone connected to or concerned with them, including friends and neighbors, is brought together in the convener's home. The therapeutic processes of networks are usually conducted in three 4-hour sessions by a minimum of three therapists who enlist the aid of everyone present on behalf of the identified patient and those who are more involved in and affected by his or her illness. It is reminiscent of an extended family coming together as a self-supporting mutual aid society. Speck and his colleagues, today including his wife Joan, and Uri Rueveni (1979), utilize tribal rituals to heighten the group's esprit de corps, sense of optimism, and willingness to participate responsibly, contributing to the family's fight for health.

Another group came together at Philadelphia Psychiatric Center; it included Al Friedman, Jack Friedman, John Sonne, Geraldine Lincoln, and Oscar Weiner (Kaslow, 1977, p. 205). Their clinical concerns included the schizophrenic family, the place of home visits in treatment, co-therapy (Sonne & Lincoln, 1966), treatment of families with disturbed adolescents (Friedman et al., 1971) and with an addict member.

In 1964 those at EPPI and PPC banded together to form the Family Institute of Philadelphia. It now has about 150 members and runs a four-year non-degree evening training institute for clinicians skilled in other disciplines who wish to become family therapists. At the end of the course work and supervised clinical practice, graduates receive a certificate.

Introducing a different orientation and much controversy to the Philadelphia scene was Salvador Minuchin, who came to the Philadelphia Child Guidance Clinic in the late 1960s from Wiltwyck School in New York (Minuchin et al., 1967) bringing with him Braulio Montalvo and Bernice Rosman. They were joined by Jay Haley and together transformed the clinic from a traditional child guidance clinic to a world-renowned family therapy training and treatment center. Their approach is called "structural"; it focuses on here-and-now transactions with little concern for causes of dysfunction or family history. Generational boundaries are clearly delineated and families are taught not to cross these inappropriately. The therapist, who plays a strong and directive role, stresses that parents should not abdicate their key role as the executives in the family and children should not be parentified (Haley & Hoffman,

1967). The structure of the family is central and restructuring is undertaken when necessary as a strategic intervention. Tasks may be assigned to help family members assume their functional and age-appropriate roles better. Often behavior therapy strategies are incorporated. The methods used by this group in treating "Psychosomatic Families" (Minuchin et al., 1978), particularly with an anorectic, asthmatic, or diabetic young member, are being used increasingly in therapy throughout the country.

The structural approach, like the Bowen approach, can be classified under the rubric of the systems school of family therapy. These two major wings share an emphasis on the family unit as patient, and share concern for the systems' properties of the family as these contribute to each member's functioning, self-image, and the interaction of the group. They differ on other important facets, notably Bowen's emphasis on the family of origin and one's personal history as it affects current behavior and relationships, and therefore the importance of the intergenerational heritage and reworking unfinished business from the past in order to improve the present. This contrasts with the structuralists' concern with the presenting family's current symptoms and dilemmas as they are expressed to the therapist in the present, and therefore the importance of intervening to restructure the current family to rapidly improve its functioning and reduce the dysfunctional or symptomatic behavior of the identified patient.

The Minuchin group, who had written *Families of the Slums* based on their experiences with delinquent boys at Wiltwyck School (1967), has had a major commitment to treating the inner city poor and has trained indigenous workers as well as professionals to serve this population. At the Child Guidance Clinic they have an excellent new facility with outstanding audio-visual capability that they utilize in treatment and training activities.

In 1973, Israel Zwerling left Bronx State-Einstein to become chairperson of the Department of Mental Health Sciences at Hahnemann Medical College and Hospital in Philadelphia. Already on the faculty teaching family therapy when he arrived were several well-trained and respected family therapists including Jean Barr, Ilda Fisher, Pirooz Sholevar, John Sonne and the current author. Determined to make Hahnemann a major training center in family therapy, Zwerling asked Boszormenyi-Nagy to become the (part-time) chief of the family therapy section. In 1976, a two-year masters in family therapy program was begun under the directorship of Robert Garfield and it was the first such degree-granting program to be funded by NIMH. Since the inclusion of family therapy in many of the department's other teaching programs—psychology, creative arts therapy, mental health technology, and residency training—is an atypical development in a medical school, it is worthy of mention. Family therapy has also become an integral part of the treatment services offered at the Hahnemann Community Mental Health Center, another somewhat unusual occurrence attributable to the chairperson's commitment and the faculty's involvement in training activities.

Several others who have made noteworthy contributions during the first two periods are John E. Bell, in such areas as family group therapy and incorporating concern for families of hospitalized patients (nonpsychiatric as well as psychiatric) into hospital structure and function, (1963; 1975); Fred and Bunny Duhl and David Kantor (Duhl, Kantor, & Duhl, 1973) at the Boston Family Institute (particularly in family sculpture and other spatial techniques of treatment); Norman Paul, in cross-confrontation approaches, grief and mourning as well as the use of EST in conjunction with family therapy; and Edgar Auerswald in ecosystems.[3]

REFLECTIONS

From 1950 to 1954 much work in family therapy took place underground. The ideas of the leaders were considered heresy and no platform was readily available to them at major professional conferences. Their writings were not welcome in the standard journals. The family movement surfaced nationally at the 1957 meeting of the American Orthopsychiatric Association when John Spiegel chaired a panel on family research in schizophrenia. Bowen and Theodore Lidz were two of the panelists. They were joined several months later on another panel, organized by O. Spurgeon English, by Ackerman and Jackson at the 1957 meeting of the American Psychiatric Association. A loose network of psychiatrists in family therapy emerged. Twenty years later, in 1977, the network was formalized with the organization of the American Family Therapy Association (AFTA) with Bowen as President and Spiegel as Vice President. AFTA held its first membership meeting, attended by 160 family therapists[4]—mostly psychiatrists by training—in April, 1979, in Chicago.

By contrast, the membership of AAMFT (begun as AAMC in 1942) is multidisciplinary and comprised of psychologists, social workers, family sociologists, pastoral counselors, as well as psychiatrists. It currently numbers over 8,000 members. It is too early to predict exactly the direction AFTA will take but reports of this meeting and of executive meetings indicate that the intention is for growth to take place slowly and for a main purpose to be the exchange of ideas regarding theory and technique at the level of a scientific society. The annual spring meeting is an in-gathering of the luminaries of the field. AAMFT plans to continue its manifold activities of 1) education through its annual national and regional conferences and its newsletter; 2) accrediting of nondegree- and degree-granting training and education programs;[5] 3) spearheading of licensing and certification efforts in states that do not yet have licensing or certification laws; 4) influencing national legislation on family policy and on reimbursement for marital and family therapy; and 5) sponsoring the *Journal of Marital and Family Therapy.*

The family of family therapists was almost exclusively a patriarchy in its first generation. Virtually all the leaders were male psychiatrists; the lone female who figured prominently on the national scene was Satir, a social worker. What did it mean to patients and to therapists that the doctors were male and the female therapists Miss or Mrs.? How much did this perpetuate chauvinism in the profession and serve to reinforce disequality in patient families? Apparently a great deal. One need only analyze the Tables of Contents of the edited collections of important books in family therapy in the 1950s and early 1960s to see that the male editors asked the male (doctor) therapists to be the contributors. A scanning of the lists of participants on panels at professional conferences will yield similar findings. Yet, a so called co-therapy or co-teaching pair cannot model an egalitarian relationship for patients when a disequality in status is inherent. Although such a disequality does not always accompany differences in educational level or title attainment, it is clear from reading the literature and case studies that indeed the male therapist usually took the dominant role. He was more highly regarded as he was the "doctor and expert." This was not beneficial to female members of the families being treated who were trying to shed their subservient roles and who looked to female therapists for validation of their aspirations.

In the second generation, some women with doctorates have become family therapists. Among the best known are: Kitty LaPerriere, Director of Training at Ackerman Institute (LaPerriere, 1979); Rachel Hare-Mustin, particularly notable in advancing equality for women; Sandra Coleman in research and treatment of addict families (Coleman & Stanton, 1978); and the author in treating families where one member has a learning disability (1978), treating prisoners and their relatives (1978), using photographs in therapy (Kaslow and Friedman, 1977; Kaslow,

1979), supervision and training of family therapists (1977), and as editor of the *Journal of Marital and Family Therapy*.

Women therapists without an M.D. or a Ph.D. such as Peggy Papp, Lynn Hoffman, Monica Orfanidis, Olga Silverstein, Betty Carter, Geraldine Spark and Marianne Walters have all become well respected; yet, it was not unusual through the late 1970s to see major conference presentations by male panelists only, a sad commentary on the role and status of women in the family of family therapists.

Many wives of well-known therapists have been motivated to obtain graduate training to serve as co-therapists with their husbands. Such persons often become competent in their own right but, unfortunately, may still be viewed as spouse-assistants, with deleterious effects on their development and on their patients' quest for maximizing their own potential fully.

Co-therapy Teams

If we are to enter family systems in order to change them, the message implicit in a co-therapy team in which the male therapist is clearly the leader must be scrutinized. Conversely, it is important to understand the impact of a dominant female therapist who overshadows her male counterpart on a family in which the husband-father is very weak in exercising his parental role. Pairing of co-therapy teams requires artistry at a level much higher than mere assignment according to convenience and *the team must have as its main concern the needs of the family and not the competitive struggles or power needs of team members* (Russell & Russell, 1979, pp. 38-48).

When the families seen are large and chaotic with numerous serious problems, co-therapy may be advisable. The team should be well balanced, have respect for one another, and be presented as co-therapists only if they are co-equal. If one is a trainer and the other a trainee, this difference in levels of knowledge and experience should be communicated to the patients so they understand the reality base for the disequal components of the team relationship (Kaslow, 1977). Just as co-therapy serves as a model of parenting, of healthy communications, and of mutual appreciation, so too can it serve as a model for authentic and ethical sharing with patients of information about the therapists which is pertinent to their treatment (Kaslow, Cooper, & Linsenberg, 1979).

TRAINING AND EDUCATION IN FAMILY THERAPY

Originally, in the training of therapists, an apprentice model evolved. As those engaging in individual therapy began to hear about the trials and triumphs of the practitioners of conjoint therapy, they became curious and asked to observe them. Since several family members attended each session and since a co-therapist was apt to be present, strict confidentiality was not observed. Therapists explained to patients, particularly in teaching and training institutions, that colleagues and students were interested in observing their work and obtained permission for the sessions to be watched either through a one-way mirror or on videotape. The drama inherent in the process of family therapy itself and the flair and flamboyance of some of the therapists made viewing a worthwhile way to learn, and people flocked to view and study with the experienced pioneers.

The locus of training has shifted from the preceptor model of the 1950s to a broad-based education and training pattern which now includes didactic course content, research, clinical practicum, and various methods of individual and group supervision. Although originally most of the training occurred in service agencies and institutions, the preponderance of activity is now based in Family Institutes, in graduate departments of family studies, home economics, or marital and family therapy in universities, and more recently, at medical colleges.

As yet, no typical model of training has emerged. Whether one attends a post-graduate institute after earning a degree, enters a two-year masters in family counseling or therapy, or trains for a doctorate in this specialty, certain components are found in all programs. Teachers seek to inculcate a basic knowledge of individual and family dynamics; growth and development in the individual and family life cycle; healthy and dysfunctional family structure and functioning; different theories of marital and family therapy; human sexuality; techniques of intervention in marital, sex and family therapy; and legal issues of concern to clinicians and their patients. Skill is acquired through clinical practicums with all programs requiring a minimum of one year of supervised internship in treating couples and families. Most programs consider two years of clinical experience essential. Teaching and supervision may be done through didactic lectures, having students view the work of experienced practitioners through one-way mirrors or on videotape. Other teaching techniques include assigned readings which are discussed; case presentations by trainees using written records, audiotapes or video-tapes of their work; having trainees serve with the supervisor as part of a therapy team; and viewing students conducting therapy sessions while calling in instructions by phone or a bug-in-the-ear device or by actually entering the session and interviewing directly.

Although some programs require that trainees enter marital or family therapy (Guldner, 1978) most simply recommend it highly. Many also urge trainees to make a voyage home to reconsider their own relation-ships with members of their family of origin in order to finish incomplete episodes from the past and reconnect as an adult in the family. I believe this is a crucial ingredient in preparing novice family therapists to help patients in reworking their own family relationships. (For comprehen-sive discussions on training of marital and family therapits see Kaslow, 1977, pp. 119-234; *Journal of Marital and Family Therapy*, July, 1979; and Liddle & Halpin, 1978).

The practice of family therapy has become international in the 1970s and family institutes for treatment and training have begun in many countries including Argentina, Australia, England, Germany, Israel, It-aly, Mexico, and South Africa. Journals devoted to family therapy are being published in Spanish, Italian, German, Norwegian, and French.

Several international conferences have been held in Italy. At the one in 1978, the work of Mara Selvini Palazzoli and her colleagues from Milan on systemic hypotheses, paradoxes and ritualized prescriptions (Selvini Palazzoli et al., 1974; 1978), was featured. The Third Interna-tional Congress of Family Therapy was held in Israel in July 1979, and among those who presented were J. Howells from England, M. Andolfi from Italy, the Framos and the author from the United States, Judith Landau from South Africa, and I. Charny, A. Barcai, and S. Davidson from Israel. There continues to be a cross-fertilization across international lines as family therapists guest lecture, sponsor workshops, and attend conferences where they exchange ideas with and demonstrate their work to one another.

SCHOOLS OF THOUGHT

The various theoretical approaches which undergird treatment have already been mentioned in the history section of this paper. Thus, the following will be a brief summation expanding the scheme recently de-vised by Gurman (1979) and extending it from the dyad to the larger family system. The reader can fit the work of the different leaders discussed earlier in this paper into this taxonomy. Gurman categorizes the various schools according to three perspectives: 1) Psychoanalytic; 2) Systems, subdivided into two major approaches: Bowenite and Communications; and 3) Behavioral.

In terms of the "role of the past and the unconscious," the psychoanalytically oriented therapist considers it important to help members of the couple understand the conscious and unconscious reasons for choice of mate. The therapist pays attention to the unconscious dynamics within the relationship and is concerned about the history of the family and past conflicts in each spouse's family of origin as these are manifested in the family of creation. Systems theorists generally concur, with the exception that, although they verbally discount the importance of individual unconscious dynamics, they appear to assess them and respond to their diagnosis. Those of the communications school deem past conflicts and experience to be of only academic interest. The behaviorists diverge in believing that knowledge of unconscious reasons for choice of mate and of the history of the family is irrelevant to treatment. They are also not concerned with unconscious dynamics or past conflicts and experiences (Gurman, 1979, p. 8).

All consider the nature and meaning of presenting problems and the role of assessment in therapy important, with communication and behavioral therapists emphasizing that it is most critical during the first phase of treatment. For those of the analytic group, assessment reflects the idiosyncratic interests of the therapist. For systems practitioners, assessment also relies on the therapist's clinical judgment but centers on key themes in all families. Behaviorists follow a standardized procedure and utilize carefully tested and researched instruments. Among the other differences in assessment is that psychoanalytically oriented therapists believe that each member of the family as well as the relationships between them comprise elements of "the patient." Only the relationships are central to systems' clinicians, and behaviorists focus on the relationships and the skills deficits of family members.

From the twenty-one mediating goals in therapy that Gurman discusses in terms of comparative importance, a few have been selected here as illustrative. Therapists of all persuasions consider specification of problem(s) to be critical. The communications group stresses clarification of attempted solutions most, the Bowenites least, and analytic and behavioral clinicians consider this of moderate import. All see the following as salient: redefining or reframing the problems; recognition that each person contributes to the difficulties; clarification of each member's desires and needs in the family system; increased reciprocity, decreased coercion and blame; and recognition and modification of family communication patterns and rules. Only the analysts, however, rate the establishment of a therapeutic alliance and later the resolution of the patient-therapist transference as a high priority. For the others this is of low to moderate import. The communications group gives greatest emphasis to the inclusion of children and of the spouses' parents in therapy. The Bowenites are very concerned with multigenerational projections through triangulation but deal with the family of origin more through the patient's visit home than by bringing parents into therapy (Bowen, 1978). Other notable differences are that developing insight is important to the analysts, less so to Bowenites, and not significant for the communications and behavioral practitioners.

Gurman's similar comparison of twelve ultimate goals reveals that each school places great importance on therapy helping patients to achieve role flexibility and adaptibility, resolution of the presenting problem(s), a more equal balance of power between spouses, and clearer communication. However, whereas the analytic group believe increased intimacy and an improved sexual relationship and "gender identity" are salient goals, for the others, these rank from low (communications) to moderate (Bowenite and behaviorists) in consequence. There is much divergence regarding the necessity of improving the family's relationship with the parents' family of origin, with behaviorists disregarding this as a goal and Bowenites valuing it highly. And whereas both Bowenites and analysts strive for resolution of neurotic conflicts, neither the behaviorists nor communicationists espouse this as an objective of therapy (Gurman, 1979, p. 11).

When it comes to the comparative emphasis the several schools place on "various therapist roles and functions," there is little agreement. Only on one role of Gurman's thirteen (1979, p. 12) do all concur that it is crucial: the clarification of communication. The analysts ascribe high value to interpreting patients' feelings and behavior and facilitating insight; to heightening and interpreting the transference; and to sharing their values and using the self actively. This includes discussing countertransference feelings. The others do not see these functions as significant. Instead, the behavioral therapist seeks to model new modes of interpersonal behavior and directs or structures sessions and sequences goals (as do systems therapists). Behavioral therapists offer practical advice and support and provide rationales for the difficulties and treatment offered—also a common role for psychoanalytic and Bowenite therapists. Homework or tasks are assigned across all groups with some divergence within the psychoanalytic school as the more orthodox clinicians would discount the value of such a practice.

Not mentioned in Gurman's categorization is the relational or contextual family therapy of Boszormenyi-Nagy and Spark (1973). Their approach is concerned with multigenerational dynamics, legacies and ledgers of balances incurred in one's biological family. One may see a single patient or members of three or four generations, but the context is always the intergenerational backdrop. Within the Gurman schema, I would place relational family therapy somewhere between psychoanalytic and Bowenian.

In addition, I would further subdivide the Systems School leaving the Bowenian as is, but separating out in the communications school those who designate themselves as strategic or tactical family therapists from the structuralists. The former group include many at Mental Research Institute in Palo Alto, Harold Goolishian and his colleagues at the Galveston Family Institute, as well as the Milan group headed by Selvini Palazzoli. It is also reflected in the work of others like Lynn Hoffman of the Ackerman Institute. An underlying key assumption in strategic family therapy is that therapeutic change occurs through the interactional processes set in motion when a therapist intervenes directively and actively in the family system (Haley, 1971, p. 7). The therapists attempt to substitute new behavior sequences for the repetitive, dysfunctional feedback patterns that characterize the family. They differentiate between first-order change, that which is permitted since it only involves superficial alterations of the system or its members, and second-order change, which causes a major modification in the system.

It is this second-order change which is essential, according to the strategic interventionists, for therapy to be successful (Watzlawick, Weakland, & Fisch, 1974). In order to bring about such change, paradoxes and counterparadoxes may be introduced (Selvini Palazzoli et al., 1978). The structural family therapists, most notably represented by Minuchin and Montalvo, focus more on changing the structure of the family by setting up clear generational boundaries, clarifying roles, and making certain that the parents are the executives in the family. They believe that by changing the organization of the family context, the position of its members will be changed and this will produce alterations in their experience and consequently in their behavior. As with all the nosologies, categories are not mutually exclusive and there are few exclusive theories and purists in the field.

Although Gurman's taxonomy, as of 1979, was probably the most comprehensive, for purposes of clarifying terminology it seemed useful to consider one other schema. The systems school is often called structural family therapy (Ritterman, 1977). These terms are used interchangeably. In Ritterman's "Paradigmatic Classification of Family Therapy Theories," (1977, pp. 29-48) the theories are grouped according to the ideal categories from which they derive in order to establish the relationship between the theory of family therapy and a more general world view. Her major proposed headings are 1) *mechanistic model*—which subsumes learning paradigms and the communications model; and 2) *organismic model*—which includes systems concepts and properties, and the structural model. She posits that her system allows for clarity and consistency in classifying and affords a solid base for research efforts. It seems inadequate as it does not include analytic or relational family therapy.

RESEARCH

The major purpose of this article is to integrate and recapitulate the mainstreams in the history of family therapy. However, a disservice would be rendered if nothing more were included about the current research in this practice area. The research has been sparse. Solid studies on a complex unit such as the family are methodologically difficult to construct. Given the multitude of variables to be taken into account, data analysis is a formidable task. Yet good work is under way and more will be done in the next decade.

The report by the Committee on the Family (1970) indicated that of 250 articles published on family therapy during the 1960s, few were research studies and those that were were predominantly geared to interaction-oriented research on schizophrenic families. Also in 1970, Olson included a review of the research in family therapy in his comprehensive article "Marital and Family Therapy: Integrative Review and Critique" (pp. 523-525). He cites Minuchin's work (1967) and that of a few others as worthwhile, but concludes by emphasizing that "little attention has been paid to the systematic evaluation of the process and outcome of family therapy . . . (and that) there has been a strong tendency to rely on traditional self-report measures which were not developed to capture the rich dynamics of family process." He concludes with "one can only hope that the traditional disregard for research evaluation will change in order that a more systematically and empirically based approach can be developed for treating families."

Framo's "Family Interaction: A Dialogue Between Family Researchers and Family Therapists" (1972) reported on a conference held in 1967 that was attended by twenty-nine family therapists, theorists and researchers. An earlier review of this book states:

> Methodological problems receive much attention. So does the selection of problems for investigation in family interaction research . . . .The urgency of collaboration between researchers and practitioners is keenly felt throughout . . . .The book leads the reader into a critical posture that incorporates willingness to evaluate what one is doing, how one is doing it, and why. It is not easy reading because it is highly theoretical, intellectual, and concerned with methodological issues. The dearth of longitudinal studies of families and . . . on the relationship of psychophysiology to family interaction becomes apparent. Difficulties in various research approaches are recognized, dealt with, and deemed not insurmountable. This volume . . . contains a wealth of data, and challenges the reader to participate in research endeavors (Kaslow, 1973, pp. 205-206).

One of the exciting research efforts to date took place at the Timberlawn Foundation in Dallas under the leadership of Jerry Lewis and W. Robert Beavers. The results of their study are reported in "No Single Thread" (Lewis, Beavers, et al., 1976) and further elaborated in Beaver's "Psychotherapy and Growth: A Family Systems Perspective" (1977), in which he synthesizes communication, systems, and family theories, and family therapy and research, with the philosophy of science. It is within this framework that the findings from the Timberlawn study are explained.

One hundred and three intact, white, middle and upper middle class families comprised the study population. Families were divided into dysfunctional, mid-range, or healthy after being observed and rated on interactional variables. They found high levels of interrater reliability on estimations of overall family competence and functioning. Given the significant levels of agreement as to what constellation of factors characterized the dysfunctional, mid-range and healthy families and a general picture of how each of these groups tend to function on a day-to-day basis, it became possible to establish for each a profile. For example, healthy families are affiliative, they enjoy being together but also accept one another's need for privacy and non-family involvements. Parental authority and responsibility are clear and are not abdicated. The boundaries are etched in that they are aware of the family as a definite unit. At the same time they are flexible enough for friends to be with the family comfortably and for family members to leave when it is time to go their separate ways. By contrast, in dysfunctional families, generation lines are blurred, parental responsibility is either converted into authoritarianism or "parentifying" a child to take over, and boundaries to the non-family world are chaotic. Messages are ambiguous and rules unclear.

Not only is the work of the Timberlawn group to be commended because it is basically sound methodologically and had a large enough sample to generate useful data, but also because it shifts the focus from illness and pathology to a factually based profile of a healthy, optimally functioning family prototype. Given such a broad-based portrait of a healthy family, it should follow that therapist interventions with dysfunctional and mid-range families would be geared to moving them in the direction of greater health on each of the eight dimensions identified.

Gurman and Kniskern's voluminous chapter "Research on Marital and Family Therapy: Progress, Perspective and Prospect" (1979) resulted from an ambitious, meticulous survey and analysis of the published and unpublished literature. They solicited research reports from colleagues throughout the country and located over 200 relevant studies. Each study was rated in accordance with a rating formula based on 14 variables they had designated including: pre-post measurement of change, follow-up, treatment carried out as described or expected, and outcome assessment allowing for both positive and negative change. The important data are presented clearly in table form and, therefore, are easily accessible to refresh one's memory on salient points. Based on research findings, comparisons are made between improvement and deterioration rates when patients have received behavioral and non-behavioral marital-family therapy in both inpatient and outpatient settings. One critical finding is that "every study to date that has compared family therapy with other types of treatment has shown family therapy to be superior or equal" (Gurman & Kniskern, 1978, pp. 840-843).

Some of their most pertinent conclusions are:

1. Systems therapies are the choice for treating such problems as anorexia, certain childhood behavior problems, and sexual dysfunction. Specific effective treatment strategies exist for some of these problems and should be taught in any marital-family training program.

2. Behavioral family therapies, while offering testable models and relatively precise intervention packages, currently offer insufficient research support to justify the training of neophyte therapists in this framework alone. Non-behavioral therapies, of course, also lack a sufficient evidential base to support "single system" training.

3. Short-term and time-limited therapies appear to be at least as effective as treatment of longer duration. The most positive results of open-ended therapy were achieved in less than five months. Goal-oriented and problem-centered training experiences constitute an important aspect of teaching beginning family therapists.

4. The father, long the absent family member in child-oriented treatment, plays a major role in the efficacy of family therapy initiated because of a child or adolescent identified patient. "The wisdom of the traditional mother and child guidance model of practice and training is questionable" (Gurman & Kniskern 1979).

5. Deterioration of patient improvement appears to be as common in marital-family therapy as it is in individual psychotherapies. While only a few of the salient factors in producing negative effects have been tentatively identified, it appears that therapist variables and patient-therapist interaction account for negative effects far more often than do patient factors alone. Furthermore, therapist factors which contribute to both improvement and deterioration in individual psychotherapy are equally powerful in the treatment of relationships within couple and family units.

6. Therapist relationship skills have major impact on the outcome of marital-family treatment regardless of the orientation of the clinician. Training programs must inculcate conceptual-technical and relationships skills in neophyte family therapists.

Gurman and Kniskern (1979) offer suggestions in response to a series of interrelated issues involved in assessing change in marital and family therapy regarding 1) what familial *units* should be assessed, 2) by what *measures* and on what *factors* these units should be assessed, and 3) what *perspective(s)* should be utilized in assessing these units and factors. It is recommended that the reader interested in the existing research in family therapy and in undertaking future research consult Gurman and Kniskern's definitive work.

THE FOURTH DECADE: A FORWARD LOOK

As the field enters young adulthood, a process of refinement should occur: a sharpening of conceptual clarity, broadening of the leadership base, and an increase in the availability of well-qualified, well-trained practitioners. In classrooms, clinics, and research laboratories, the question of what works for which kinds of families and why will receive additional attention as family therapy process and outcome research results become assimilated into the knowledge base of the field. Given tightening budgets and peer review boards, therapists will have to be able to demonstrate and justify the efficiency and efficacy of their therapeutic endeavors. Gone is the period of attributing success to one's own efforts using the excuse that no valid criteria for measurement and no longitudinal studies to determine the durability of positive results existed, or because a "guru" mystique surrounded the therapist who therefore was not to be challenged.

Currently, work is being done which integrates knowledge of the developmental phases of adulthood with an understanding of the developmental stages of the family cycle (Vines, 1979). As these two trends in the individual's life occur simultaneously, knowing the personal growth stage of the individual as well as where the family is in its history will help therapists select the most appropriate intervention strategies.

A multiplicity of techniques have been developed which are reasonably easy to teach. Unfortunately, too many are being utilized as a "bag of tricks" by novices who do not know when to judiciously select a given technique to facilitate the therapy process. Hopefully, such techniques will only be employed when they enhance the therapy by adding to the therapist's understanding and aiding therapists and patients in the realization of treatment goals. Such techniques include family sculpting and choreography (Duhl, Kantor, & Duhl, 1973; Constantine, 1978); photo reconnaissance (Kaslow & Friedman, 1977); family art therapy; and the adaptation of various Gestalt and encounter techniques.

Abroms (1978) has written a thoughtful article on "The Place of Values in Psychotherapy." He indicates that we are increasingly confronting the myths of the amoral stance and of the value neutrality of the therapists. It is important that therapists recognize their biases and learn to use these in a disciplined, rational way in caring for patients. When we espouse ideas such as parents should be the executives in the family, or it is healthy for adolescents to individuate, these are value statements and need to be honestly posited in the therapy.

On the national scene, training programs may continue to proliferate *if* funding is available. The freedom of the earlier periods when each center virtually did whatever it deemed appropriate will diminish. With the Department of Health and Human Services designating the American Association for Marriage and Family Therapy as the official accrediting agency for marriage and family training programs in 1978, and the establishment of the Commission on Accreditation, nationally recognized standards are being promulgated. Also, as more universities and medical schools establish specific degree programs, curriculum is becoming more formal and academic criteria and expectations which exist in graduate and professional schools are beginning to permeate the field. Some of the programs are requiring research dissertations which may produce practitioner-researchers competent to undertake controlled analytic, developmental, evaluative, and outcome studies as called for by Olson (1970) and Gurman and Kniskern (1978).

The trend toward formalization of the field is further underscored by the number of organizations beginning, such as AFTA in 1977, and those that are growing rapidly, like AAMFT and the National Council on Family Relations (NCFR). The pressure for inclusion of marital and family therapists in National Health Insurance legislation is mounting as is pressure to have insurance companies reimburse for services to couples and families—an effort that met with success in relation to Champus during the late 1970s.

By 1982, eight states had licensing laws for marital and family therapists. An effort to have the New Jersey law repealed failed in January 1979. I predict that more states will enact certification or licensing laws so that unqualified people are restrained from hanging out a shingle and there can be a modicum of legal protection of the public's interest. To realize the seriousness of this problem, one need only look in the yellow pages of any telephone directory under marriage and family counselors and assess the listings of some of the untrained or under-trained whose names appear.

Until the mid 1970s, *Family Process* was the only American Journal devoted to family therapy. In 1974, AAMFC (now AAMFT) began publication of the *Journal of Marriage and Family Counseling* wth William C. Nichols as editor. By 1980 it had acquired the largest circulation in the field (over 12,000). Its name was changed in 1979 to *Journal of Marital and Family Therapy* as this more accurately reflects the increased emphasis on family theory, therapy, research, and training for clinical practice. The *American Journal of Family Therapy* originated around the same time.

Several other journals were also founded in the late 1970s as commercial publishing firms saw the family therapy market as a profitable one. No doubt several more will be introduced before the market is saturated. And, as indicated earlier, the number of foreign journals being published devoted to this specialty is also growing rapidly and probably will continue to do so during the 1980s.

During the past three decades family therapy has become a valuable addition to the treatment armamentarium. Much more needs to be done to validate its efficacy and efficiency. It is not a panacea, and to treat it as such potentiates failure and frustration for patients and therapists alike. But when family therapy constitutes the treatment of choice and is practiced as an art and science by a skilled clinician, it is a potent intervention strategy.

Despite spiraling divorce rates and the thousands of young people leaving families to join cults, the family remains for many a viable institution and preferred life style. According to Lewis and Beavers (1976; 1977), Sussman (1971), Whitaker and Wynne, and the author, who are finding and studying healthy families, in some quarters the American family is indeed alive and well and family therapists are helping others in their quest to grow in this direction.

REFERENCE NOTES

1. The early Palo Alto group consisted of Jackson, Bateson, Haley and Weakland. Satir joined them shortly after they began working together.
2. Guerin erroneously speaks of Geraldine Lincoln Spark as one person (1976, p. 11). There are two Geraldines in the Philadelphia group; Geraldine Lincoln (now Grossman) and Geraldine Spark.
3. See Olson (1970, pp. 501-538) for an excellent analysis from a different vantage point of the historical developments in which he traces and integrates the evolution of both marital and family therapy. It is not possible to include everyone who has made valuable contributions to the formulation of concepts, theory, and techniques. The work cited is reasonably inclusive but by no means exhaustive and undoubtedly reflects that with which the author is most conversant.
4. From Report of First National Organizational Meeting of American Family Therapy Association (mimeographed report sent to members.) The author is a member of both organizations and writes with the hope that the organizations will supplement each other's functioning rather than compete. There is a small but growing number of individuals who hold membership in both AAMFT and AFTA and see them as having different purposes and fulfilling different needs.
5. For a list of accredited programs see the Jan. 1981 issues of the *Journal of Marital and Family Therapy.*
6. For a fairly comprehensive history of the American Association of Marital and Family Counseling see Kaslow, 1977.

REFERENCES

Abroms, G.M. The place of values in psychotherapy. *Journal of Marriage and Family Counseling,* October 1978, 4, (4), 3-18.

Ackerman, B. Relational paradox: Toward a language of interactional sequences. *Journal of Marital and Family Therapy,* January, 1979, 5, (1), 29-38.

Ackerman, N. The unity of the family. *Archives of Pediatrics,* 1938, LV, (1), 51-62.

Ackerman, N., Beatman, F.L. & Sherman, S.N. *Exploring the Base for Family Therapy.* New York: Family Service Association of America, 1961.

Ackerman, N. & Sobel, R. Family diagnosis: An approach to the preschool child. *American Journal of Orthopsychiatry*, 1950, *XX*, (4), 744-753.

Bandler, R. & Grinder, J. *The Structure of Magic I: A Book about Language and Therapy.* California: Science and Behavior Books, 1975.

Bateson, G. *Steps to an Ecology of the Mind.* New York: Ballantine Books, 1972.

Bateson, G., Jackson, D.D., Haley, J. & Weakland, J. Towards a theory of schizophrenia. *Behavioral Science*, 1956, *I*, 251-264.

Beavers, W.R. *Psychotherapy and Growth: A Family Systems Perspective.* New York: Brunner/Mazel, 1977.

Bell, J.E. A theoretical position for family group therapy. *Family Process*, 1963, *2*, 1-14.

Bell, J. E. *Family Therapy.* New York: Jason Aronson, 1975.

Berger, M.M. (Ed.) *Beyond the Double Bind.* New York: Brunner/Mazel, 1978.

Boszormenyi-Nagy, I. & Framo, J.L. (Eds.) *Intensive Family Therapy.* New York: Harper and Row, 1965.

Boszormenyi-Nagy, I. & Spark, G.M. *Invisible Loyalties: Reciprocity in Intergenerational Family Therapy.* New York: Harper and Row, 1973.

Bowen, M. Toward the differentiation of a self in one's family of origin. In F. Andres & J. Lorio (Eds.) *Georgetown Family Symposium Papers I.* Washington, D.C.: Georgetown University Press, 1974.

Bowen, M. Family psychotherapy with schizophrenia in the hospital and in private practice. In I. Boszormenyi-Nagy & J. Framo (Eds.) *Intensive Family Therapy.* New York: Harper and Row, 1965.

Bowen, M. *Family Therapy in Clinical Practice.* New York: Jason Aronson, 1978.

Brown, G.W. Experiences of discharged chronic schizophrenic patients in various types of living groups. *Milbank Memorial Fund Quarterly*, 1959, *XXXVII*, (2), 105-131.

Coleman, S.B. & Stanton, M.D. The role of death in the addict family. *Journal of Marriage and Family Counseling*, January 1978, *4*, (1), 79-91.

Committee on the Family, *The Field of Family Therapy.* New York: Group for the Advancement of Psychiatry, 1970.

Constantine, L.L. Family sculpture and relationship mapping techniques. *Journal of Marriage and Family Counseling*, April 1978, *4*, (2), 13-24.

Duhl, F., Kantor, D. & Duhl, B. Learning, space and action in family therapy. In D. Bloch, (Ed.) *Techniques of Psychotherapy: A Primer.* New York: Grune and Stratton, 1973.

Fairbairn, R. *Object Relations Theory of Personality.* New York: Basic Books, 1952.

Ferber, A., Mendelsohn, M. & Napier, A.Y. (Eds.) *The Book of Family Therapy.* New York: Science House, 1972.

Fisch, R., Watzlawick, P., Weakland, J. & Bodin, A. On unbecoming family therapists. In A. Ferber, M. Mendelsohn, & A.Y. Napier (Eds.), *The Book of Family Therapy.* New York: Science House, 1972.

Flugel, J.C. *The Psychoanalytic Study of the Family.* London: Hogarth Press, 1921.

Framo, J.L. *Family Interaction: A Dialogue between Family Researchers and Family Threapists.* New York: Springer, 1972.

Friedman, A.S. et al. *Therapy with Families of Sexually Acting-Out Girls.* New York: Springer, 1971.

Freud, A. *The Ego and the Mechanisms of Defense.* New York: International Universities Press, 1946.

Freud, S. Analysis of a phobia in a five year old boy (Little Hans). In S. Freud, *The Sexual Enlightenment of Children* (written in 1909). New York: Collier Books, 1963.

Fromm-Reichman, F. *Psychoanalysis and Psychotherapy: Selected Papers.* Illinois: University of Chicago Press, 1959.

Grinder, J. & Bandler, R. *The Structure of Magic II: A Book about Language and Therapy.* California: Science and Behavior Books, 1976.

Guerin, P.J. Family Therapy: The first twenty five years. In P.J. Guerin (Ed.) *Family Therapy and Practice.* New York: Gardner Press, 1976.

Guerin, P.J. & Fogarty, T. Study your own family. In A. Ferber, M. Mendelsohn, & A.Y. Napier (Eds.) *The Book of Family Therapy*. New York: Science House, 1972.

Guldner, C.A. Family therapy for the trainee in family therapy. *Journal of Marriage and Family Counseling*, January 1978, *4*, (1), 127-132.

Gurman, A.S. Dimensions of marital therapy: A comparative analysis. *Journal of Marital and Family Therapy*, January 1979, *5*, (1), 5-18.

Gurman, A.S. & Kniskern, D.P. Research on marital and family therapy: Progress, perspective and prospect. In S.L. Garfield & A.E. Bergin (Eds.) *Handbook of Psychotherapy and Behavior Change: An Empirical Analysis*. 2nd edition, New York: Wiley, 1978.

Haley, J. *Strategies of Psychotherapy*, New York: Grune and Stratton, 1963.

Haley, J. & Hoffman, R. *Techniques of Family Therapy*. New York: Basic Books, 1967.

Haley, J. A Review of the family therapy field. In J. Haley (Ed.) *Changing Families*. New York: Grune & Stratton, 1971.

Horney, K. *Neurotic Personality of Our Times*. New York: Norton, 1937.

Jackson, D.D. Family interaction, family homeostasis and some implications for conjoint family psychotherapy. In J.H. Masserman (Ed.), *Science and Psychoanalysis: Individual and Familial Dynamics*. New York: Grune and Stratton, 1959.

Jackson, D.D. & Satir, V. A review of psychiatric developments in family diagnosis and therapy. In N.W. Ackerman, F.L. Beatman, & S.N. Sherman (Eds.), *Exploring the Base of Family Therapy*. New York: Family Service Association of America, 1961a.

Jackson, D.D. & Weakland, J.H. Conjoint family therapy: Some considerations on theory, technique and results. *Psychiatry*, 1961b, *24*, 30-45.

Journal of Marital and Family Therapy, January 1981, *7*, (1) 112-113.

Kaslow, F.W. Family therapy: Viewpoints and perspectives. *Clinical Social Work Journal*, 1973, *1*, (3) 196-207.

Kaslow, F.W. Therapy within the family constellation. In W. Adamson & K. Adamson (Eds.), *A Handbook for Specific Learning Disabilities*. New York: Gardner Press, 1978.

Kaslow, F.W. Training of marital and family therapists. In F. Kaslow (Ed.), *Supervision, Consultation and Staff Training in the Helping Professions*. California: Jossey-Bass, 1977, 199-234.

Kaslow, F.W. Marital or family therapy for prisoners and their spouses or families. *The Prison Journal*, Spring-Summer 1978, *LVIII*, (1), 53-59.

Kaslow, F.W. What personal photos reveal about marital sex conflicts. *Journal of Sex and Marital Therapy*, Summer 1979, *5*, (2), 134-141.

Kaslow, F.W., Cooper, B. & Linsenberg, M. Therapist authenticity: A key factor in family therapy effectiveness. *International Journal of Family Therapy*, Summer 1979, *1*, (2), 184-199.

Kaslow, F.W. & Friedman, J. Utilization of family photos and movies in family therapy. *Journal of Marriage and Family Counseling*, January 1977, *3*, (1), 19-25.

Keith, D.V. & Whitaker, C.A. Struggling with the impotence impasse: Absurdity and acting in. *Journal of Marriage and Family Counseling*, January 1978, *4*, (1), 69-78.

LaPerriere, K. Family therapy training at the Ackerman Institute: Thoughts of form and substance. *Journal of Marital and Family Therapy*, July 1979, *5*, (3), 53-58.

Lewis, J.M., Beavers, W.R., Gossett, J.T. & Phillips, V.A. *No Single Thread: Psychological Health in Family Systems*. New York: Brunner/Mazel, 1976.

Liddle, H.A. & Halpin, R.J. Family therapy training and supervision: A comparative review. *Journal of Marriage and Family Counseling*, October 1978, *4*, (4), 77-98.

Luthman, S. & Kirschenbaum, M. *The Dynamic Family*. California: Science and Behavior Books, 1974.

Mahler, M. Autism and symbiosis: Two extreme disturbances of identity. *International Journal of Psychoanalysis*, 1958, *39*, 77-83.

Minuchin, S., Montalvo, B., Guerney, B.G., Rosman, B. & Schumer, F. *Families of the Slums: An Exploration of Their Structure and Treatment*, New York: Basic Books, 1967.

Minuchin, S., Rosman, B.L., & Baker, L. *Psychosomatic Families: Anorexia Nervosa in Context*, Boston: Harvard University Press, 1978.

Napier, A.Y. & Whitaker, C.A. *The Family Crucible*. New York: Harper and Row, 1978.

Olson, D.H. Marital and family therapy: Integrative review and critique. *Journal of Marriage and the Family*, November 1970, *32*, (4), 501-538.

Parsons, T. *The Social System*. Illinois: Free Press, 1951.

Richmond, M. *Social Diagnosis*. New York: Russell Sage Foundation, 1917.

Ritterman, M.K. Paradigmatic classification of family therapy theories. *Family Process*, 1977, *16*, 29-48.

Ruesch, J. & Bateson, G. *Communication and the Social Matrix of Psychiatry*. New York: W.W. Norton, 1951.

Russell, A. & Russell, L. The uses and abuses of co-therapy. *Journal of Marital and Family Therapy*, 1979, *5*, (1), 39-46.

Rueveni, U. *Networking Families in Crisis*. New York: Human Sciences Press, 1979.

Satir, V. *Conjoint Family Therapy*. California: Science and Behavior Books, 1964 (revised 1967).

Satir, V. *Peoplemaking*. California: Science and Behavior Books, 1972.

Satir, V., Stachowiak, J. & Taskman, H. (Eds.) *Helping Families to Change*. New York: Jason Aronson, 1975.

Selvini Palazzoli, M., Boscolo, L., Cecchin, G. & Prata, G. A ritualized prescription in family therapy. *Journal of Marital and Family Therapy*, July 1978, *4*, (3), 3-9.

Selvini Palazzoli, M. Boscolo, L., Cecchin, G. & Prata, G. *Paradox and Counterparadox: A New Model in the Therapy of the Family in Schizophrenic Transaction*. New York: Jason Aronson, 1978.

Selvini Palazzoli, M., Boscolo, L., Cecchin, G. & Prata, G. The treatment of children through brief therapy of their parents. *Family Process*, 1974, *13*, (4).

Sonne, J. & Lincoln, G. The importance of a heterosexual co-therapy relationship in the construction of a family image. Reprint: *Psychiatric Research Report 20*, American Psychiatric Association, February 1966.

Speck, R.V. & Attneave, CN. *Family Networks*. New York: Vintage Books, 1974.

Stierlin, H. *Psychoanalysis and Family Therapy*, New York: Jason Aronson, 1977.

Sullivan, H.S. *The Interpersonal Theory of Psychiatry*. New York: W.W. Norton, 1953.

Sussman, M. & Associates. White House Conference on Children. Final Report Form 14. Washington, D.C.: U.S. Government Printing Office, 1971.

Vines, N. Adult unfolding and marital conflict. *Journal of Marital and Family Therapy*, April 1979, *5*, (2), 5-14.

Watzlawick, P., Weakland, J. & Fisch, R. *Change: Principles of Problem Formation and Problem Resolution*. New York: Norton, 1974.

Whitaker, C. Psychotherapy of the absurd: With a special emphasis on the psychotherapy of aggression. *Family Process*, March 1975, *14*, (1), 1-16.

Whitaker, C.A., Malone, T.P. & Warkentin, J. Multiple therapy and psychotherapy. In F. Fromm-Reichman & J.L. Moreno (Eds.), *Progress in Psychotherapy*. 1956, Vol. I. New York: Grune and Stratton, pp. 210-216.

Wynne, L., Cromwell, R. & Matthysse, S. *The Nature of Schizophrenia: New Approaches to Research and Treatment*. New York: John Wiley, 1978.

Wynne, L., Ryckoff, I., Day, J. & Hirsch, S.H. Pseudo-mutuality in schizophrenia. *Psychiatry*, 1958, *21*, 205-220.

Zuk, G.H. *Family Therapy: A Triadic-Based Approach*. New York: Behavioral Publications, 1971.

Editor's Commentary: Additional Historic Highways and Byways

How pleased I was when *Marriage and Family Review* selected one of my papers as its nominee for inclusion in this collection! It seemed a fitting one to open the book and set the tone, pace, and context for what is to follow. In rereading it and reediting it as I have done with all the other papers in this volume, I became aware of some of the gaps in this article as it was originally written in 1978. Some updating has been included in the text and more will be encompassed in this quasi-addendum. It seems imperative to fill in two major gaps.

Charles Kramer, a psychiatrist, was another person who sallied into the terrain of marital and family therapy in the mid 1950s and quickly undertook to supervise, teach, and consult about this modality to mental health professionals in Chicago and environs. In 1968 he founded The Family Institute of Chicago. By 1975 the Institute had expanded and became the Center for Family Studies of the Institute of Psychiatry, a department of Northwestern Memorial Hospital and Northwestern University Medical School. In addition to offering treatment at the center, it sponsors a large training program and workshops. Chuck, and his wife Jan, also a physician, conduct growth workshops for family therapists and their partners. They serve as co-therapists. Chuck's work has a warm, sensitive, and whimsical quality. This flavor is apparent in the maxims in the last chapter of his book "Becoming a Family Therapist" (Kramer, 1980). A few of his gems are:

1. There is no way you can learn a new technique without changing yourself.
2. Learn . . . to admit gracefully when you have been wrong.
3. You can get yourself out of your family, but you cannot get your family out of yourself.
4. Never underestimate the power of helplessness.

5. No matter how loudly the family members protest to the contrary, any pair that stays together deserves each other.
6. None of us is all-giving or all-understanding.
7. Therapy is an induced crisis.
   and
8. Don't be too impressed by all the preceding advice.

The work of Nathan Epstein and his colleagues formulated originally in Canada has been called "The McMaster Model of Family Functioning" (Epstein et al., 1981). This is a problem-centered systems therapy which goes step by step from elucidating the problem to gathering data, through considering alternatives for resolution, to assessing the procedures evolved in learning to cope more effectively, in order to help families understand their own interaction and build mechanisms for evaluating their functioning and newly acquired coping skills. With Epstein having relocated several years ago from McMaster Hospital to the Chairmanship of the Section of Psychiatry and Human Behavior at Brown University in Providence, Rhode Island, this approach is now receiving more attention and gaining more adherents in the United States. The "McMaster" group write with great specificity and this approach has a persuasive advantage in that it is comparatively easy to articulate, demonstrate, and teach. It also can be comprehended by patients.

During the past four years, I have become increasingly interested in culling from the variety of approaches now extant that which I find useful and integrating it into a more holistic framework, which I call "Diaclectic Family Therapy" (Kaslow, 1981). (All schools of thought need a label to become respectable it seems.) I have placed eight major schools on a continuum: Psychodynamic-Psychoanalytic; Bowenian; Relational-Contextual; Experiential; Structural; Communications-Interactional; Strategic-Systemic; and Behavioral. The Diaclectic or Integrative Model is the ninth one and becomes overarching. It appears that all other schools can be subsumed under these major headings, with Cognitive as described in Chapter 10 by Waring and Russell being added as a hyphenated word so that it would become Cognitive-Behavioral.

For me history is dynamic and not static. It is today as much as yesterday. I hope this paper and the ones that follow will make it come alive for our readers and that they will resonate to it as they place themselves, their professional heritage, and their orientation in historical context.

REFERENCES

Epstein, N.B., Bishop, D.S., & Baldwin, L.M. McMaster model of family functioning: A view of the normal family. In F. Walsh, (Ed.), *Normal Family Problems.* New York: Guilford Press, 1981.

Kaslow, F.W. A diaclectic approach to family therapy and practice: Selectivity and synthesis. *Journal of Marital and Family Therapy,* July 1981, *7,* (3), 345-351.

Kramer, C.H. *Becoming a Family Threapist.* New York: Human Sciences Press, 1980.

Chapter 2

The Personal and Family
Mental Health of
Family Therapists

By Israel W. Charny

Disappointing as it may be, family therapists do not appear any more immune to family problems than other people. In fact, there are probably several influences of family therapy work which heighten the possibilities of family difficulties and breakdowns. The central issue may well be whether family therapists tend to look in their own family lives for something that does not exist. Family therapists need to accept both their own and their family's limitations and to struggle against these limitations—a dialectical process. It may be time to consider much more seriously the recommendation of systematic family therapy for family therapists and their families, much like the time-honored recommendation of individual therapy for serious clinicians.

Mental health professionals naturally are concerned with their own mental health, and in recent years there has been increasing concern with what has been called "burnout." There is, moreover, mounting firm evidence for heretofore bemused popular observations of a high incidence of serious emotional disturbances among mental health practitioners and their families.

Invited Address to the Third International Congress on Family Therapy, Tel Aviv, 1979.
Israel W. Charny, Ph.D., is an Associate Professor of Psychology, School of Social Work, Tel Aviv University; Past Founding President, Israel Association of Marital and Family Therapy.

41

We also know that often mental health professionals originally embark on their careers in a search for their own improved mental health and that many clinicians fervently embrace a particular ideology in the mental health field in an effort to solve their personal anxieties and problems so as to arrive at a new certainty and confidence for their own troubled selves. Family therapy, like all psychotherapy, seems to offer hope of resolving one's own marriage and parenting problems, as well as of improving one's mental health and professional satisfaction in general.

HOW DOES FAMILY THERAPY HELP FAMILY THERAPISTS?

On the positive side of the ledger, family therapy really helps many therapists to feel better. From the very outset of family therapy, there has been a steady stream of reports from many therapists that family therapy, in contrast to other modes of treatment, helped them to feel better about themselves in their work and about themselves as people. The late Don Jackson (whom some consider one of the "fathers" of family therapy) concluded a now-classic paper on the then-discovery of family therapy, in the course of efforts to research the family dynamics of schizophrenics, with the following observation:

> Finally, though it often appeared a severe course of treatment, all of our therapists seem to have been helped, without exception (1969, p. 248).

What seems to happen in family therapy, in contrast to individual treatment, which tends to maintain differences between therapist and patients, is that the therapist experiences himself as far more human, more of a kindred soul to his so-called "patients." The very physical structure of the family therapy situation invites therapists out from behind their desks to sit with their fellow human beings. The role situation of working with several people who are not identified as bonafide "patients" or disturbed people removes structural temptations from the therapist to play omniscient "doctor" or authority. The very content of family therapy, as it involves universal problems of relationships and intimacy, draws many therapists into self-disclosure of some of their own everyday experiences and struggles which revolve around much the same issues. In family therapy, patients share everyday hurts, angers, dilemmas and crises in their human interactions within their families that inevitably present variations on the therapist's own family situation. The family therapist, in short, is likely to become far more human himself, hence more genuine, and a more effective and happier person. Consequently, many therapists have reported over the years that doing family therapy changed for them their basic experience of being mental health professionals, from a painful struggle to deal with abnormal behaviors to an engaging, heart-warming experience of kinship with fellow human beings who are seeking to improve their personal relationships (Ferber, Mendelsohn, & Napier, 1972).

In the process, family therapy has brought about a major and long-needed revision of what might be called "the era of psychoanalytic idealization," namely the belief, and more correctly the pretense, that well-analyzed people, and certainly those who themselves are psychoanalytic therapists, would be spared the most serious personal and family problems and disappointments. A mock style of maturity developed in the subculture of psychoanalysis: The "complete" psychoanalytic practitioner or ambitious student knew to walk with a quiet dignity, speak with measured restraint, and present a pleasant if cool affability. The problem was that, in the long run, these seemingly well-adjusted therapists proved vulnerable to the same range of human despairs as everyone else. Family therapy at least put it on record that there is no illusion of personal completeness or freedom from problems in intimate relationships (Charny, 1974). Rather, the goal of personal and family mental health is to cultivate the strength to live out the process of being ourselves and living with our significant others, with all the inevitable ups and downs, times of deep hurt, and at least a few clear-cut failures in the course of everyone's life.

Moreover, family therapy seems to have contributed a powerful new insight (our knowledge of which is still unfolding) of the dialectic process of human experience or the continuous reconciliation of opposites and polarities as a basis for emotional strength, satisfaction, and health. In family therapy one has a uniquely rich opportunity to see, in the simultaneous focus on several family members, how both individuals and the family group as a whole cannot afford to stay rigidly stuck with any one side of emotion or experience, such as being too intellectual or too emotional, too tender or too tough, too close or too distant. Personal and family mental health requires that we flow with the imbalances and contradictions of these opposite sides of experience, gauge our imbalances, and correct ourselves (Charny, 1980).

Consider, for example, the issue of closeness and distance. Intimate relationships prove equally susceptible to disturbances of undue closeness and to those of undue distance. Enmeshed relationships turn out to be breeding grounds for every conceivable emotional and mental disaster because they do violence to people's needs for separateness, and too much separateness or lack of closeness means a breakdown or absence of belongingness.

Similarly, too much responsibility for the emotional well-being of an intimate other turns out to be as disastrous as too little responsibility or abandonment of family members in favor of one's own narcissistic pursuits. Overresponsibility for someone else's growth lays a burden of guilt on that person which inhibits growth and stimulates negativism, and also traps the overresponsible family member into being so obligated to this mission that he/she cannot be his/her own relaxed self. Conversely, it is no secret that narcissistic lack of responsibility for one's marriage or parenting is one of the great curses of our times (Lasch, 1979).

Knowledge of dialectical processes is hardly unique to family therapists (see, for example, Assagioli's interesting formulations of "psychosynthesis," 1965), but family therapy provides, in my opinion, a concentrated vantage point for seeing the quest for dialectical integration, first in each of the several individuals in the family, and second in the family unit as a whole as a systematic collective process. In this context, family therapists too have special opportunities to accept the different contradictory sides of themselves and to give up much of the strain at pseudo-maturity and ostensible completeness that was characteristic of the early psychoanalytic professional mode. Family therapy makes it much more possible for therapists to be more of the different aspects of themselves, rational and emotional, friendly and angry, relaxed and stern, and so on, which is very different from the "steady-state" mode of rational wisdom, sparingly delivered, that was called for from psychoanalytic therapists.

Finally, working with family groups and not with just a single identified patient seems to invite therapists to a greater degree of friendliness and friendships with some patient families—where it is appropriate without violating the basic professional responsibility—and also to a greater degree of friendliness with colleagues and personal friends and family. Family therapy is a constant reminder to all participants that we are all no more than people and need one another's caring and respect—a far cry from the vaunted goals of yesteryear of being resolutely "healthy," "mature," or "self-actualized."

THE NEGATIVE SIDE OF FAMILY THERAPY

On the other hand, family therapy, like every mode of human experience, imposes its own particular set of constrictions and distortions of human experience. This modality may be conducive to a loosening of the professionalism and necessary boundaries of therapy. In psychoanalysis, clear-cut boundaries between patient and therapist are crucial to the successful penetration of the inner emptiness that is an inevitable part of all human beings, therapists included. *The ultimate testing point of each human being's emotional survival and quality of life is the ability to live within and with oneself—no mean task. Being in oneself is, in effect, a precondition for intimate relationships.* The forte of psychoanalytic therapy is that the patient (and in a sense also the therapist) is confronted with his or her aloneness and vulnerability. In psychoanalysis, the therapist is purposely not responsive to the patient much of the time so that the patient, frustrated and angry, is driven progressively towards his deepest weaknesses and emptiness. Menninger (1958) explains the disciplined use of silence very well. Even in psychoanalytically oriented therapy, there is a large degree of relative deprivation through a disciplined use of silence and declining to respond to requests and demands for attention.

Family therapy, by its very nature, is interactional and involves much less imposed deprivation, hence much less experiencing of one's aloneness and emptiness. The prevailing context in family therapy is clarification of feelings through actual emotional contact, thus replacing the frustration and circumspection of psychoanalytic therapy with more immediately gratifying experiences of being with and talking with. In the process, patients and therapists are drawn away from coping with their loneliness and nothingness. Some family therapists pay a high price for carrying over to their own family relationships an expectation for the kind of continuous responsiveness and involvement they experience in the therapy. Moreover, some family therapists become so accustomed to expecting active interaction with their family therapy patients that they become smug and cocksure about themselves as "real people," and are unable to empathize with the lingering emotional hunger and fear of closeness of their spouses and children who are not in family therapy all day. Family therapy, along with other modes of encounter and group experiences, which have been encouraged to no small extent by the family therapy movement's breaking down old barriers to interaction and closeness, may lead some people, including therapists, to a search for continuous stimulation from others and to too little being with themselves.

The saddest fact of all is that, whatever the reasons, family therapists themselves seem to have a considerably high rate of serious family problems and breakdowns. The stories of the problems and disappointments in the personal lives of some of the greats and near greats in family therapy are legion. It is said of one of the leaders of family therapy that his marriage broke down not long before he took ill with a terminal illness; of another that he finished his life as a near-alcoholic. There is no end to trainers and consultants in the field who are marvelous, warm, brilliant workshop leaders and teachers, but whose own family lives are replete with disastrous breakdowns of relationships. I did an informal survey of the distinguished and visibly senior leadership of family therapists in two cities in which I have lived, as well as in several major family therapy congresses, and discovered that the majority, including myself, had been divorced at least once. The number of family therapists who struggle with serious chronic marital and family problems hardly seems much different than what we know is the commonplace story of never-ending problems in nonprofessional families. Overall, family therapists seem to fare no better than other people and families in our beleaguered society, so far as marriage and family life are concerned.

Of course, it has always been the case that many psychotherapists could help other people to recover from serious emotional difficulties even while they themselves were suffering from some considerable problems. Moreover, it is my personal conviction that psychotherapy, generally, is far more effective—I believe often remarkably effective—in helping people recover from actual emotional distress, but that we really do not know nearly as much about how to *prevent* emotional problems.

Nobody really knows fully why human experiences and relationships are so troubled, but it seems like a worthwhile exercise to try to understand the particular problems family therapists face in their own lives, not only because we are human like everyone else, but because we are therapists in general and family therapists in particular.

SOME PERSONAL AND FAMILY TRAPS OF THE FAMILY THERAPIST

1. Like many professionals, family therapists often work too hard and too long and leave too little energy and real tolerance for the "staying-with-itness" of family life.

2. Family therapists are often captives of the "simple" structural trap that, having listened all day so well to so many others, they find it difficult to listen well to their own families when they return home.
3. Family therapists tend to set very high standards for marital and family functioning, based on the idealistic treatment goals they set all day long at work. Ivan Nagy has commented: "As a result of family therapy work I have become more secure in human relationships—but also more demanding. I am afraid. Many things that I would have accepted in the past as satisfactory responses appear now to me as phony or lacking openness" (Ferber, Mendelsohn, & Napier, 1972, p. 84). Moreover, the particularly vaunted ideals that are the goals of so many professional workshops away from home several times a year leave everyday life at home distinctly dull in comparison.
4. Like other male professionals with nonworking spouses, the male family therapist may develop over the years more worldliness and self-confidence than his wife who has stayed at home to bring up the children.
5. The family therapist, whether male or female, is likely to develop more with regard to the very issues of warmth, intimacy, decency, and fairness in solving problems of family life than his or her mate, whether the mate is at home or in another line of work. If, moreover, the family therapist tells the non-expert mate so, the latter becomes increasingly resentful of the ostensibly lesser-status in matters of relationship; besides, it becomes increasingly rewarding to drive the family therapist-partner crazy with repeated relationship frustrations, since this is obviously a powerful way to get to him/her.
6. The problem is further complicated by the fact that plain human beings are almost never successful or competent in all respects in family life. Guerin (1976) has pointed out that in marriage, husbands and wives are called upon to play at least three major roles: wage earners and/or homekeepers, lovers and friends, and parents. It is rare, if ever, that one finds the same person is able to succeed in maintaining a high standard in all three of these roles, notwithstanding the fact that each is clearly essential to complete marriage and family lives. Before long a series of *legitimate* disappointments and complaints is focused on the obvious failings of each mate in the one or more areas where they are, by all objective standards (and in comparison with their own greater competence in whatever they are good at), falling short of effective functioning. It is doubtful that any school of family therapy has yet learned how to teach people

how to live with this built-in dilemma, which is universal for all families, but especially for family therapists with their tendency to set unrealistically high ideals of family life.

7. The family therapist inevitably finds much of his daily satisfaction, like any successful person, in the pleasures of work, where so many times the finer human spirit triumphs. After hours of victories over anxiety and alienation in the office, the family therapist comes home to an assortment of human creatures operating for the most part at the usual level of disconnection from genuineness and resorting to common unappealing defenses to ward off and cover up anxieties. To say the least, home life pales by comparison, and more and more, the family therapist is drawn to feel more meaningful in and through the therapy he/she does than in personal relationships.

8. There is a seduction in the professional role to superiority and feelings of pseudo-wholeness attributable to the appreciation and affection of patients. The same therapist then comes home and cannot possibly understand how his/her own spouse and children do not see the same hero that he/she has been all day long in the office.

   Zweben and Deitch (1976, pp. 78, 80) have described artfully "the emergence of prima-donnahood in prominent psychotherapists," and how a sequence builds up of increasing neglect of intimate relationships at home, to a point where the prominent therapist is cut off from meaningful *human* contact with the people with whom he/she really needs to be most human and caring.

   One of the more troubling consequences of success in the "training business" is the gradual disappearance of peer group contact for the therapist and its replacement by leader-disciple relationships. . . . The fact that he is lonely is not surprising; his ongoing contacts have all but disappeared. Many colleagues have become alienated by his emerging prima donnahood and many of those who remain do not wish to jeopardize their own potential mobility by too much negative criticism. . . . Since the effort to sustain his heroics eventually leaves him exhausted, he is increasingly prone to adopt a single "do for me" attitude when he returns home. . . . The mundane demands of his children become less tolerable than the dependencies of his disciples and he becomes further alienated from his family.

9. Although family therapy is very much a laboratory of family life, *the transactions of family therapy take place on a different level than normal family life.* There is in family therapy a special climate of commitment

to growth and an unusual letting down of airs and letting go of lies. In addition, there is the comfort of having a warm and knowing authority conducting the interaction. In family therapy the situation is also ideal for raising problematic issues and developing confrontations which families find hard to manage on their own. These are not conditions which apply in everyday family life. The same processes which the family therapist stewards so masterfully for other families are enormously difficult to manage in the therapist's own family, where issues and feelings that the therapist is accustomed to handling easily in the office are often thwarted and blocked by members of his/her own family.

10. In real family life there is, normally, considerable regression. Since family life is being what we really are with those who are most likely to know us for what we really are, it is also an opportunity, let alone a necessity, to let go through cycles of weakness, trouble-making and madness, along with caring, loving, triumphing, and well-organized experiences. Too often, however, clinicians who are overly concerned with being well, and getting well, and becoming ever more mature, see in such regressions spectres of emotional disturbances and insult and problem, and do not allow regressions and weaknesses in their own family members to play themselves out sufficiently. For the family therapist's mate or children, symptoms of emotional trouble then also take on enormously gratifying and power-serving means or are exaggerated in their worrisome implications.

11. Some relatives of family therapists must, like in all families, oppose, hurt, enter into conflict with the husband-father or wife-mother therapist, therefore with all that he/she stands for, which in this case is a family therapy orientation. The result is that some therapists' families have a battle raging around the very central values of family communication, emotional support, and commitment, which are dear to the therapist. This anti-mental health motif is not only problematic, but is, additionally, symbolically insulting, even maddening, to the professional family therapist. Since therapists are, after all, "experts" on human relationships and family lives, the assaults of their spouses and/or children try them and hurt them and expose their terrible weaknesses that much more. In ever so slight variations, this same basic problem long has been well-known in the family lives of older established professionals such as ministers, educators, as well as other "important people" in the public eye, such as government and business leaders.

In a discussion of the etiology of emotional impairment in physicians, Elaine Knutsen (1978, p. 38) observed:

> Physicians frequently have difficulty in voluntarily allowing
> their humanness to be seen, responded to and acknowledged.
> They build a facade of competence which can then imprison.
> They can develop a need to appear immune to life's give-and-
> take, including the normal developmental crises. Family ther-
> apy offers many opportunities for a greater humanness. At the
> same time this seems to be one reason why physicians are
> particularly resistant to family therapy.

FAMILY THERAPY AND LEARNING TO LIVE WITH IMPERFECTION

The central issue may well be whether family therapists tend to look in their own family lives for something that does not exist. In treatment, the clinician often succeeds in helping troubled marriages and families, but in the excitement of the process one may forget how much of real life is built around the incomplete and damaged and missing, in our patients and in ourselves. After all, we are only human.

In successful therapy, one should learn that there is a special significance to being oneself in all one's limitations, including one's ultimate mortality, and that *"simply being," and enjoying being alive, is the central goal of existence.* Family therapy tends at this time still to be messianic and romanticized, and does not yet teach sufficiently that we need to be ourselves in our families, including tolerating various and serious limitations, while enjoying all there is to enjoy in our families.

Carl Whitaker has indicated about his work with families that each of his observations of the limitations of people elaborates a part of himself: "I sense that I am struggling with a problem of how to reparent myself, to prepare for my death by practicing dying, which in a strange paradoxical way is also practicing a fuller way of living in today's joy" (1976, pp. 66-67).

At a Vermont Conference on the "Primary Prevention of Psychopathology," Seymour Sarason (1979) described adulthood as a process in which "blinders are removed from the eyes of individuals to recognize that far from being free individuals they are always part of and restricted by a social matrix." Too often such recognition is accompanied by bitterness and resignation. Sarason continues, "Many people take it personally as if it was all arranged to defeat them." In a different symposium on adulthood, Samuel Osherson of Harvard's Laboratory of Social Psychology (1979) presented research on how men cope with mid-life turmoil by career change, and concluded that "one of the major challenges of the life cycle is developing the ability to resolve adaptively experiences of loss and change. This capacity to tolerate ambivalence—the linchpin of integrative resolutions—seems a crucial personality characteristic."

The same is true about one's family life. Family therapists in particular need to be aware of ambivalences and incompleteness in family life. In their clinical practices they are so busy providing other people with the opportunity for breakthroughs towards resolving conflicts and achieving mutuality that they may forget or deny the irrepressible core of problems in all family life.

Is this a pessimistic view? *I think not, for what I see and propose is a continuous dialectic: accepting the facts of our own limitations and those of our family as a whole, and at the same time struggling against these weaknesses, in ourselves and our loved ones—in effect, an aliveness that is generated from the clash and integration of both negative and positive.*

It is a synthesis that derives from the ultimate dialectic between life and death that defines the experience of everyone as an individual, and I am suggesting that it extends also to our marriages and our families which, at best, are also alive and dying simultaneously. Admittedly, any number of marriages do, in fact, die and should not be kept artificially alive, but even some of these *might* have been saved and brought alive at an earlier time, had there been less of an effort or struggle around producing an entirely "successful" family or feeling really "joyous" and "whole" in the family.

Michael Rossman (1979, p. 21) has written:

> Confronted with chaos, cognitive dissonance, unresolved ambiguity, and tension, the primal impulse both within the self and in society is to close these out and simplify things, make secure our frames of understanding once again, by whatever means. Yet if there is one prime educational need for us as citizens of our times, it is to learn how to endure chaos, to appreciate it, survive in it, build in and from it our structures of meaning anew, accepting their dissolution and re-creation as the process of life. . . . As in any rich solution, it is a slow process of crystallization, rather than a hasty gelling, that produces the rich forms of which our substance is capable.

To conclude, I suggest that some of the problems inherent in family life for those who are family therapists or their mates and children are virtually inescapable and become insoluble, as they do for anyone else, once a spiral of provocation, bad faith, and mutual chronic dissatisfaction takes a hold. But we will only do ourselves a favor if we do some more thinking about these built-in problems, and how, wisely, to prevent them or reduce their toll. The main point of this essay's contribution to a topic about which surprisingly little has appeared in the literature is that family therapists should be more careful to create a climate of acceptance at home for the weaknesses and problems and regressions, and also, many times, the anti-mental health postures of some of their family members. Moreover, it may be time to consider a lot more seriously the recommendations of systematic family therapy for family therapists and their families, much like the time-honored recommendation of individual therapy for serious clinicians.

Several family therapy trainers do in fact recommend a good deal of self-disclosure by family therapists in training, and some trainers, like Bowen, clearly recommend family therapy for students (see Goldenberg & Goldenberg, 1980), but overall, the concept that family therapy is a necessary qualifying experience for professional therapists has not been widely promoted or evaluated. The whole subject deserves to be taken out of hiding and given a healthy airing, and this article is intended to help stimulate more thinking in a somewhat taboo area.

REFERENCES

Assagioli, R. *Psychosynthesis*. London: Turner Books, 1965.
Charny, I.W. The new psychotherapies and encounters of the seventies: Progress or fads? *The Humanist*, 1974 (2-part series, May-June, July-August). Reprinted in *Reflections* (Merck, Sharp and Dohme, 1975, *10*, [2-parts: 1-13, 3: 1-17]). Reprinted in I.D. Welch, G.A. Tate, & F. Richards (Eds.), *Humanistic Psychology: A Sourcebook*. New York: Prometheus, 1978.
Charny, I. W. Modern psychology—friend or foe of marriage. *Ptachim*, 1979, (3-4), 45-46, 12-19 (Hebrew).
Charny, I.W. Why are so many (if not really all) people and families disturbed? *Journal of Marriage and Family Therapy*, 1980, *6*, (1), 37-37.
Charny, I.W. Structuralism, paradoxical intervention and existentialism: The current philosophy and politics of family therapy. *Fokus på Familien*, 1981, *9*, (1), 14-30 (Norwegian). English text in L.R. Wolberg & M.L. Aronson (Eds.), *Group and Family Therapy 1982*. New York: Brunner/Mazel, 1982.
Ferber, A., Mendelsohn, M., & Napier, A. *The Book of Family Therapy*. New York: Science House, 1972.
Goldenberg, I., & Goldenberg, H. *Family Therapy*. Belmont, California: Wadsworth, 1980.
Guerin, P.J., Jr. (Ed.), *Family Therapy: Theory and Practice*. New York: Gardner Press, 1976.
Jackson, D.D., & Weakland, J.H. Conjoint family therapy: Some considerations on theory, technique, and results. In D.D. Jackson (Ed.), *Therapy, Communication and Change*. Vol.

2. Palo Alto: Science & Behavior Books, 1969, pp. 222-248. (Original publication in *Psychiatry*, 1961.)

Knutsen, E. On the emotional well-being of psychiatrists: Overview and rationale. *American Journal of Psychoanalysis*, 1977, 37, 123-129.

Knutsen, E. Conference Proceedings: "What You Need to Know About Impairment in Physicians . . . ". Sponsored by the California Medical Association , March 20, 1978, San Francisco.

Lasch, C. *The Culture of Narcissism*. New York: Warner, 1979.

Menninger, K. *Theory of Psychoanalytic Technique*. New York: Basic Books, 1958.

Osherson, S. As reported in *American Psychological Association Monitor*, January, 1979.

Rossman, M. The pedagogy of the Guru. *Association of Humanistic Psychlogy Newsletter*, March, 1979.

Sarason, S. As reported in *American Psychological Association Monitor*, January, 1979.

Whitaker, C. A. Family therapy and reparenting myself. *Voices: The Art and Science of Psychotherapy*, Fall 1976, 12, (4), 66-67.

Zweben, J.E. & Deitch, D.A. The emergence of prima-donnahood in prominent psycho-therapists. *Voices: The Art and Science of Psychotherapy*, Spring 1976, 12, (1), 75-81.

Editor's Commentary: Affective Responses to Charny's Analysis of the Unique Problems of Family Therapists

Charny has a wonderful ability to pierce the orthodox therapeutic veil while still maintaining the sanctity of the sanctuary. He touches deeply the hidden wellsprings of caring, sharing, and the quest for meaning, which leads one toward a dialectical synthesis. In this, as in his other works (for example, Charny, 1972, 1980), he allows us to see him as a warm and sensitive human being who has gone through his own personal trials, tribulations, and triumphs as he has continuously grown in the process of becoming and being a family therapist. I feel a quickening of my own heartbeat as I sense his own episodic pain and pleasure.

This is a man whose writing has a timelessness and a universality; his work reflects his profound knowledge derived from having allowed himself to be vulnerable in love and in work. He is able to use his own experience to help his patients explore their agony, seek ways to resolve the intrapsychic and interpersonal turmoil, and move to resolution which might even encompass ephemeral moments of joy.

Because he is bright and articulate and well-grounded theoretically, his work integrates a cognitive knowledge of the theory of therapy, wisdom and skill, and, in implementing the therapeutic process, a humane value stance and an ability to enter into the affective domain to significantly influence the lives of those he treats.

While reading and considering the section on "Some Personal and Family Traps of the Family Therapist," I experienced moments of instant connection to the points he so succinctly makes—recognition of some of these dilemmas in my own life and in the marriages of colleagues. I've treated other therapists, with their families or using a family systems perspective, for exactly the kinds of conflicts he elucidates, most notably the "high" they derive from being the admired teacher or trainer "guru," followed by the "low" that ensues when they go home and are expected to do the myriad chores normal mortals do or are treated as an ordinary spouse, mom or dad, rather than as someone super-special and talented. At times, moving in and out of the worlds of contrasting "ego trips" and not feeling valued and appreciated seem conducive to a fragmented rather than integrated sense of self. This portion of the Charny article contains many wise gems, reminiscent of the candid self-disclosures which appeared a decade ago in Ferber, Mendelsohn and Napier's *The Book of Family Therapy* (1972), yet presented in a more objective and organized manner.

We concur that family therapy for the trainee on the way to becoming a family therapist is an important component of the cognitive and affective learning—in fact, an essential ingredient for absorbing the intricacies and subtleties of the dynamic process and for learning about oneself in the complex web of family relationships. Without experiencing this from the recipient end of the process, how can one become cognizant enough of the inner world of the family to conduct therapy as the "expert" clinician?

REFERENCES

Charny, I.W. *Marital Love and Hate,* New York: Macmillan, 1972.
Charny, I.W. Why are so many (if not really all) people and families disturbed? *Journal of Marital and Family Therapy,* 1980, *6,* (1), 37-47.
Ferber, A., Mendelsohn, M., & Napier, A. *The Book of Family Therapy.* New York: Science House, 1972.

Chapter 3

Family Theory and the Epistemology of Humberto Maturana

By Paul F. Dell

Family therapists' recent interest in epistemology is linked to a variety of factors, including the development of systemic family therapy, the polarization between strategic and nonstrategic family therapists, the shortcomings of existing theories of family therapy, and the death of Gregory Bateson. In particular, family therapy's popularization of epistemology is considered to be synchronous with the theoretical breakthrough of Humberto Maturana, whose work casts serious doubt on several important concepts in the family therapy field: homeostasis, resistance, paradox, open and closed systems, information, hierarchy, and linear versus circular causality.

During the past few years, a variety of authors have claimed that epistemology is vitally relevant to the family therapy field. This paper examines the encounter between epistemology and family therapy and attempts to answer several questions: What is epistemology? What are

This is a revised version of an invited plenary address on "Practical Consequences of the 'New' Epistemologies," 39th annual meeting of the American Association for Marriage and Family Therapy, San Diego, California, October 1981.

Paul F. Dell, Ph.D., is Director of Clinical and Theoretical Studies, Colonial Institute, Newport News, Virginia. (This paper was written while the author was a visiting faculty member in the Behavioral Science Program of the University of Houston at Clear Lake City.)

the so-called " 'new' epistemologies"? Why are family therapists talking about epistemology? Is epistemology relevant to theory? Is it relevant to practice? What, if any, are its practical consequences?

Epistemology is the study of theories of knowledge. It is a branch of philosophy which investigates the origin, nature, and limitations of knowledge. Given this definition, the difference bewteen the old and the so-called " 'new' epistemologies" would seem to amount to the difference between old theories of knowledge and new theories of knowledge. This, however, is not what family therapists mean when they talk about the " 'new' epistemologies."

With rare exceptions, family therapists have used the word "episte-mology" not to mean theory of knowledge, but rather something like "paradigm," "foundational theory," or "world view" (Dell, unpublished). Thus, the " 'new' epistemologies" are not new theories of knowledge, but new paradigms. Whereas in years past one referred to the Ptolemaic paradigm of the world, the Copernican paradigm, Newtonian paradigm, Einsteinian or relativistic paradigm, today it seems to be the fashion to refer to Ptolemaic epistemology, Copernican episte-mology, Newtonian epistemology, and Einsteinian epistemology. Thus, in keeping with this fashion, family therapists speak of individual and systemic epistemologies, linear and circular epistemologies, Aristotelian and ecosystemic epistemologies.

This altered meaning of the word seems to have originated with Gregory Bateson, who spent the last decades of his life influencing the family therapy field and arguing that epistemology is crucially important to all human endeavor. Bateson, in fact, used the term in a variety of different ways (Dell, unpublished), but the meaning which seems to have caught on with family threapists is "epistemology-in-the-sense-of-paradigm." Thus, the average family therapist requires no knowledge of philosophy to be able to read most of the articles in the family therapy literature which deal with "epistemology." The reader must simply remember that, almost invariably, such literature is describing theories whose essential characteristic is that they involve considerably different paradigms or world views.

There are, I think, a variety of reasons for this recent popularization. To begin with, Bateson always used the word in conjunction with his commitment to a systemic view of the world. He described human interactions in terms of systems theory and, in turn, discussed systems theory in terms of epistemology (Bateson, 1972b; 1979). Thus, Bateson brought to the family therapy field a tradition of talking about systems theory and cybernetics in terms of epistemology. In doing so, he provided a language for advocates of family systems theory. This Batesonian tradition is simultaneously the primary source for infusing epistemology into family therapy and the second key to translating the term when it is used in the literature. That is, family therapists who talk about epistemology not only mean "paradigm"; almost invariably, they also mean *the systemic paradigm.*

Nevertheless, the question remains: Why has the family therapy field been so attracted to this usage of the term? And why now? Bateson began introducing epistemological issues into the field during the 1950s, but, with the exception of a few widely-spaced publications, there had been little talk of epistemology in family therapy until the last few years.

There seem to be four significant reasons for the sudden interest. First, the family therapy field has always had a loose, general allegiance to some form of systems theory, but recently some new, explicitly systemic approaches to therapy have evolved. In particular, Selvini Palazzoli, Boscolo, Cecchin, and Prata (1978) in Milan, and Hoffman (1981) and her colleagues at the Ackerman Institute in New York have devised a systemic therapy which they describe and explain in terms of Batesonian epistemology. Therefore, as the field has grown more interested in the work of Selvini Palazzoli et al. and Hoffman et al., so too has the field grown more interested in Batesonian epistemology.

Second, since at least 1974 when the book *Change* (Watzlawick, Weakland & Fisch, 1974) was published, there has been a growing polarization between strategic family therapists on the one hand, and nonstrategic, or even anti-strategic, family therapists on the other hand. The last three meetings of the American Association for Marriage and Family Therapy (1978 in Toronto, 1979 in Washington, D.C., 1980 in Denver), for example, have been marked by serious and often emotional debates between strategic and nonstrategic family therapists. Strategic therapists (who take their heritage from the work of Jackson, Haley, Erickson, Watzlawick, Weakland, Fisch, and Selvini Palazzoli) argue that families should be understood in terms of patterns of interaction or in terms of the structure of the system. Their approach to therapy emphasizes planned, strategic interventions, often employing so-called "paradoxes," which are designed to alter or disrupt the existing family system. In contrast, nonstrategic or anti-strategic therapists have taken exception to, and often taken offense at, the strategic therapists' apparent worship of technique, commitment to formula approaches to therapy, and insistence upon describing the human beings in a family in terms of the abstract language of systems. Fred Duhl (1979) neatly capsulized these objections when he reminded the strategic therapist that, "You can't kiss a system."

Having been charged with a certain callous insensitivity to the human feelings of family members, many (but by no means all) strategic therapists have fought back with the language of systemic epistemology. Many strategic therapists have accused their nonstrategic colleagues of being nonsystemic, linear thinkers who fail to grasp the fundamental circularity that is described by the " 'new' epistemology." This tactic of epistemologic one-upmanship was aptly labeled "systemic chic' by Liddle and Saba (1981) in a fine, satiric article which hopefully will do much to reduce some of the epistemologic excesses of the strategic/systemic therapists. It should also be noted that at least one family therapist has turned the tables on the strategic therapists by using epistemologic arguments *against* them. In a forthcoming article, Keeney (1982) revives the Bateson-Haley debate by criticizing the strategic therapists' overemphasis upon pragmatism and technological power. Instead, Keeney argues in favor of an aesthetic, growth-oriented approach to therapy which is based upon ecosystemic epistemology.

Third, Williamson (1980) recently asserted that the theories in the family therapy field are more poetic than scientific. His point is well taken. The theories of family therapy are not very rigorous. Family therapy is an American phenomenon and Americans, by and large, do not value theory. Americans want techniques; they want to know how to do it. As a result, the major developments in the family therapy field have too often been technological rather than theoretical. Ironically, those family therapists who dislike the overemphasis on techniques *also* tend to dislike theory. These more humanistic therapists consider both theory and technique to be artificial devices which may hinder, if not dehumanize, the therapist-family relationship. Thus, given that theory is an underdeveloped aspect of family therapy, it is not surprising that those who *do* like theory are strongly attracted to the " 'new' epistemologies."

Finally, the current interest in epistemology must also be attributed to the death of Bateson. Bateson was the first intellectual giant to endow the family therapy field with his ideas. Certainly, family therapy is now paying its tribute to him. It is interesting in this regard that family therapy's renewed interest in epistemology more or less coincided with Bateson's hospitalization for cancer in 1978. Today, as the field grieves his loss, there are more and more therapists who are clearly identifying themselves with his ideas.

These, then, are the sources which have energized the interest in the "new" epistemologies, but what exactly *are* the "new" epistemologies? Their names are legion: cybernetic epistemology (Bateson, 1972a), circular epistemology (Hoffman, 1981), systemic epistemology (Dell, 1980; Colapinto, 1979), ecological epistemology (Auerswald, 1972), evolutionary epistemology (Dell and Goolishian, 1981), ecosystemic epistemology (Keeney, 1982), and so on. A close reading of the literature on these " 'new' epistemologies" yields a very curious finding. They are all strikingly similar. Each of them is so heavily indebted to Bateson as to be almost indistinguishable from the essential ideas of *Steps to an Ecology of Mind* (Bateson, 1972b) and *Mind and Nature* (Bateson, 1979). As does Bateson, each of them elevates cybernetics or systems theory to the status of an epistemology. All of them strive to be totally, purely, and consistently systemic. By and large they succeed in this aim and, thereby, constitute the best existing thinking about systems theory that is to be found in the family therapy literature.

But what is so new and exciting about systems theory? Why all the ferment? It seems that there is more going on than the previously listed reasons can account for. There is more happening than just one-upmanship or an attempt to deify systems theory by calling it an epistemology. I think the reason that there is a great deal of ferment in the field is that *something is really fermenting*. People are struggling to achieve a more fundamental understanding of systems than systems theory has previously made possible. This was certainly Bateson's quest and I think many people are intuitively and, perhaps, unconsciously convinced that such a fundamental breakthrough in understanding is close at hand. This, I think, is what the excitement is all about. Moreover, I would contend that the excitement if well founded. I think that the breakthrough has happened.

A MAN NAMED MATURANA

During an interview several years ago, Bateson was asked who else was studying the epistemological premises which he believed in so deeply (Keeney, unpublished). His reply was prophetic: "a man named Maturana." Humberto Maturana is a biologist in Chile who has made a breakthrough in understanding living systems which, I think, is comparable in magnitude to Einstein's theories of relativity. Bateson wanted to discover the correct epistemology; Maturana may have discovered the correct ontology (Maturana, 1970a; 1970b; 1974; 1975; 1978; Maturana & Varela, 1973).

Maturana's ontology does not define the correct epistemology; for ontological reasons there can be no correct epistemology. Instead, Maturana has defined the *necessary* epistemology. He argues that his ontology specifies what the epistemology of all systems must necessarily be (because any other way is ontologically impossible). If Maturana is correct, and I believe that he is, then the consequences of his work are enormous. In fact, they are quite literally "mind-boggling" because they destroy so many of the foundations of our thinking.

To begin with, Maturana's epistemology is not a theory of therapy. His work provides no new techniques, nor does it tell us how or when to use our old techniques. The guidelines for therapy which *can* be extracted from his work are not positive, but negative. They do not tell us what to do; they tell us what *not* to do. They do not tell us how to think about therapy; they tell us how *not* to think. Similarly, they do not tell us what is possible; they tell us what is *not* possible.

I cannot provide all of the reasons or details for what I am about to say. That is not the task of this paper. These reasons have been described elsewhere (Dell, 1981, unpublished). In this paper I will summarize my understanding of the consequences for family therapy of Maturana's necessary epistemology.

Maturana's work demolishes, or at least seriously damages, seven major concepts in the family therapy field: homeostasis, resistance, paradox, open and closed systems, information, hierarchy, and the whole idea of linear and circular causality. First, the concept of family homeostasis is seriously in error and should be abandoned (Dell, 1982). The idea of a family maintaining the *status quo* by resisting change is, to use Bateson's phrase, an epistemological error. Before Copernicus, people considered the daily passage of the sun across the sky to be certain proof that the sun revolves around the earth. It does not. Yet, it is still very easy for us to succumb to our *experience* of the sun revolving around us; we still talk in terms of "sunrise" and "sunset." It is only our awareness that our inertial perspective (being on the earth) is misleading, and it is only our certainty that it is indeed the *earth* which is moving (rotating), that allows us to give up the idea (and ignore our experience) that the sun revolves around the earth.

In a similar fashion it can be said that, before Maturana, family therapists considered the imperviousness of families to their interventions to be certain proof that families are homeostatic. They are not (Dell,

1982). However, unlike our understanding of the relationship between the movement of the sun and the movement of the earth (which allows us to overcome our misleading experience), family therapists still succumb to their *experience* that families resist change by maintaining the status quo. Family therapists have not yet acquired knowledge about the *relationship* between the phenomena of a family system and the phenomena of its environment. Only when such knowledge is acquired will family therapists be aware that it is our observational perspective which creates homeostasis.

Second, the concept of resistance is completely wrong (Dell, 1982). Neither families nor individuals are resistant. The concept of resistance is an epistemological error. People do not resist one another. They simply continue to be who they are. If I try to push over a building, do I say that the building is resisting me? No, because I know that people cannot push over buildings. More importantly, however, the building is just being itself. What does a building do when you push it? Nothing. What does a family do when you make an intervention? It does whatever it does. It does not resist; it just continues to be what it is. To claim that it is resisting *you* is a very egocentric point of view.

Third, there is absolutely no such thing as "a paradox" (Dell, 1981). All paradoxes exist solely in the mind of the beholder. The world functions in a very orderly way and has no paradoxes. There is nothing in the world which is paradoxical in and of itself. Paradox exists only in the crack between human expectation on the one hand and the actuality of the world on the other hand. Therapists do not use paradoxes on their clients. They make interventions. If a therapist is said to use a paradoxical intervention, then that means that the observer—for whom that intervention is paradoxical—does not think in the same way as the therapist who chose the intervention. Similarly, if an intervention is said to produce a paradoxical result, then that means that the observer—for whom that result is paradoxical—does not understand the system which is being treated. In either case, there is no paradox, for such a phenomenon does not exist.

Fourth, the description of families in terms of open and closed systems is fundamentally wrong (Dell, 1982). Open and closed systems belong to the world of thermodynamics where systems are open or closed to the transport of matter and energy. Thermodynamics has nothing to do with the patterns of human interaction which constitute a family system. A system may be *thermodynamically* open, but a pattern cannot be. In what sense could a pattern be open? To "open" a pattern is to destroy it. All patterns are, by definition, closed. All families, as patterns, are closed. Admittedly, family therapists are usually not talking about matter and energy when they say a family is open or closed. They usually mean that the family is open or closed to *information*. This, however, is precisely the problem.

The very concept of information is misleading and inaccurate. This is probably the most startling aspect of Maturana's thinking and it is very difficult to explain. Maturana insists that *all systems are closed to information*. He argues that it is ontologically impossible for a system to be *open* to information. Instead, all systems are "information tight" (Ashby, 1956, p. 5). If information really existed, that is, if systems were really open instead of closed, then parents would never have trouble raising their children; clients would always hear what their therapists were saying; students would always get A's on their exams; you would fully understand every book you have ever read; you would fully understand everything which you hear; you would completely understand what I am telling you now. The problem is that human beings are sufficiently *well-coupled* (Maturana, 1978) to the world around them that the experience of giving and receiving "information" is overwhelmingly convincing. Nevertheless, this perception is an illusion. In fact, believing in information is probably the second most convincing epistemological illusion that is harbored by human beings. The *most* convincing epistemological illusion is believing in control. Control of *anything* by *anybody* is ontologically impossible (Maturana, 1978)—despite our experience to the contrary. The impossibility of control and the impossibility of information are, in fact, two sides of the same coin. Together, they constitute an extremely dangerous epistemological illusion which is single-handedly responsible for most of the interpersonal miseries on this planet.

Sixth, the concept of a hierarchically organized system is a contradiction in terms. Hierarchy is an inherently linear concept which implies that the higher part of a system *controls* the lower part of the system. The idea of one part of a system controlling another part of the system contradicts the wholism upon which systems theory is founded. Systems are circular. The idea of a circular hierarchy makes no sense and there is simply no way that a linear hierarchy can be embedded in a circular system. Thus, although families and other systems can be *described* as having a hierarchical organization, we must remember that that is not the way that systems actually operate. In short, family therapists should probably abandon the concept of hierarchy because it is an intrinsically fallacious metaphor which constantly threatens to seduce us into believing in control.

Seventh, the dichotomy between linear and circular causality is a mistake. Family therapists have been justifiably suspicious of the notion of linear causality, but the alternative of circular causality does not solve the problem. In fact, the concept of circular causality is every bit as erroneous. The reason for this is probably the most controversial aspect of Maturana's thinking. Specifically, Maturana insists that the entire concept of causality is *itself* an epistemological error. The world, says Maturana, does not operate on the basis of causality. This is obviously a shocking claim, but I think that he is correct. In fact, it is my belief that family therapy's preoccupation with linear versus circular causality actually represents the field's intuitive, but poorly grasped, awareness that Maturana may be right. That is, the field has long recognized that there are serious problems with the idea of linear causality. The problem, however, lies not with linear causality, but with the idea of causality itself. Interactions do not involve Newtonian efficient causation, but rather a relativistic structure determinism (Maturana, 1978).

These are seven implications of Maturana's work for family therapy. What would our field look like without these concepts? How will we understand family systems if we give up the concepts of homeostasis, resistance, paradox, open and closed systems, information, hierarchy, and linear and circular causality? In my opinion, we will understand everything much better because our thinking will be clearer. The implications of Maturana's work are not all destructive; there are constructive implications as well. For example, Maturana provides us with a new perspective on the relationship between individuals and the systems to which they belong. Maturana's epistemology makes it clear that it is the *individual* who is primary, not the system; the system is secondary (Maturana, 1978; Dell, 1981, unpublished). For years, the family therapy field has witnessed a sort of creeping systemic imperialism which has increasingly subordinated individuals to the systems of which they are part. Maturana has redressed this imbalance in a way which I think will ultimately please almost everyone.

I realize that much of what I have said in this paper is minimally explained and often flies in the face of currently accepted theory and even our experience and common sense. Given the magnitude of the shift in perspective that Maturana's work entails, it is unlikely that the reader can gain more than some bewildered intuitions from the material that I have presented. I have not explained Maturana; that is a task which would require a far longer paper. Instead, I have summarized my opinion of what his impact on family therapy will be. It is my hope that the reader will be sufficiently intrigued to pursue the matter further.

Maturana's work is radically important. He simultaneously integrates perception, cognition, learning, language, and communication within a new understanding of the human condition. His ontology constitutes a unified field theory of at least the life sciences and the social sciences. I think his work represents some of the most important thinking of this century. I urge the family therapy field to give Humberto Maturana its most serious attention.

REFERENCES

Ashby, W.R. *An Introduction to Cybernetics.* London: Chapman and Hall, 1956.
Auerswald, E. Families, change, and the ecological perspective. In A. Ferber, M. Mendelsohn, & A. Napier (Eds.), *The Book of Family Therapy.* New York: Jason Aronson, 1972.
Bateson, G. The cybernetics of "self." A theory of alcoholism. In G. Bateson, *Steps to an Ecology of Mind.* New York: Ballantine, 1972a.
Bateson, G. *Steps to an Ecology of Mind.* New York: Ballantine, 1972b.
Bateson, G. *Mind and Nature: A Necessary Unity.* New York: Dutton, 1979.
Colapinto, J. The relative value of empirical evidence. *Family Process,* 1979, *18,* 427-441.
Dell, P.F. Researching the family theories of schizophrenia: An exercise in epistemological confusion. *Family Process,* 1980, *19,* 321-335.
Dell, P.F., Paradox redux. *Journal of Marital and Family Therapy,* 1981, *7,* 127-134.
Dell, P.F. From systemic to clinical epistemology. Invited plenary lecture presented to the Seventh International Symposium of the Institute für Ehe und Familie, Zurich, Switzerland, September, 1981. Unpublished manuscript.
Dell, P.F. Beyond homeostasis: Toward a concept of coherence. *Family Process,* 1982, *21,* 21-41.
Dell, P.F. & Goolishian, H.A. "Ordnung durch fluktuation": Eine evolutionare epistemologie für menschliche systeme. *Familiendynamik,* 1981, *6,* 104-122.
Duhl, F. Remarks made during the 37th annual meeting of the American Association for Marriage and Family Therapy, Washington, D.C., 1979.
Hoffman, L. *Foundations of Family Therapy.* New York: Basic Books, 1981.
Keeney, B.P. Ecosystemic epistemology: An alternate paradigm for diagnosis. *Family Process,* 1979, *18,* 117-129.
Keeney, B.P. Ecosystemic epistemology: Critical implications for the aesthetics and pragmatics of family therapy. *Family Process,* 1982, *21,* 1-19.
Keeney, B.P. On paradigmatic change: Conversations with Gregory Bateson. Unpublished manuscript.
Liddle, H., & Saba, G. Systemic chic: Family therapy's new wave. *Family Therapy News,* July 1981, *9,* 12.
Maturana, H.R. Biology of cognition (1970a). In H.R. Maturana, & F.J. Varela. *Autopoiesis and Cognition: The Realization of the Living.* Boston: Reidel, 1980.
Maturana, H.R. Neurophysiology of cognition. In P. Garvin (Ed.), *Cognition: A Multiple View.* New York: Spartan, 1970b.
Maturana, H.R. Stratégies cognitives. In E. Morin & M. Piattelli-Palmarini (Eds.), *L'Unité de l'Homme.* Paris: Du Seuil, 1974.
Maturana, H.R. The organization of the living: A theory of the living organization. *International Journal of Man-Machine Studies,* 1975, *7,* 313-332.
Maturana, H.R. The biology of language: The epistemology of reality. In G.A. Miller & E. Lenneberg (Eds.), *Psychology and Biology of Language and Thought.* New York: Academic Press, 1978.

Maturana, H.R. & Varela, F.J. Autopoiesis: The organization of the living. In H.R. Maturana & F.J. Varela. *Autopoiesis and Cognition: The Realization of the Living.* Boston: Reidel, 1980.

Selvini Palazzoli, M., Cecchin, G., Boscolo, L. & Prata, G. *Paradox and Counterparadox.* New York: Jason Aronson, 1978.

Watzlawick, P., Weakland, J., & Fisch, R. *Change: Principles of Problem Formation and Problem Resolution.* New York: Norton, 1974.

Williamson, D. Presidential address. Thirty-eighth annual meeting of the American Association for Marriage and Family Therapy, Toronto, Canada, 1980.

Editor's Commentary: Some
Cardinal Principles Demolished

Dell may be the foremost American interpreter of the implications of Maturana's work on family systems theory. This is probably a logical extension of his prior immersion in Batesonian epistemology and its ramifications in the work of other schools of epistemology. Dell has in his previous writings dealt with such abstract and highly theoretical issues as our Aristotelian logical heritage and its incompatibility with Hopi or systems family therapy (Dell, 1980) and the anatomy of paradox and its relationship to self-recursive phenomena (Dell, 1981). This chapter represents his latest excursion into the realm of expanding, or one might more accurately say confounding, the theoretical horizons of the field of family therapy.

In his decisive, unequivocal manner, Dell takes a fearlessly outspoken stance against seven dearly held mainstream concepts, utilizing Maturana's thinking as the foundation for his arguments. These concepts are homeostasis, resistance, paradox, open and closed systems, information (communication), hierarchy, and ideas on linear and circular causality. He posits, for example, that the idea of a "family maintaining the status quo (its homeostatic balance) by resisting change is an epistemological error." Similarly, he asserts that "there is absolutely no such thing as a 'paradox' "; this abstraction only exists in the mind of the observer. How can his logic lead to "the truth" when so many other key theorists arrive at a different truth—as did Selvini Palazzoli and her colleagues in *Paradox and Counterparadox* (1978)? Tomm, in the chapter which follows, embodies some of the very same concepts in his Calgary Model that Dell seeks here to debunk—particularly those of open and closed systems, hierarchy and circular causality. Does this lead us to believe that Dell's own non-Aristotelian, anti-either/or position (1980) provides a pathway out of the either/or polarity he confronts us with when holding that fundamental concepts of the field are erroneous? Is the proof he presents of his (and Maturana's) rightness sufficient? Is it so because he says it is? Or, is there more than one truth?

For instance, Dell states that the concept of resistance is an epistemological error, and cites that "If I try to push over a building, do I say that the building is resisting me? . . . What does a family do when you make an intervention? . . . It does not resist; it just continues to be what it is. To claim that it is resisting *you* is a very egocentric point of view."

It seems to me that, when Dell says "it just continues to be what it is," he is promulgating the concept of a family's maintaining its static equilibrium; yet earlier he claims the concept of homeostasis is an epistemological error. Herein lies a confusing contradiction. Perchance the therapist does not (narcissistically) think that the patients are resisting him or her, but rather they are resisting becoming engaged in the painful process of changing themselves and their interaction.

In a chapter certain to be thought-provoking, one of the areas most likely to be highly controversial is Dell's postulating that the concept of circular causality is every bit as erroneous as linear causality. He argues in a way tautologically that this is so because "Maturana insists that the entire concept of causality is *itself* an epistemological error." If Maturana and Dell are correct, all of our beliefs in cause-effect sequences, psychic and economic determinism, and circular and reciprocal interactions fall by the wayside. If this turns out to be correct, and we are open to corrective input, one can only ponder what might replace them in our interpretive schema for understanding human behavior. This challenging of our existing formulations opens vast space for new, more precise, and accurate formulations. We seem to be moving along a trajectory from thesis to antithesis and then, hopefully, a new, more advanced synthesis.

I do agree with the effort to reemphasize the primacy and centrality of the individual, since I too have come to believe we have reified "the family system" and fallaciously lost sight of the individuals, in all their humaneness, who interact to establish and maintain the system.

This intriguing chapter, like Chapter 4 by Tomm, Chapter 9 by Pollack, N. Kaslow and Harvey, Chapter 11 by Andolfi, and Chapter 25 by Lang, addresses itself to issues of epistemology and paradox. Historically, these came to the forefront in family therapy in the 1970s and seem especially salient in the 1980s. It is striking that they are generating concern in many regions of the globe, as represented in the array of chapters alluded to here. They herald the fact that the field remains dynamic, volatile, and open to new questions, answers, arguments, and paradigms.

REFERENCES

Dell, P.F. Paradox redux. *Journal of Marital and Family Therapy,* April 1981, *7,* 127-134.
Dell, P.F. The Hopi family therapist and the Aristotelian parents. *Journal of Marital and Family Therapy,* April, 1980, *6,* 123-130.
Selvini Palazzoli, M., Boscolo, L., Cecchin, G. & Prata, G. *Paradox and Counterparadox.* New York: Jason Aronson, 1978.

Chapter 4

Towards a Cybernetic Systems Approach to Family Therapy

By Karl Tomm

A general open hierarchical systems approach to family therapy was developed at the University of Calgary by integrating a number of concepts from other clinical approaches. Within this context a concrete application of the cybernetic notion of feedback led to the elaboration of a very simple but useful conceptual tool—the circular pattern diagram. This diagrammatic model has proven helpful in facilitating a shift from linear to circular thinking and in guiding therapeutic action.

In initiating the Family Therapy Program at the University of Calgary in 1973, an effort was begun to develop a reasonably comprehensive yet coherent and teachable model of family therapy. The initial major influence on the Calgary Program was the family therapy approach taught at McMaster University in the early 1970s, where the author obtained most of his psychiatric training. Nathan Epstein, who initiated the McMaster Program, had in turn been heavily influenced by Nathan Ackerman, the founder of the well-known Institute in New York. The other major influences came from the Palo Alto Group inspired by Gre-

This is a revised version of a chapter originally published in *Perspectives on Family Therapy*, David S. Freeman (Ed.), Vancouver, British Columbia: Butterworth and Co. (Western Canada).

Karl Tomm, M.D., F.R.C.P. (C), is an Associate Professor, Department of Psychiatry, and Director, Family Therapy Program, Faculty of Medicine, University of Calgary, Calgary, Alberta, Canada.

gory Bateson and from the Philadelphia Group led by Salvador Minuchin.[1] In the course of trying to integrate ideas from these and other sources, some idiosyncratic features emerged in the Calgary systems model. One of these was an explicit emphasis on cybernetic principles. This chapter outlines the basic systems concepts upon which the overall model is built and describes how the cybernetic concepts are applied.

Systems-oriented family therapy is now widely practiced and includes a number of variations (Gurman & Kniskern, 1981). Two of the more prominent "pure" schools are structural and strategic family therapy. Structural therapists deliberately manipulate interpersonal alignments and depend on joining, unbalancing, and confrontation (Minuchin, 1974; Minuchin & Fishman, 1981). The Palo Alto version of strategic therapy emphasizes perceptual punctuation and beliefs and uses reframing, paradoxical injunctions, and behavioral prescriptions (Watzlawick, Weakland, & Fisch, 1974). These different systems approaches may be explained, at least in part, by the different focus each school uses when assessing family systems. Structural therapists attend predominantly to interpersonal distance, coalitions, and boundaries, while strategic therapists attend more to problem-solving attempts, communicational paradoxes and family myths.

In comparison to these approaches, the Calgary systems model is more concerned with cybernetic regulatory mechanisms. The focus when assessing the family is on identifying and clarifying circular patterns that maintain problematic behavior. Core interventions include stimulating family interaction to observe behavior patterns and to explore interpersonal perceptions, behavioral effects, and catastrophic expectations. The specific skills involved in this approach are outlined in detail in another paper (Tomm & Wright, 1979). There are, of course, areas of overlap and similarity in these systems models. Like the structural approach, interviewing in the Calgary model is directive and seeks to initiate new adaptive interaction during the session itself. Like the Palo Alto approach, considerable attention is paid to family belief systems and the need for cognitive reframing. Unlike both of these approaches, however, the Calgary cybernetic model encourages explicit awareness of maladaptive circular patterns and conscious deliberate action on the part of the family to effect change.

---

[1]Since this paper was originally written in 1978-79, there has been another major influence on the Calgary Program, i.e., the Milan group led by Mara Selvini Palazzoli. At the time of this republication both the cybernetic approach described in this paper and the Milan approach described by Selvini et al. (1978) and summarized by Tomm (1982) are being practiced and taught in Calgary.

THEORETICAL FOUNDATIONS

The primary theoretical basis of the Calgary model is general systems theory (von Bertalanffy, 1968). Within this context a number of ideas from cybernetics, communications theory, ethology, psychodynamics, and learning theory have been incorporated. The essential core concept is that the family may be regarded as a holistic unit. For systems-oriented therapists, the family is seen as a system that is composed of individuals embedded in a structure of mutual interaction patterns and which functions in a collective, goal-oriented manner. Thus, when an individual presents with an emotional or behavioral problem, it is assumed that the symptoms are a manifestation of the structure or functioning of the interpersonal system of which he is a part. For instance, a child's perpetually disruptive behavior may be in the service of the family goal to maintain the integrity of the system when covert conflict between the parents threatens to break up the family. The negative feelings stemming from unresolved marital conflict are displaced onto the child, who consequently "acts out" the tension. This misbehavior evokes parental concern which, being common to both spouses, temporarily brings them together and thus reduces the immediate threat of marital confrontation and separation. The symptom is functional for the family as a whole. Hence treatment should be aimed at the whole system, not just a part of it. Behavioral change in the symptomatic child in this case, if it is to be enduring, requires complementary change in other members of the family. The absence of such complementary change in others is often a major factor that impedes the effectiveness of individual therapy.

The assumption that the family is a stable organismic system has certain distinct advantages. However, if held too strongly, it may constrict the clinician's perspective and result in erroneous conclusions. The most significant factors contributing to a particular problem may not derive from patterns of interaction in the family but may lie within an individual or between the family and its social context. For instance, the husband may have grossly unrealistic expectations derived from early experience in his family of origin. On the other hand, the external social network and community may be promoting conflicting marital roles or male/female stereotypes which do not suit this couple. To allow for a broader base of theory and practice, a conceptual framework of *open hierarchical systems* is emphasized. Within this perspective each element or unit at a particular level of the hierarchy represents both a holistic system at that level and part of a larger system at the next higher level. For instance, the central nervous system is both a discrete body system *and* part of the individual. The individual is both a whole self *and* part of the family. The family is both a basic social unit *and* part of the larger community or sociocultural system. Whatever the level, any particular unit simultaneously reflects both self-assertive tendencies as a holistic unit and integrative tendencies as a part (Koestler, 1967). Such dual characteristics in the hierarchical framework allow for the inclusion of many biological, psychological, and social concepts in the overall model.

Open hierarchical systems theory suggests that a change in a unit at one level will have an impact at other levels. For instance, a change at the biological level through disease, inebriation, or psychotropic medication will have an impact on behavior at the individual level, which in turn may have family and social or institutional ramifications. Any significant new life experience resulting in psychological growth within an individual will alter his or her family relationships. This process of lower level input effecting higher level change is referred to as "upward" causation. On the other hand, "downward" causation is said to occur when input at a higher level results in change at a lower level. The impact of family therapy on individual psychological problems and on some biological ones (Minuchin et al., 1978) may be said to reflect downward causation. Increasing experience suggests that for many common behavioral problems clinical approaches relying predominantly on downward causation are more efficient (Langsley & Kaplan, 1968) and more effective (Gurman & Kniskern, 1978) than the more traditional medical and individual psychotherapy approaches which rely primarily on upward causation. Further research is, of course, required to clarify and substantiate these claims. However, one distinct advantage of the practice of working with whole family units is that the therapist may intervene at multiple levels simultaneously, thus taking advantage of both upward and downward influences to effect change.

The manner in which a problem is conceptualized heavily influences assessment procedures and intervention methods. Hence problem definition is a crucial process. Hierarchical systems theory orients the clinician to consider more carefully the level (biological, psychological, or interpersonal) at which a particular problem should be defined. Problems at the interface between susbystems or systems at the same level are best defined at the next higher level. For instance, the difficulty that a particular behavior pattern of one family member constitutes for another is best defined as a problem at the interpersonal level. A problem between two families in a neighborhood should be defined at the community level. However, problems that appear to overlap between levels or that are very complex are usually best described at multiple levels (at least initially). For instance, the unrealistic expectations that an adolescent has of his privileges in the home should be defined not only at the individual level but also at the parent-child subsystem level. A case of diabetes which is difficult to manage may reflect problems that can be defined at the biological level, the individual psychological level, and the family level (Tomm et al., 1977). This hierarchical systems orientation is reflected in the problem list of the problem-oriented family therapy record which has been developed for the Calgary Program. For any particular family, multiple problems are identified and described at different levels: individual problems (e.g., hearing loss, thought disorder), marital subsystem problems (overadequate-inadequate reciprocity), parent-child subsystem problems (ineffective behavioral controls), sibling subsystem problems (intense sibling rivalry), whole family system problems (maladaptive family rule), and family-community suprasystem problems (racial discrimination). As issues are clarified, problems are redefined and the list is revised.

Although the family system level remains the primary focus in the Calgary Program, both in theory and in clinical practice, therapists are by no means constrained to working only with whole family groups. Therapeutic interviews are conducted with individuals or with marital, parent-child, or sibling subsystems when indicated. Occasionally medication is prescribed. At the higher family-community level, consultative conferences are arranged for the family with relevant community resources such as school, legal, welfare, or mental health personnel. The therapist and family also form a transient system during the process of treatment. Thus, when therapeutic goals are not being achieved, problems at the therapist-family system level should also be explored.

Another central notion of systems theory is expressed in the truism: The whole is greater that the sum of the parts. The whole system consists of the sum of the parts *plus* their goal-directed organization. It is the organizational aspect of the system that yields the peculiarly systemic qualities to the collection of parts. Aspects of family organization include: interpersonal and subsystem boundaries, attachments and coalitions, regulatory mechanisms, family rules, and collective beliefs and goals. One of the skills that should characterize a systems-oriented family therapist is the ability to focus attention on the purely systemic aspects of the family. This means that the therapist should be able to sit down with a family and "see" the interpersonal structure of family relationships and remain "blind" to separate individuals (when conceptualizing at the family systems level). To use the dichotomy of figure versus ground, the family therapist needs to be able to focus on the ground. In reference to the Rubin figure, he needs to study the shape of the goblet or vase and not remain conceptually locked into seeing only two separate faces (see Figure 1). To develop and maintain the conceptual gestalt to focus on the organizational structure of the "family ground" (i.e., the systemic elements of the family) is not easy. This is because family organization per se cannot be observed directly but must be inferred from redundancies or patterns of interaction between family members.

One method to aid in systemic conceptualization is to visualize interpersonal structures as geometric forms. Triangles and circles are commonly used. Murray Bowen (1972) emphasizes the value of regarding the triangle, that is, a three-person system, as the basic social unit. The assumption is made that each person in a particular triangle in some way contributes to the maintenance of a particular relationship structure and hence promotes the homeostatic stability in the system. For instance, the problem of the symptomatic child cited earlier may be conceptualized as part of a triangular relationship structure. Not only do the parents scapegoat the child by displacing onto him, but the child also actively interrupts the parents when they express negative feelings directly to one another. One would also hypothesize that were the parents to refrain from both direct confrontation and displacement, the boy would initiate

Figure 1. The Figure-Ground Gestalt

disruptive behavior to recreate the pattern and maintain the triangulation process. The concept of interpersonal triangles facilitates the recognition of subtle family coalitions and family splits. (The application of the geometric notion of the circle as a basic organizational structure of relationships will be described in some detail in the section on circular pattern diagramming.)

Early in this section the family was described as goal-oriented. In order for any system to function in a goal-directed manner, coordinated action of its parts is necessary. This implies some degree of regulation and control, which represents another important aspect of systemic organization. Cybernetics has emerged as a scientific discipline devoted to the study of communication and control in both mechanical and living systems (Weiner, 1948). Thus, cybernetics has become relevant to family assessment and to family therapy. Control theory (an aspect of cybernetics) distinguishes between feedforward and feedback regulation (McFarland, 1971). Feedforward regulation is governed by input variables, whereas feedback regulation is governed by output or results. Feedforward is an open loop and linear process, whereas feedback is a closed loop and circular process. However, within a very brief time frame feedback may appear linear and within an extended time frame feedforward may appear circular.

Deliberate conscious planning for goal-directed action (on the basis of prior information) may be regarded as a feedforward process. With feedforward control, the eventual consequence or outcome of the regulatory activity does not influence its present application; *anticipated* outcome does. By anticipating future consequences, feedforward mechanisms still can, however, contribute to the maintenance of homeostasis. For instance, upper-class families usually arrange for superior education for their children in the interests of maintaining their privileged position in the community.

In feedback control the consequences of an action are monitored and directly influence further regulation of that action in an ongoing manner. There are two types of cybernetic feedback: postive feedback and negative feedback. Positive feedback exists when the consequences of an output serve to *increase* the same output. For instance, if yelling at a misbehaving child intensifies the misbehavior, positive feedback is said to occur. Negative feedback occurs when the monitored consequences of a particular action result in a *decrease* in that output. Thus, if the yelling results in a decrease of the child's misbehavior, negative feedback is said to have occurred. The terms "deviation amplifying" (Hoffman, 1971) and "escalating" are used to describe positive feedback, whereas "deviation minimizing" and "homeostatic" describe negative feedback. It is important to note that the terms positive and negative feedback are being used in the technical cybernetic sense and are value-free. The regulatory patterns that they describe do not necessarily correspond to the colloquial usage of negative feedback as criticism and positive feedback as praise.

Positive feedback regulation tends to operate within a certain range, while negative feedback is activated at the limits of the range. Both processes are important for the system to maintain itself in a steady state (homeostasis), to achieve the same final goal when starting from different initial conditions (equifinality), and to guide change to achieve alternative goals (morphogenesis). Thus, in an ongoing relationship there may be intermittent bursts of positive feedback regulation (morphogenesis) limited by negative feedback regulation (morphostasis). In families these patterns of control tend to become quite stable and predictable. For any substantial change to occur in a relationship, the regulatory limits must be readjusted so that a new range of behaviors is possible or an entirely new pattern (transformation) can emerge. Family beliefs and family rules are the additional organizational elements that determine the points at which feedback regulation is activated. In the process of applying these cybernetic regulatory concepts, a method of diagramming patterns of interpersonal interaction was developed.

CIRCULAR PATTERN DIAGRAMMING

One of the major problems confronting beginning (and experienced) therapists is the overwhelming amount of data available when working with families. Fortunately, information may be "compressed" by pattern recognition. Thus, one method of coping with all these data is to develop skills in recognizing patterns which summarize and simplify the "organized complexity" of family systems. Two types of interaction patterns may be identified: linear and circular (triangles may be considered special forms of circular patterns). Everyday experience of interpersonal events occurring in chronological time tends to promote the perception of interactional sequences as linear patterns. However, when a certain block of time that contains repetitive sequences is conceptually "collapsed" onto a flat plane, circular as well as linear patterns may emerge. Circular patterns have the advantage of summarizing more data and of revealing stable organizational structure with feedback regulation.

A simple diagrammatic model was developed in the Calgary Program to concretize the rather abstract cybernetic concept of feedback as it is applied to family systems. The model is easiest to apply when used to understand an ongoing interaction pattern within a dyadic relationship. The simplest circular pattern diagram (CPD), when applied to a dyad, includes two observable behaviors and two inferences of meaning which connect these behaviors. Figure 2A diagrams the structural relationship between these four basic elements. The small enclosures represent the two persons involved in the dyad (square = male, circle = female). The inference is entered inside the enclosure, and represents an internal process, that is, what presumably is going on inside the interactant. The external arrows represent information conveyed from each person to the other through their behaviors. The circular linkage implies an interaction pattern that is repetitive, stable, and self-regulatory. Figure 2B elaborates on the component elements and connections of the basic model. The behavioral output of one person provides the communication which becomes the perceptual input of the second person, and vice-versa. Two types of inferences may be used: affective or cognitive. An affective inference refers to the motivational response set which is activated in the individual and which "drives" his or her behavioral output. The cognitive inference reflects the idea, concept, or belief which is used to attribute meaning to the perceptual input and which triggers the affective set.

When constructing a CPD (Figure 3), it is helpful to remember that there are multiple channels and levels of communication (Watzlawick et al., 1967). To a large extent it is the nonverbal communication that serves to regulate the structure of ongoing interpersonal relationships

Figure 2. Basic Elements of a Circular Pattern Diagram

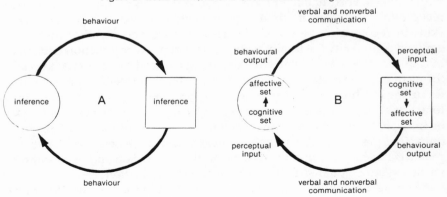

Figure 3. Construction of a Circular Pattern Diagram

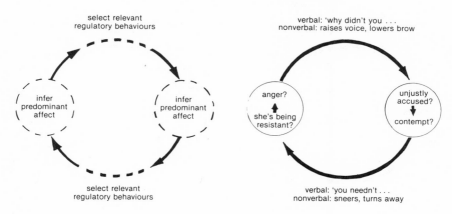

(Scheflen, 1973). Thus, nonverbal behavior may be expected to yield important information regarding appropriate inferences. Facial expression, for instance, usually reflects specific affective states (Ekman & Friesen, 1975) and is a valuable source of data to determine the appropriate affect to be used as the affective inference. Asking people how they feel may be helpful but verbal communication is more easily "managed" to create a certain impression. If there is a discrepancy between what is being said and what is being conveyed, the inference should be based on the nonverbal data which are less liable to be deceptive. Finally, it is important to select those behaviors and inferences that are in fact associated with one another and that would follow logically in a sequence to complete a circle.

In practice it is through a series of successive approximations that a succinct CPD is created. The diagram is then used to represent a basic structural component of a particular ongoing relationship. Human interaction is far too complex for any one simple diagram to describe the totality of any relationship. However, a well developed CPD often can capture a core pattern that is paradigmatic. As such it provides a valuable aid in retaining a systemic gestalt of the structure of the relationship. From the point of view of dyadic interpersonal structure (cf. the shape of the vase), two fundamentally different forms of circular patterns may be described: symmetrical and complementary. The particular form of relationship structure is not inherently adaptive or maladaptive, but its contents and stability may be. Complementary patterns that are maladaptive and relatively fixed are particularly pathogenic.

Figure 4. Common Circular Patterns

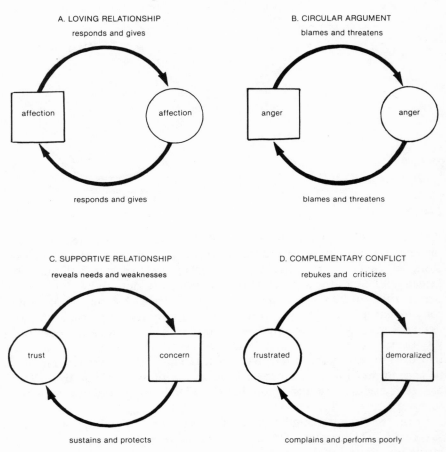

A few common circular patterns are represented in Figure 4. Both "vicious" and "virtuous" circles (Wender, 1968) are illustrated. The mutual affection and circular argument (Figure 4A and 4B) are symmetrical, whereas the support and conflict relationships (Figure 4C and 4D) are complementary. One interesting feature of complementary patterns is that they vary in reversibility. A relationship which is complementary but whose interactants can readily exchange roles is reversible and thus has symmetrical characteristics. A friendship, for instance, usually includes patterns of alternating emotional support, whereas a therapist-patient relationship tends to be unidirectional. The complementary conflict pattern in Figure 4D includes onus-putting and onus-taking. The female (in this diagram) not only rebukes and criticizes the male for what he does wrong but also places the onus of responsibility for the problem in their relationship on him. To complement her projection, he introjects and takes the onus onto himself, thus intensifying his own depressive demoralization. Bowen (1966) aptly described this as overadequate-inadequate reciprocity. When this pattern becomes fixed, the male appears chronically depressed and the female perpetually angry. All too often this type of problem "presents" as an individual one, usually the depressed member of the dyad. If conceptualized only at this level, the "patient" would be treated with medication (antidepressants or tranquilizers) or individual psychotherapy while the underlying pathogenic relationship structure remained unchanged. Hence, one would expect the improvement, if any, to be transitory.

All these relationship patterns are self-perpetuating and are sustained by positive feedback processes. As noted earlier, cybernetic theory defines positive feedback as deviation amplifying (Maruyama, 1963) and therefore the pattern should escalate. While escalation may occur, there are several reasons why these relationships tend to manifest as stable maintenance patterns and not as rapidly escalating ones. Considerable energy is required to sustain an organized relationship, that is, to resist the entropic tendency toward gradual dissolution. Communication theory suggests that information may be lost in the interaction between signal and noise in the communication channels and that "slippage" may occur in the encoding and decoding process (Dittman, 1972). Thus, some amplification is required to ensure that the message gets across. More significantly, however, each behavioral pattern has certain limits which are governed by rules of the system. That is, as positive feedback escalates the pattern, a point is reached at which another negative feedback pattern is activated to resist further change in the same direction.

Figure 5 illustrates the homeostatic limitations that negative feedback may introduce in a positive feedback pattern of mutual affection. Either participant in the relationship may become satiated and, having his or her needs met, tire of the interaction and seek outside interests or involvements. Or the intimate interaction may arouse anxieties of becoming engulfed, suffocated, or controlled. Consequently the participant will withdraw or push away. In both situations the intensity of the intimacy subsides. The response of the partner to the negative feedback signals in these new behaviors will influence subsequent interaction. If they are met with acceptance and tolerance, there is a good probability

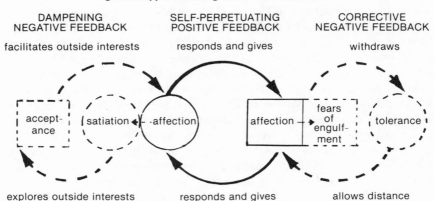

Figure 5. Upper Limit Regulation of a Stable Pattern

that the affectionate pattern will later be resumed and continue. If, on the other hand, the partner fails to recognize or respond to these behaviors (as negative feedback regulation), but tries to continue further intimate interaction, the negative feedback signals will be intensified, become actively rejecting, and hence conflict-promoting. As a result, a sudden "flip" into circular argument may occur. Figure 6 illustrates this and also shows how the fear of loss (or a reemergence of a need for intimacy) could likewise limit the severity of the conflict by activating conciliatory behaviors such as apology and appeasement (negative feedback for the conflict). The resultant intimacy-conflict cycle is quite common in some marriages and is elaborated by Feldman (1979). This cycle reflects the phenomenon of oscillation, another characteristic of cybernetic systems, which if extreme can be highly pathological.

Figure 6. An Alternating Intimacy-Conflict Cycle

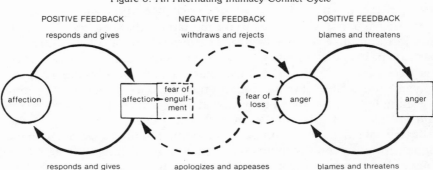

The CPD model may also be applied to help clarify parent-child interaction. Figure 7A outlines a pattern that is often found when a child presents with an emotional or behavioral problem. If the mother is stimulated to see herself as inadequate as a mother (cognitive inference), she is liable to become angry or depressed (affective inference). This may be reflected behaviorally in her irritability or lack of responsiveness to the child. As a result, the child may perceive himself as unwanted or bad, which generates anxiety or guilt. The child tends to become preoccupied with these thoughts and feelings, has more difficulty attending to his usual instrumental and developmental tasks, and thus performs poorly at home and school. In addition, he may misbehave as a ploy to stimulate more responsiveness and attention from the mother. The child's poor performance and misbehavior, however, actually feed into the mother's cognitive set of "inadequate mother" and thus the vicious pattern comes full circle and is perpetuated.

If the father is included in the interaction noted above, a triadic circular pattern may be conceptualized, as in Figure 7B. The child's poor performance and inappropriate behavior may feed into the father's perception of seeing the child as unlikable and bad. He may react with disgust, anger, or contempt, which may be manifested behaviorally by his avoidance of the whole situation or in overt expressions of disapproval towards his wife (or son). These reactions feed into the mother's sense of inadequacy, depression, and anger, and the pattern is maintained with yet additional input. The triadic circle could, of course, also be drawn in the opposite direction to illustrate the self-perpetuating sequence: father→ son→ mother→ father, etc. Or the combined triadic circles

Figure 7. Dyadic and Triadic Parent-Child Patterns

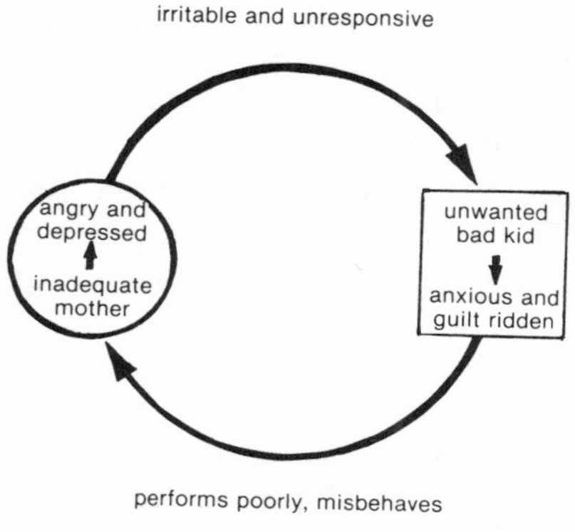

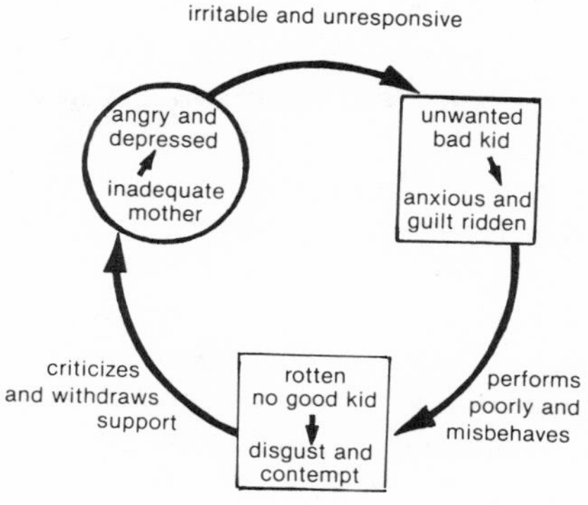

could be drawn as three interrelated dyadic patterns. However, the triangle is considered a more economic geometric form to grasp three-person relationship structure.

THERAPEUTIC APPLICATION AND UTILITY

In order to use this model of circular pattern diagramming, it is useful to see family members conjointly. A more accurate account of interactional events is likely to be obtained when all members of the relationship are present. Family members readily correct one another when descriptions are ambiguous or distorted. Even when explicit description or correction is disallowed and the interactants collude to give a false impression because of the rules of the system, there is still a great deal of nonverbal leakage which may implicitly validate or contradict what is said. A more important reason for conjoint interviewing is the opportunity to "sample" the relationship directly by observing the interaction in the immediacy of the session. To do this the therapist encourages and deliberately stimulates spontaneous interaction between family members during the session. If the clinician is interested in understanding a particular aspect of the relationship, it is important to focus on this area and note the interactants' responses to one another while they are discussing the relevant issues.

Although it is a simple and concrete tool, the CPD promotes integrative and abstract conceptualization. It helps the student or experienced clinician focus specifically on a systemic element of the family. Usually when the family initially describes a problem, it is in linear terms and there is a tendency to blame particular individuals for causing difficulties. If the therapist is drawn into the family's way of perceiving and conceptualizing, he or she too is liable to end up focusing on and covertly blaming the individual (albeit with somewhat more empathy) and to overlook the interpersonal systemic problem. The use of CPDs facilitates the shift from linear to circular thinking. For instance, one benefit of using CPDs rapidly emerges when *parts* of a circular process are not readily evident. In struggling conceptually to complete the circle, the therapist's perceptions and questions are oriented towards discovering the missing links. In this way significant but nonobvious regulatory behaviors are more likely to be elicited and identified. When certain events are connected and reinterpreted as circular rather than linear, specific behaviors are recontextualized and take on different meaning.

When the therapist can clearly see the full circular pattern(s), it is easier for him/her to maintain his/her neutrality and avoid taking sides inappropriately. When a problem is defined as being circular, the issue of initiator or "first cause" becomes irrelevant. A circle by definition has no beginning or end. It is often helpful to draw a CPD on a blackboard or piece of paper and explain it to the family. As family members transcend their individual linear conceptualizations, a flash of insight may occur and be accompanied by considerable relief of underlying guilt feelings. Sometimes this is enough to precipitate change. However, when the pattern is tenacious, such insight is transitory. The family quickly regresses back to linear thinking and more vigorous interventions are required.

The reason that linear thinking can be so problematic is that it mobilizes predominantly feedforward regulation and fails to take advantage of the constructive potential of negative feedback. For instance, the male in the circular argument described earlier (Figure 4B) does not usually deliberately try to maintain or escalate the conflict by generating positive feedback with his blaming or threatening. Instead, he sees himself simply as trying to correct the female on the basis of limited perceptual input. "She keeps blaming me. If she would stop, we would get along fine. Therefore, I must correct her." This negative feedback *intent* actually constitutes feedforward regulation (on the individual level) and inadvertently has a positive feedback *effect* (at the interpersonal level) that keeps the maladaptive pattern going. However, if the therapist is able to shift the perceptual punctuation of events so that the husband's perceptual input *includes* his own output, feedback rather than feedforward regulation can occur. "When I try to correct her, she just gets angry and blames me. To get different results maybe I should try something else." When he recognizes the consequences of his own problematic behavior, the possibility of activating negative rather than positive feedback responses is increased. With the component parts of a CPD clearly in mind, the therapist is able to redirect a family member to explore the specific problematic consequences of his/her own behaviors and thus help repunctuate the member's perceptions to be output- as well as input-based.

Ultimately, the greatest advantage of using CPDs is that they suggest a multiplicity of potential therapeutic strategies. The diagram clearly indicates multiple points of entry to break up the maladaptive pattern. Because of the clarity of links in the circle, interventions may be more specific and precise. If one is behaviorally oriented, one may focus primarily on altering the communicative behavior described on the connecting arrows. If one is psychodynamically oriented, one may direct interventions towards modifying the affective set or response tendency. If one is cognitively oriented, the target would be the cognitive inference. A broad-based, eclectic clinician may probe to find those points that provide the greatest leverage to initiate change or intervene at multiple points simultaneously to break up the homeostatic cycle (Hoffman, 1976). Thus, this particular model of circular pattern diagramming serves to integrate a number of behavioral, psychodynamic and cognitive concepts and techniques.

Figures 8 and 9 outline possible psychodynamic and cognitive interventions to alter the common complementary pattern of blame-withdrawal. This pattern is often seen in conflicted marriages. The psychodynamic approach is oriented towards an exploration of deeper affective experience related to the predominant surface affects of anger and fear entered as the affective inference in the basic maladaptive pattern (the conceptual CPD in Figure 8). By identifying and mobilizing underlying feelings of guilt and fear of loss in the angry wife, for instance, the husband is liable to respond with concern and take initiative to offer support rather than react with his usual fear and withdrawal. Experiencing his support, she in turn is more liable to disclose her vulnerability further and thus the couple may enter a more adaptive pattern (as illustrated in the left CPD of Figure 8). Likewise, by uncovering the husband's underlying anger and guilt, a change may be initiated in the wife's response. As indicated in the figure, each uncovering exploration carried out in the presence of the spouse opens the possibility of the emergence of a more constructive marital pattern. In practice these psychodynamic explorations are usually accompanied by cognitive explorations as well. The upper CPD in Figure 9 shows the same basic pattern but with cognitive inferences. The figure illustrates some cognitive intervention strategies that lead to an adaptive pattern to replace the maladaptive one.

Figure 8. A Psychodynamic Intervention Strategy

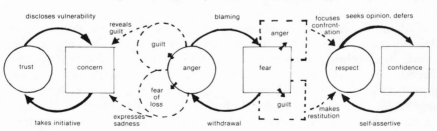

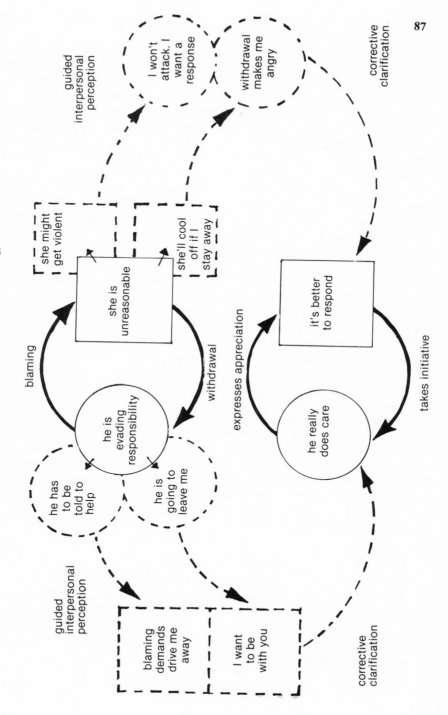

Figure 9. A Cognitive Intervention Strategy

Expressed affect functions not only as an interpersonal regulator but also as a "marker" of intrapsychic events and of the specific cognitions involved in maintaining the maladaptive pattern. For instance, by being able to identify the wife's underlying sadness or fear of loss, one is led to uncover her catastrophic expectation that he may leave her. It is easy to see how his withdrawal behavior helps keep her fears of loss alive. In attempting to explore her expectations and revise any unrealistic beliefs, it is useful to stimulate direct interaction between the spouses concerning their interpersonal perceptions. She would be encouraged to inquire directly from him whether he expects to leave, and how imminent he thought the possibility was. Finally, he would be given the task of providing her with convincing corrective evidence (verbal and/or behavioral) when there is a discrepancy between their expectations.

As implied in Figures 8 and 9, the model of circular pattern diagramming also offers a method of conceptualizing an adaptive goal for the relationship. The therapist or family may construct a virtuous pattern to replace the vicious one and use this as a template to work towards. As the appropriate initiatives or conciliatory behaviors occur in the interview, the therapist stimulates the spouse to respond to them. As a result, an adaptive positive feedback loop emerges. By exercising these adaptive or virtuous circles in the session and learning the skills of cognitive restructuring through interpersonal inquiry, the spouses become more competent in solving their own problems and less dependent on the therapist.

While some of these interventions may appear to be individualistic, they are derived from the context of the relationship and are guided by an interpersonal systems concept. The CPD helps clarify discrepancies between individual intentions and interpersonal effects and thus allows for more focused and specific therapeutic interventions. Perhaps it is the increased precision that is possible at the individual level when the problem is conceptualized at the interpersonal level that contributes to the increased efficacy of family therapy.

CONCLUDING COMMENTS

Many students and therapists have already found this model of circular pattern diagramming useful in their work with families. Some families report on follow-up that they found the circular explanations one of the most helpful aspects of tharapy. However, the CPD is only one simple application of the concept of the circle. The full potential of cybernetic conceptualization has not yet been realized; it is only beginning to be explored. Further development of circular models that are simple and easy to use, yet facilitate systemic understanding, is required. As hinted in Figure 6, interpersonal circular patterns are related to each other in higher level interlocking circles. Initial efforts have been made to conceptualize circular patterns at the individual intrapsychic level as well. With further clarification of circular process at different hierarchical levels and also between levels, it may be possible to delineate problems more precisely, to estimate the relative effectiveness of interventions at different levels, and to determine whether an upward, horizontal, or downward therapeutic strategy would be optimal.

Family systems theory, although very appealing, still has relatively little research support. A major reason for this is the difficulty in measuring systemic phenomena. Individual measures, although helpful, are not adequate. Specialized techniques such as markovian sequence analysis (Rausch et al., 1974) are developing but are rather complex and cumbersome to use. There is a real need for new research approaches and methods to study the family system and family therapy. Much needs to be understood about contraindications, side effects, and deterioration as a result of family therapy. The major research question that needs to be addressed is the same as that for the psychotherapies in general, namely the specificity question: What specific problems in what specific families respond to what specific interventions by what therapists, when and in what way? The answer to this question is still a long way off, but perhaps it is time to begin to compare the outcomes of various systems-oriented techniques and approaches.

REFERENCES

Bowen, M. The use of the family in clinical practice. *Comprehensive Psychiatry*, 1966, *VII*, (5), 345-374.

Bowen, M. Toward the differentiations of a self in one's own family. In J. Framo (Ed.), *Family Interaction: A Dialogue Between Family Researchers and Family Therapists*. New York: Springer, 1972.

Dittman, A. *Interpersonal Messages of Emotion*. New York: Springer, 1972.

Ekman, P. & Friesen, W.V. *Unmasking the Face: A Guide to Recognizing Emotions from Facial Clues*. Englewood Cliffs, NJ: Prentice-Hall, 1975.

Feldman, L.B. Marital conflict and marital intimacy: An integrative psychodynamic-behavioural-systemic model. *Family Process*, 1979, *18*, (2), 69-78.

Gurman, A.S. & Kniskern, D.P. Research on marital and family therapy. In S.L. Garfield & A.E. Bergin, (Eds.), *Handbook of Psychotherapy and Behavior Change*. New York: Wiley, 1978, pp. 817-902.

Gurman, A.S. & Kniskern, D.P. *Handbook of Family Therapy*. New York: Bunner/Mazel, 1981.

Hoffman, L. Deviation-amplifying processes in natural groups. In J. Haley, (Ed.), *Changing Families*. New York: Grune and Stratton, 1971, pp. 285-311.

Hoffman, L. Breaking the homeostatic cycle. In P. Guerin, (Ed.), *Family Therapy: Theory and Practice*. New York: Gardner Press, 1976, pp. 501-579.

Koestler, A. *The Ghost in the Machine*. London: Hutchison, 1967.

Langsley, D.G. & Kaplan, D.M. *The Treatment of Families in Crisis*. New York: Grune and Stratton, 1968.

McFarland, D.J. *Feedback Mechanisms in Animal Behaviour*. London, New York: Academic Press, 1971.

Maruyama, M. The second cybernetics: Deviation-amplifying mutual causative processes. *American Scientist*, 1963, *51*, 164-179.

Minuchin, S. *Families and Family Therapy*. Cambridge: Harvard University Press, 1974.

Minuchin, S. & Fishman, H.C. *Family Therapy Techniques*. Cambridge: Harvard University Press, 1981.

Minuchin, S., Rosman, B.L., & Baker, L. *Psychosomatic Families: Anorexia Nervosa in Context*. Cambridge: Harvard University Press, 1978.

Rausch, H.L., Barry, W.A., Hertel, R.K., & Swain, M.A. *Communication, Conflict and Marriage*. San Francisco: Jossey-Bass, 1974.

Scheflen, A.E. *Communicational Structure: Analysis of Psychotherapy Transaction*. Bloomington: Indiana University Press, 1973.

Selvini Palazzoli, M., Cecchin, G., Prata, G., & Boscolo, L. *Paradox and Counterparadox*. New York: Jason Aronson, 1978.

Tomm, K. The Milan approach to family therapy: A tentative report. In D. Freeman, & B. Trute, (Eds.), *Treating Families with Special Needs*. Ottawa: Canadian Association of Social Workers, 1982.

Tomm, K., McArthur, R.G., & Leahey, M.D. Psychologic management of children with diabetes mellitus. *Clinical Pediatrics*, 1977, *16*, (12), 1141-1155.

Tomm, K. & Wright, L.M. Training in family therapy: Perceptual, conceptual, and executive skills. *Family Process*, 1979, *18*, (3), 227-250.

von Bertalanffy, L.P. *General System Theory: Foundations, Development, Applications*. New York: G. Braziller, 1968.

Watzlawick, P., Beavin, J.H., & Jackson, D.D. *Pragmatics of Human Communication*. New York: W.W. Norton, 1967.

Watzlawick, P., Weakland, J., & Fisch, R. *Change: Principles of Problem Formation and Problem Resolution*. New York: Norton, 1974.

Weiner, N. *Cybernetics or Control and Communication in the Animal and the Machine*. Cambridge: MA: Technology Press, 1948.

Wender, P. Vicious and virtuous circles: The role of deviation amplifying feedback in the origin and perpetuation of behavior. *Psychiatry*, 1968, *31*, (4), 309-324.

Editor's Commentary: Circular Pattern Diagramming: The New Geometrics of Family Therapy

Concern with cybernetic regulatory mechanisms in the family has increased markedly in the field of family therapy in the past two decades. Tomm's discussion of feedforward and feedback loops, of open heirarchical systems theory, and of upward and downward causation is a particularly lucid one that should serve as a clear introductory guide for the novice newly exploring this body of knowledge. For the "old pro," his elaboration should enhance the depth and breadth of understanding. It follows Dell's exposition because both deal, in their idiosyncratic and erudite fashion, with conceptualizations of the inherent properties of the family system and its regulatory processes. They are complementary and yet provocatively contradictory.

Tomm prefers circular pattern diagramming (CPD) to using triangles à la Bowen (1978) as the major geometric figure. His various figures cogently present what he is trying to depict regarding the vicious circularity of repetitive, dysfunctional interaction patterns. I am particularly drawn to the Calgary CPD model because it serves to integrate a number of behavioral, psychodynamic, and cognitive concepts and techniques. As such, it is compatible with my own "diaclectic model" (Kaslow, 1981) which seeks to cull what is most applicable from the various theoretical schools in making the decision as to what is likely to be the most efficacious approach for treating this family at this point in time. In addition, the CPD offers therapist and patients a way of formulating a realizable goal and "a template to work towards." Without rigidly structuring the therapeutic process, this model offers enough specificity for flexible mapping of anticipated outcomes and of the best pathways to be pursued. The diagramming lends itself to simplifying the mass of data a family communicates about its organizational complexity and to charting inferences about both verbal and nonverbal behavior. Each diagram represents a basic structural component of a particular ongoing relationship; it may capture a core paradigmatic pattern. Further, one can assess functioning at three different levels—biological, psychological, and interpersonal—and consider the interface of the different subsystems, problems which exist at one level only, and those which are multilevel.

The CPD not only should be an effective tool for assessing and conceptualizing a problem and for formulating of treatment goals, but might also be adaptable for comparative research on family therapy treatment outcomes across settings and therapists. It is a model that is at once sophisticated and highly understandable—a rare and laudatory combination.

REFERENCES

Bowen, M. *Family Therapy in Clinical Practice*. New York: Jason Aronson, 1978.
Kaslow, F.W. A diaclectic approach to family therapy and practice: Selectivity and synthesis. *Journal of Marital and Family Therapy*, July 1981, 7, (3), 345-351.

Part II

Family Therapy:
Theory, Process, and Technique

Chapter 5

Family Paradigm and Family Coping: A Proposal for Linking the Family's Intrinsic Adaptive Capacities to Its Responses to Stress

By David Reiss
and Mary Ellen Oliveri

Recently, there has been an increased interest in delineating the strategies by which families cope with stressful and challenging events and circumstances. This essay is an effort to explore the range and variety of such coping strategies. More important, it attempts to show how these strategies are related to one another and to more fundamental adaptive capacities of families; these capacities are manifest in the routines that are typical of the quiescent periods of the families' lives. The relationships we posit are shaped by a theory developing out of an extended series of laboratory and field studies in our center. Kuhn's concept of paradigm has been a helpful organizing metaphor for this theoretical work. It has led us to suspect that a family's adaptive capacities—both its everyday routines as well as its

This paper was originally published in *Family Relations,* Oct. 1980, *291*, 431-444. Slight modifications have been made in the current chapter.

The work described in this paper was supported by DHEW Grant MH 26711.

David Reiss, M.D., is Director, Center for Family Research, and Professor, Department of Psychiatry and Behavioral Sciences. The George Washington University School of Medicine, Washington, D.C.

Mary Ellen Oliveri, Ph.D., is Investigator, Center for Family Research, and Assistant Research Professor, Department of Psychiatry and Behavioral Sciences, The George Washington University School of Medicine, Washington, D.C.

attempts to cope with unusual and stressful events—are shaped by its abiding conception of the social world in which it lives.

Careful, direct observational studies of families in their natural settings—their homes and communities—are indicating that large segments of family life are humdrum and routine. Although the routines of daily life doubtless serve important functions for families during stable times, occasional events and circumstances challenge the family's well-formed habits. It is then that the family is called upon to exert some unusual effort: to observe, to experience, to define, to understand and to take some kind of special action so that it can return to the more orderly routines of its daily life. These sequences of experiences and actions, at times of challenge, are occasionally imaginative and inspired, and other times banal and tragic. All of them in their endless variety are coming to be known in our field by the somewhat prosaic term of "coping strategies."

This essay is an attempt to picture some of the variables of these strategies of coping with stress and to show how they derive from underlying intrinsic adaptive capacities of families that, while stable and enduring, may be little noticed during the more ordinary routines of everyday life. More specifically, our aim is to refine a model of family coping so that we may measure a family's intrinsic adaptive capacities at a quiescent period in its life, and use those measurements to predict the family's response to stress. Our efforts along these lines have proceeded through three phases. First, we have over many years developed a set of laboratory procedures which highlight variations in how families solve externally-given problems. We have explored what underlying adaptive capacities are expressed by the various problem-solving styles we observe (Reiss, 1967; 1968; 1969; 1971b; 1971c). This phase of our work has been aided by a developing theory and set of methods which conceive of a broad variety of family problem-solving routines as shaped by an enduring conception each family holds about the fundamental nature of its social world and its place in that world (Reiss, 1971d). Although our theoretical work draws on several sources, Kuhn's (1970) concept of paradigm has been a particularly helpful organizing metaphor. A second phase has been the development of hypotheses about what sorts of coping strategies a family with a particular set of adaptive capacities would develop in the face of stress. Third, we test these predictions by comparing our laboratory findings with assessments of actual coping strategies families use in times of stress.

The first of these phases has to some degree been accomplished and is summarized in the first part of this essay. The second phase is outlined in the main portion of this essay. The final phase is under active investigation in our laboratory now.

THE CONCEPT OF THE FAMILY PARADIGM

Family Problem Solving and Shared Constructs

For many years we have investigated several aspects of family problem solving. Initially, we used a well-controlled and precise series of laboratory methods, and our interest was in distinguishing different styles or patterns of problem solving. Indeed we found marked differences among families along three principal dimensions (Reiss, 1971d). First, families differed in the extent to which they could detect patterns and organization in the complex stimulus arrays with which we presented them as a group. Second, families differed in their degrees of coordination, cooperation, and agreement as they progressed through the many phases of our problems. Finally, families differed in their openness to new information: some families reached decisions early whereas others delayed closure as long as possible.

Our first question about these differences in problem-solving style concerned their correlates in the actual lives of families, and several studies have suggested that there are some remarkably detailed parallels. For example, in a recent series of clinical studies we have been able to use families' problem-solving styles, measured in the laboratory, to make fine-grained predictions successfully about their patterns of adjustment to the psychiatric hospitalization of an adolescent member (Reiss, Costell, Jones, & Berkman, 1980). Also, in recent studies of nonclinical families, problem-solving styles have correlated with the patterns of relationships between families and their extended kin (Oliveri & Reiss, 1981).

Since the problem-solving styles we were observing seemed to reflect more general modes of family adaptation, we wondered what factors or circumstances shaped and controlled them. We examined the most obvious variables to answer this question, but in our samples (we have now tested well over 400 families), social class, family structure, race and the religion of the family, as well as the intelligence, problem-solving skills, and perceptual styles of individual members, have had no relationship with the family group's problem-solving style. However, detailed observation of our families in the laboratory, and interviewing of them after the formal procedures had been administered, gave us our first clue about what did shape their problem-solving styles. It seemed that a specific family's problem-solving style arose less from its understanding of the problems we presented them, and more from their perception of the research setting and the research team. For all families, the research setting is ambiguous and moderately stressful. Despite the careful oral and written instructions we give them before they come, and once again when they arrive, families really do not know why we are doing the research, what we expect of them, and how they are being assessed. Each family must come to its own conclusions on these matters. These conclusions, we have found, are formed early (often before the family arrives at our doorstep) and seem to determine all that comes afterwards.

For example, some families mistrust us from the outset. They feel that we are giving them an insoluble puzzle whose *real* (although concealed) purpose is to humiliate them or strain the ties of one member to another. For them, the true problem is not to solve the logical puzzle we give them but rather to stick together to finish the puzzles and then, as quickly as possible, beat a hasty though decorous retreat. Hence, they show a particular "problem-solving style": very tight consensus, early closure and crude pattern recognition (they have not really tried to look for patterns). In sharp contrast are families who trust us (whether or not we, in fact, deserve it). They assume right from the start we have given them a soluble puzzle and that we are being honest when we tell them "this is a study to learn more about how families solve problems." They go about their business cooperatively, efficiently, waiting for the maximum amount of data before making a final decision. Thus, they show another kind of "problem-solving style": one of cooperative and effective search for patterns with delayed closure.

From the outset we doubted that these shared family perceptions of the situation resulted from anything we did, purposively or not (Rosenthal, 1969, notwithstanding). First, the reactions of our families were quite varied even though our approach to them was relatively uniform. Second, the beliefs about us seemed to be held with great and profound conviction. We began to feel that our laboratory problem-solving procedure had serendipitously uncovered, for each family, a pervasive orientation to the social environment. We reasoned that this orientation might be built into the family and condition the quality of its engagement with any social setting, particularly if the setting were at all ambiguous. This would be a good explanation not only for the variety of problem-solving styles we had observed in the laboratory but, more importantly, for the pin-point predictions regarding families' relationships with social communities in their everyday worlds (e.g., the social community of the psychiatric hospital or of the extended family).

We have begun to look at this issue directly, and have been developing measures to assess the family's perception of a variety of communities and groups with which it comes into contact. For example, we have recently published a report exploring how a family perceives other families and again have shown surprising, but by now understandable, correlations between problem-solving style and these shared perceptions of other families (Reiss, Costell, Berkman, & Jones, 1980). Our recent work has revealed, in each family, a rich and ordered set of beliefs about the social world. These beliefs seem sensibly connected to the ways families actually respond to and interact with their social world.

Our attention has now turned to exploring these shared beliefs, assumptions and orientations that families hold. Since our evidence suggests that they are built-in and enduring components of family life, we have asked what function they serve. It was not enough to argue that they played a role in regulating the family's transactions with its social environment. We now want to know why families develop such shared beliefs and assumptions to perform such a function. Equally important, we want to know how such belief systems develop and what circumstances lead to major changes. This line of theorizing has been described in some detail elsewhere (Reiss, 1981) along with evidence in support of it. We will only summarize our thinking here in preparation for our discussion of family stress and coping.

The Nature and Function of Shared Constructs

This line of theorizing has been supported and shaped by the ideas on individual psychology of Heider (1958) and Kelly (1955) and on social process by Berger and Luckman (1966). A beginning premise is that each individual must develop his own set of constructs of social phenomena, bound together with his theory of how the social world works. This personal system of ideas, opinions, hunches, assumptions, hypotheses and convictions is a constant guide to individuals in any novel situation. It shapes their hypotheses about that situation, their investigations and conclusions, and is a constant guide for their behavior. In our work on theory, we have added to these familiar notions some ideas about the individual's need to share with others this task of developing personal theories. Indeed, we have argued with the assistance of thoughts from

Berger and Luckman (1966) that lengthy, intimate, face-to-face relationships cannot go forward without a reconciliation, integration and shared development of the basic premises of these personal theories. In other words, when two or more individuals develop an intimate relationship, they engage in a process of reconciling the basic premises of their personal construct systems. Thus, a shared system of construing in a family reflects the progressive and crucial integration, over time, of the personal explanatory system of each member. Conversely, the dissolution or splitting of families develops out of the disavowal of shared premises and personal constructs.

The concept of shared beliefs has been a little difficult to accept for people who recognize how much disagreement and conflict are invariably components of family life. Our view is that the presence of conflict or disagreement itself does not necessarily mean these underlying shared beliefs are absent. Indeed, what family members often share at times of dissension are beliefs about what is important to argue about and how such arguments may ultimately be resolved. For example, a husband and wife quarrel bitterly about whose responsibility it is to clean the children's toys from the sidewalk in front of their house. They accuse each other of risking criticism from their neighbors. The wife becomes more strident and the husband sulks away to clean up. We may say this couple, despite its argument, shares at least two conceptions. First, both share an extreme sensitivity to the opinion of their neighbors. Second, they share an assumption that the most strident arguer must win out. Underlying, shared beliefs of this kind cannot easily be reported verbally by the family. Often, they must be inferred from observations of the family's behavior. Our own data are tentative but do seem to support the idea that beliefs or orientations of this kind are truly shared (Reiss, 1971a; Reiss & Salzman, 1973). We also have reported some preliminary evidence that these shared beliefs are more evident in a family's nonverbal behavior than in its discussion (Reiss, 1970).

Our model acknowledges that there are, in all likelihood, several mechanisms by which shared constructs develop and change. Our main interest has been in the role of serious and disabling crisis in family life. We have seen in this circumstance, though rare in the life of an ordinary family, an opportunity to understand some of the fundamental aspects of the development and change of family constructs. Drawing on clinical experience and the theoretical work of Kantor and Lehr (1975) we have argued that in severe family crisis, whatever the cause, the family's typical mode of conceptualizing its position in the world becomes more clear, stark, simple. It loses its background position as a gentle coordinator of family affairs and becomes a conspicuous eminence with which no family member feels entirely comfortable. As the crisis becomes more severe, members start to disown this eminence which has come to seem oppressive. Dissolution of the family or a split of one member from the rest is imminent and often occurs.

At this point in the progressive decay of a family, a reorganization of their mode of construing their position in the world is often possible. In a clinical setting it may be influenced by a therapist; a religious family may draw on a priest or a clerical community. The recovery and reconstruction from extreme crisis can bring a new organization to family life and more importantly, for our purposes, to their typical mode of perceiving events. Surface manifestations of these shifts are seen in the way some families respond: to the unanticipated death of a child, to a prolonged and disabling illness in an older member, to a move or a job loss. Crisis provides the raw material for a fundamental revision of its shared mode of construing the environment. The new system of constructs can become a point around which the family organizes. Consider, for example, a family that finds it can thrive following the death of a dominant grandmother who controlled the family through dire predictions of danger only she could thwart. A new set of concepts about the family's relationship to the social world can emerge through grief and crisis following grandmother's death. The family can develop an entirely new sense of its own potency. The important point here is that the force, persistence and pervasiveness of the new construct system comes from its initial and continuing role in providing family coherence after a time of crisis. We have argued that this force continues even after the crisis is no longer consciously remembered.

This crisis-oriented group dynamic, as we propose it, bears an interesting relationship to that described by Kuhn for scientific revolutions (Kuhn, 1970). His familiar formulation pictures, in effect, scientists as a quasi-social group whose behavior is shaped by a set of fundamental assumptions about the natural world. When these assumptions fail to account for new data, dissolution occurs; the community of scientists can no longer function as a smoothly working "group," and crisis arises. A clever new solution to existing problems serves as a continuing model or paradigm for the rebuilding of a new system of framing assumptions. Whatever difficulty Kuhn's ideas have encountered in the philosophy of science (Suppe, 1977) they have been a useful set of metaphors for our work. We now refer to the *family paradigm* as that new idea or approach, born in crisis, which serves as a background and orienting idea or perspective to the family's problem solving in daily life. A family paradigm serves as a stable disposition or orientation whenever the family must actively construe a new situation.

We do not have a clear idea, as yet, of the circumstances under which crisis produces a genuine change or "revolution" in family life. After crisis, some families return to the old order whereas others undergo major transformations. Some hypotheses in this regard have been formulated elsewhere (Reiss, 1981) but this matter is an important area for future investigation.

DIMENSIONS OF FAMILY PARADIGM

If our argument thus far is on the mark, then it follows that if we know the family's paradigm we should be able to predict a wide range of its responses to ambiguous and stressful events in its social world. We are just beginning to examine these possibilities in a series of related research programs. We are aided by two factors of immense practical importance. First, it appears possible to delineate, at least in part, these underlying orientations in family life by our laboratory problem-solving techniques. They serve in part as a group Rorschach: an ambiguous field on which the family can project its own assumptions. However, unlike the Rorschach, our procedures require the family to *act* rather than just talk. These actions are measurable by precise quantitative techniques. A second factor of practical importance is that a great deal of variation in problem-solving behavior, and we believe in the underlying paradigms that produce it, can be accounted for by three conceptually distinct dimensions. Thus, if we know a family's position along each of these three dimensions we should be able to successfully predict a great range of their responses to challenging social situations. It is the burden of this essay to specify these predictions. First, however, we must summarize our cardinal dimensions. The conceptualization and validation of these dimensions is based on work carried out in our own laboratory. Although the findings from this work are internally consistent, it must be emphasized that the findings themselves, and the interpretation we attach to them, need to be corroborated by other investigators in different settings.

Configuration

In our problem-solving tasks we recognize this dimension by the degree to which the family can discover the hidden or underlying patterns in the stimulus arrays we present them. Our data suggest that this problem-solving behavior reflects a fundamental conception, by the family, that the social world in which they live is ordered by a coherent set of principles which they can discover and master through exploration and interpretation (Reiss, 1971b; Reiss, 1981; Reiss et al., 1980). For example, families who recognize patterns in the laboratory problem-solving task also have well-worked out, ordered and subtle conceptions of other families they know (Reiss et al., 1980). Also, in our clinical studies, they are sensitive to subtle cues, particularly emotional ones, in developing their impressions of an in-patient treatment program to which their adolescent child has been admitted (Costell et al., 1981). The sense of potential mastery over the social environment characterizing families high on configuration has also been revealed in the patterns of social network interactions of nonclinical families: configuration is positively associated with the degree of autonomy of individual family members in relation to the network of the extended family (Oliveri & Reiss, 1981). Elsewhere, we have proposed that families high or low on configuration can be recognized by observing their everyday household routines. For example, families high on configuration practice rituals which tie them firmly to wider social groups outside the home, such as the home celebration of ethnic rituals or the regular invitation of guests to dinner (Reiss, 1981). They also arrange their household activities to clearly reflect an ordered and comprehensive grasp of the family's role in the community. For example, a child will be given space to study and a mother space to conduct meetings if her vocation or avocation requires it. In contrast, the rituals of low-configuration families reflect idiosyncratic ties to their own past and are incomprehensible and separate from the larger community. Their households are either an inchoate jumble or a frozen idealization of the past. An example of the latter is the family of a physician's widow who kept the deceased doctor's desk, medical equipment and books in place for over a decade after his death.

Coordination

We recognize this dimension by the care with which each member dovetails his problem-solving efforts with others in the family. This is more than a measure of simple agreement on the nature of the problem's solution. Our measurement of coordination is based on the degree to which members attend to the details of each other's problem-solving efforts. These problem-solving patterns reflect the family's belief that they, in fact, occupy the same experiential world, a world which operates in the same way for all of them. Beyond that, families high on this dimension see themselves as facing their social world as a group; they feel themselves to be a group, but even more important, feel the world treats them as a group. Thus, what happens to one will have implications for the rest. Our data do indeed suggest that families who are high on this dimension carefully compare and integrate their impressions about many aspects of their social world. For example, members in high-co-ordination families take care to develop similar views of the in-patient treatment program (Costell, Reiss, Berkman, & Jones, 1981) and are precisely attuned to one another's efforts to explore and understand other families (Reiss, 1981). It is also of interest that these families are embedded in nuclear families who are close and well connected; in these cases the wife's and husband's families often know and relate to one another (Oliveri & Reiss, 1981). We have proposed that families high in coordination, as measured in the laboratory, also show a great deal of synchrony and coordination of planning and scheduling in their daily lives. The dimension of coordination is similar, in some respects, to the recently re-conceptualized dimension of cohesion as presented by Olson, Sprenkle, & Russell (1979). Our dimension focuses more specifically on the family's conception or belief about their experiential world. Unlike Olson et al., we do not regard either the extreme or moderate values on this dimension as adaptive or non-adaptive. As we will briefly review at the end of this essay, in our view family adaptiveness must take into account the family's own goals as well as the social setting in which it lives.

Closure

In our problem-solving situation, this dimension is measured by the degree to which families delay their final decisions until they have all the evidence they can obtain. Families who show delayed closure are rated high on this dimension. They have a strong engagement in the novelty and uniqueness of each new setting which they experience with a relative freshness and little preconception. Low-scoring families reach decisions early and stick with them. They seem dominated by the convictions and forms of their own past. They see the world as constantly reminiscent, as pre-figured and, at most, a modest reshuffling of past experience. In some cases they truly see the world through the eyes of their ancestors. (Olson's dimension of adaptability [1979] is similar in some respects). It is particularly interesting that, in our studies of social network, families with delayed closure are significantly invested in the largest number of extended family members. This is a reflection, we argue, of their thirst for access to maximum breadth and variety of input from the environment that assures continued openness of the family to new experiences (Oliveri & Reiss, 1981). We have proposed that, in their own home, early-closure families will show a leisurely pacing of activities, what Kantor and Lehr have referred to as slow "clocking." A more frenetic pacing of events, rapid clocking, will be seen in delayed-closure families. The rituals of early-closure families will invoke the family's past. Consider for example the ritual where every Christmas night a family writes an account of the evening, round-robin style, and then reads the accounts of previous Christmases. In contrast, the rituals of the delayed-closure families will cut them off from the past. For example, a mother and father who have grown up in an orthodox Jewish family fail to celebrate Jewish holidays in their home but annually help their two children to hang Christmas stockings.

In repeated samples of clinic and non-clinic families we have seen that these dimensions are orthogonal. Thus a family may have any combination of high and low scores on all three.

STRESS AND THE FAMILY PARADIGM

A Working Definition of Family Stresss

In this essay, a preliminary attempt at theoretical synthesis, it seems wise to begin simply. Thus, we will want to consider only those events and circumstances that are relatively brief and circumscribed, lasting weeks or at most months, but not years. Further, we will want to focus on events or circumstances that happen to the family such as neighborhood changes and physical illness, rather than events that happen within the family, such as marital separations and the birth of children. The latter internal, rather than external, stress events are every bit as important as the former for a general theory of family stress and coping. However, they are particularly difficult conundrums since they are simultaneously stressful events and, in all likelihood, responses to stress. This dual role is easy to see for such an obvious internal event as marital separation. More subtly, La Rossa (1977) has shown quite convincingly how conceiving and bearing children can also be a strategy by which couples cope with preexisting stress. It must be acknowledged, however, that it is no easy matter to distinguish internal and external events. Neighborhood changes, such as a new road or a significant demographic shift, may be relatively beyond the control of the family and hence qualify as truly external. Physical illness, on the other hand, is another matter. Numerous studies have shown that physical illness in one or more member may be part of the family's effort to cope with some other stress, chronic or acute, in their lives. Nonetheless, we will focus on those events and circumstances that seem primarily or substantially to be external.

The next problem concerns some definition of what kinds of external events or circumstances may be regarded as stressful for families. Equally important, for our purposes, is to conceive of a way of judging the magnitude of stress that inheres in the event. Hill (1965) has proposed two factors which interact to establish the stressfulness of an event and the magnitude of that stress. The first is the objective hardships for a particular family which accompany the event. Second is the definition the family makes of the event: how stressful this event seems to them. From our perspective this second factor, the definitional process, is part of the family's *response* to the event; it does not inhere, in any sense, in the stressful qualities of the event itself. Indeed, we will try to show in the last portion of this essay that the full range of a family's response to a stressful event can be shown to be related to these definitional processes, not only as their definitional processes are activated at times of stress but as they operate to regulate the routine transactions of a family with its outer world.

Hill's first factor, the actual hardships associated with an event, is not an entirely satisfactory way of judging the magnitude of stress in an event. Hardships do not arrive objectively and unvarnished at the family's boundary for them to define and respond to. Hardships, of whatever magnitude, are transformed by the culture (Hill recognized this process as "cultural definition"). For example, in Navajo society, physical illness is regarded as a failure of fit between the ill person and supernatural forces; it becomes the community's responsibility, under the guidance of the shaman, to provide healing through a reestablishment of harmony between the ill person and the supernatural (Kluckhohn & Leighton, 1958). All the objective hardships accompanying illness may be identical for a Navajo family and a neighboring Anglo family, but the meaning to the average family within each culture will be different. The Anglo family will see illness as its unique burden to bear, the Navajo as a burden to be shared with its community. It is useful, then, to distinguish conceptually between two aspects of stress. First, the magnitude of a stressful event is determined by the interaction of hardship and cultural definition. Second, the family's definitional processes constitute the core of all the coping responses which follow. Cultural definition shapes the magnitude of the stress; family definition shapes the style of the response.

It is now a practical matter to determine the "cultural definition" of stressful events. Quite unintentionally, the tradition of life events research begun by Holmes and Rahe (1967) has given us some preliminary tools. When these researchers ask a group of judges to rate the "magnitude of stress" inherent in a set of events they are, in effect, asking them to read their own culture. They are asking: "In your culture how much stress or life change will this event produce in the average person?" In the most careful study to date, for example, Dohrenwend, Krasnoff, Askenasy, & Dohrenwend (1978) found significant and interpretable differences between Black, Puerto Rican, and White subcultures in New York City.

Our question, however, is somewhat different from that of investigators in the life events tradition. We want to know, for any particular culture, what events are regarded as stressful for the average *family*. We believe the most sensible approach here requires two steps. The first is to interview a sample of families representative of a particular subculture. In this interview of the whole family as a group the aim is to determine what recent events have significantly altered or disrupted the family's usual routines. The next step is to recruit a second representative sample of families, from the same subculture, and ask each family to work as a group to rate the events, which were provided by the first sample, for the stress or magnitude of change those events will induce in the average family in their community, and for the "externality" of those events. We are already engaged in a study of this kind and have found some intriguing results. For example, families are regularly reporting to us when we interview the family group the importance of neighborhood changes to them. They have included changes such as demographic ones, alterations in the age or race of neighbors, and spatial changes, such as the construction of new highways with consequent changes in traffic patterns and access routes. No events of this kind appear on any of the standard life events lists constructed for individuals.

Now that we have working concepts and methods to determine the magnitude of stressful events, our interest will focus on events of *moderate* severity. As we have explained elsewhere, severe stress may overwhelm any semblance of family organization. The family's set of beliefs, organized by its central paradigm, may be shattered. Its coping strategies may be determined as much by the nature of the support it receives from the surrounding community (church, neighborhood, therapists, extended family) as from its pre-existing patterns. Thus, it is more difficult to predict from a knowledge of the family's paradigm how it will respond to severe stress. Moderate stress, on the other hand, will more often than not be encompassable by the family paradigm. Here a knowledge of the family's paradigm can help us predict, organize, and understand the family's repertoire of coping strategies.

Stages of a Family's Response to Moderate Stress

It is important to distinguish different phases or stages of a family's responses to moderate stress, since different coping strategies are likely to be employed during different phases. We have drawn on two promising sources. The first is Joan Aldous' (1971) adaptation of the problem-solving perspectives originally developed by John Dewey (1910) and applied to individuals and families by Brim (1962). This approach views the family's response to any significant problem or stress as a quasi-logical, rational process in which options are developed and explored, and decisions are made based on these options. Aldous lists the following six stages:

1. Identification and definition of the problem.
2. Collection of information about the problem.
3. Production of alternative solutions.
4. Deciding among alternatives.
5. Taking action to solve the problem.
6. Evaluation of action taken.

Although useful, this system of stages implies a stark rationality to family process. It needs to be brought closer to actual sequences in family life. Concepts drawn from work phases in small task groups are useful here. A good source is the work of Chris Argyris who has been a leader in conceptualizing adaptive work in task groups (1965a; 1965b). Borrowing freely from his work, we may revise the specific stages of a family's response to a stressful event as follows:

1. Definition of the event; delineating it as a problem or as a routine occurrence; accepting or rejecting group or individual responsibility for response.
2. Information seeking; encouragement or discouragement of individual explorations.
3. Self-organization, role allocation, selection or confirmation of competent or incompetent leadership in the group.

4. Trial solutions, risk taking.
5. Decision-making; consensus or dissension.
6. Self-evaluation; sense of group confidence; *élan*.
7. Commitment or failure of commitment to group decision.

There are still problems with this scheme. As Weick (1971) and others have pointed out, any notion of a family's response to a stressful or problematic event must recognize particular features of family life. For example, the stages of a family's response may interpenetrate, be skipped entirely, or not follow in an easily-recognizable sequence. Thus, it seems reasonable, at the very least, to combine the stages derived from Aldous and Argyris. Further, it seems best to regard these stages as three conceptual vantage points for examining a family's response to a stressful event rather than considering them as sequential phases which follow one another in regular or predictable order. Somewhat arbitrarily, we have combined the Aldous-Argyris phases as follows:

1. Definition of the events and search for additional information.
2. Initial response and trial solutions.
3. Final decisions or closing position and family's commitment to this.

We regard these as three forms of family process: definition, trial action, and commitment to decision. *They may occur in any order or simultaneously.* As an example of how the order may be reversed, consider the Jones family's response to a new family, the Smiths, who moved in next door. The family who had lived in the house before the Smiths moved in was friendly and open. Accordingly, the Jones' first response to the Smiths is on the entirely implicit and unstated assumption that, like the old neighbors, they would be open and friendly. However, their first interactions (initial response and trial solution) are unhappy; they are rebuffed by the Smiths. The Jones family begins to develop a shared sense that they have difficult neighbors who must be avoided or closely watched (closing position). Only then do they begin to recognize, after taking trial action and assuming a closing position, that they have defined a difficult problem.

Dimension of Paradigm and Coping Strategies

Let us now consider the relationship between our three cardinal dimensions of paradigm—configuration, coordination and closure—and the three aspects of the family's response to stressful events. Our hypotheses are summarized in Table 1. We have reasoned that each of the

Table 1

Hypothesized Influence of Family Paradigm Dimensions on the Three Aspects of the Family's Response to Stressful Events

Paradigm Dimensions	Definition of the Event and Search for Additional Information	Phases of Family Coping — Initial Responses and Trial Solutions	Final Decision or Closing Position and Family's Commitment to This
Configuration: Mastery			
High:	1. Owning up Family takes responsibility for event and/or coping	2. Exploration Family's initial responses are designed to seek information and outside resources, or are in response to information and outside support	3. Response to outcome The family is proud of accomplishment, or feels it has learned something of value in failure
Low:	Family feels victimized and blames outside forces	Initial reactions are unrelated to information or explanation	The family feels fortunate if successful or victimized if not
Coordination: Solidarity			
High:	4. Family Identity Readily perceived as family issue; information exchanged quickly	5. Organization or response Organized, integrated response by all family members; roles clear	6. Consensus on decision Decision was reached with clear consensus and family remains committed to it
Low:	Slowly or not perceived as family issue; information exchanged slowly; events are seen as happening to individual members	Individuals act on own; overt or covert conflict possible	The consensus was forced on the family by a single individual; the status of agreement unclear, or no consensus is reached
Closure: Openness			
High: (Delayed)	7. Reference to the past Focuses on current experiences; past family history unimportant	8. Novelty of responses First responses include trying something new; individual experiences, intuitions, and guesses are encouraged	9. Self-evaluation As a result of coping, family alters conception of itself in some way
Low:	Past determines current perception and action; little interest in raw experience; more interest in convention or tradition	First responses mostly typical or familiar	As a result of coping, family confirms conception of itself

three dimensions should relate to each of the three aspects of the family's response to stress.

Configuration, as we have defined it in many contexts, refers to a sense of mastery in the family. Families high on this dimension feel they can gain control in a novel or challenging environment through investigation and understanding. Thus, their definition of a problematic or stressful event is organized around a concept that as a family they can do something in response. In effect, the outcome of the solution is, at least in part, their responsibility. Argyris has referred to this as "owning up." Families low on this dimension feel their future is in the hands of fate. Stressful events enhance their sense of being victimized. Rather than owning up, they disown or disavow responsibility. Some of these families will have faith in an abiding and providing destiny; others will feel pessimistic and victimized. In terms of initial responses and trial solutions, families high on configuration should be oriented toward investigation, information gathering and, in general, exploration and use of people and resources outside the family. Probably there are few instances where families entertain a specific, clearly-articulated hypothesis; nonetheless, high-configuration families during this phase probably have some implicit idea or question which is modified, sharpened, or answered with increasing information and experience. When the high-configuration family reaches a decision, a solution or a closing position, there is some pride, sense of accomplishment, or tangible growth. In contrast, a low-configuration family does not sense any connection between its own response to the problem, the outcome, and its own characteristics as a group. If things have gone well, the family feels fortunate; destiny has smiled. If the outcome or closing position is somehow negative or disappointing, the family's sense of victimization is enhanced.

Coordination refers to solidarity in family organization. Solidarity, then, should be the hallmark of the adaptive or coping style of high-coordination families. These families should often define any problem as one that somehow involves or concerns the whole family. Stressful events in the environment are often experienced as happening to the family as a unitary group rather than to a particular individual. As a result, information and/or feelings about these events are quickly shared. Low-coordination families, in contrast, rarely perceive stress events as happening to the family. Rather they perceive events as befalling individuals only; as a consequence, information about the event is exchanged slowly, if at all. The initial responses and trial solutions of high-coordination families are carefully dove-tailed. People work in recognizable relationships to one another, role allocation is clear and individuals pay attention to what others do and find out. In low-coordiantion families individuals act on their own; in some families they do so in lonely isolation, and in others, in endless struggle and competition. When they finally reach a closing position or decision, high-coordination families forge a genuine agreement. All members remain committed to this position until or unless they forge a new consensus on a new position. In low-coordination families, an apparent consensus will turn out to be forced on the group by a single individual. Quite often the family cannot or does not reach any consensus, or the status of their agreement is unclear.

Closure refers to the role of tradition in the family's attempt to cope with the here and now. High-closure (which means delayed-closure) families emphasize the here and now; the immediacy of current experience is the major determinant of what they believe and how they act. Families low on closure are oriented toward their past. Over long periods, family traditions and perspectives play an enormous role in their efforts to interpret the present. Over shorter periods, the family cannot tolerate uncertainty; they reach decisions quickly and stand by them rather than remaining open to fresh experience and ideas. This stance toward experience influences families in all three phases of their coping with stressful events. With respect to problem definition, high-closure families value and search for immediate data. The nature of the problem is often left somewhat up in the air; clarification is expected in time, but not necessarily fashioned immediately. The family does not have a rich sense of its own past and a sense of family convention. The initial responses and trial solutions in high-closure families are often novel and intuitive. The family encourages the members to take risks, and to be responsive to idiosyncratic and uncanny experiences. Low-closure families try to routinize experience (Aldous has provided a laboratory study of this form of routinization in family life [Aldous et al., 1974]). The family's initial responses and trial solutions are conservative, drawing on a repertoire of established or traditional behaviors and attitudes in the family. After they come to a closing position, high-closure families will alter the conception of themselves in some way. The decision or closing position will be reached relatively slowly and some aspects or phases of the family's response to the problem should clearly precede the closing position. In low-closure families, the final decision confirms rather than alters the family's conception of itself. Often the decision or closing position is reached early or may even be the family's first recognizable response. In low-closure families the problem definition and trial solutions are shaped by an abiding conception of what the closing position or decision is or should be.

Table 1 identifies nine different tasks of family coping beginning with (1) "owning up," which is the acceptance or rejection of family responsibility for responding to the stressful event; the table ends with (9) the family's evaluation of its own response. The numbering is meant for ease of reference; we do not mean to imply that the coping process is in any sense sequential according to this numbering system. Families may begin almost anywhere, skip some steps, and end almost anywhere else. Within each task are two contrasting coping strategies. Thus, within task 1 a family may either acknowledge responsibility for dealing with the stress or disown that responsibility. If a family's paradigm is located high on the configuration dimension, we would predict that it would, in most circumstances, own up to its responsibility to meet or deal with the stressful event. Also, a high-configuration family should, during the time when the family makes its initial response (second column), actively explore its environment for useful information, people and resources. Finally, when at (2) closing position, high-configuration families should feel pride in accomplishment, or learn from failure. Likewise, a family's position on the coordination dimension should predict which of the coping strategies it will pick in the task areas: (4) family identity, (5) organization of response, and (6) consensus on decision. A family's position on the closure dimension should predict which of the pair it will pick in: (7) reference to the past, (8) novelty of response, and (9) self-evaluation. We should be able to predict which of these 18 coping strategies any particular family will use based on its typical problem-solving patterns as measured in our laboratory and we are currently engaged in a series of investigations to explore just this point.

It is helpful to consider the similarity between the concepts represented in Table 1 and other work on family stress and coping. First consider, in more general perspective, the contents of the three main columns. The coping strategies we list under "definition of the event" are similar to what Hill (1965) has called by the same name. Hill evidently regarded family definitional processes as coming conceptually and temporally prior to the family's active coping responses to the stressful situation. We see definitional process as more action oriented, as initiating a series of family actions in response to stress, as continuing throughout the family's response to stress, and as ending only when closure is complete (which, in some families, it may never be). Indeed, we see definitional and action processes as intertwined throughout the family's response to and efforts to cope with stress; we do not separate off, as does Hill, the "definition of the event" as a distinct conceptual component. To our knowledge the sequences of action and experience outlined in the last column, "closing position," are ordinarily not perceived as coping strategies by other investigators. In our view, however, the process by which closure is reached, and even more important, the process integrating the family's final resolution in the continuing stream of its life and development, are as critical in coping as the other strategies deployed during other phases of their response. Boss' study of families of servicemen missing in action suggests that some families may never reach a closing position (Boss, 1977). Many of her families could not accept the father's status years after he was reported missing. They continued to act as if he were alive and were thus unable to bring to closure their response to his loss. Her data suggest that, paradoxically, it may be our early-closure families who stand in greatest risk of this form of failed closure. Their inability to make major shifts and the importance to them of maintaining tradition may make them unable to reach closure in times of grief and give up someone or something that has been treasured.

On a more microscopic level, some of the strategies we are proposing are similar to coping strategies described by McCubbin (1979) and Boss (1977) for wives of absent husbands. For example, our "exploration" seems a prototype of what they call Establishing Independence and Self-Sufficiency. McCubbin and Boss describe the latter as the wife's acquisition of skills, experience, and training to deal with the objective hardships entailed by her absent husband. They describe another strategy, "Maintaining the Past and Dependence on Religion." This seems similar, in some respects, to each of the lower strategies in cells 7, 8, and 9 of our table. Finally, their strategy of "Maintaining Family Integration and Structure" is similar to the strategy of organizing the family, described in the upper portion of cell 5.

Hill, McCubbin, and Boss, as well as other scholars in this field, have attempted to define strategies that are most adaptive. We, quite emphatically, do not. More specifically, we do not suggest that the strategy labeled "high" within any of the nine cells in Table 1 is more effective or adaptive than the strategy labeled "low." For example, it is likely that the average Navajo family would not "own up" to its responsibility to bring relief to an ill member but would, in effect, disown such responsibility in the service of joining in communal healing rights. The question of the adaptiveness of coping strategies must take into account the family's own objectives and the nature of the social community in which it lives. In our fledgling science of family stress and coping we may be rushing to judgment, on every slender evidence, concerning which strategies are "best."

Our aim in this paper has been to emphasize the extraordinary variety of coping strategies families employ in response to stress. We have tried to show how these strategies may be related to an enduring structure of beliefs, convictions, and assumptions the family holds about its social world. Kuhn's concept of paradigm, used as a metaphor, helps us understand how these shared beliefs shape family action.

REFERENCES

Aldous, J. A framework for the analysis of family problem solving. In J. Aldous, T. Condon, R. Hill, M. Straus, & I Tallman (Eds.), *Family Problem Solving: A Symposium on Theoretical, Methodological and Substantive Concerns.* Hinsdale, IL.: Dryden, 1974.

Argyris, C. Explorations in interpersonal competence—I. Journal of Applied Behavioral Science, 1965, *1,* 58-83 (a).

Argyris, C. Explorations in interpersonal competence—II. *Journal of Applied Behavioral Science,* 1965, *1,* 147-177 (b).

Berger, P.L., & Luckman, T. *The Social Construction of Reality.* New York: Doubleday, 1966.

Boss, P. A clarification of the concept of psychological father presence in families experiencing ambiguity of boundary. *Journal of Marriage and the Family,* 1977, *39,* 141-151.

Brim, O.G., Jr. *Personality and Decision Processes, Studies in the Social Psychology of Thinking.* Palo Alto: Stanford University Press, 1962.

Costell, R., Reiss, D., Berkman, H., & Jones. C. The family meets the hospital: Predicting the family's perception of the treatment program from its problem-solving style. *Archives of General Psychiatry,* 1981, *38,* 569-577.

Dewey, J. *How We Think,* New York: D.C. Heath, 1910.

Dohrenwend, B.S., Krasnoff, L., Askenasy, A.R., & Dohrenwend, B.P. Exemplification of a method for scaling life events: The PERI life events scale. *Journal of Health and Social Behavior,* 1978, *19,* 205-229.

Heider, F. *The Psychology of Interpersonal Relations.* New York: Wiley, 1958.

Hill, R. Genetic features of families under stress. In H.J. Parad (Ed.), *Crisis Intervention.* New York: Family Service Association of America, 1965.

Holmes, T.H., & Rahe, R.H. The social readjustment rating scale. *Journal of Psychosomatic Research,* 1967, *11,* 213-218.

Kantor, D., & Lehr, W. *Inside the Family.* San Francisco: Jossey-Bass, 1975.

Kelly, G. *The Psychology of Personal Constructs,* New York: Norton, 1955.

Kluckhohn, C., & Leighton, D. *The Navajo.* Cambridge: Harvard University Press, 1958.

Kuhn, T.S. *The Structure of Scientific Revolutions.* Chicago: University of Chicago Press, 1970.

La Rossa, R. *Conflict and Power in Marriage.* Beverly Hills: Sage, 1977.

McCubbin, H.I. Integrating coping behavior in family stress theory. *Journal of Marriage and the Family.* 1979, *41,* 237-244.

Oliveri, M.E., & Reiss, D. The structure of families' ties to their kin: The shaping role of social construction. *Journal of Marriage and the Family,* 1981, *43,* 391-407.

Olson, D.D., Sprenkle, D.H., & Russell, C.S. Circumplex model of marital and family systems: I. Cohesion and adaptability dimensions, family types and clinical applications. *Family Process,* 1979, *18,* 3-28.

Reiss, D. Individual thinking and family interaction II: A study of pattern recognition and hypothesis testing in families of normals, character disorders and schizophrenics. *Journal of Psychiatric Research,* 1967, *5,* 193-211.

Reiss, D. Individual thinking and family interaction III: An experimental study of categorization performance in families of normals, character disorders and schizophrenics. *Journal of Nervous and Mental Disease*, 1968, *146*, 384-403.

Reiss, D. Individual thinking and family interaction IV: A study of information exchange in families of normals, those with character disorders and schizophrenics. *Journal of Nervous and Mental Disease*, 1969, *149*, 473-490.

Reiss, D. Individual thinking and family interaction V: Proposals for the contrasting character of experiential sensitivity and expressive form in families. *Journal of Nervous and Mental Disease*, 1970, *151*, 187-202.

Reiss, D. Intimacy and problem solving: An automated procedure for testing a theory of consensual experience in families. *Archives of General Psychiatry*, 1971, *22*, 442-455 (a).

Reiss, D. Varieties of consensual experience I: A theory for relating family interaction to individual thinking. *Family Process*, 1971, *10*, 1-28 (b).

Reiss, D. Varieties of consensual experience II: Dimensions of a family's experience of its environment. *Family Process*, 1971, *10*, 28-35 (c).

Reiss, D. Varieties of consensual experience III: Contrasts between families of normals, delinquents and schizophrenics. *Journal of Nervous and Mental Disease*, 1971, *152*, 37-95 (d).

Reiss, D. *The Family's Construction of Reality*. Cambridge: Harvard University Press, 1981.

Reiss, D., Costell, R., Berkman, H., & Jones, C. How one family perceives another: The relationship between social constructions and problem solving competence. *Family Process*, 1980, *19*, 239-256.

Reiss, D., Costell, R., Jones, C., & Berkman, H. The family meets the hospital: A laboratory forecast of the encounter. *Archives of General Psychiatry*, 1980, *37*, 141-154.

Reiss, D., & Salzman, C. Resilience of family process: Effect of secobarbital. *Archives of General Psychiatry*, 1973, *28*, 425-433.

Rosenthal, R. Interpersonal expectations: Effects of the experimenter's hypothesis. In R. Rosenthal & R. Rosnow (Eds.), *Artifact in Behavioral Research*. New York: Academic Press, 1969.

Suppe, F. Exemplars, theories and disciplinary matrices. In F. Suppe (Ed.), *The Structure of Scientific Theories* (Second Edition). Urbana: University of Illinois Press, 1977.

Weick, K.E. Group processes, family processes and problem solving. In J. Aldous, T. Condor, R. Hill, M. Straus, & I. Tallman (Eds.), *Family Problem Solving: A Symposium on Theoretical, Methodological and Substantive Concerns*. Hinsdale, IL: Dryden Press, 1971.

Editor's Commentary: Dealing with Stressful Life Events: An Extension of the Family's Typical Problem-solving Patterns

Reiss and Oliveri, writing in the mainstream of family sociology, present an illuminating conceptual framework that should prove useful to family therapists by way of expanding their knowledge of the family's intrinsic adaptive capacities for responding to stress. They posit that the family's various coping strategies are all related to each other. It seems likely, based on their laboratory findings, that if one has observed and analyzed a family's adaptive capacities and techniques as these are manifested in the "routines that are typical" during the quiescent periods of the family's life," then it should be possible to predict how they will function in response to stressful life events. Insightful families should be able to articulate their problem-solving strategies and will know what process of deliberation and resolution has worked for them in the past. Clinically, having this information should enable the therapist working with dysfunctional and midrange families that are very troubled by either internal or external stress-inducing situations or both to determine what kinds of interventions will facilitate new and better coping behaviors.

Within the context of Kuhn's concept of paradigm used as metaphor they describe how shared beliefs contribute to shaping a family's actions and reactions. They also underscore how the intensity of the hardship experienced in relation to the stressful event or condition is partially predicated upon the family's definition of the situation. This in turn is partly determined by the cultural definition of what constitutes stress and appropriate response patterns in the society in which the specific family lives and from which it derives its beliefs and values. This line of reasoning is akin to the one pursued by Landau-Stanton, Griffiths

117

and Mason in Chapter 20 on link therapy with East Indian families in transition in South Africa; the traditional cultural determinants of behavior in response to stressful changes are manifold.

Although Reiss and Oliveri indicate that, given cultural variability, they do not define which coping stretegies are most adaptive and beneficial, they do imply that reaching a "closing position" (arriving at closure) in regard to such situations as acceptance of the finality of death, even in the case of a dear one long missing in action, constitutes effective coping. From my perspective, based on a good deal of work in the areas of the healthy family (Kaslow, 1980/1981a) and re-equilibration after divorce (Kaslow, 1981b), it is evident that healthy individuals and families engage in creative, fruitful problem-solving processes, evaluate and improve their strategies, and do not leave many loose ends open. Instead they work on issues, including losses, until they bring them through to resolution and closure. In accepting their own mortality, they can better deal with death—going through the grieving process and being able to offer one another support and sustenance. When the process is complete, they are again able to live in the present rather than dwell in longing for the memories of the past.

Table 1 presents an excellent, therapeutically useful summary of nine different tasks families must cope with during their development cycle and 18 coping strategies, which we highly recommend for serious perusal.

REFERENCES

Kaslow, F.W. Profile of the healthy family. *Fokus på Familian* (Norwegian Journal of Family Therapy), 1980; & *Interaction,* Spring/Summer, 1981, *4*, (1&2), 1-15.(a)

Kaslow, F.W. Divorce and divorce therapy. In A.S. Gurman & D.P. Kniskern (Eds.), *Handbook of Family Therapy.* New York: Brunner/Mazel, 1981b.

Chapter 6

The Therapist as Director
of the Family Drama

By Maurizio Andolfi and
Claudio Angelo

The authors compare the therapist's function to that of a theatrical director who revises a play, the family drama, which the actors continue to recite according to an old script with a foregone conclusion. To achieve his goal, the therapist uses certain contextual (or "nodal") elements to construct an alternative "reading" of events which neutralizes the actors' persistent efforts to make the course of therapy conform to their old patterns.

The Director: "Who are you, please? What do you want?"
The Father: ". . . we have come here in search of an author."
The Director: "And where is the script?"
The Father: "It is in us! The drama is in us, and we are the drama. We are impatient to play it. Our inner passion drives us on to this!"

Luigi Pirandello

This paper was originally published in the joint international issue of *Terapia Familiare,* June, 1981, and the *Journal of Marital and Family Therapy,* July 1981, 7, (3), 255-264.

This paper and the illustrations presented here are a product of a research program of the Family Therapy Institute of Rome on methods of intervention in rigid systems, particularly in families with a schizophrenic member.

Maurizio Andolfi, M.D., is Director of the Family Therapy Institute of Rome, and President of the Italian Society for Family Therapy.

Claudio Angelo, M.D. is Assistant at the Mental Health Services of Bolzano, and teacher at the Family Therapy Institute of Rome.

There are many ways of defining psychotherapy, corresponding to methods of intervention based on different conceptions of the individual and his basic interpersonal relationships. The choice of a *method* of intervention, together with the significance attributed to it, is inspired by a particular philosophy of change and by a particular way of defining the therapeutic relationship. Similar methods can be utilized in different ways by emphasizing certain aspects rather than others; that is, the method varies according to the *significance* attributed to it by the therapist and patient in the therapeutic context.

Although no one has yet succeeded in providing an exhaustive explanation of what psychotherapy is, we believe that learning constitutes an important part. In this paper we will describe a learning model in which therapist and family are the protagonists in a re-edited version of the family drama that is played out in the therapeutic scenario. However, before going further, it may be useful to state some of our initial suppositions.

Family functioning is maintained by a state of dynamic equilibrium. This equilibrium is the product of repetitive interactions (which have become interactional rules) that permit each member to fulfill specific functions that define his or her identity. This state of equilibrium assures system *continuity*. However, to promote the *differentiation* of family members (and therefore to promote change), every family has to tolerate certain states of disorganization in order to move from a functional equilibrium consonant to one phase of its development to a new equilibrium consonant with the successive phase (Hoffman, 1971). In families where changes in relations that are essential to developmental processes are experienced as threatening, the interactional patterns and individual functions become progressively more rigid. Ultimately, the greater the system's need for stability becomes, the more severe and irreversible the individual pathology grows.

In such cases, the mental disturbance is a metaphor of the dilemma of a family that *would like to change without changing* (Angelo, 1981). The family's request for therapy is motivated by this same dilemma. A new element, the therapist, enters the scene and is invited to accept the family's paradoxical request—*to help them to change without changing*. Thus the groundwork is laid for a relation in which the therapist and family implicitly agree to play complementary roles: the therapist will be the judge, savior, or expert; the patient will play incompetent, sick or irrational. The other family members will favor one side or the other depending on their age, sex, or profession, or according to the specific situation.

If what the family really fears is change, and *not the contrary*, then the identified patient and the other family members will unite in proposing a plan for therapy that will not alter existing equilibriums. If the therapist accepts this plan, or is drawn into it, he will eventually reinforce the family's static-pathological tendencies. Should this occur, the family would learn nothing substantially new. It would merely utilize its dysfunctional patterns in a more sophisticated manner, while each member would maintain his assigned role. Individual identity would be inhibited and progressively stifled by repetitive, highly predictable functions (Piperno, 1979). In a context of this type, the function of the therapist becomes equally repetitive and predictable, for he too fears change and shies away from uncovering new parts of his self to utilize in his relations with others.

Conversely, if we hypothesize that the therapeutic encounter is capable of provoking a *change in values* (considered as the totality of cognitive and emotional meanings the family attributes to its own reality), then the intervention can be viewed in a completely different light; the problem then becomes *how* to change those meanings which have led to the formation and maintenance of pathological behaviors, including both the mental disturbance expressed by one of the family members and the 'reactive' behaviors of the others.

THE FAMILY DRAMA IN THERAPY

A drama is a game, intensely emotional in content, having a plot that evolves toward a foreseeable and usually unhappy conclusion. The characters have little possibility of escaping from their rigid, assigned roles. Unlike the actors in other games, such as comedy, the characters in a drama lack the ability to smile benignly at themselves or at others. They cannot see humor in human events or accept life's inevitable contradictions, and thus they seem to lack the premises for overcoming the limitations of their rigidly patterned relations.

It is difficult to say how important the game is to each of us. It is nonetheless certain that in the course of every individual's life, he must continually play a 'game' in order to find an equilibrium in his relations to external reality and to the persons with whom he lives. Usually, the game begins and evolves within the family, in the relations between parents and between children and parents. The more the family's affective needs lead to a rigid and complementary distribution of roles, the more sterile the game becomes and the more interactions lose their capacity to transmit information. Each members's personal space (that area still free of attributes and fixed rules), where he elaborates the significance of his interactions with the others, progressively empties out and is filled by functional demands (Andolfi, Menghi, Nicolo, & Saccu, 1980). Eventually each member adapts himself to a view of reality complementary to that of another: there will be the sick member and the sane one, the aggressor and the victim, the wise one and the incompetent, with progressively more rigid specifications concerning when and where each function must be actuated in the relationship. As Bowen has observed, the functional value of the behavior of family members increases proportionally to their degree of symbiosis and lack of differentiation (Bowen, 1971). As the family game becomes more repetitious, it forms the script for a drama which conforms more and more to the family myth (Ferreira, 1963). The efforts of the individual members to differentiate themselves fail, and their guilt feelings increase.

By the time a therapist has his first contact with a rigid family system, the family has long since lost its capacity for playing creative games. *As in a classical drama, each character wears the mask that best expresses his function.* The expectations associated with each mask are so completely taken for granted that the members can foresee all future events, the behavior of the other members, and even the function of the therapist. To perform the family drama, the plot must unfold in predictable, interrelated sequences that lead to the foreseen conclusion—despite the family's request for help in changing the final act.

The therapeutic situation differs from the family's daily life because, with the introduction of the therapist, functions are redistributed and a new entity, the *therapeutic system,* is created. Some of the functions originally "assigned" within the family system are now "projected" onto the therapist (for example that of judge, savior or expert), so that the "performance" seen in therapy is not identical with what would be seen if the family were acting only for its own members. Moreover, in therapy, as in the theater or in play, the actions and sentiments manifested are by definition not the same as those manifested in reality, although they are expressed as though they were real. They are experienced in such a way that the boundary between "actors" and "observers" is alternately defined and dissolved. The therapeutic relation is not a "real relation," but it becomes one in fact during the course of patient-therapist interactions. This is precisely the game in which the crystallized family reality can regain its capacity for movement, which is the premise for the emergence of new developmental processes.

In Pirandello's play *Six Characters in Search of an Author* (Pirandello,

1922), each character appears to be imprisoned by his role, but only wants the director to help him to play his part better. In the same way the family seems to ask the therapist to help them recite their own "drama" better, preferably without altering their preconceived "script," even though the participation of a new character has already altered it. If the therapist wants to avoid being trapped in a role (like the director in Pirandello's play) by passively accepting the functions that others assign to him and by participating in a drama with a foregone conclusion, then he must take part in the action. He has to redefine each player's role (including his own) and alter the timing and modality of each sequence, introducing new ways of playing the game (Andolfi, 1979).

We have found that the therapist can achieve this if he is able to promptly propose a different version of the family's script, changing it by amplifying the significance of the various functions. He will be effective as a director if the family group accepts him, and if, in the situation presented to him, he is able to individuate the *nodal elements* on which to base his proposal for an alternative structure. These nodal elements exist in the contextual data most clearly indicative of the functional patterning of the system and of the relation that each member seeks to establish with the therapist. These data will be further enriched by "historical" contents later on, when their significance in the family's developmental cycle is explored. This exploration will not be easy because the family will oppose its own definitions, insisting on the importance of more obvious and predictable data and indicating interconnections which deny any personal involvement.

But despite the family's spasmodic efforts to present itself as a stable unit, elements of potential instability[1] can be discerned. Once these have been determined, they can be related to other elements that emerge from the therapist's imagination and from his participation in the therapeutic system, providing an alternative key for "reading" the problem.

In recomposing a mosaic, the addition of new fragments enables one to fit more pieces into place. Similarly, in the therapeutic scenario the individual family actors are encouraged to perform utilizing parts of their self which they had hoped to keep concealed, fearing their strong emotional implications. For this game of recomposition to take place,

---

[1]We are referring to those elements that acquire particular significance because they represent the fusion of contradictory elements in the reality to which they refer. The most obvious example is a symptom which expresses a conflict between tendencies toward maintenance and tendencies toward disruption of a system's equilibrium. A symptom successfully congeals processes that are evolving in opposite directions; however, it also provides indications for intervening to restructure interactional rules (Angelo, 1981).

the therapist too has to risk exposure, utilizing his own fantasies in his relation with the family. These fantasies, in which the elements supplied by the family are reintroduced in the form of images, actions or scenes, stimulate the others to offer new information or to make further associations, in a circular process. An *intensification of the threapeutic relationship* occurs, as the nodal elements of the family script are brought together and organized by the therapist's suggestions.

Following is an example taken from the opening phase of a first session, which demonstrates the importance of promptly evaluating and opposing the family's attempts to introduce their own script. The identified patient, Tiziana, a woman of 50 years and married for the second time, telephoned the therapist requesting an appointment. She wanted help in curing her depression of 20-year duration. She stated that she had previously tried psychotherapy and other forms of treatment without success. The mournful and theatrical tone in which she described her "hermit's" life—ten years in which she had avoided outside contacts and had completely lost interest in life—was punctuated by sobs and weeping. Efforts by her family and friends to draw her out of her apathy had failed: she insisted that only the therapist could "save her," (even though this phone call was her first contact with him). The therapist concluded from this that the patient's magical expectations concerning him concealed an attempt to induce him to play the role of the "impotent hero," previously played by her other psychiatrists and probably by all of the men in her life. Her message seemed to be, "You act for me, I am helpless."

The therapist, therefore, after gathering information on the composition of her present family and her previous one, told her that *since there was clearly nothing that could be done to help her, he was willing to see her only if she brought in her family to help make them feel less imprisoned by her depression.* While Tiziana was complaining that she no longer had the strength to live, the therapist asked her to find the energy to bring in her family so that they could liberate themselves from her. In this way the therapist prepared the script for the first session and forced her, contrary to her expectations, to mobilize latent resources.

On the appointed day the patient appeared with the members of her family: her first and second husbands (her first husband still managed the family's finances), and her daughters from both marriages. She was still an attractive woman, meticulously dressed and made-up despite her "depression." Her way of moving and speaking conveyed her claim to center all attention on herself. She wore a turban and brandished a long cigarette-holder, final touches to her image as a "femme fatale." The two husbands had an unassuming and detached air, as though they just happened to be there by chance. The daughters looked like poor little orphans in search of a refuge. The general atmosphere suggested a group of people who had fallen under the curse of some malign fate.

Therapist:	*(While entering, before sitting down)* Would you mind clearing off one of those armchairs for mother? *(pointing to two armchairs in a corner on which personal belongings have been piled up)* *(To the patient)* Madame, would you please sit there? *(To the others)* Now, can you close the circle and forget about Tiziana? After all, you realize there's no hope in that direction *(indicating Tiziana in the corner armchair)*. This meeting will be useless unless all of you, or some of you, can escape from the curse. Or have you already given up hope? All of you?
1st husband:	*(Showing surprise)* I don't understand.
Therapist:	I mean, is there any hope for the rest of you? Who has more hope? Who has less?
Giulia:	*(Age 27, oldest daughter from the first marriage, in a funereal tone)* I think that each of us is looking for a way to live well.
Therapist:	Yes, I can understand what you are looking for, but what you have found is a different matter.
Giulia:	I think all of us are looking for something . . . .
Therapist:	Have you escaped from the curse, for example?
Giulia:	What curse do you mean? This . . . this suffering because of things in the family? . . . No, I haven't escaped, I really haven't.
Therapist:	Are you the one most imprisoned by the curse?
Giulia:	Well, I'm certainly suffering from it. There are lots of things that can happen now that may have consequences later on. For example, she is the youngest. *(She indicates Sabina, the youngest daughter, who is 11)*
Therapist:	You mean she may be damaged by the curse even at a distance?
Giulia:	I don't know, she has probably been damaged already, or she may suffer more later on. I feel responsible for her too, in some ways. She's still a child . . . .
Therapist:	Is it the curse that makes you play mother to Sabina?

Giulia:	It's not that I play mother . . . sometimes I worry about a lot of things that happen to her, apart from what troubles me personally.
Therapist:	Have you no children?
Giulia:	No, I don't . . . I don't . . . think I want any because I wouldn't be capable . . . of . . . I wouldn't be calm enough, I wouldn't have anything positive to offer to children.
Therapist:	So the curse has gotten to your uterus. *(Turning to Grazia, the firstborn of the second marriage)* And what about you? Have you more hope or less hope of escaping from the curse?
Grazia:	More or less like her *(turning toward Giulia)*.
Therapist:	So you won't have children either?
Grazia:	Oh, definitely not!
Therapist:	For how long have you been under the curse?
Grazia:	*(With a mixture of anger and resignation)* Well, I think I always have been, or almost . . . well, I can't say exactly.
Sabina:	*(Interrupting and showing that she doesn't want to be left out)* I don't like children. I can't stay with kids for more than fifteen minutes. Then I lose my patience . . . .
Therapist:	*(To the two men, seated facing each other and somewhat apart from the three girls)* Where do the men stand in this situation?
1st husband:	I really think I'm outside the curse. I feel sorry for Tiziana, for my wife whom I love like a sister, and naturally I feel sorry for my daughter, too . . . she suffers indirectly from the situation. But as for me, I'm out of it.
Therapist:	Help me to understand one thing. The curse has the power to let you save yourself, but not your daughter? Have you ever thought that if your daughter had lived with you she might have escaped the curse?
1st husband:	Hmm! Maybe I never thought about it very seriously because I'm an egoist . . .I mean, I feel independent.
Therapist:	*(To the second husband)* And where do you stand? You have taken over . . .
2nd husband:	. . . The job . . . well, I do suffer in some ways . . . but I manage to keep pretty detached from what's going on.
Therapist:	According to what you all have told me here . . . he *(indicating the first husband)* has escaped intact, and so much the better for him . . . he is egoistic but independent. But these three young people seem to be imprisoned in a jail.

You two *(to the two husbands)* have passed an injection of egoism from one to the other. When you *(to the first husband)* left, you told your successor, "Look, the only thing that can save you is to be egoistic and ignore what happens to all these women, otherwise the curse will get you too . . . .

As we can see from this example, the therapist utilized only a few of the elements supplied by the family. These are magnified and made to serve as structural supports for an alternative script. Emphasis is placed on the *functions* of the various members, which are revealed through their nonverbal communications such as posture, physical characteristics, the spatial positioning of the patient and of the others. The "historical" and "emotional" elements that characterize the various functions in the particular situation are added gradually, as the therapist calls attention to them in order to provoke personal responses from each member.

It is the family that supplies the "material" while the therapist traces a course for the flow of associations. That is why, instead of collecting impersonal data, we find it more effective to take in only a limited amount of historical information in the initial phase and to amplify or change its emotional resonance in the rest of the session so that interconnections can emerge. What counts are not the facts in themselves, but *each member's personal interpretation* of the story, the way that each person relates to himself, his needs, his functions in the family.

An illustration of this can be drawn from the first session with the family of Giorgio, a 26-year-old psychotic patient. Present besides the patient are: his 72-year-old father, who wears a hearing aid and sits at a considerable distance from the others, slumped over, giving the appearance of a man long dead whose position in the family has been taken over by his own ghost; his mother, seated next to the patient, with a suffering expression; and an older brother and his wife who take the responsibility for relating the history of Giorgio's "illness." The brother's description emphasizes the organic aspect, tracing the origins to a cranial trauma caused by an automobile accident. He speaks with an air of competence, using a plethora of psychiatric terms (like "delusional syndrome," "paranoid traits"). He details the various diagnoses that have been made and the drugs that have been prescribed, continually asking the therapist which ones are most effective. A distinctly medical context is emerging, in which the symptoms discussed are seen as organically caused.

At this point the therapist interrupted the sequence by introducing a question to disrupt the script proposed by the family for this encounter. In trying to redefine the context, the language employed is of crucial importance. The therapist introduced a new language which translated and integrated the various nodal elements, individuating interconnections that the family has not yet discerned, and about which they are now forced to furnish new information. Once this occurs, the family has to take cognizance of this new input, thus laying the basis for change.

Therapist: *(To Giorgio, who has been obtusely silent until now)* When did your father die, before or after you got sick?

Giorgio: *(Clearly perplexed, he stalls for time, asks for explanations; finally, sighing)* . . . Your question makes me feel uncomfortable, really uncomfortable, yes, because . . . *(silence)*. Excuse me, I have to go to the bathroom for a minute.

Mother: Yes, go ahead, you wanted to go even earlier.

Therapist: I think you can answer before you go.

Giorgio: Yes, I can say that . . . *(goes off the track)*.

Therapist: Before or after?

Giorgio: Well, it happened after I got sick.

The same question is now posed to the other family members.

Brother: The truth is, I don't think he sees my father any more as a person he can . . . .

Therapist: But I'm not talking about Giorgio, I'm trying to find out how long your father has been dead.

Brother: *(The mother interrupts: she hasn't been able to stand it these last four years, the worries . . .)* For about a year, I'd say, ever since he completely lost his hearing.

Therapist: After, then?

Brother: Yes, yes.

Mother: After *(silence)*.

Therapist: Did he die of heartbreak?

Mother: Well, sure . . . after, you see, a little bit at a time.

Therapist: So now you have a new head of the family?

Mother: That's just it, we don't know what to do. We have to find the right medicine. *(She continues talking about how hard it is for her to bear the situation)*

Therapist: *(He takes out a prescription pad and leans toward the mother, as though intending to comply with her request to prescribe effective medication)* If I am to prescribe the right medication, you will have to help me understand whether it should be medicine for a crazy guy who suddenly had to take over his father's place, or medicine for a crazy guy who purposely killed his father so he could take his place. I think that's the problem, and we can't continue until we get an answer.

In this example, as in the preceding one, we can see how the family selects from its entire history only those elements that conform to its preferred script—the elements it selects—diagnoses, medicines, or cranial traumas—become the framework. Then the therapist tries to change the significance of the script and to introduce other elements which modify their original framework by defining the function of each member in the system. What enables him to grasp the distribution and characteristics of the reciprocal functions rapidly? In the first contact and during the course of the first session, the family supplies many elements through their verbal and nonverbal communications and through interactional redundancies. These elements are perceived by the therapist in the form of a comprehensive "gestalt" on which he bases his effort to redefine the situation. In the case cited above, he noted the father's posture and spatial position, the older brother's behavior, the mother's position next to the patient and her obtuse expression, and the fact that she sat between her two sons. These elements all seemed to indicate that the father had long since lost his position in the family and that his two sons had been delegated to take over for him, one with the function of "the wise one"; the other of "the crazy one." The therapist actively organized the elements supplied by the family to construct a new framework which was gradually built on during the course of the session as new information emerged.

In other words, the material that the family presents contains certain elements that are particularly significant and pertinent to any redefinition of the existing relations among the family members. These elements which we describe as "nodal" represent points of intersection of the different and mutually exclusive scripts proposed respectively by the family and the therapist as a framework for ordering the family's history.

This concept is illustrated in Fig. 1. Diagrams of two different suits of clothing are represented in a limited space which they in part share. Imagine that the outer circle enclosing the diagrams contains all of the available information concerning the family's history. If we suppose that the model proposed by the family corresponds to the "dress" outlined by the black dots and continuous lines, then the model constructed by the therapist corresponds to the "shirt and pants" represented by the

Figure 1

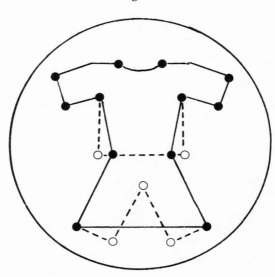

same black dots plus the white dots and the broken lines. With the introduction of a few "nodal" points, we can draw new outlines which change the gestalt and the overall significance of the image.

Utilizing such nodal points as structural elements, the family will try to impose its own "suit of clothes," describing it in minute detail and inviting the therapist to share its own frame of reference. If he lets himself become enmeshed in this operation, he risks accepting the family's model as his own. He may implicitly confirm this model not only by his verbal communications, but also through other secondary behaviors that accompany and define transactions within the therapeutic system. For example, in the case described above, if the therapist had allowed the family to continue at length describing all of the patient's past medical and psychiatric history, he would have automatically reinforced the family's image of the patient and of the correlated functions of the other members.

The analysis presented can easily give rise to misunderstandings: for example, it may seem as though the therapist is trying to impose on the family an arbitrary framework that is "extraneous" to the family's problems. Similar doubts may be reinforced by the therapist's extremely active behavior, which may at times seem "manipulative." However, it is our view that the therapist does not introduce "extraneous" elements into the script that is being dramatized by the family in its encounter with the therapist. Everything the therapist says or does during the session is based on material that emerges from the transactions. He merely *restructures* the elements that are offered: emphasizing some which have previously gone unnoticed; relegating others that had been overemphasized to the background, or altering their sequential positions. He proposes an alternative structure by introducing isolated and vaguely defined images which stimulate the family to elaborate on them further. These images serve as an armature for the family to build on, which takes form gradually only as new information is added. By information we mean not static historical data but information concerning interactive patterns.

On the other hand, utilizing the data in the family history enables the therapist to create a strong bond with the family, and this is a prerequisite for the continuation of therapy. Certain interventions which seem totally arbitrary and interrupt interactive sequences in reality serve to translate on a verbal level what the therapist has perceived nonverbally or through his own associations. The organization of the material is clearly the result of an active process on the part of the therapist, and is influenced by his personal history. In this sense, we can say that the therapist's personality and his perceptive power are the "extraneous" elements that are introduced into the system.

If we ask what it is that the therapist is trying to achieve, the immediate answer is: to change the family's rules. If the therapy is successful, the family's initial functional rigidity gradually gives way to increased elasticity in the attribution of individual functions. At the same time, the therapist's self-confidence in rewriting the family's original script, and his willingness to enter into even the most obscure family myths and phantoms guarantee a *containing structure* in which the actors can either follow the old script or experiment with new roles.

The moment the family accepts the new "suit of clothes" proposed by the therapist, he begins to deny its importance, so that an element of change will not be transformed into another crystallized reality. The original highly stabilized family structure must gradually be replaced by a new organization, the therapeutic one, which is *unstable* and *provisory*. The process is completed when the family members have learned to make their own choices, free from rigid models; this is when they have gained the capacity to accept the unpredictable—when the unexpected itself becomes part of their "rules."

REFERENCES

Andolfi, M. Redefinition in family therapy. *American Journal of Family Therapy*, 1979, *7*, 5-15.

Andolfi, M., Menghi, P., Nicolo, A.M., & Saccu, C. Interaction in rigid systems: A model for intervention in families with a schizophrenic patient. In M. Andolfi, & I. Zwerling, (Eds.), *Dimensions of Family Therapy*. New York: Guilford Press, 1980.

Angelo, C. The use of the metaphoric object in family therapy. *American Journal of Family Therapy*, 1981, *9*, (1), 69-78.

Bowen, M. The use of family theory in clinical practice. In J. Haley, (Ed.), *Changing Families*. New York: Grune and Stratton, 1971.

Ferreira, A.J. Family myths and homeostasis. *Archives of General Psychiatry*, 1963, *9*, 457-473.

Hoffman, L. Deviation-amplifying processes in natural groups. In J. Haley (Ed.), *Changing Families*. New York: Grune and Stratton, 1971.

Piperno, R. La funzione della provocazione nel mantenimento omeostatico dei sistemi rigidi. *Terapia Familiare*, 1979, *5*, 39-50.

Pirandello, L. *Six Characters in Search of an Author*. In L. Pirandello. *Naked Masks*. New York: Dutton, 1922.

Editor's Commentary: Real Life
Script Reformulation

Perhaps the real cognoscenti of personality dynamics and interpersonal relationships are the authors of great plays and novels whose classic works transcend time and space, illuminating man's inner quest and outer directedness, rather than the therapists who minutely dissect the patient in order to assess and treat. In utilizing Pirandello's scenario depicting the passionate search for identity as their frame, Andolfi and Angelo deftly meld the finest of the world of theater with the dramatic universe of therapy. The analogy between the author-director and re-creator-therapist is an apt one; the alternating currents of sadness-happiness, tension-resolution, regression-progression characterize the human experience in both theater and therapy. Each has a script and a momentum that unfolds—sometimes slowly, sometimes rapidly in a mounting crescendo.

The authors sculpt a collage—sometimes static, sometimes dynamic—in which, in therapy, "as in classical drama, they reveal that each character wears the mask that best expresses his function." To be able to decipher the symbolic meaning of the idiosyncratic mask is to begin to know that "patient" or "character." Perhaps this is akin to Reich's (1928) starting each character analysis by piercing the first defensive layer in the top armor ring around the eyes.

As the therapist decides which intervention to utilize, he/she defines his/her role vis-à-vis the character-patients, helping them rewrite the possible alternative scripts they might prefer. This is a delightfully appealing way to articulate the therapeutic dictum about "conscious use of self." As in all music, dance and drama—the rhythm and sequencing of the therapeutic choreography are critical. The therapist is attentive, active or silent, provocative or reassuring—depending on the drama being enacted, the emotion being evinced, and the desired finale.

That the finale is unpredictable is an irony of therapy; that the post-treatment, continually evolving script must remain fluid is part of the intriguing yet disconcerting paradox of the therapeutic scene.

We appreciate the authors' nugget of brief theatrical enchantment. It has the liveliness and ingenuity which have become one of the hallmarks of the Italian contribution to family therapy.

REFERENCE

Reich, W. *Character Analysis* (1928). New York: Noonday Press, 1963.

Chapter 7

The Problem of the
Referring Person

Mara Selvini Palazzoli, Luigi Boscolo,
Gianfranco Cecchin, and Giuliana Prata

This paper is a preliminary contribution to the potentially insidious problem of the referring person in family therapy. In our experience, our failure
to examine this problem according to the systemic epistemology was the
root of several unsuccessful therapies. A description of those who, most
often, are the referring persons to be suspected of having become homeostatic members of the family is given. We also present sketches of the
behavior we most often observe in families which are maintaining a homeostatic bond with the referring person. Lastly, we explain and give examples of the tactics devised by our team to reveal and resolve this
problem.[1]

The problem of the referring person in family therapy is one of the
most insidious and potentially compromising to the success of treatment.

This paper was originally published in the *Journal of Marital and Family Therapy*, Jan.
1980, 6, (1), 3-9.

Translated from Italian by Elizabeth V. Burt, Milan.

Mara Selvini Palazzoli, M.D., is founder and Research Director of the Milan Center
(Centro per lo Studio della Famiglia). Luigi Boscolo, M.D., and Gianfranco Cecchin, M.D.,
were members of the research team at the Milan Center when this article was written.
Now they are co-directors of training at the Milan Center. Giuliana Prata, M.D., is a
member of the research team.

However, this problem is overlooked in the literature dealing with family therapy; we have not been able to discover more than its merest mention in publications to date. During workshops and seminars we have noted occasional allusions to a "hostile referral," but in these cases we are dealing with no more than sporadic observations, and, while they demonstrate a certain awareness of the existence of this problem, they do not show the full appreciation of its gravity which would lead to a detailed analysis.

We carried out our research in family therapy for years without paying particular attention to this specific problem. Even while being aware that in certain cases the referring person could constitute a grave problem, and even after establishing (in 1972) that on every family's chart, the first question should be, "Who referred the family?", we continued to regard the referring person according to the traditional model, considering above all his rapport with us and underevaluating that which he had with the family.

But certain failures in therapy forced us to go over entire cases in an effort to discover where we had gone wrong. We were able to understand that our error was very basic; we had failed to build our study of the family upon the systemic model in that we had been dealing with a family that was missing one of its members who occupied a nodal homeostatic position in that family, the referring person. Therefore the essential question which we should always ask ourselves is, "What is the present position of the referring person in the family group? Has he/she become involved to the point of becoming an important member in the family system?" Our failure to consider him/her as a member of the family was further aggravated by the fact that the referring person, in not participating in the session, had the power of the "absent member" (Sonne, Speck, & Jungreis, 1965).

The problem of the referring person, which may occur in every type of family, reaches the maximum frequency and the maximum insidiousness when we are dealing with families presenting psychotic patients, particularly those characterized by the type of communication defined as schizophrenic. We observed that in such families there is a certain "stickiness" that characterizes the various relationships. Wynne and Singer, in their classic work on the disorder of communication in the families of schizophrenics, were the first to observe this phenomenon and speak of it, coining the splendid metaphoric expression, "rubber fence." The "rubber fence" is something that encircles the family, something which absorbs anything or anyone who ventures near it (Wynne and Singer, 1963; 1965).

The professional who assists the index patient belonging to such a family is particularly exposed to this phenomenon. If he passes the family's "entrance exam," the rubber fence silently swallows him whole and he becomes installed in the position of a full-right member of the family. As such, he loses any operative possibility. Not only this, but having become a member of a family characterized by a highly homeostatic tendency, he will become, paradoxically, an essential prop to the family.

The individual who is absorbed unknowingly by the family commonly passes through three stages. First he experiences gratitude and fulfillment for having been welcomed by the family as its helper. However, bit by bit, as all his efforts and urgings towards change in the family go unheeded and, as at the same time, his endeavors are met by subtle disqualifications from the family, he will enter into the second stage which is characterized by a growing sense of discomfort and uneasiness, by the vague sensation of being trapped. Thus, in the third stage, pushed to exasperation and seeking some solution, he sends the family to family therapy. We can describe these stages because, in our professional careers, we ourselves have had this experience, and are sure that anyone who has worked with schizophrenic families can confirm it.

The reaction of the family bundled off to family therapy is usually one of total obedience. The referring person has become essential to its homeostasis, and he must be kept as a member of the family at all costs. The family will do anything to please him, anything apparent, that is. If the family therapist inquires into the motive which has led the family into therapy, he will usually receive the following stereotype, redundant answer: "Well, we've tried everything else, we might as well try this too." Implicit in this answer is the certainty, "If everything else has failed, this will too." However, after going to family therapy, they will be able to return to the referring person, their consciences appeased, with an apologetic smile on their lips, in order to resume their idyll where they had left off.

As stated above, the problem of the referring person may occur in the most diverse types of families, though it may be less insidious and take place with less frequency in families other than those of the schizophrenic type. Therefore one must consider its possibility in all cases and gather accurate information in this respect.

WHAT TYPE OF REFERRING PERSON IS MOST SUSPECT

Those who are most commonly susceptible to becoming homeostatic members of the family and are therefore the most to be suspected are:

a) Child psychiatrists, neurologists, pediatricians and family physicians who have been treating one member of the family for years, and have ended up by forming a friendship with them.

b) Young psychiatrists and psychologists, so-called "supportive" therapists, who have become involved with the family of the patient, most often with the mother, who maintains contact through long telephone chats, special requests, and invitations. In this case, it is almost always the young therapist who contacts our Center, or else comes personally, with notable anxiety and embarrassment, usually without an appointment, to present his case.

c) More rarely, social workers who are assisting a chronic psychotic or are acting as middlemen between the patient and the family and the patient and the eventual clinic to which he is sent.

How Do Suspect Families Behave?

Through observation and careful examination of the relationship between the referring person and the family, we have come to note that when the former occupies a homeostatic position as a member of the family, the latter often displays three different types of behavior patterns in the session which can be sketched as follows:

a) *The smiling family:* This is usually a courteous, good-humored family, without the least anxiety in spite of the poverty of its present relational situation and the serious condition of the index patient. Its analogical message seems to be, "Here we are at your complete dispositon, now what can we do for you?" This attitude may remind one of the smiling cheerfulness and generic helpfulness of the expert public relations person. The information supplied by the family is just as generic in that it gives us nothing meaningful. This type of family has adapted itself to the index patient, who is more of a problem for the referring person than for his family. This family is the most able in sucking in whomever approaches it.

A family of this type, which presented as the index patient a daughter who had been diagnosed as hebephrenic from the age of ten years, had maintained a close friendship with the referring psychiatrist for years. The young psychiatrist had been a guest in the family's home for long periods of time. During the session with this family, the daughter caricatured to a certain degree the general attitude of the other family members in a curious and redundant behavior. Throughout the session she slouched in her chair, with her chin lolling on her chest. It was impossible to see if she was awake or asleep. When, every once in a while, the therapist spoke to her, a tremor passed through her body as if she had heard an alarm bell, and she jerked up her head, with a leering grin on her face.

b) *The angry family:* This type of family appears to be irritated to the point of hostility. The members present a unified front, drawn up in ranks, and express in analogical language, especially in body language, the complete exclusion and rejection of the therapist. We had an eloquent example of such behavior in the first session of a family presenting an anorexic patient.

This family, of a low educational level, but at the same time financially well-off, came from the countryside, where their village doctor had insisted upon their entering into family therapy at our Center. The family had agreed to do so out of respect for the doctor, towards whom they felt a longstanding sense of obligation. On our videotape of the session, it is amusing to observe the following sequence:

The family is sitting in a line facing the therapist (Selvini). As she speaks to them, the therapist leans slightly forward. She fails to solicit a positive response from them. The family lineup draws closer together. The therapist hitches her chair a bit closer, leans towards them, puts more expression in her face and more empathy in her voice. The family moves back and closer together, the expression on their faces becomes stonier and more impenetrable. The observing members of the team, moved by compassion for the obvious frustration of their colleague, repeatedly call her out of the session to give some advice or other, but even when following these suggestions, she is unable to make a dent in the armor of the family. Within the next few sessions, the index patient lost weight alarmingly and her mother consulted two famous local magicians whose magic prescriptions she followed diligently. (They advised her that if her daughter's condition was caused by envy, she would find wood chips in the feather pillows. She opened all the pillows in the house and found the indicated wood chips in all the pillows but her own.) In the fifth session, the therapist declared her own impotence and interrupted the family therapy. In that moment, she saw the family members smile for the very first time.

c) *The complaining family:* This family complains about the discomfort it suffers in coming to the session, the length and cost of the trip, the inconvenience of the appointment time or day, the expense of the therapy, the lack of progress on the part of the index patient. Characteristically, this type of family does not follow prescriptions. It is in a hurry to finish therapy, to free itself of these pests (the therapists) and return to the referring person to declare that this experiment has been a failure.

WHAT TO DO

In order to fully understand the problem of the referring person and to place it in its proper perspective, the family therapist must obtain adequate information concerning him. If the referring person has made contact by phone, or has come in person to present his case, we try to take into account any information or behavior which bears upon his relationship with the family.

In our experience this occurs only in a minority of cases. More often, it is a member of the family who contacts us and either volunteers the name of the person who has sent him or responds in answer to our questions concerning the referral service. At times the situation is immediately clear if the family member says, "Dr. so-and-so sent us, and he's been treating our daughter (son, etc.) for years, and he told us he won't see us anymore if we don't come to see you for family therapy. . . ." Here it is obvious that the therapy cannot begin without placing this information in a position of prime importance. In most cases, the referring person who sends the family to therapy with this type of ultimatum rarely places himself in personal contact with the Center, thus leaving it up to the therapists whether or not they should contact him.

We shall now describe what we do in these different cases.

1) *The suspected referring person is invited to attend a session with the family.* We are not speaking of the case of a family therapist who has turned to our Center for assistance. In this case, we always make an appointment for a consultation session in which the therapist is also present so that he may eventually continue the therapy on his own. Rather, we are dealing here with the case of a referring person belonging to the categories previously described, who has ordered the family to come to our Center.

The first session with the family is dedicated to gathering information concerning the relationship the various members of the family have with the referring person and the reasons for which he has sent the family to our Center. If it appears that the relationship has existed over a significant period of time and/or that it is an intense relationship, we can hypothesize that the referring person has become a homeostatic member of the family. At the end of this session, we state that we can continue the therapy only if the referring person is willing to attend personally in order to help us, given his profound knowledge and understanding of the family. We decline any suggestion made by the family to substitute for the physical presence of the referring person with records, charts, or letters from his office. We insist that he come, given his understanding and concern.

In the next session, which is attended by the family and the referring person, we work primarily with the latter, turning to him as a colleague who has been invited in order to supply essential information. By using this approach, we are able to see to what extent he has become a member of the family and to what point he has become exasperated with the total lack of change on the part of the family in spite of all his efforts and advice. At the conclusion of the session, far from criticizing him, we positively connote the work he has done with the family, and congratulate his failure. Here it is essential to avoid any sarcasm or irony, but rather to express our understanding of the feeling of frustration he must experience. During the session we have been careful to gather data which can be presented at this moment as reason for strict prevention of any change in the family system, stressing the dangers such change would present.

At this point, whether we decide to delay the next session for an appreciable period of time so that everyone involved can reflect upon the dangers presented by family therapy, or whether we accept the family in therapy by making a definite appointment for the next session, *we no longer make the mistake of advising or prescribing the interruption of the relationship between the family and the referring person.* In dealing with this fundamental point, we are careful to use the "prescription of the symptom," advising, even insisting upon the continuation of that friendship which has revealed itself as being so comforting and necessary for the cohesion and stability of the family. In this way, the position of the referring person as a member of the family group is implicitly pointed out.

The termination of the game between the referring person and the family, and thus the solution of the problem, should be the result of a session which has been properly handled. Then, and only then, can the therapists begin their work of treating the family.

2) *The suspected referring person is not asked to participate in the session.* In the first meeting with the family, we inquire closely into the family's relationship with the referring person. We are careful to avoid any tone of judgment or disapproval. If anything, we adopt an attitude of acceptance and good-naturedness. We ask in detail about the length of the relationship, the frequency of meetings and telephone calls, eventual gifts given on the holidays or on particular occasions. Above all, we seek information with which we can construct a graduated scale indi-

cating the position of each family member in the relationship with the referring person, beginning with the member who has the strongest bond and working down to the member who has the weakest. (This inquiry is not always carried out at the beginning of a therapy. At times we are compelled to make this detailed examination in a more advanced phase of the therapy, when we first begin to observe behavior in the family such as we have described earlier in this paper. In such cases, we discover that the family has minimized or held back significant information concerning its relationship with the referring person.) Once this has been accomplished, and, basing tactics upon the information obtained, we choose not to invite the referring person to attend the next session, but to make instead an intervention which includes him.

For example, this is a case that dealt with a family of three: mother, father, and a 15-year-old daughter, Christina. The mother had called the Center for a meeting because of Christina, who, from the age of two years, after an attack of meningitis, had been in treatment with a well-known children's neurologist, Dr. Maria Finzi (a fictitious name). The mother explained that they had been sent by Dr. Finzi because at this time Christina was going through a difficult period: she was rebellious, made scenes continuously, and refused to take the pills prescribed. However, Christina was doing well in school, and, in our opinion at the time, seemed to show no particular signs of being gravely disturbed.

In our discussion preceding the first session, we decided that the first problem to examine was that concerning the neurologist who had been treating Christina for the past 13 years and who, it appeared, had sent the family to our Center because Christina refused to take the medication she had prescribed (an anti-epileptic).

In response to our questions concerning the family's relationship with the neurologist, we learned that the mother maintained an intimate friendship with her, with frequent visits, chats, and presents. The neurologist, besides controlling the EEG's of Christina and prescribing sedatives for her, also concerned herself with the girl's education, discussing it frequently with the mother and less frequently with the father (who, during the session, showed a marked disagreement with his wife on several points, especially those concerning the way to deal with Christina).

When we tried to clarify the motive for which the neurologist had referred the family to family therapy, we encountered a powerful resistance which indicated that here lay some vital issue. By insisting, we were able to learn that approximately six months before, the family, which had been paying the neurologist rather high fees for years, had by accident discovered that they had the right to free medical assistance for Christina at a regional neurological clinic. It was the father who was interested in bringing the girl to the clinic for examination and later returned for the results of these examinations. He had come home full of enthusiasm, having had a "marvelous" discussion with the specialist who had examined Christina. The results had been normal, and all medication had been suspended.

The mother, not at all convinced, had immediately made an appointment with Dr. Finzi. The moment they entered the office, Christina had declared petulantly that she had been examined by another doctor who had found her normal and who had said she should not take any more medicine. "From that moment," sighed the mother, "even though I tried to explain how it had happened, Dr. Finzi ignored me completely and only talked to the child. She told her to stop taking the medicine if she wanted to, but that after the summer holidays (it had been June) she wouldn't see us anymore unless we came to your Center. She said that you would have to study our family in order to discover why Christina is so unbearable, and then tell us what to do. I'm waiting for you to do that so that I can call Dr. Finzi."

Until this point, Christina had maintained an air of complete disinterest in everything that was being said. She kept glancing at her watch, and would answer in monosyllables or with the irritating phrase, "I don't know." whenever she was asked a question.

During the discussion of the team before the conclusion of the session, we decided unanimously to exclude any offer of treatment. The family as a whole was not at all interested in treatment; it had been the mother who had dragged them to the Center in order to obtain, *expressis verbis*, an appointment with the neurologist. As for the neurologist, it seemed evident that she had sent the family to our Center because she felt powerless and professionally disqualified as well as entangled in the competition and internal conflicts of the family. We finally agreed upon a paradoxical conclusion that had as its target the relationship of the mother with the neurologist. Here follows our conclusion of the session:

Ther.: Our team is in complete agreement in excluding family therapy for Christina, because Christina is not sick. She does everything she does for a reason, even if she isn't aware of it. She is trying to maintain the relationship between her mother and Dr. Finzi, and she's trying to keep it in the right balance. Christina has known for years that her father isn't enough for her mother, that her mother needs someone she can confide in, depend on, and she knows that she found all that in Dr. Finzi. But then Christina became afraid that the friendship between her mother and Dr. Finzi was getting too close, and that her father was beginning to feel left out. So Christina got naughty with Dr. Finzi, who got mad enough to send you all here to us. But, when you arrived here today, Christina began to worry again. If you really started family therapy, there was the danger that her mother would lose her dear Dr. Finzi. That's why Christina didn't cooperate today, why she was always looking at her watch, why she never answered our questions—to discourage us from taking you into therapy! *(turning towards Christina)* In fact, Christina, we're not going to do family therapy with you. But you have to keep on doing what you've been doing until now, even if you get fed up, even if you decide you don't want to anymore! Keep on behaving in exactly the same way so that your mother can keep her friendship with Dr. Finzi, but with the right balance! Not too little, or your mother will suffer and feel alone, and not too much, or your father will feel left out.

In other cases where the family relationships appeared seriously dysfunctional, as in families presenting members designated as schizophrenic, we have dealt with the problem of the referring person through systemic interventions which, while exposing the ongoing family game by connoting it positively, at the same time included, in an elusive and implicit manner, the referring person also, paradoxically encouraging and prescribing the continuation of the relationship.

CONCLUSIONS

The systemic model furnishes the therapist with the adequate means of defining and resolving the problem of the referring person. The systemic model, being of a superior logical level in respect to the linear-causal model, allows the therapist to place and to maintain himself in a meta-level in respect to family and referring person. Moreover, it seems quite important, even if only secondary, that the systemic model permits valid solutions without creating friction with the referring person, especially since the professional situation is already touchy.

Obviously a correct methodology would have required the consulting of all the files and records concerning the families treated at our Center in the ten years of its existence. Unfortunately this proved to be impossible, since for many years we had underevaluated this aspect of family therapy, and therefore the necessary information was totally or in part missing. From now on we shall systematically collect data concerning the referring person.

All the same, we felt it useful to report these observations because in themselves they are indicative of the seriousness of this problem.

REFERENCE NOTE

[1]It is important to specify that the discussion of the problem presented in this paper is based upon the experiences of an autonomous and private center. Family therapy carried out in the ambience of an institutional context will obviously meet different problems.

REFERENCES

Selvini Palazzoli, M., Boscolo, L., Cecchin, G.F., & Prata, G. *Paradox and Counterparadox: A New Model in the Therapy of the Family in Schizophrenic Transaction.* New York: Aronson, 1978.

Sonne, J.C., Speck, R.V., & Jungreis, K.E. The absent member maneuver as a family resistance. In A. Friedman et al. (Eds.), *Psychotherapy of the Whole Family.* New York: Springer, 1965.

Wynne, L.C. & Thaler-Singer, M. Thought disorders and the family relations of schizophrenics. *Archives of General Psychiatry,* 1963, *9,* 191-206; 1965, *12,* 187-212.

Editor's Commentary: The Specialness of the Source

When I first received this chapter from the Milan group as a submission to the *Journal of Marital and Family Therapy*, I read it and became intrigued by it. Although I had routinely asked, as they had traditionally done, who referred the patients, it had been more as a contact point and to determine if any exchange of summary data might be in order. No additional significance was attached to the referral source, by me, or to my knowledge, any of my colleagues. Certainly the referring person was not conceptualized as a quasi-member of the family system. Yet, their brief, eloquent presentation had a compelling logic. Once described, it seemed so important and so obvious that the shared oversight was almost embarrassing.

Since reading this gem, I have paid much more attention to the response to the series of queries about "who referred you" and sometimes incorporate the approaches Selvini Palazzoli et al. recommend. Following them has proven fruitful.

From my clinical experience, I would like to add two additional categories of persons to their typology of referring persons who are suspect. First are mental health professionals who are *relatives*. Because they are members of the extended family, they realize they should not assume the role of therapist. Nonetheless, they are vitally concerned about the well-being of their sister, brother, parents, or cousins, and their recommendation of a therapist is solicited and respected. They are likely to state that they believe they are referring their relatives to the best person in town, which places an extra burden on the therapist to live up to this salutary reputation. The referring relative therapist seems to hover in the wings, ever interested in the patient's impressions of the treatment and the therapist. He or she also may deliberately or inadvertently slip into functioning as an auxiliary post-session therapist, perhaps a well-intentioned maneuver but one likely to impede the therapy.

146

For example, recently a professional couple in their early thirties were referred to me by his sister, who is a prominent therapist in another state. One of the presenting problems is that the wife is no longer sexually responsive to her husband. Probably not coincidentally, the referring sister is best known for her work in sexual dysfunction. When it became increasingly evident that she is acting as a behind-the-scenes coach for her brother, I got their permission and called to invite her to join them with me for a session as soon as possible. The call was met with surprise. Unfortunately, but perhaps not coincidentally, the couple dropped out of therapy before we could schedule this session.

It is perhaps a tribute to one's skill to be considered a therapist's therapist. However, it is a mixed blessing, as anyone who treats other therapists and their families will attest. When a *therapist self-refers him- or herself* (the second group I would add to the typology) and family, it is fraught with potential difficulties—not the least of which is the referring therapist's change of status in the family and perhaps in the treating therapist's eyes as he/she is in the unfamiliar and less comfortable terrain of the patient. He or she may try to compete with the therapist or shift into a co-therapy alliance. If the referring person here has other ties, such as being on the therapist's agency board or being a frequent source of referral to the therapist in his/her private practice, the situation can be extremely sticky and must be handled with great aplomb—or sent elsewhere!

We are indebted to Selvini Palazzoli and her colleagues for heightening our consciousness about this special component of the therapeutic process.

Chapter 8

A Method for Organizing the Clinical Description of Family Interaction: The "Family Interaction Summary Format"

By Peter Loader, Charlotte Burck,
Warren Kinston, and Arnon Bentovim

Family therapy emphasizes the family as the basic unit of study and treatment for psychological problems. Family therapists view the symptoms of an individual as predominantly meaningful within the context of his family relational system, and place emphasis on interactional processes occurring between family members. As part of any psychiatric assessment, a systematic written description of family functioning, brief or lengthy depending on the circumstances, is required. Clinicians' descriptions suffer excessively from idiosyncrasy and incompleteness. Review of the literature revealed the lack of an accepted systematic method for describing family interaction. The Family Interaction Summary Format was devised

This is a slightly revised version of an article originally published in the *Australian Journal of Family Therapy*, 1981, 2, (3), 131-141.

Peter Loader, M.D., is a Research Fellow, The Department of Psychological Medicine, The Hospital for Sick Children, London, U.K. Charlotte Burck, M.S.W., is a Social Worker, formerly of The Department of Psychological Medicine, The Hospital for Sick Children, London, U.K. Warren Kinston, M.D., is Honorary Senior Lecturer, Academic Department of Child Psychiatry, Institute of Child Health, London; Senior Research Fellow, Brunel Institute of Organisation and Social Studies, Brunel University, Uxbridge, Middlesex, U.K. Arnon Bentovim, M.D., is Consultant Psychiatrist, The Department of Psychological Medicine, The Hospital for Sick Children, London; and The Tavistock Clinic, London, U.K.

to fill this gap. This paper describes the logic of the Format and is a guide to its use.

Investigation of family therapy at the Hospital for Sick Children in London commenced in 1973 when we became convinced of the effectiveness and efficiency of the approach. We discovered that basic clinical research was impeded by the lack of an agreed upon terminology. In addition, there were no widely used methods of assessment, no order in the variety of treatment methods, and the development of clinical theory was limited and without substantial validation.[1]

This led us to commence a research program rooted in our clinical determination to help families with problems (Kinston, 1981). The clinical description of family interaction was an immediate task. Studies conducted within the Department revealed that different clinicians focused on different aspects of interaction and their descriptions were rarely comprehensive or comparable; the briefer the description, the more idiosyncratic. We therefore decided to devise a standard framework for description.

CRITERIA FOR A METHOD OF DESCRIPTION

A clinically suitable method for describing family interaction needs to be:

1. Systematic and clear. It requires a logical format, with terminology defined and agreed upon, and with each conceptual area of interaction broken down into mentally-manageable and observable component parts.
2. Comprehensive. All major areas of interaction should be covered rather than an emphasis on one or two particular aspects.
3. Brief. With familiarity, it should be able to be completed quickly.
4. Widely-applicable. It should be useful to clinicians of different theoretical orientations and of varying degrees of experience, including newcomers to the field.

The "Family Interaction Summary Format" has been developed with these criteria. (Copies are available on request.)

STRUCTURE OF THE FAMILY INTERACTION SUMMARY FORMAT

The Summary Format described here is the version currently in use. It has been reformulated and modified several times, and is expected to require continuing revision as our understanding of families develops.

The Summary Format considers the total family system, including its relationship to the environment, and its component subsystems, as well as relevant aspects of individual functioning which contribute to the assessment of family functioning. It is concerned only with family interaction and functioning as observed here and now. It is therefore only one aspect of a full assessment of a family which would also consider such factors as the presenting problem, the developmental history of the family, and crises and stresses.

The Summary Format delineates eight conceptual groupings (dimensions) of family interaction and function, each on a separate page. These are: Atmosphere, Communication, Affective Status, Boundaries, Family Operations, Alliances, Parental Function, and Relation to the Environment. Each of these is divided into sub-sections which offer guidelines to aid the description, with space for clinicians to write notes.

A front page allows notation of family members present and absent, and offers general instructions for the use of the Format. These include that clinicians: consider the family-as-a-whole, describe only what they see, minimize inferences, be brief and specific, and avoid repetition.

CONTENTS OF THE SUMMARY FORMAT

In this section, the eight dimensions and their sub-sections are outlined. Our aim is to convey for clinical, **not** research, purposes the nature of the Format. We are not intending to be comprehensive or definitive and references have been kept to a minimum.

Atmosphere

The concept of "family atmosphere" receives relatively little attention in the family therapy literature, and generally its definition is left vague. Ackerman (1958) described it as "the changing manifold of emotional currents and crosscurrents within the family."

TABLE 1

Page 2 of Summary Format (condensed)

ATMOSPHERE

Describe the mood and tone of the family, including the degree of comfort and tension.

Is humor available and used? What sort of laughter occurs?

Comment on the supportive-appreciative interactions; and the attacking-oppositional patterns.

Other Comments:

The phenomenon of family atmosphere is well-recognized by clinicians, even though they may find it hard to define or describe what they mean by the term. We think it refers to the overall "feel" of the family, a pervasive quality as distinct yet as intangible as a smell or a taste. It is a global, subjective response of the therapist to all the family do and say, and is best appreciated by being in close physical proximity to the family. Colleagues watching through a one-way screen may be too distant to fully sense it. Families can be so "poisonous" that a therapist just longs to get out of the room.

We have attempted to tease out the observable family characteristics of particular relevance to atmosphere. We started from the idea that "atmosphere" is the emotional affect of family members being together. Then, we distinguished two aspects that we labeled family "mood" and "tone." We remain unsatisfied with these labels. "Family mood" refers to the prevailing sense of safety/warmth or danger/coldness. "Family tone" refers to the quality of social ease: whether the family is comfortable and relaxed being together, or whether there is some degree of discomfort, stiffness or embarrassment. Families who are close and warm may present at a clinical interview as embarrassed or uncomfortable.

The presence of a sense of humor in the family seems to belong here. It is a strength which receives too little mention. The capacity of a family to use gentle irony and see the humorous side of things is important in dealing with the trials and tribulations of daily living. Humor needs to be distinguished from sarcasm, ridicule, contempt or mockery which promote a very different family atmosphere. The ability of family members to laugh together should be noted, as well as the kind of laughter that occurs. Is it the consequence of genuine good humor, or is it bizarre, embarrassed, or a screen to conceal misery or aggression?

Finally, the overall quality of interactions between family members must be considered. Relationships may be characterized by support and appreciation, disinterest and apathy, or attack and opposition. In some families the members never let themselves come together at all.

The nature of family interactions must be viewed in the light of their contextual appropriateness, for example, critical behavior on the part of a parent to a child may be supportive when benevolently performed in certain circumstances. The overall context must also be considered. For instance, the atmosphere of a family in mourning will inevitably be pain-filled.

Communication

Table 2

Page 3 of Summary Format (condensed)

COMMUNICATION
Comment on Clarity: i.e., communication of meaning, articulation, explicitness of content, verbal/nonverbal congruence.
How were themes and topics taken up, focused upon, developed and changed?
Describe the overall patterns of communication: the pathways, the noise level, the equality of participation, the conversational style.
Comment on the giving and receiving of messages: the frequency and nature of control (orders, demands, requests, questions, etc.), information exchange, listening and acknowledgement.
Other Comments:

Both clinical experience and review of the literature demand the inclusion of communication as a major heading.

By contrast to atmosphere, it seems to be clearly located in the family itself and can be objectively assessed. Unfortunately, the term "communication" means different things to different people. Following the pioneering work of Bateson et al. (1956), it has become an approach to families and therapy. The communication theorists take an extreme view by regarding all behavior as communication, so that one ends up asking, what is **not** communication? Family researchers have attempted to deal with the complexity of the communicational process by focusing on specific aspects. For example, linguistic analysis has been applied to family therapy transcripts, and the order in which family members speak and the frequency with which one person follows another have been investigated. This theoretical approach typically fails to provide definitions of communication which are meaningful and operational in the clinical setting. However, Riskin and Faunce (1970) have contributed to the field by delineating low-inference, relevant, and manageable components within the broad concept.

Our use of the term "communication" refers to directly observable verbal interchange, paraverbal indicators (such as tone of voice), and related nonverbal cues (like body movements). The Format provides guidelines for the description of family communication in terms of the overall patterns, the expression and reception of messages, and the predominant nature of those messages.

The overall patterns of family communication refer to such general characteristics as noise-level, conversational style (for example, flowing, fragmented), and equality of participation. Do all family members join in appropriately, or is conversation dominated by one or more members with others excluded or opting out? Who talks to whom in the family? It may be that all family members talk to each other openly and freely as the need dictates or that communication is routinely restricted between some, or all, members. There may be a preferred or mandatory pathway for the whole family, e.g., all communication may go through mother, "the family switchboard." Another feature is the family's ability to share a focus of attention and to develop topics and themes. This may occur easily and naturally, or family members may be unable to maintain a shared focus and/or to develop a topic coherently. Equally important is the capacity to move from one topic of conversation to another. Does this occur, or does the family rigidly adhere, or repeatedly return, to one particular subject? Are such changes in topic smooth and appropriate, or illogical, even bizarre?

Clarity of expression is crucial for communication of meaning; disturbed families often have difficulty in this area. Messages may be unclear when they are whispered or poorly articulated, or if the content is muddled or vague or masked. This may result in misunderstanding. Even more difficult to deal with may be the misunderstanding inherent in verbal/nonverbal incongruence. Nonverbal cues may confuse, negate or disqualify explicit verbal content. What is a child to make of a father who tells him to "stop fighting this instant," while sitting passively in his chair, and speaking in a flat tone of voice? Clear communication also demands that the message goes to the person for whom it is intended. Here too nonverbal cues such as eye contact are important.

Effective family communication is as dependent upon the way messages are received and responded to as upon the clarity with which they are expressed. Family members may fail to receive messages because they do not pay attention or listen to one another. They may receive messages but fail to acknowledge them, either verbally or nonverbally, so that the sender cannot be sure whether or not his message got through. In addition, messages that are received can be misinterpreted or responded to in an inappropriate way.

Finally, the predominant type of message is important. Are family members able to exchange information freely and spontaneously? Is communication characterized by too many or too few control messages such as orders, demands, requests, questions?

Affective Status

TABLE 3

Page 4 of Summary Format (condensed)

AFFECTIVE STATUS
Comment on the range and intensity of feelings. Are they differentiated, and how are they expressed?
Describe the family's sensitivity to and valuation of its members' inner experiences, i.e., feelings, wishes, etc.
Comment on the communication of, and about, emotion.
Other Comments:

We experienced considerable difficulty devising this section of the Format and giving it a label. The central problem is the complex relationship that exists between individual and family functioning.

Is it meaningful to speak of the experiential aspects of family life, when it is individual members who have feelings and fantasies, not families? On further reflection it became clear that we were not concerned with individual psychodynamics, but with a particular family phenomenon. The family does have an "emotional life" and is bound together by shared common meanings and intersubjective experiences which constitute a "family reality" (Kinston & Bentovim, 1980).

Emotional experience may be located within the individual, but it is regulated by, and regulates, the interaction between family members, particularly with regard to how they express, respond to, and talk about feelings. The affective dimension of family life involves more than the communication of, and about, feelings which could have been subsumed under Communication. Communication does not take into account factors like range, differentiation and intensity of emotions. Nor does it encompass family methods of responding to members' wishes, needs, fears, fantasies and expectations. The emotional world of the family lies somewhere between the social world of public expression and the personal world of private experience. This aspect of family life demands far more investigation. We believe careful observation, without undue dependence on inference, yields a wealth of detail about emotional experience within a family.

The family may show access to a broad or narrow range of feelings, or restrict experience to a single valence, positive (e.g., love, tenderness, happiness, joy), or negative (e.g., fear, anger, sadness, hate). Sometimes inner experience appears to be absent with consequent deadness or blandness. Differentiation of experience is probably related to the capacity to use words, but the family may promote this or accept global responses such as good," "okay," and "bad." Feeling states must be considered in relation to the provoking situation. They may be congruent, inappropriate, or bizarre; the intensity can be heightened, appropriate, or diminished; and their duration can be viewed along a continuum from prolonged through appropriate to transient or poorly sustained.

The second major component of affective status involves the expression of experience. As with other forms of communication, clarity and directionality are important, but there are some special attributes as well. Is expression primarily verbal or nonverbal and what is the degree of congruence between these? Are physical or psychological symptoms used as a mode of emotional expression within the family? The expression of feelings may occur naturally and spontaneously, or family members may show signs of discomfort and attempt to conceal their feelings. In some families, emotional expression is used primarily for manipulative purposes, for example, one member may control others by being depressed or angry.

The third observable component of affective status is the recognition and valuation of inner experiences within the family. Experiences can be distorted, disqualified, devalued or rejected by family members. It may be that any emotional expression is unacceptable, or there may be selective acceptance and encouragement of some states (e.g., excitement), with a rejection of others (e.g., depression). This may be a whole family of a subsystem phenomenon. Conversely, the family environment may be one where all experiences are accepted as an essential, important part of family life and where members sensitively recognize and suitably respond to feelings and needs in themselves and in others.

Families vary in the capacity of members to talk meaningfully about events that affect them. At one extreme, the family may be so inward-looking that day-to-day living is interfered with, and at the other, so impoverished that major events, such as death, cannot be assimilated.

Boundaries

TABLE 4

Page 5 of Summary Format (condensed)

BOUNDARIES
Describe the degrees of individuation shown by the members.
Comment on the intergenerational and sexual roles. How distinct are they?
Comment on the balance of connectedness and separateness, i.e. enmeshment and disengagement, reactiveness and responsiveness.
Responsibility of members for their own inner states and behavior. Intrusions, interference and mind-reading between members.
Other Comments:

Minuchin's structural model of family functioning promoted the concept of boundaries as a parameter for the evaluation of family functioning and a useful focus for therapeutic work (Minuchin, 1974). Boundaries refer to the degree of separateness and connectedness that characterizes the family system. They must always be considered in the light of individual and family development. The concept is applicable at all levels of functioning: there is a boundary around the family, boundaries within the family, and boundaries around the individual family members. (The boundary around the family defines its relationship to the outside world. We thought this aspect of family functioning needed its own section: Relationship to the Environment.)

Boundaries within the family can be described with reference to the family-as-a-whole (defining the separateness and connectedness of family members), and to the various family subsystems. Minuchin conceives all families as falling somewhere along a continuum whose poles are the two extremes of very diffuse boundaries (the "enmeshed" family) and overly-rigid boundaries (the "disengaged" family). Diffuse boundaries are excessively permeable, so that family members are over-joined. They are over-reactive and over-responsive to one another. The mutual over-involvement is such that change in any one family member reverberates throughout the entire family. Interruption and intrusiveness with regard to the thought, talk, feelings and the relationships of others are commonplace. Boundaries may be generally so diffuse that individuals be-lieve they always know what other family members are thinking. When the boundaries defining family relationships are overly-rigid, there is a sense of disconnectedness between family members. Communication and cooperative effort are very difficult and empathic responses virtually impossible. Family members are isolated and tend to go their own way, with little interest shown by, or to, others. Between these two extremes fall the majority of families, with effectively-functioning boundaries. Ideally, these are firm-but-flexible, well-differentiated but appropriately permeable. Family members are able to mesh in and cooperate with one another in accordance with circumstances. At the same time, they do not intrude upon or interfere with each other's autonomous functioning, and there is a healthy balance of separateness and connectedness.

Boundary properties are not necessarily consistent throughout the whole family, so that it is possible to have both extremes simultaneously present. For example, one parent may be over-involved with a child (diffuse boundary) while the other is isolated (rigid boundary). The parents may alternate, mother being over-involved at one time and father at another. In this case, not only are both extremes present, but their distribution within the family varies at different times. There are many possible subgroupings of family members; the rules determining who participates in them, and how, constitute the boundaries of the family's subsystems.

Particularly important boundaries exist between the generations, de-fining the parental and sibling subsystems, and between the sexes, de-fining the male and female subsystems. When the intergenerational boundary is weak, a child may be "parentified," or a parent "infantil-ized." At the other extreme, the intergenerational boundary may be excessively rigid with parent and child roles fixed and stereotyped. Dis-tinction between the sexes can also be poorly-defined or undesirably exaggerated. Yet parents may show a reversal of the usual mother/father roles, while still making a clear male/female distinction.

Finally, at the individual level of functioning, there are boundaries that determine the family members' identity and degree of individuation. Interpersonal differentiation may be so poor that family members are unable to act independently or even to acknowledge their differences. They may rarely accept responsibility for their own feelings and actions and tend to see these as being caused by others. Despite excessive togetherness, the sought-after sense of belonging is more apparent than real, as any genuine relationship requires a view of oneself as a separate, unique human being. Over-involvement may also be manifested as excessive self-assertion, identity struggles, or avoidance of belonging. Optimally, family members have a secure sense of belonging and exhibit an age-appropriate degree of autonomous behaviour. They are aware of, and accept, both their similarities and their differences, and are able to assert themselves in an atmosphere of mutual self-respect.

Family Operations

TABLE 5

Page 6 of Summary Format (condensed)

FAMILY OPERATIONS
Conflict Resolution—describe the acknowledgment, acceptance and resolution of inter-member conflicts.
Decision-making—comment on the process and outcome.
Problem-solving Ability—can the family recognize problems and their complexity, can it organize itself flexibly and efficiently? Is there tolerance of ambiguity and uncertainty?
Family Life Cycle—comment on the handling of the current family tasks.

This section includes a number of family tasks: conflict resolution, decision-making, problem-solving and specific family-life cycle issues. These operations are central to family functioning and both influence and are influenced by other qualities and characteristics of the family.

Conflict resolution refers to the ability of the family to acknowledge and resolve the inevitable differences that occur between members. If the existence of conflict is not recognized or not openly acknowledged, resolution is problematic. Some families attempt to deal with conflict by never disagreeing. Other families may require continual disagreements as evidence of concern and an indication of closeness. Resolution of disagreements may take a variety of forms. It may only occur intermittently, with intervening periods of withdrawal and breakdown of communication; or conflictual issues may become diffused and lost; or insincere simplistic solutions may be accepted. One family member may always act as mediator in the conflict of others, or draw attention away from the issues. This often impedes resolution, and if the child has this central role, the family is almost certainly dysfunctional. In a healthy family, conflicts are not overly disruptive and are resolved by negotiation, creative endeavor or compromise, and family members can accept that they may be "wrong," or that everyone is "right."

Families have to make decisions frequently. This task has three aspects: the participants, the process, and the implementation.

Families not only have to make decisions which affect everyone, but also decisions which concern only some of their members; each individual also has to make his own choices. Who takes part in the decision-making process needs to be noted. Members may involve themselves inappropriately or interfere in some way in the decisions of others, or may be left out when they should have a say. The process of making decisions may be more or less flexible, and more or less fair. One person may be elected as decision-maker, or choices may be routinely made autocratically. A family may ignore the need to make a decision, or be unable to make one and drift into the decision by non-action. In other families the decision reached may not correspond at all to any of the individual's wishes. Some families make a decision and then proceed to do something completely different, or not act at all; some may carry out the decision in only a limited way; others will implement it fully.

Problem-solving refers to the family's ability to deal with difficulties encountered with regard to an individual's behavior, the relationship between family members, or environmental demands and stresses. Some approaches to family therapy focus on helping the family develop its problem-solving ability (Haley, 1977; Epstein et al., 1978). The operation of problem-solving involves a number of steps. First families must be able to perceive relevant problems accurately. If problems are continually denied or mislabeled or unhelpfully redefined or over-simplified, they accumulate and become overwhelming. Following identification of the problem, the family organizes itself to deal with it. Are the most appropriate participants involved, and how flexible is the family in seeking and considering alternatives? The family must then make a realistic plan and proceed to put it into action. Uncertainty and ambiguity must be tolerated during the time from problem identification through to problem solution. The final stage involves evaluating how effectively the problem has been dealt with. Without this, a family is unable to learn from its experiences and develop its problem-solving ability.

A large number of conflicts, decisions and problems are met with as part of the family life-cycle. Duvall (1967) has described the various stages, each of which presents the family with various tasks which need to be mastered. Symptoms may be a signal that a family is having difficulty in completing a stage or in moving on to the next. In the Summary Format we are concerned with the family's handling of current tasks. As an example, we consider the stage of the family life-cycle which comprises the period from when the oldest child commences school to the onset of puberty. Tasks include a) helping the child relate to the outside world by developing bonds to peers and loosening dependence on family members; b) parents reviewing their marital relationship as they face the eventual departure of their children, renegotiating their differences about rearing as these become more manifest with their child's greater range of possibilities; c) reorganizing the family to link with outside systems like schools and to deal with the development of new interests and activities.

Alliances

TABLE 6

Page 7 of Summary Format (condensed)

ALLIANCES
Alignments, splits, scapegoating (a diagram may be helpful).
Marital subsystem (affection, support, maturity, balance of assertion).
Sibling subsystem (acceptance, affection, sharing parents, common play, rivalry).
Child/Parent relationships (compliance with controls, demands on parents, preference for one parent).
Other Comments:

Alongside consideration of the family-as-a-whole, it is essential to look at the subsystems which make up the family. These dyadic and triadic relationships are referred to as the allliances of the family.

There are two main ways of looking at these alliances. One of these is to examine the overall pattern of the relationships and to note any important groupings. The other is to look at each subsystem, particularly the component dyads. The marital subsystem is the core dyad of the family; sibling-sibling, child-parent, and parent-child relationships may contain a number of dyads. We have considered parent-child interaction in a separate section because it is of such central clinical importance in our child psychiatry setting.

In a well-functioning family, relationships are appropriately strong and close, depending on age, sex and role, and they show flexibility.

Strong relationships between members have been termed alignments or coalitions. These may serve to strengthen or weaken family functioning. The family may split into warring or distant groups, or may gang up on one member. Triangulation is the inclusion of a third person to reduce tension between two family members. Scapegoating does not refer simply to an excess focus on one member, but to a situation where all that is bad is dumped on that member without respite. These patterns can often be easily represented in diagrammatic form.

Some aspects of the marital relationship have been described elsewhere in the Format, such as under Communication. We have selected four areas to be noted at this point: affection, support, maturity, and balance of assertion. How affectionate are the marital partners? Do they show warmth to each other, or is there frequent mutual hostility? Do husband and wife support each other? Do they respect each other's opinions and encourage each other? How mature is the relationship? Do husband and wife relate as equals, or do they behave as if in a parent-child relationship, or even as two siblings? Is there a balance of assertion? Are the partners able to give and take with a sharing or satisfactory delegation of decisions? Is one partner dominant with the other submissive? Is there continual competition between the partners for dominance? Is interaction wishy-washy because neither marital partner is able to assert him/herself, or is there no pattern of dominance because husband and wife do not relate at all?

In our experience, sibling interaction is often neglected in clinical work unless there is extreme pathology. There are several aspects to this relationship which merit our attention. In interview, siblings usually have the opportunity to play together. How affectionate and helpful to each other are they? How do they handle their rivalry; in particular, how do they share their parents?

Child/parent relationships also need examination. Does a child do what his parents ask? And does he make reasonable demands on his parents or are these excessive or insufficient? Does he go to each parent equally or show marked preference, perhaps when he needs comforting? Child/parent relationships influence and are influenced by the nature of parent/child interaction, which is considered in the next section.

Parental Function

TABLE 7

Page 8 of Summary Format (condensed)

PARENTAL FUNCTION
(Check appropriate column and clarify by commenting as required).

	Very Poor	Defic-ient	OK	Good	Comments
A. *Interaction between parents*					
Sharing of care					
Division of care					
Agreement on rearing					
Support and cooperation					
B. *Tasks of Parenting*					
Spontaneity/pleasure in children					
Imposition of routines					
Consistency in relating and expectations					
Adaptation to children's needs					
Discipline and control					
Demands on the children					
Anticipation of physical needs					

General Comments:

Although the quality of the marital relationship affects the kind of parenting which occurs, the parental roles can be considered separately. This refers to how husband and wife relate to each other as parents and how the specific tasks of nurturance and socialization of the children are carried out.

One facet of parental interaction concerns how the parents divide the care of the children between them. Families will vary in how they do this, but it is important for parents to come to a mutually satisfactory arrangement. Another essential aspect is whether the parents are able to agree on how the children should be reared. Not only do parents need to come to some agreement or compromise but they should be able to offer each other support and cooperation when dealing with the children. Do they back each other up when a child is being difficult, or do they undermine each other? Does one parent join the children against the other parent? Do they exclude each other in relation to the children? Parents may act independently because of their mutual isolation or because they are unable to negotiate and compromise with one another, or to express hostility.

How do the parents carry out the particular tasks of parenting? They must meet the child's physical requirements appropriately—neither neglecting nor over-protecting him. Parents also need to meet a child's emotional needs, which include giving him a sense of belonging and helping him gain a sense of autonomy. Other aspects of this include enjoying the child and feeling pleased and proud of him; being consistent in responding to the child and in their expectations of him; setting up routines which meet the needs of both the family and the child and give a consistency and structure to everyday life; relating to him in a way suited to his characteristics, capacities and needs; and making appropriate demands of the child to help him develop. Parents also need to be able to control their child and to set limits which are appropriate to his needs and age. Difficulties with discipline may present as intrusive, insufficient, or deviant control.

The concepts in this section and the assessment of parenting are familiar to clinicians. We therefore designed the page in the form of a checklist.

Relation to the Environment

TABLE 8

Page 9 of Summary Format (condensed)

RELATION TO THE ENVIRONMENT
Describe relations with extended family.
How does the family relate to people outside, i.e., friends, neighbors, strangers, the interviewer?
What are the family's connections with the community (school, church, clubs, and helping-agencies)?
Other Comments:

It is essential to look at the family in terms of the wider social system of which it is a part. Therapists often neglect this area and focus solely on the family, just as they previously neglected the family system and focused on the individual. Consideration of the larger system and its interaction with the family may lead to the location of pathology in these outside relationships. This may lead to network therapy, or family therapy which includes the extended family. In a clinical setting, one should always obtain some information about the way the family interacts with the environment. In other settings, this aspect may be more open to direct observation.

It is possible to assess three sets of relationships the family has with the outside world: those with relatives, those with individuals outside the family, including the interviewer, and those with neighboring systems.

Of prime importance is the need to establish how the family interacts with relatives. In a well-functioning family, parents have achieved independence but are able to continue to relate intimately with their families of origin. Other families continue to be a minor subsystem of a larger extended family. Depending on the nature of the family and on sociocultural factors, this may or may not work. At the other extreme, a family may have cut off all connections with relatives.

The relationship the family establishes with the interviewer and the treatment setting is directly observable. Families may perceive non-family persons as basically friendly, and will relate to them openly and warmly. Other families seem to be self-sufficient and do not relate much to outsiders. Some families perceive outsiders as threatening or confusing and relate with suspicion and hostility. Others suck outsiders in to fulfill certain functions such as mediator, confidante, or as the person who provokes family conflict.

Families also relate to other neighboring systems and institutions. Some cannot function without helping agencies. A healthy family will use outside agencies appropriately and have a constructive two-way involvement with the community.

RESPONSE TO USERS OF THE METHOD

A small group of family therapists, including the authors, have used the Summary Format routinely to describe families they are assessing and treating. The Format has also been presented at various workshops and conferences[2] where participants have used it to describe family interaction viewed on videotape. These events have raised a number of issues and difficulties in the use of the Format.

The immediate reaction was two somewhat contrasting criticisms of the Format's structure: It was overwhelming, confusing and too complicated; or it was limiting, oversimplified and too precise. In answer to these objections, we would argue that the Format does justice to the undeniable complexity of family life, and that disciplined thinking and observations are essential components of clinical work.

A more substantial problem was the uncertainty of users as to where to record particular observations of family interaction. There is a good deal of overlap between different sections of the Format to allow for the predilections of clinicians and to ensure comprehensive coverage. However, we found users initially had difficulty allocating observations they did make. Instead they reported some particular aspect of interaction in every section and omitted other clinical phenomena.

Some users criticized the inclusion of terms and observations apparently centering on individual functioning e.g., affect, individuation. They reported being confused as to what level of description was being required. Our intention is that the family be considered as a system, as a number of subsystems and as a collection of individuals. The aim of the Format is to facilitate recording of current directly observed and reported family functioning, and the nature and patterning of certain aspects of individual functioning must be included to provide a meaningful account.

The Format has been criticized as being too long and time-consuming for routine clinical use. This time factor became inevitably compounded with other initial difficulties described above. Any form of systematic information-gathering is time-consuming; for example, a full clinical neurological examination may take up to an hour. However, once familiarity is attained and the needs of the current problem established, neither a neurological examination nor our Format is unduly time-consuming to complete. The user must internalize the Format with its underlying principles, theories and implications and then he can abbreviate his report as appropriate.

In our experience, these problems of discipline, decision, detail and difficulty rapidly recede with continued careful use of the Format. Clinicians have found that it sharpens their use of terminology, clarifies their perception of interaction, and enhances their ability to formulate therapeutic plans. Tomm and Wright (1979) divided family therapy skills into three competencies: conceptual and perceptual and executive. The conceptual and perceptual work forms the basis for the overt actions on the family—the executive work. The Format encourages the development of conceptual and perceptual skills and aids executive work by facilitating evaluation of particular strategies and techniques.

CONCLUSION

The work we have described has been built on our own and others' experience in observing and treating families and is based on the belief that careful observation and description is a component of theory-construction and testing.

Our concern was to break down the complexities of family interaction for the practicing clinician. He/she requires a method for conceptualizing and describing that is close to what he uses intuitively, or that is an extension of unused intuitive and observational capacities. Our whole effort has been guided as much by pragmatism as by theory. With experience and repeated use, the Format can be mentally abbreviated and family interaction can be meaningfully and non-idiosyncratically summarized in a paragraph or two as part of a diagnostic or therapy summary.

A Summary Format will stand or fall insofar as it actually meets clinical needs. We have found that it aids communication between family workers, assists formulation of family problems and treatment goals, and also provides a written record of family functioning for future reference. It has proved a valuable teaching tool in recent years. Issues of validity and reliability are pertinent but not problematic within this clinical context.

There are two common major criticisms. The first is that we have made false distinctions in determining our dimensions. In the real world, of course, everything is interconnected and any family event is simultaneously communication, experience, alliance and so on. It is the task of the human observer for his purposes, artificially and temporarily, to make the disconnections. The second is that we mix observation and conceptualization. In reply to this we point out that conceptualization must precede clinical observation and that the Format does not demand subtle judgments or deep intuition, but rather clear statements of what is seen.

The Summary Format gives considerable latitude to those who use it, but does demand that effort of careful, self-disciplined description without which family therapy cannot progress.

REFERENCE NOTES

[1]The cooperation of members of the Department of Psychological Medicine, The Hospital for Sick Children, the Academic Department of Child Psychiatry, and The Institute of

Child Health is appreciated. Ms. Oonagh O'Brien provided secretarial assistance. The Research Unit of the Family Studies Group receives financial support from the Leverhulme Trust.

²These include: Society for Psychotherapy Research European Conference, 1979; Tavistock Training Conference, 1979; Annual Conference of The Association for Family Therapy (UK), 1979, 1980; International Conference of Group Psychotherapy, 1980; American Association for Marriage and Family Therapy, International Conference, 1980.

REFERENCES

Ackerman, N.W. *The Psychodynamics of Family Life,* New York: Basic Books, 1958.

Bateson, G., Jackson, D.D., Haley, J., & Weakland, J. Toward a theory of schizophrenia. *Behavioral Science,* 1956, *1,* 251-264.

Duvall, E. *Family Development.* Philadelphia: Lippincott, 1967.

Epstein, N.B., Bishop, D.S., & Levin, L. The McMaster Model of Family Functioning, *Journal of Marriage and Family Counseling,* 1978, *4,* 19-31.

Haley, J. *Problem Solving Therapy.* San Francisco: Jossey-Bass, 1977.

Kinston, W. In M. Pines, and L. Rafaelsen, (Eds.), *The Individual and the Group: Boundaries and Interrelations in Theory and Practice.* (Proceedings of VII International Congress of Group Psychotherapy, Copenhagen, 1980.) New York: Plenum Publishing Corporation, 1981.

Kinston, W. & Bentovim, A. Creating a focus in marital and family therapy. In S. Budman, (Ed.), *Forms of Brief Psychotherapy.* New York: Guilford Press, 1980.

Minuchin, S. *Families and Family Therapy,* Cambridge: Harvard University Press, 1974.

Riskin, J. & Faunce, E.E. Family interaction scales. 1: Theoretical framework and method. *Archives of General Psychiatry,* 1970, *22,* 504-512.

Tomm, K. & Wright, L.M. Training and family therapy: Perceptual, conceptual and executive skills. *Family Process,* 1979, *18,* 227-250.

Editor's Commentary: Toward
Systemization of Assessment

In developing the "Family Interaction Summary Format," Loader, Burck, Kinston and Bentovim have taken a giant step forward in systematizing and categorizing the dimensions clinicians should consider when assessing a family. Not only should this Format for organizing the clinical description of family interaction be extremely valuable as an evaluation tool, but it also seems to constitute an instrument that makes possible comparative research between therapists, and across settings and different countries. It is striking that as they were developing this Format for assessment in England, Tomm was developing his Circular Pattern Diagram in Canada. Clearly the need for such an instrument has been felt by researchers and clinicians alike in many countries; these two chapters offer two interesting possibilities. A third which I would like to call to the reader's attention is Duhl's Chronological Chart (1981); this could be used in conjunction with either of the aforementioned approaches since, whereas these two present primarily here-and-now interactive data, Duhl's chart seeks to obtain a longitudinal, cross-sectional view and provides the opportunity to record much more historical background data.

Like Pollack, N. Kaslow and Harvey (Chapter 9), Loader and his colleagues chronicle the evolutionary process through which they arrived at the Summary Format. We are permitted to glimpse their personal thought processes and self critique. This style is consonant with the somewhat unusual family therapy mode which I initially encountered in *The Book of Family Therapy* a decade ago and found intriguing and viable then (Ferber, Mendelsohn, & Napier, 1972). I still do, as it represents one of the strengths of those who gravitate to the family therapy approach in clinical practice—to be appropriately self-disclosing and reveal their own dynamic path in arriving at their formulations.

Their eight dimensions which characterize families and are used in systematizing the data mesh quite well with those delineated by Lewis, et al. (1976), further elaborated by Beavers (1977), and expanded and amplified in my work on the healthy family (Kaslow, 1980/1981). In some instances different terms are used and where data are subsumed varies slightly. Yet the threefold division of families as healthy, midrange and dysfunctional is consistent in the writings of all of these authors—and the eight dimensions are sufficiently similar that perhaps this indicates that a schema has been delineated for analysis and description which might begin to be accepted and utilized by many therapists. It does not seem grandiose to believe that the time for such universalization is near. Certainly, this chapter contributes to the theory construction and theory testing in which these authors and many others believe it is essential to engage.

In candid style they attempt to handle the criticisms already leveled at their work. I concur with them that it is necessary to make decisions, albeit at times arbitrary and by one's own determination, as to what the dimensions are and where particular data should be classified. Otherwise, scientific investigation and replication studies are not possible and we each work in semi-isolation without benefit of sharing concepts that are useful, having then to work by trial and error, each fashioning our own typology. Given the complexity of family life and the great science and artistry necessary to turn treatment into a truly therapeutic experience, an hour, or even two, utilized in making and recording an accurate assessment seems precious little time to invest to enter and come to know what Loader et al. call "the emotional world of the family."

REFERENCES

Beavers, W.R. *Psychotherapy and Growth: A Family Systems Perspective.* New York: Brunner/Mazel, 1977.

Duhl, F.J. The use of the chronological chart in general systems family therapy. *Journal of Marital and Family Therapy*, July 1981, 7, (3), 361-374.

Ferber, A., Mendelsohn, M. & Napier, A. *The Book of Family Therapy.* New York: Science House, 1972.

Kaslow, F.W. Profile of the healthy family. *Fokus på Familien*, 1980 and *Interaction*, 1981, 4, 1 & 2, 1-15

Lewis, J.M., Beavers, W.R., Gossett, J.T., & Phillips, V.A. *No Single Thread: Psychological Health in Family Systems.* New York: Brunner/Mazel, 1976.

Chapter 9

Symmetry, Complementarity, and Depression: The Evolution of an Hypothesis

By Stephen L. Pollack, Nadine J. Kaslow, and David M. Harvey

This paper traces the development of an interactional model of depression from a simple schismogenic model to a more complex, nonschismogenic model. The initial model viewed depression as the result of a runaway sequence of symmetrical or complementary interactions. The nonschismogenic model, our working hypothesis, portrays depressive interaction as a knot of interlocking symmetrical and complementary relationship processes. The model explains both observed interpersonal and intrapsychic depressive interactions which focus on the depressed person's affect and behavioral competence. The model suggests that therapeutic strategies should aim to unravel the depressive knotting through facilitating progressive differentiation.

Although family therapists have identified models for a number of different problems, a search of the literature reveals only a few articles written on depression from a systems theory perspective (Coyne, 1976;

Stephen L. Pollack, Ph.D., is a Senior Faculty Member at the Houston-Galveston Family Institute, Houston, Texas. Nadine J. Kaslow, M.A., is a doctoral candidate in clinical psychology at the University of Houston, Houston, Texas. David M. Harvey, Ph.D., is Associate Professor, Counseling Psychology Program, at the University of Texas, Austin, Texas.

Feldman, 1976; Hogan & Hogan, 1975; Rubinstein & Timmins, 1978; Watzlawick & Coyne, 1980). The following details the development of a systemic, interactional model of depression. A passage from Bateson (1972) encouraged us to think that his theory of systems was specifically applicable to the problem of depression.

It is unfortunate that these abstractions (love, hate, fear, anxiety, hostility) referring to patterns of relationships have received names, which are usually handled in ways that assume that "feelings" are mainly characterized by quantity rather than by precise patterns. This is one of the nonsensical contributions of psychology to a distorted epistemology (p. 140).

In an attempt to understand those patterns of relationships in which depression is embedded, we initially proposed a simple schismogenic model. This model was then refined to be more specific to depression.

Finally, we produced a more complex, nonschismogenic model which accounts for both intra-individual and interpersonal depressive processes, and defines depression in terms of patterns of symmetrical and complementary interactions.

FUNDAMENTAL CONCEPTS

Some important concepts which Bateson used to explain patterns of relationships are applicable to a systemic view of depression. These include schismogenesis, symmetrical relationships, and complementary relationships, each of which will be discussed below.

Schismogenesis

Bateson described schismogenesis as the process of progressive differentiation of interactional patterns resulting from cumulative interaction, or the repetition of an interactional unit over time, as the basis for interactional evolution. Between individuals, these processes are associated with the evolution of norms of individual behavior as well as the hierarchical relationships associated with social control (Bateson, 1936). Between groups, schismogenesis contributes to the differentiation of interactions which distinguish subcultural groupings (Bateson, 1941). Bateson contended that many relationship systems show this tendency toward progressive change and differentiation. However, he proposed that when cumulative interactions exceed some upper limit of repetition and intensity, a schismogenic runaway results, of either a symmetrical or complementary nature, which is characterized by increased strain and distortion of behavior and affect.

Symmetry and Complementarity

Bateson identified two types of schismogenic processes: symmetrical and complementary. Although Bateson refined these notions repeatedly and they have received substantial attention in the field of family therapy (e.g., Haley, 1963; Hoffman, 1981; Selvini Palazzoli, Boscolo, Cecchin, & Prata, 1978; Watzlawick, Beavin, & Jackson, 1967), they have only been used descriptively and have not been central to models of family dynamics or other social systems since *Naven* (Bateson, 1936). Nevertheless, since symmetry and complementarity are Bateson's only classificatory concepts which define processes of interaction, they seem critical for understanding depressive interaction. According to Watzlawick et al. (1967), symmetrical interaction is characterized by "equality and the minimization of difference by the participants"; partners in a symmetrical exchange are said to "mirror" each other. Complementary interaction is based on the "maximization of difference," such that the behavior of the participants "fits" together. One partner occupies the "one-up" position, the other the "one-down" position.

Bateson used the behavior of the individual, as well as interactional criteria referring to the relationship, in defining symmetrical and complementary processes. A behavioral view of symmetrical processes refers to literal physical acts showing a progressive minimization of behavioral differences between the participants, while a behavioral view of complementary processes refers to progressive maximization of behavioral differences. The processes of minimizing and maximizing differences in behavior result in progressive behavioral change. Although actual behaviors are one such source of useful information in determining relatedness, they are not sufficient. Additionally, relationship observations, which are the product of inferential judgments about the quality of the interaction of the individuals involved, are required. An observation of a relationship between people requires the judgment that the two parties are somehow coordinating their conduct.

Recalling the children's game "Simon Says" clarifies the importance of determining symmetry and complementarity at the relationship level if one is to understand the patterning of interaction. In the game, one person, called "Simon," commands *behavioral* limitation with the phrase beginning "Simon Says." The remaining portion is a verbal description of the behavior to be produced accompanied by an actual demonstration. One is "out" when mimicking a behavior described and demonstrated, but not commanded. The mistake is believing that the game concerns the symmetry of behaviors, when, in fact, the game prioritizes one style of complementary relating.

All of this exploration led us to definitions of symmetrical and complementary relationships that were only slight modifications from our starting views and were similar to those found in the literature (e.g., Haley, 1963; Hoffman, 1981). Symmetry and complementarity are defined in the following way throughout the paper. With respect to any particular interactional context, the identification of a relationship as *symmetrical* depends on the observers' decision that over some period of time two parties are behaving as if they perceive themselves as equals in terms of power, control over the other, or influence. Thus, *complementarity* must then depend on an observer's judgment of inequality. Embedded in such a definition is the idea that two sets of relationship judgments are crucial: those of the participants and those of the observers of the participants. Although there may be considerable congruence between the perceptions of participants and observers about an interaction, there will always be some differences. We speculated that to an observer a symmetrical relationship might look like a progressively escalating struggle between equals, while each of the participants believes themselves just "a bit more equal" than the other. Similarly, complementary relationships probably seem more equal to the participants than to outsiders.

In New Guinea, Bateson (1936) observed that the Naven ceremonial contained both complementary and symmetrical sequences. Bateson suggested that unrestrained schismogenic processes ("runaway sequences") of either type eventually resulted in systemic breakdown. Excessive symmetry leads to "extreme rivalry" and "hostility" while too much complementarity promotes "progressive unilateral distortion of the personalities" and then, "destructive mutual hostility."

It is as if there is a disastrous consequence for exceeding some maximum value parameter on each of these processes. We began to see depression as one such disastrous outcome of a runaway sequence.

Given this view, one must determine how such runaway sequences are naturally constrained. Bateson observed the temporal contiguity of symmetrical and complementary processes and judged that the two were, in effect, incompatible opposites, reasoning that each acted to balance or cancel the other. Interactions of the opposite type functionally prevent excessive escalations. Apparently, a little bit of complementarity goes a long way to reducing too much symmetry and vice versa. This principle of the mutual constraining effect of contiguous symmetrical and complementary processes becomes important in constructing therapeutic interventions for interrupting schismogenic runaways.

A SCHISMOGENIC MODEL OF DEPRESSION

As is common in problem-focused, systemic conceptualizations, depression is viewed here not as an inherent attribute of an individual but as a complaint referring to certain perceived aspects of an individual's behavior or experience. Individuals come to therapists complaining about something they label "depression" or one of its synonyms. For depression to actually become a problem, there must be a complaint which defines the behavior or experience as problematic, as well as interactions which promote and sustain this definition.

Depressive interactions which include the depressed individual and significant others who are intensely involved with the complaint have been described by a number of writers (Coyne, 1976; Dell, 1981; Feldman, 1976; Hogan & Hogan, 1975; Rubinstein & Timmins, 1978; Watzlawick & Coyne, 1980). Our initial schismogenic model of depression proposed that family interactions with a depressed member can be classified as either symmetrical or complementary, and furthermore, that these interactional sequences are problem-escalating or schismogenic. In other words, symmetrical or complementary runaways relative to the complaint of depression prompt people to come into treatment, since such runaways are associated with strain and the possibility of breakdown. An example of a symmetrical schismogenesis would be the repetition of the following interaction: "You shouldn't be so sad, why don't you get going?" "I'm just sad and useless."

An example of a complementary schismogenesis involving depression would be the following communication repeated over time: "You are sad and helpless, let me cheer you up and help you." "Please do, I am so depressed and incompetent." Of course, the content of these communications sequences, as well as the mode of communication, may vary. It is more crucial to identify the type of interactional sequences as symmetrical or complementary than to be concerned with the content of these sequences. Once the type of schismogenic interaction which escalates the depressive complaint is identified, therapeutic maneuvers which will interrupt and restrain the runaway can be selected. In general, the therapeutic strategy for restraining a symmetrical runaway is to reframe the interaction as complementary or to make prescriptions which initiate complementary interactions. The reverse process would be applicable to complementary runaways. This strategy follows directly from Bateson's assertion that the contiguous occurrence of these opposing processes restrains the escalation such that no further runaway can occur. For example, the wife of a depressed husband may state, "I keep telling him he's got to stop being so down in the dumps because it's wrecking our family," while the husband replies, "If only you would stop nagging me, I could be less depressed and everybody would be happier." In this instance, the two participants are relating symmetrically around the complaint of depression. The therapist's aim is to introduce some complementary relating into their interaction around the husband's depression. For example, his depression might be redefined positively (positive reframe) as helpful to the family in some way, or the wife could be invited to prescribe her husband's symptoms.

Another strategy suggested by Bateson (1936) for restraining a symmetrical runaway entails shifting the symmetrical struggle away from the two participants involved to a similar and more salient struggle with some new, third party. A naturally occurring and potentially unfortunate example of this would be a depressed husband and his wife who shift the focus of their attention away from the issue of depression to their child's bad temper. Thus, an original schismogenic pattern of relating may be constrained through other interlocking patterns involving more members of the system. Although the original runaway may be constrained, the new struggle would itself be liable to escalation.

Besides depressive interpersonal interactions, depressive cognitions or self-statements (Beck, 1967) can also be understood within our schismogenic model. In this view, self-statements are viewed as intrapsychic interactions between two internal observers (cf. Maturana, 1978), in which the silent comments an individual makes on his or her affective state or functioning are always made as if directed to another internal observer. For example, a person might say, "I have been depressed almost all my life. It's pretty clear there is nothing I can do about this. I guess it's in my genes and I will always be this way." In such a sequence, one internal observer has taken a complementary position relative to the depressed other observer. Therapeutic intervention should aim at inviting the person to take a more symmetrical position relative to his/her complaint about him/herself. Without directly challenging the basic premise, a therapist might try to promote symmetry by encouraging the person to try to "make the best of your handicap."

Behavior modification, jogging, and even carefully prescribed medication all seem to fall into a category of invitations to the person to presume to be equal to their depression and fight back.

The Definition of Affect in a Relationship

The schismogenic model of depression described above seemed to us to be deficient in that the processes delineated were not sufficiently specific to depression. The issues around which persons interact symmetrically or complementarily could involve any behaviors or experiences as long as they are labeled "depression" by the participants. Responding to this criticism, the model was refined to specify that the interactions most pertinent to depression are those where the definition of one person's affect is negotiated. In a complementary schismogenesis, then, the participants repetitively define one person's affect as depressed with all the consequences that definition entails (e.g., the comforting of a despondent person). In this complementary interaction, there is no disagreement or variation about the definition of depression; it appears as if one person has the power to define the affect in the relationship. In a symmetrical schismogenesis involving depression, the participants struggle for control over the definition of the affect in the relationship; one person defines him/herself as depressed while the other shows his/her equality by asserting an alternative definition. (In this case of symmetry, "depression" reflects an attempt to control *not* the self or others [cf. Dell, 1981], but rather the definition of the affective aspects of the relationship.)

One can see the negotiations over the definition of affect or the labeling of internal states are not inconsequential for persons in an ongoing relationship. Affects are like context markers in that they offer information regarding what behaviors are called for (e.g., nurturance, sympathy, criticism) and hence, promote the coordination of conduct. For example, in our culture, the consequences of labeling affect as fatigue would be different from the consequences of labeling it depression or disease. Thus, the consequences make the negotiations over the definition of affect a critical process in any relationship.

This refined schismogenic model of depression suggests an additional therapeutic strategy—redefining the context of interactions. In effect, a therapist can propose that the negation concerns not affect, but some other class of issues. Because such a redefinition shifts the consequences and culturally prescribed patterns of appropriate interaction, it should interrupt a schismogenic runaway. An example is found in Madanes'

(1981) case of the "Depressed Man." In this case the husband's depression was redefined as irresponsibility, shifting the problem from the realm of affect to the realm of volitional behavior. The wife was a therapist herself so this redefinition took the problem out of the wife's area of expertise, which presumably introduced different patterns of interaction around the problem. Such redefinitions of relationship contexts allow participants to interact within a different domain of meanings.

Although this particular schismogenic model defined depression and its escalation as a problem in interactional terms, it did not fit our clinical observations in three important ways. First, the model proposes that *either* symmetrical or complementary runaways will be observed to escalate depression; yet we had more commonly observed both patterns occurring simultaneously in a family. The model seemed too simplistic in assuming depression would involve only one type of schismogenic process. Second, the refined model, with its emphasis on affect, seemed depression-specific, but it did not account for non-affective symptoms (e.g., helplessness) which have been so thoroughly documented and investigated as prominent aspects of depression (Bibring, 1953; Seligman, 1975). *The model needed to address behavioral functioning as well as the affective life of the individuals involved in depressive interactions.* Third, viewing depression as part of an escalating process did not seem to fit the "stuckness" which is a salient aspect of the phenomenon of depression. By "stuckness" we mean the behavioral inertia, enduring dysphoria, the persistence of the problem, and the subjective sense of being caught in a hopeless mire. The schismogenic model of depression seems an appropriate view of how things get worse, but does not seem to account for how things stay bad. These considerations led us to try to evolve a more complex, nonschismogenic model of depression.

WORKING HYPOTHESIS

Given the problems associated with a schismogenic model of depression, we developed a radically different nonschismogenic model to account for the "stuckness" which characterizes depressive interactions. The image of a knot of interwoven symmetrical and complementary processes seemed helpful. It became evident that schismogenesis was not to be restrained, as in the previous model, but rather that schismogenesis was a desirable resolution to a depressive interactional knot. Bateson's (1958, 1979) later modifications of symmetry and complementarity parallel the changes in our thinking. While symmetry and complementarity still referred to interactional processes which are opposing under certain circumstances, they also refer to self-corrective, circular-causal chains of interactions. In other words, a symmetrical schismogenic process, if allowed to run its course, should resolve itself through transformation into a complementary process, and the reverse is true for a complementary escalation. Given this modified view of the outcome of schismogenic processes as self-corrective or self-healing, we began to delineate the nonschismogenic model of depression described below.

One domain of human interaction and communication concerns the naming of internal states. It is commonly assumed that affects are describable in terms of the quantity or intensity of an internal attribute which exerts linear, causal influence over other parts of the organism. This line of thinking has exhausted itself and is useful only to the extent that it invites new views.

For our hypothesis, we refer to this same phenomenon in interactional terms as the interpersonal or intrapersonal negotiation over the naming of affects or feelings. This negotiation always involves at least two observers, whether they be two organisms or two "as if" observers experienced inside organisms. Terms referring to the intensity of affect are pertinent only to the participant's experience.

In such negotiations, the typical observer comments on two domains of information as if they were substantively related to characterizing feelings. One, reference is made to a continuum of pleasantness/ unpleasantness of internal states; and two, reference is made to aspects of behavior, usually judgments about "normal" body functioning and/or some type of "productivity." "Behavioral competence" refers to both of the latter judgments. More concretely, the negotiators typically ask two types of questions, "How do you feel?" and "What are you doing?" We are concerned with those negotiations where at least one observer concludes that the other is best characterized as "depressed."

This model suggests that the *relation* between any internal state and an observer's names for such states is continuously changing. The best label at one moment becomes something else the next. The progressive differentiation of affect is ongoing, recursive and interactional. In other words, individuals increase the complexity of understanding of their own internal states through interactions with other observers about these states.

Progressive differentiation of this sort entails the maximization of single relationship themes. In other words, one relationship pattern (i.e., symmetry or complementarity) for negotiating the definition of affect becomes the only pattern for such negotiations. The process depends on distortions of the relationship characterized by an increasing frequency of pattern repetition. At their most persistent, such patterns are experienced as distressing and sometimes as potentially disastrous. But such schismogenic processes are self-correcting, except when certain relationship patterns exist which do not allow them to run their course. The contiguity of symmetrical and complementary relationships is one such pattern.

Bateson asserted that the language needed to talk about actions will always be of a different order of complexity than the language of changing actions. Symmetry and complementarity categorize those interactions which therapists observe concomitant with depressive complaints. Symmetry refers to a perceived relationship between two observers of affect which is best described as an interaction between "equals in contest" for influence over the definition of feeling states. Complementarity refers to a relationship vis-à-vis affect best described as one in which both participants appear to believe that only one observer has input and control over the naming process. Runaway sequences of either sort are the path of affective learning and differentiation. From the observer's point of view, moments of relationship distortion are necessary to the process because they stand as invitations to the participants to interact differently. Progressive differentiation via pattern repetition and relationship distortion eventually promotes relationship changes and pattern disruption which, in turn, promotes differentiation, and so on. Similarly, the participant's experience of increasing distress is inextricably tied to the subsequent relief.

"Depression" then refers to interference with this ongoing process. It is not a reflection of the epistemological error of trying to control that which cannot be controlled (e.g., Dell, 1981), but rather an inadvertent co-occurrence of relationship patterns which constrain the process of affective differentiation. Persons should be most likely to complain about depression when there is a convergence of symmetrical and complementary relationships, all focusing on the affective complaint. Such co-occurrence of relationships around depressive complaints should be associated with a certain "stuckness" manifested in the repeated application of labels referring to either feelings or behavioral competence or both.

Symmetry and complementarity are analogic descriptions of the quality of relationships. Such judgments require examination over time of interactions between observers of affect. By specifying domains of information and domains of observer interactions, we are indicating where to make such relationship inferences, and hence, where to observe the knots.

As was noted previously, there are two domains of information relevant to characterizing feelings: internal states and behavioral competence. Depressive knotting should occur when the relationship observed in one domain is different from the other. For example, if individuals relate in complementary fashion on the issue of internal states (e.g., "I know you're depressed . . ."), and relate symmetrically vis-à-vis the issue of competence (e.g., "But why don't you go to work?"), then problems should develop.

In order to understand such knotting, it is important to remember that observer interaction can occur both interpersonally and intrapersonally. More complex and therefore more "stuck" depressive relationship knots occur when the type of interaction (symmetrical or complementary) differs both between issues (affect vs. behavioral competence) and between interactional domains (intrapersonal vs. interpersonal). For example, if symmetry is the relationship pattern which characterizes the interpersonal discussion of competence, then complementarity should characterize intrapersonal interchanges concerning this same issue.

To complete the knot, then, the interpersonal negotiations concerning affect should show evidence of symmetrical relating while interpersonal exchanges should show complementarity. Table 1 depicts the two types of relationship knots which could occur.

Although this model offers a more effective view of depressive interactions, it is less precise than our previous one with respect to the guidance it offers for interventions. With the interactional knots proposed here, it is clear that one would attempt to promote runaway

TABLE 1

Two Types of Interactional Knots Maintaining Depression as a Problem

	Interpersonal Interactions	Intrapersonal Interactions
Type #1	Affect (S)	Affect (C)
	Competence (C)	Competence (S)
Type #2	Affect (C)	Affect (S)
	Competence (S)	Competence (C)

Note: "S" and "C" refer to symmetry and complementarity, respectively.

relationship sequences of either a symmetrical or complementary type. The model does not suggest where to begin, nor does it place any particular premium on either style of relating. It only proposes that shifts to one type of relationship, whether between or within interactional domains, should increase the likelihood that the process of affective differentiation will once again proceed.

Case Example

The following is a hypothetical case example intended to illustrate the general features of our working hypothesis. We have chosen not to present actual case material, since we are only in the initial stages of systematic clinical use of the model.

Mrs. M. is a successful, hardworking professional who has been chronically depressed since the birth of her second child. At that time, a pattern of interaction emerged which has persisted. Mrs. M. began to find that it was more difficult to fulfill her responsibilities as mother and professional. Mr. M. responded to his wife's frustration, self-criticism, and feelings of despair by becoming more involved in household tasks and generally being more helpful to his wife. At the same time, however, he also began offering rational arguments to the effect that she had so much going for her that she had no reason to be depressed. Mrs. M's response was to accept his help while rejecting his "rational" reassurances. Cumulatively, these interactions resulted in a symmetrical struggle over the definition of affect (whether she had the right to be depressed) and a complementary interaction in the domain of her behavioral competence.

Mrs. M. entered individual therapy where she revealed the following redundant internal dialogue: "I feel very down in the dumps. I have so much work to do and I'm not doing any of it as well as I should. It's as if there's a part of me that I can't get into gear." Her internal dialogue seemed to cycle from self-acceptance of her depressed affect by her observing self (complementarity) to a struggle with her self in the area of behavioral competence: "It's as if there's a part of me that's oppositional when it comes to work" (symmetry). In this example it is as if there are four dances concurrently performed around the depression which balance and constrain each other in a harmonious round. It is predicted that the alteration of any of these relationships could begin to unravel the interactional knot around the problem. For example, if Mr. M. could be encouraged to become more supportive and accepting of his wife's sadness and despair, a complementary relationship in the realm of affect would then parallel the already observed complementary relationship in the realm of competence. The resulting exaggeration of the sympathy-helpfulness/depressed-helplessness relationship between the husband and wife should reach some limit beyond which continuation of this pattern is not tolerated and the self-corrective nature of such processes would facilitate a resolution.

Much like other systems theorists, we have assumed that clinical phenomena are best described in terms of interactions. We have gone beyond a simple interactional description of depression, however, and developed several relationship concepts in order to describe how depressive interactions evolve and how they can be changed. The resultant model of problematic interactions emphasizes "stuckness" and relationship impasses without assigning homeostatic mechanisms to the interactional system or any of its "parts."

We are convinced that ideas are best represented developmentally, not as statues, unchanging and timeless, and so we have chronicled the life of our idea. By contrasting our final, working hypothesis against its precursor, we have portrayed the historical context in which the final model is best understood.

REFERENCES

Bateson, G. Culture contact and schismogenesis. *Man*, 1935, *35*, 178-183.
Bateson, G. *Naven*. Cambridge: Cambridge University Press, 1936.
Bateson, G. Experiments in thinking about observed ethnological material. *Philosophy of Sciences*, 1941, *8*, 53-68.
Bateson, G. Morale and national character. In G. Watson (Ed.), *Civilian Morale*. Boston: Houghton Mifflin, 1942.
Bateson, G. *Naven*. 2nd ed., with added "Epilogue 1958." Stanford: Stanford University Press, 1958.
Bateson, G. The cybernetics of "self": A theory of alcoholism. *Psychiatry*, 1971, *34*, 1-18.
Bateson, G. Style, grace, and information in primitive art. Report of the Wenner-Gren Symposium on Primitive Art and Society, held June 27-July 5, 1967, at Burg Wartenstein, Austria. Reprinted in *Steps to an Ecology of Mind*. New York: Ballantine, 1972.
Bateson, G. *Mind and Nature*. New York: E. P. Dutton, 1979.
Beck, A.T. *Depression: Clinical, Experimental and Theoretical Aspects*. New York: Hoeber, 1967. (Republished as *Depression: Causes and Treatment*. Philadelphia: University of Pennsylvania Press, 1972.)
Bibring, E. The mechanisms of depression. In P. Greenacre (Ed.), *Affective Disorders*. New York: International Universities Press, 1953.
Coyne, J.C. Toward an interactional description of depression. *Psychiatry*, 1976, *39*, 28-40.
Dell, P. The Interactional Basis for Depression. Paper presented at American Psychological Association Division 29, San Antonio, March 1981.
Feldman, L.B. Depression and marital interaction. *Family Process*, 1976, *15*, 389-395.
Haley, J. *Strategies of Psychotherapy*. New York: Grune and Stratton, 1963.
Hoffman, L. *Foundations of Family Therapy*. New York: Basic Books, 1981.

Hogan, P. & Hogan, B.K. The family treatment of depression. In F.F. Flach & S.C. Draghi (Eds.), *The Nature and Treatment of Depression*. New York: Wiley and Sons, 1975.

Madanes, C. *Strategic Family Therapy*. San Francisco: Jossey-Bass, 1981.

Maturana, H.R. Biology of language: The epistemology of reality. In G.A. Miller and E. Lenneberg (Eds.), *Psychology and Biology of Language and Thought*. New York: Academic Press, 1978.

Rubinstein, D. & Timmins, J.F. Depressive dyadic and triadic relationships. *Journal of Marriage and Family Counseling*, 1978, 4, 13-23.

Seligman, M.E.P. *Helplessness: On Depression, Development, and Death*. San Francisco: W. H. Freeman, 1975.

Selvini Palazzoli, M., Boscolo, L., Cecchin, G., & Prata, G. *Paradox and Counterparadox*. New York: Aronson, 1978.

Watzlawick, P., Beavin, J., and Jackson, D. *Pragmatics of Human Communication*. New York: W. W. Norton, 1967.

Watzlawick, P., & Coyne, J.C. Depression following stroke: Brief, problem-focused family treatment. *Family Process*, 1980, *19*, 13-18.

Editor's Commentary: The Interactive
Anatomy of Depression

Pollack, N. Kaslow and Harvey are representatives of the fourth generation of family therapists. Their chapter, written expressly for this volume, reflects that they are already deeply steeped in the literature of several fields, including family systems theory and therapy and depression—from a cognitive, behavioral perspective. Their writing reveals a lively freshness, a new way of grasping the essence of depression and a grappling with this syndrome in an interactive context uncontaminated by years of immersion in repetitive dialogue. In spanning material drawn from Beck and Seligman on depression, from Bateson on schismogenesis, complementarity and symmetry, and from Coyne, Madanes, Rubinstein, Selvini Palazzoli et al. and Watzlawick on family dynamics, functioning and change processes, they bring together a novel and illuminating formulation. In taking us step by step through their thought processes as they shift from a schismogenic to a nonschismogenic model of depression, they offer a sounder understanding of the rationale for their recently evolved model, and I, for one, find it intellectually persuasive. We look to them to test their model and report their findings in the near future.

Their definition of depressive interaction as a "knot of interlocking symmetrical and complementary relationship processes" enables the reader to visualize what might otherwise be the elusive aspect inherent in the interchange of a depressive dyad. It evokes memories of reading the touching, tortured book *Knots*, written by Laing (1970), about the inner experiences of some of his patients. They elucidate how much untangling is essential for individuation, the proposed antidote to depression, to be able to occur. The therapeutic strategy which emerges entails "unravelling the depressive knotting through facilitating progressive individuation" or in Bowen's terms, disengaging them from "the undifferentiated (family) ego mass" (Bowen, 1978).

The discussion of symmetry as a relationship in which differences are minimized, the partners mirror one another, and power and control are equalized is crystal clear. Each member contributes to defining what constitutes depression. So, to the exposition of complementarity as a relationship in which differences are maximized, there is a coordinated fit in which one is up and the other down in the balance of power and influence. Only the one in control can label behavior or affect "depressed." The authors point out that, contrary to the usual belief that only one of these patterns is operable at a given time, they can coexist. A runaway sequence in either or both processes leads to systemic breakdown, but, as they point out cogently, the disruption also can become the precipitating factor which makes it possible for the system and the individuals within it to become "unstuck." Symmetry and complementarity can be opposing processes or they can intertwine in such a way as to become self-corrective. If each runs its full course, it may be transformed into its opposite, at least from the perspective of circular causality. While this is occurring, the individuals can begin to extricate from the enmeshment; this differentiation of affect is ongoing, recursive, and interactional—and ultimately curative.

What is perhaps missing here is something on the intrapsychic aspects of depression. There is no mention of depression as an affective mood disorder nor of the biological components which have led some to conclude that there is a physiological base to depression. To only deal with the interactive and learned helplessness elements is, to this writer's way of thinking, inadequate. This is another hurdle to be crossed so that seemingly discrete or contradictory material can be synthesized into a more meaningful whole. (APA, 1980).

The sense of a process occurring over time, both in the authors' evolution of their hypothesis and in their description of the depressive interaction process, lends rhythm and elegance to their chapter. Perhaps most salient is their conclusion that description and definition of a phenomenon take place on one level of thought and the changing of the pattern or problem occurs at quite another level of being. We look to them and their contemporaries to join us in gleaning new insights that will lead to further breakthroughs in theory development and intervention strategy.

REFERENCES

American Psychiatric Association. *Diagnostic and Statistical Manual of Mental Disorders, III,* Washington, D.C.: American Psychiatric Association, 1980.

Bowen, M. *Family Therapy in Clinical Practice.* New York: Aronson, 1978.

Laing, R.D. *Knots.* New York: Random House, 1970.

Chapter 10

Cognitive Family Therapy

By E. M. Waring
and Lila Russell

Cognitive family therapy is a new short-term psychotherapy which facilitates cognitive self-disclosure. The paper defines self-disclosure and differentiates cognitive self-disclosure from self-exposure and emotional self-disclosure. The role of cognitive self-disclosure in facilitating marital intimacy is discussed. A case history is presented which describes the therapeutic process and suggests possible future research.

Cognitive family therapy (CFT) is a new technique of psychotherapy which facilitates self-disclosure in order to increase intimacy in the interpersonal marital relationship. The therapy is theoretically derived and based on empirical data from family interactional research.

Self-disclosure refers to the process of making the private self known to other persons. *Cognitive self-disclosure* refers to revealing one's ideas, attitudes, beliefs, and theories regarding one's relationships and behavior and is differentiated from *emotional disclosure*, which reveals one's feelings. This is also different from self-exposure which reveals secret or fantasized behavior which may be detrimental to a relationship. Self-exposure of secretive behavior is seen as motivated by lack of closeness

This is a revised version of an article which originally was published in *Journal of Sex and Marital Therapy*, 1980, 6, (4), 258-273.

E. M. Waring, M.D., is Associate Professor of Psychiatry, Assistant Dean-Continuing Medical Education, and Director of Psychiatric Education, University of Western Ontario. He is also a Consultant Psychiatrist at Victoria Hospital, London, Ontario. Lila Russell, M.S.W., is Coordinator of the Human Sexuality Clinic in the Department of Psychiatry at Victoria Hospital.

in the relationship; emotional disclosure, especially of negative feelings, often produces distance rather than closeness.

Cognitive family therapy facilitates the revelation by the spouses of their ideas, attitudes, beliefs, and theories regarding why the marital relationship is maladjusted, as well as enabling them to disclose their ideas regarding the influence of their parents' marital relationship on their own. It is based on the theory which states that an "affective dysfunctional potential" in the marital dyadic interpersonal relationship is a necessary but not sufficient etiological variable in all families with individual psychopathology (Waring, 1978). This "affective dysfunctional potential" is operationally defined as a failure of the spouses to develop interpersonal intimacy (Russell, Russell, & Waring, 1980).

Intimacy is an interpersonal dimension which describes the quality of a marital relationship (Waring, Tillmann, Frelick, Russell, & Weisz, 1980). Let us start by operationally defining intimacy in marriage as a multifaceted dimension of an interpersonal relationship at a point in time; the level of intimacy is a composite of: 1) conflict resolution—the ease with which differences of opinion are resolved; 2) affection—the degree to which feelings of emotional closeness are expressed by the couple; 3) cohesion—a commitment to the marriage; 4) sexuality—the degree to which sexual needs are communicated and fulfilled; 5) identity—the couple's level of self-confidence and self-esteem; 6) compatibility—the degree to which the couple is able to work and play together comfortably; 7) autonomy—the couple's degree of positive connectedness to family and friends; and 8) expressiveness—the degree to which thoughts, beliefs, attitudes and feelings are communicated within the marriage. Recently, reliable and valid techniques for measuring interpersonal intimacy by self-report questionnaires and structured interviews have been developed (Schaefer & Olson, 1981; Waring & Reddon, 1981).

The importance of intimacy as an adult psychosocial task, an interpersonal dimension of marriage, and a developmental variable of personality generally has not led family theorists or therapists to the corollary that "intimacy" may be the primary determinant of family functioning, particularly at the beginning of the family life cycle (Harlow & Zimmerman, 1953; Waring, 1980b).

The theory that the emotional relationship of the marital dyad has profound influence on family functioning and individual development is not new or startling (Lewis, Beavers, Gossett, & Phillips, 1976). However, the insight that the primary determinant of marital intimacy may be "cognitive self-disclosure" and the empirical evidence supporting this observation has implications for the understanding of normal and clinical families (Grinker, 1967; Jourard & Laskow, 1958). Family interactional research has consistently demonstrated greater hostility, marital maladjustment and criticism between the parents of psychiatric patients, as compared to normal controls, particularly in the presence of the offspring (Doane, 1978; Jacob, 1975). These findings may represent the clinical manifestation of a failure to develop intimacy. Further, Beck has demonstrated that the manipulation of a cognitive variable in cognitive behavior therapy can alter emotional depression (Beck, 1967). Thus, self-disclosure, which reveals one's ideas, attitudes, and beliefs, may be the primary determinant of an affective variable, the couple's feelings of intimacy (Berman & Lief, 1975; Waring et al., 1980).

CFT attempts to decrease marital maladjustment, hostility and parental criticism by increasing intimacy through facilitating cognitive self-disclosure. The therapy was developed clinically by one of the authors (EMW) for the treatment of families with schizophrenic and psychosomatic members (Waring, 1978; Waring, 1980a). The specific technique, to be described below, derives its *form* from the work of Bowen (1975), Zuk and Boszormenyi-Nagy (1967) and Framo (1972). Bowen's concept that the therapist should respond (*cognitive*), rather than react (*emotional*), to the couple suggests a specific and explicit suppression of affect throughout therapy sessions (Bowen, 1975). Zuk's concept of the therapist as a "go-between" suggests the direct prohibition of the couple from talking to each other during the session. Finally, Bowen (1975) and Framo (1972) both focus on helping the couple to understand the reasons for their lack of intimacy by self-disclosure of their beliefs, theories and ideas about why their parents were or were not close and the influence of this on their relationship.

Finally, self-disclosure is facilitated when the biographical material is perceived as appropriate in the context of the current relationship and the partner is perceived as supportive and willing to disclose in a reciprocal pattern. The more an individual speaks on topics regarding the self, the more intimate the disclosures become (Waring, 1981).

COGNITIVE FAMILY THERAPY—THE TECHNIQUE

Cognitive family therapy begins with an evaluation interview with all family members present. The focus of the evaluation is to elicit each family member's "theory" of why the presenting problem or symptom has appeared. The children's cognitive explanation of why the family is not functioning optimally and the parents' theories regarding their parents' relationships are elicited. A developmental history of the parents' courtship and marriage is obtained and they are asked for similar information about the marriages in their respective families of origin.

The interviewer asks only "why" or "theory" questions, and avoids and suppresses affective interchange and/or behavioral interpretation or confrontation. The interviewer evaluates the eight dimensions of marital intimacy using the Victoria Hospital Intimacy Interview form: affection, cohesion, expressiveness, compatibility, conflict resolution, sexuality, autonomy, and identity. This facilitates the identification of the couple's strengths, as well as the dimensions which are determining their lack of intimacy (Waring, McElrath, Mitchell, & Derry, 1981).

The interviewer then explains to the entire family the theory on which CFT is based and the parents are offered ten one-hour sessions to increase their intimacy (or improve one of the specific eight areas of intimate relationships) and, as a result, improve family functioning and the symptomatology of the presenting patient. Then, the specific rules and behaviors of the CFT sessions are outlined and a specific treatment contract is negotiated.

Only the parents are involved in the CFT sessions. The session begins with the therapist stating, "We are here to understand why you are not close." As the therapy proceeds, each session begins with the major "why" questions from the previous session, as will be demonstrated in the case history to follow. The couple may talk *only to the therapist* in an alternating pattern during the sessions. No feeling or behavior is identified, confronted or interpreted. The spouses alternate in talking about any biographical or theoretical material which they think is relevant to the "why" question.

When a spouse cannot answer the "why" question, the therapist *in a standardized manner* asks the other spouse, "What were you thinking while your spouse was talking?", thus facilitating cognitive self-disclosure. The therapist may also ask one spouse for a theory on the question which the other spouse cannot answer. The therapist may share his or her cognitive theories but does not use interpretation or cognitive restructuring to identify the current conflict. When the couple understands a particular "why" question, a more sophisticated "why" question becomes apparent.

Although the description of this stereotypic format sounds tedious for the therapist, the material and revelations are surprisingly fascinating and clinical skills develop through the perceptiveness of the therapist's "why" questions.

CASE EXAMPLE

This particular couple sought a marital assessment six months after their marriage. Both partners were professionals in their late twenties. The presenting problem was a difference of opinion regarding whether the husband's career or their relationship should have priority in their lives. They also had a difference of opinion regarding the wife's wish to have a child and the husband's wish to delay it until their relationship improved. The final presenting problem was an imbalance in expression of affection, with the husband being critical and the wife withdrawing affection when hurt. The couple had many strengths in their relationship, including their commitment to the marriage, a good sexual relationship, similar backgrounds, and a willingness to talk about the relationship.

The couple accepted that their differences of opinion regarding issues of control and the subsequent arguments were producing increasing distance and they agreed to participate in cognitive family therapy.

In the first session, the husband disclosed that he had a strict, overbearing father who dominated him through fear, but was isolated both from his wife and the children. He described a passive but undermining mother, who was emotionally invested in the children. His parents differed markedly in their attitudes towards parenting. The wife disclosed that she had not been close to either of her parents and had been involved in considerable acting-out behavior at about the time her father had been involved in an affair. She was forced to keep this affair a secret from her mother. The therapist focused their attention on answering the following cognitive questions: 1) Why did his mother undermine his father and why was his father so strict? 2) Why did her father cheat on his wife and why did her mother stay in the relationship?

In the second session, the wife revealed that her mother was a cold, suspicious, and proud woman who had picked a man who had a reputation as a "ladies' man." Her mother had a brother who had had two divorces and had married a very disturbed woman. The husband disclosed that giving his wife what she wanted would be considered a weak and shameful thing in his family. He related this weakness to his father's alcohol abuse. The cognitive questions for the wife in this session were: Why was her father so dishonest and why was her mother unwilling to face the truth about the relationship? For the husband: Why did his father drink and why was his mother subtly dominating?

In the next session, the wife revealed her desire to get close and have a companion for a husband. This was important to her as she had not seen it in her own parents' marriage or her childhood. The husband reported a need to be needed by a stranger, but not by his wife, again, because if you need a wife you will be seen as weak and effeminate. During this session a shift occurred in which the husband, who had previously seen his alcoholic father as dominating, began to perceive the isolation and ineffectiveness of his father within the family setting. The wife began to identify her mother's coldness and lack of reality-testing, which she thought may have been an explanation for her father's cheating.

In sessions five, six, and seven, the wife revealed that her father's father had committed suicide at the death of his wife. Her father had a brother who also committed suicide and another brother who was divorced. She disclosed that her father was totally cut off from his brothers, but had no idea what grudge had led to this. She revealed that her mother's family had a reputation for emotional coldness. The wife of her mother's divorced brother had told her that her grandparents were both cold, unemotional people as well. In these sessions the husband revealed that his father also had had a brother who was an alcoholic. His father's father had been an alcoholic and a weak, ineffectual man who was dominated by his wife. His maternal grandmother was a big woman who dominated her husband.

In these sessions the cognitive questions shifted dramatically for the wife to an attempt to understand: "Why did the men in her family commit suicide?" and "Why were the men so helpless in their interpersonal relationships with women?" and "Why were the women so powerful?" In the eighth session, the original conflict was identified as the wife's demand that she be put first or the husband might die literally and figuratively. The husband's demand was that she directly ask for companionship and affection rather than forcing it out of him by emotional coldness. The clarification of this family issue led to self-disclosure of both the husband and wife about how violent their arguments had been; they even involved physical abuse. The husband explained his views that his wife came from a disturbed family in which neither parent had expressed any interest in her, revealing his understanding of her profound need for companionship and closeness; he also had not observed closeness in her parents' marriage. He understood that his parents had had a battle for control, although now he had a different and new theory regarding the power balance. The wife revealed that she now understood she had come from a seriously disturbed family and marriage, but she was uncertain whether facing this reality helped or hindered her adjustment. She believed that understanding how her husband's family also was seriously distressed provided some relief. The husband disclosed that he felt that, if he gave his wife the companionship and affection that she demanded, he would lose some of his own self-esteem and that her demands would be incessant. The wife disclosed that her husband's insecurity and need for understanding had not been apparent to her.

In the ninth session, they revealed that they wanted to have a child in order to be able to give the love which they felt deprived of while growing up in their families. The husband wanted to give the child closeness and companionship. The therapist presented the theory to them that these were the things they wanted from each other and asked the cognitive question: "Why is it so difficult for them to give each other what they want?" The wife disclosed that she was willing to give him what *she* wanted, closeness or companionship. Like her parents she was unwilling to accept that this was not what *he* wanted in terms of his wish for understanding and acceptance. The husband disclosed that he was unwilling to give the closeness or companionship unless she gave the understanding he wanted. He feared loss of his self-esteem if he gave her what she wanted.

In the tenth session, the couple discussed their clinical progress and also gave their subjective opinions about what in therapy had led to improvement. Their arguments had decreased both in severity and frequency. They felt closer to one another, and were better able to listen and talk about both their own families and their personal situation. The husband had made professional changes in order to spend more time with his wife, and the wife was spending more time listening to his concerns and insecurities. They both thought that their parents had not been close and had had a battle for control strikingly similar to that which they had experienced. An increased understanding of why the parents had behaved like this had a powerful impact on them.

They both thought their needs had been clearly stated and were understood within the context of their own upbringing and background.

TREATMENT ISSUES

The clinical material presented in this case report is typical of the disclosures in the course of cognitive family therapy, which elicits never before discussed family issues of suicide, alcoholism, power conflicts, sexual frigidity, and extramarital affairs. The couple's experience of increasing self-disclosure regarding serious psychological difficulties in their parents' interpersonal relationship and in their families as a whole is typical. A specific theoretical interpretation often is not developed or apparently important to the couples being treated.

What specific aspects of the therapy account for clinical improvement? This question must be answered by research which is designed to evaluate the components of this therapy. Theoretically, the self-disclosure which occurs facilitates understanding and increases the couple's level of intimacy. Several other possibilities exist. First, when the initial assessment is of the family, but the therapy excludes the children and focuses on the marital interaction in the ten sessions, a component of Minuchin's structural family therapy is introduced (Minuchin, 1974). This intervention results in increasing the strength of the wife-husband structure in the family by excluding the children from this interpersonal relationship (Grinker, 1967). Second, the spouses really learn to listen to one another, as each spouse talks about his/her theories regarding the personal relationship without the option of emotionally reacting to what is heard. The specific technique of *not* allowing interaction between the spouses during sessions and of allowing them to respond only to the therapist's cognitive questions immediately reduces tension as each session begins. Also, the therapist is modeling a specific form of communication for the couple which involves cognitive understanding. Finally, the revelations about parental interaction and the marital interaction in the grandparental generation provide cognitive restructuring as both new information and understanding may produce a therapeutic impact.

As so often happens in neurotic interaction in marital pathology, the spouses enter marriage unconsciously wishing to meet *a need they feel deprived of* in their upbringing, but irrationally pick a spouse who has serious difficulties in providing satisfaction for these needs. They then focus their attention on their spouse's areas of difficulty as a method of disowning their own neurotic needs through projection and self-justification. Often one partner identifies traits in the spouse similar to those in the parent whom he/she believes was most responsible for his/her parents' lack of closeness and then tries to change those traits in the spouse. An understanding of the parents' marital interaction in terms of its antecedents in the previous generation seems to decrease the emotional pressure to perpetuate attempts to change the spouse or resolve the same conflict situation in the present relationship. In the course of cognitive family therapy, spouses may choose either to dissolve their relationship and seek out spouses who rationally may be able to meet their needs or, more often, to redefine the relationship in terms of areas of strengths and accept each other's weak areas.

The therapist facilitates self-disclosure about the spouses' ideas, theories, and perceptions of their parents' marriage without attempting to restructure their cognitions. The self-disclosed information is not given to the partners as fixed explanations of their relationship problems, but stimulates more sophisticated "why" questions about new information as it is revealed.

SUMMARY

Cognitive family therapy provides several advantages for family therapy outcome studies. These include that it is: 1) theoretically based; 2) empirically derived; 3) standardized; 4) short-term; and 5) can be taught and supervised. The recent development of methods of measurement of intimacy and self-disclosure suggest that therapy variables may be able to be clarified in outcome studies of CFT (Chelune, 1978; Schaefer & Olson, 1981; Waring, McElrath, Mitchell, & Derry 1981). Further research may allow conclusions to be drawn regarding the specific effectiveness of CFT with particular clinical problems.

REFERENCES

Beck, A.T. *Depression: Clinical, Experimental, and Therapeutic Aspects.* New York: Harper and Row, 1967.

Berman, E.M. and Lief, H.I. Marital therapy from a psychiatric perspective: An overview. *American Journal of Psychiatry*, 1975, *132*, 583-592.

Bowen, M. Family therapy after twenty years. In S. Arieti (Ed.), *American Handbook of Psychiatry, Volume 5.* New York: Basic Books, 1975.

Chelune, G.J. Nature and assessment of self-disclosing behavior. In P. McReynolds (Ed.), *Advances in Psychological Assessment, Volume 4.* San Francisco: Jossey-Bass, 1978.

Doane, J.A. Family interactional and communication deviance in disturbed and normal Families. *Family Process*, 1978, *17*, 357-376.

Framo, J.L. Towards the differentiation of a self in one's own family. In J. L. Framo (Ed.), *Family Interaction: A Dialogue Between Family Researchers and Family Therapists*, New York: Springer, 1972.

Grinker, R.R. *Toward a Unified Theory of Human Behavior*, 2nd Edition. New York: Basic Books, 1967.

Harlow, H.F. & Zimmerman, R.R. Affectional responses in the infant monkey. *Science*, 1953, p. 130.

Jacob, T. Family interaction in disturbed and normal families: A methodological and substantiative review. *Psychological Bulletin*, 1975, *82*, 33-65.

Jourard, S.M. & Laskow, D. Some factors in self-disclosure. *Journal of Abnormal Social Psychiatry*, 1958, *56*, 91-98.

Lewis, J.M., Beavers, W.R., Gossett, J.T., & Phillips, V.A. *No Single Thread: Psychological Health in Family Systems.* New York: Brunner/Mazel, 1976.

Minuchin, S. *Families and Family Therapy.* Cambridge: Harvard University Press, 1974.

Russell, A., Russell, L., & Waring, E.M. Cognitive family therapy: A preliminary report. *Canadian Psychiatric Association Journal*, 1980, *15*, 64-67.

Schaefer, M.T., & Olson, D.H. Assessing intimacy: The PAIR Inventory. *Journal of Marital and Family Therapy*, 1981, *7*, (1), 47-60.

Waring, E.M. Family therapy and schizophrenia. *Canadian Psychiatric Association Journal*, 1978, *23*, 51-58.

Waring, E.M. Marital intimacy, psychosomatic symptoms and cognitive therapy. *Psychosomatics*, 1980, *21*, 595-601. (a)

Waring, E.M. Family therapy and psychosomatic illness. *International Journal of Family Therapy*, 1980, *2*, (4), 243-252. (b)

Waring, E.M. Facilitating intimacy through self-disclosure. *American Journal of Family Therapy*, 1981, *9*, (4), 33-42.

Waring, E.M., McElrath, D., Mitchell, P., & Derry, M.E. Intimacy and emotional illness in the general population. *Canadian Psychiatric Association Journal*, 1981, *26*, 167-172.

Waring, E.M., & Reddon, J.R. The measurement of intimacy in marriage: The Waring Intimacy Questionnaire. *Journal of Clinical Psychology*, 1981 (in press).

Waring, E.M., Tillmann, M.P., Frelick, L., Russell, L., & Weisz, G. Concepts of intimacy in the general population. *Journal of Nervous and Mental Disease*, 1980, *168*, (8), 471-474.

Zuk, G.H., & Boszormenyi-Nagy, I. *Family Therapy and Disturbed Families*. Palo Alto: Science and Behavior Books, 1967.

Editor's Commentary: What You Think—
Not How You Feel

In cognitive family therapy, the therapists seek to facilitate cognitive self-disclosure, that is, the revelation of the patients' ideas, attitudes, and beliefs and their theories regarding their interpersonal relationships and behavior. Waring and Russell explain that self-disclosure is different from self-exposure, which entails the revealing of fantasies and/or secrets and sometimes the kinds of negative feelings which precipitate distancing rather than fostering closeness. They have carefully structured the CFT process in a ten-week time frame; thus it falls under the rubric of brief, time-limited, and goal-oriented treatment. The methodology encompasses asking "why" questions of increasing sophistication to each of the spouses, having them answer only to the therapist, and asking them not to address each other during the session so that they can listen attentively and become aware of what they are thinking while the spouse is talking, without pressing to rebut or support. The authors also posit that in this way each spouse is enabled to disclose long-standing psychological difficulties and turbulence. No interruptions are permitted. Waring and Russell claim this reduces tension and ultimately facilitates increased intimacy.

The questions they are likely to ask may deal with each partner's family of origin as well as their family of creation. Thus a multigenerational portrait is etched to illuminate and help resolve the current dilemmas. It is this aspect which justifies calling the approach family and not marital therapy.

In reading the original of this article, I found myself puzzled at their narrow definition of marriage, which they conceptualize as a relationship geared to mutual need satisfaction. This is perhaps true for many at a basic level, particularly those who have had great deficits in their emotional upbringing and bring to marriage huge cravings for filling the emptiness. These are the couples most likely to come for therapy. Waring and Russell seem to be talking about what Maslow labeled D, for Deficiency needs (Maslow, 1962). But this is only part of the reason for marrying. Continuing with Maslow's language, the healthy, self-actualized individual has B or Being needs. They enter relationships out of fullness, not emptiness, able to give and receive, wanting to share pleasure and peak experiences, and not needing to cling for sustenance and validation. Although we see few of these healthy couples in our clinical practices, a formulation that attempts to define marriage should be more inclusive.

In this volume, numerous theories have been discussed and utilized as the foundation for treatment. Cognitive family therapy, described herein, falls at one end of the spectrum in that it seeks to suppress feeling and promote intellectual awareness and rational thought. Analytic therapy as utilized by Badaracco and his colleagues in Argentina lies at the opposite end of the spectrum, seeking the return of the repressed, often by doing regressive therapy. Much remains to be done in psychotherapy process and outcome studies before it is clear what approach is most effective, with whom and what kinds of problems, and when. These are answers we should be seeking in the 1980s.

REFERENCE

Maslow, A.H. *Toward a Psychology of Being*. New York: Van Nostrand, 1962.

Chapter 11

Prescribing the Family's Own Dysfunctional Rules as a Therapeutic Strategy

By Maurizio Andolfi

The use of paradox-strategy in therapy is motivated by the fact that many families request help but at the same time seem to reject all offers of help. The therapist may be drawn into a game in which every effort on his part to act as an agent of change is nullified by the family group. In systemic terms these contradictory attitudes derive from the dynamic equilibrium existing between the tendency toward change, which is implicit in the request for help at one level, and the tendency toward homeostasis, which at another level imposes the repetition of the family's habitual rules of interaction. The coexistence of these forces can entangle the therapist in the family's paradoxical logic of "help me to change, but without changing anything."

By accepting the contradiction facing him and by "uniting" himself with this within the family, the therapist puts himself into a position opposite to that which the family expects. His response to the family's paradoxical request is a paradox, or counterparadox, because it creates the contradictory communication typical of rigid family systems. By prescribing its own dysfunctional rules to the family, the therapist can stimulate the tendencies toward change present in the family system.

This article was originally published in the *Journal of Marital and Family Therapy,* January 1980, *6,* (1), 29-36.

I am grateful to Paolo Menghi with whom I discussed and elaborated much of this material. The examples described herein are drawn from clinical work done together with Menghi, Nicolò and Saccu at the Centro Studi della Comunicazione nei Sistemi, Roma.

Maurizio Andolfi, M.D., is President of the Italian Society for Family Therapy; Director, Family Therapy Institute of Rome, Rome, Italy.

PREMISES

Taking as the point of departure the statement of von Bertalanffy (1968) that every organism is a system, that is, a dynamic order of parts and processes which interact reciprocally, one can view the family as an open system composed of many parts bound together by particular rules of behavior and dynamic functions in constant internal and external interaction.

Family processes, like those of all intrinsically active organisms, can be modified. The family's inherent capacity to change enables it to achieve *self-regulation* by means of rules which it develops and modifies over a period of time, and *to adapt* to the varying demands posed in different phases of its life cycle (Selvini Palazzoli et al., 1978). The ability of the family system to ensure both continuity and growth is derived from a dynamic equilibrium between two functions common to all systems: a tendency toward homeostasis *(H)* and a capacity for transformation *(T)* (von Bertalanffy, 1968).

To achieve change in a family group, the existing relationship between homeostasis and transformation should be modified in favor of the latter. Vice versa, in order to stabilize and maintain the new structure, the *H/T* relationship should be modified in favor of the former. Consequently, every change or adjustment is preceded by a temporary state of *imbalance* between *H* and *T*. The degree of imbalance depends on the significance of the change and consequent stabilization that takes place.

The capacity to modify an existing equilibrium between homeostasis and transformation differs from one family system to another; this can be measured objectively. Some systems can utilize alternately their capacity for change or their ability to maintain the existing state, whereas other systems find this particularly difficult. Family systems can therefore be described as *flexible* or *rigid* according to their position on a scale that goes from a maximum to a minimum degree of flexibility (Andolfi et al., 1980).

A family system may be described as more or less rigid according to the degree of difficulty it has in attaining new equilibria in response to developments that occur during its life cycle. Situations that are potentially disruptive to its equilibrium—such as individual growth, marriage, birth, aging, and death usually coincide with the normal developmental processes of the family system. Flexibility and rigidity are not intrinsic characteristics of the structure of a given system; they are relative to variation in the state and the dynamics of the system of a particular *time* and *place*.

While the evaluation of a system in terms of a temporal or historical perspective provides information concerning the system's developmental cycle and its evolution, a spatial parameter enables one to evaluate the relationships existing here and now between the functions which members of the system serve as well as their respective levels of individual growth and differentiation. Ideally the system should be capable of modifying the equilibrium between the *functions* of its members and the *growth* of each individual over time.

A family system becomes rigid when an excessive accumulation of functions or the inability to modify these functions in the course of time interferes with the member's needs for differentiation. When opportunities for self expression are reduced because of increased demands at the level of function, the group structures rigid relationships which progressively compress the energies existing in the system, and communications with the extra-familial world become impoverished.

A complicated network of functions is then created within the family group. These functions are mutually reinforcing and crystallize relationships in stereotyped roles (Andolfi et al., 1980).

The system involved in therapy, however, is not the family itself, but *the family's interaction with the therapist*. This new therapeutic system evolves dynamically; it creates its own structure whose rules are defined gradually during the course of therapy. Some families interact with the therapist in ways that tend to entangle him/her in the families' transactional rules. This, of necessity, leads to the *formation of a therapeutic system that is just as rigid as the family system*. This new system will be equally incapable of modifying its equilibrium during the course of therapy.

When intervention takes place in a family whose capacity for transformation is easily activated (that is, when the tendency toward homeostatic rigidity is not preponderant), the T of the therapist and the T of the family integrate and facilitate a rapid solution of the problem. On the contrary, if the therapist's T activates a family system whose T has been suppressed by rigid internal rules, the family will perceive the therapeutic T as threatening and will eventually neutralize it by assimilating it in its own homeostasis.

The more the therapist openly opposes the family's *H*, the more the family system will respond by reinforcing the status quo (Selvini Palazzoli et al., 1978). Even if the existing equilibrium is a source of intense suffering, it will be defended at any cost because it serves to maintain interactional solutions that the members believe to be the only ones possible. After years spent in carefully selecting acceptable transactional modalities through an arduous process of trial and error, the family sees the present situation as the best that it can achieve. In cases of this kind the therapist can promote change by disguising the therapeutic *T* as *H*, thereby supporting the family's *H*. The strategy of prescribing to the family the same dysfunctional rules that maintain the existing homeostatic equilibrium can be used. Since the family will not be able to oppose the therapist's *T*, which is now syntonic with its own *H*, it will be forced to change. It will have to liberate its own *T* in order to demonstrate that the therapist is making a mistake in confirming the family's tendency to resist change.

This strategy attempts to substitute a *new game* for the *endless game* played previously by the family. By denying the possibility of alternative behavior, the therapist acts in a way that is at once *provocative* and *liberating*. This approach enables the family group to respond with a counterprovocation (*I'll prove to you that you are wrong*). Beyond the interactional message that it contains, the counterprovocation permits the family to try out new ways of relating and solving the problem (Andolfi, 1979).

Since the therapist's intervention will be perceived as a challenge, the family will feel itself relieved of a part of the responsibility which initially weighed upon it . . . that is, the responsibility implicit in *changing only for oneself* (and not for someone else, particularly for the person whose task it is to stimulate change). *To change for the therapist* (which means demonstrating that he is wrong) signifies entering into a new state of abnormality. In many cases, however, a transitional phase of this kind is necessary. It helps the family members to free themselves from a severely disturbed reality so that they can develop more acceptable interactional patterns without resorting to scapegoating.

The family will have to decide whether to carry out the therapist's directives (which implies accepting the therapist's power) or whether to defy these directives, which signifies changing the rules. Moreover, the family members will perceive (whether or not they follow the therapist's directives) that the real game, of which they both are protagonists and prisoners, has become explicit, and that their habitual patterns of relating are becoming less effective (Andolfi, 1978).

STRATEGY

Below are three examples of the strategy under discussion.

The first concerns the case of a couple in therapy for about three months. Treatment was requested because of the husband's "alcoholism." This definition of the problem was offered by the wife and was implicitly accepted by the husband, who accused his wife of being the principal cause of his drinking. After a few sessions the dynamics of his problem seemed to be as follows.

Neither husband nor wife were willing to specify the extent of his drinking. This led us to suspect that there was some sort of complicity concerning the problem which served to maintain a certain level of equilibrium in the system. He almost never drank at home, but his wife frequently "discovered" him drinking at a bar. He seemed to arrange things so that his wife would find out about them and then "reproach" him. For example, he took his young son to the bar with him; the son then told his mother or his mother's friends what he had seen. (The wife's father had died of cirrhosis of the liver; it seemed clear that drinking had special significance for her.) The wife aggravated the problem by attempting to control her husband. She insisted on smelling his breath when he came home, and refused to have sexual intercourse with him because of his "vices." Her behavior enraged him and he retreated into nostalgic reminiscences of the good old times before their marriage. He would then drink "for consolation," leaving evidence that his wife would be sure to discover.

If we had used any of this information in a linear way, without considering the other data and the circular relation that existed between them, we would have run a series of risks. We would have risked being sucked into the rules of an endless game; we would have been tempted to take sides on the contents of the issue as presented by the husband or wife, and to enter into an alliance which would have unbalanced the system and placed the blame on the excluded spouse.

These considerations convinced us to use a paradoxical intervention to provoke a change in the couple's rules, which they seemed incapable of doing by themselves. As described by others (Haley, 1973, Selvini Palazzoli et al., 1978; Watzlawick et al., 1967), we predicted that a therapeutic paradox prescribing the very rules which had set in motion the couple's game would facilitate a change in the couple's rules of interacting. We wanted *to promote change by directing them not to change.* By instructing each spouse to supervise the other, we hoped to prevent the possibility of reciprocal control. This maneuver could succeed only after the therapist had gained power and control over the entire sequence of interactions in the couple-therapist relationship.

The prescription was formulated as follows: The wife was instructed to increase supervision over her husband and not to miss any occasion for "catching him in the act." We told her to allow her husband to consume daily a set quantity of alcohol (large enough that her husband could not easily exceed it) which she should administer to her husband herself if necessary by going with him to the bar. We explained to her that this would relieve her of her anxiety at having a "depraved" husband who was drowning himself in rivers of alcohol in some bar in Rome. In this way she would gain total control of the situation. At the same time she was told to uphold her own "moral principles" and to abstain from sexual intercourse with her husband when he smelled of alcohol.

The husband, in turn, was instructed to check up assiduously on his wife to be sure that she would not try to cheat him by increasing or diminishing the agreed daily dosage of alcohol. Any failure on the wife's part would clearly indicate her bad faith and unwillingness to help find a solution to the problem. He was also asked to be sure that his wife made absolutely no sexual requests when he smelled of alcohol.

Formulated in these terms, the task was presented to the couple. They seemed interested in collaborating in a concrete task that promised to help them escape from a situation of exasperation and continual resentment. The therapist advised the couple that they would probably meet with difficulties in carrying out the task and, in particular, he warned them that it would be very difficult to keep each other's behavior under complete control.

The next week the couple reported to the therapist about what had happened. The wife had gone to the bar with her husband, but not as often as planned. As soon as she started accompanying him, her anxiety about his drinking vanished. The husband seemed proud of his wife for her courage in accompanying him (it was the first time in their marital life that she had done this) and he verbalized his satisfaction. The husband, too, had been only partially successful in controlling his wife. They related that on some occasions it had been the husband who refused to go to the bar with her because "he didn't feel like drinking."

The wife had also made sexual advances, ignoring the prohibition that was part of her assigned task. He told us that he was very pleased by her unexpected demonstrations of affection.

The therapist responded to the couple's account by saying that although he had foreseen that they would fail to carry out such a difficult task, he had not predicted so complete a failure. He alerted them to the danger that by sabotaging the task in this way, they were demonstrating their refusal to overcome their marital problems. He then reassigned the same task, underlining certain aspects and asking each spouse to bring to the following session a written record concerning any "transgressions" made by the other.

As a result of this paradoxical intervention the spouses united in a renewed effort to sabotage the task assigned by the therapist. Consequently, the husband's alcohol problem, which until then had seemed unsolvable, disappeared. The couple was then able to reactivate the more positive potentialities in their relationship.

In this case, the paradox consisted in *prescribing the couple's own dysfunctional rules.* This produced a liberating effect on both spouses, for once they succeeded in abandoning their endless game, they were able to discover new ways of relating.

The next case illustrates prescribing the rules for an entire family group. Here family therapy served to avoid hospitalization for Renzo (age 14) and gave the family confidence in its ability to solve its own problems.

In the sixth session the rules of the spouse relationship were explored. By then, the family no longer thought it necessary to hospitalize their son. By activating the relations between sub-systems, the therapist had brought to light the redundancies which were maintaining some of the family's interactional problems. These were:

1. When the parents talked to each other they talked almost exlusively about Renzo and his problems.
2. Renzo systematically activated his parents in such a way as to make them continue to worry about him. He was always positioned between his parents.
3. Renzo continually drew attention to his parents' responsibility for his fear of being "mentally ill." He told us that he had searched in the psychology columns of newspapers for information that would diminish his fears.
4. If either of the parents irritated Renzo, he hit his younger brother.
5. Renzo made his mother the excuse so that he could avoid his com-

panions. This behavior is syntonic with the mother's need to control her son.

Shortly before the end of the session, the therapist distributed a sheet of paper to each family member and dictated the task:

a. The mother must answer all telephone calls. All calls for Renzo were to be answered with excuses to make sure that he doesn't go out "too much." If Renzo disobeyed this rule in any way, the mother was to note it in a special notebook to be kept for this purpose. If she broke the rule, then Renzo should take note of it.
b. Every time Renzo got angry at his father and mother, he should "get it off his chest" by getting mad at his younger brother. The younger brother must note in writing every time that Renzo fails to obey this rule. At this point Renzo asked whether it might not be better for him not to get mad at anyone. The therapist cut short his interruption without answering and continued:
c. The father must go to a library with Renzo to look up information on "character neuroses." The results of their research were to be written down and brought to the next session.

The central problem was the adolescent son's need to achieve autonomy and the difficulties that this process was creating in his family. The therapist "packaged" a series of directives based on material brought in by the family members. The common denominator of these directives was that they all aimed at establishing control by each member over the others. A system of reciprocal controls is one of the elements in this family system that most seriously limits the autonomy of the identified patient and of the other members. The first task assigned accepts and reinforces the rule of reciprocal control between mother and son. This rule also implies a coalition against the father. The motivation for this task given by the therapist—"so that he won't go out too much"—is really a stimulus for the boy and a challenge to his unrealized adolescent potential.

The second task makes Renzo's blackmailing of his parents appear ridiculous and absurd. Renzo avoided confronting them directly (the parents' attitude reinforces his behavior); he prefers to play the part of a crazy, irresponsible child rather than assume a more adult role, which he fears. But the task underlines the intentional aspect of his bizarre behavior. It thereby unmasks his game and makes it seem infantile and useless. Moreover, with the younger brother supervising how he implements the task, his mode of behavior—previously in some way accepted as the inevitable result of his "character neurosis"—will become progressively less justifiable.

The third task differs from the first two. Although like the others it is intended to emphasize Renzo's disturbance, it introduces an important variation: it aims at dismantling the myth of "character neurosis" (which has paralyzed the entire family) by making it a subject for intellectual research and analysis. This task will also yield information concerning the ability of the system to accept a more direct relationship between Renzo and his father. This variation in the family's usual transactional pattern temporarily excludes the mother from the father-son relationship. By excluding her, the therapist is not seconding an existing family rule: rather, he is exploring the system's ability to redistribute relationships and alliances. The fact that it is "too" early in therapy to introduce an "excessively" countersystemic move is precisely what will provoke a series of lively counterreactions on the part of the family; these will be extremely useful in guiding successive interventions. As for the other directives given, the family soon experiences difficulty in behaving according to its habitual interactional models, and finds it necessary to look for alternative ways of relating.

The following transcription is from a session held with a family with a 21-year-old daughter, Anna, who presented the kind of behavior usually defined as schizophrenic. The case was difficult because of the type of interactions common to this kind of family group. In the preceding session it had seemed to us that Anna's behavior fulfilled a protective function vis-à-vis the rest of the family, and towards the parents in particular. In this session, Anna's absence seemed to confirm this hypothesis. The family members all felt free to talk about and for her. It was clear that she was the source of great concern for all.

Therapist:	I would like each of you to phone Anna and ask whether she is willing to come to the next session.
Father:	I'm very pessimistic. (*The mother shakes her head with a dejected expression of resignation. The brother and sister are also pessimistic. A telephone is brought into the room. Each member of the family in turn asks Anna if she is willing to come, and each time Anna replies that the problem does not concern her.*)
Therapist:	(*The therapist comes to the telephone and talks to Anna*) . . . Well, if you don't want to come, there is no reason to insist. Listen, Anna, now I want to ask your family some-

thing. I would like you to listen, but without saying anything. (*To the other family members*): I would like each of you to answer me holding the receiver in hand and speaking into this microphone. I am going to lay down a rule: you are not to speak to Anna . . . you must speak only to me. This is the question: What is the problem in this family? (*The family members take turns answering the question into the receiver and Anna listens without replying. The first attempt of the mother to elicit a reply from her daughter is immediately blocked by the therapist. There are no further attempts to break the rule. After the family members have spoken, the therapist comes to the phone and puts the same question to Anna*). Anna, in ten minutes I would like to ask you and your family another question. Can you please call us back?

Anna: Yes.

Therapist: All right, I'll give you the number . . . so long.

In this phase of therapy the therapist is making *exploratory* moves to sound out his relationship with Anna and to establish a basis for negotiating with her. This information will help the therapist to join the family system. Exactly ten minutes later Anna called.

Therapist: Hello, Anna. I would like you to listen at first, the way you did last time. (*To the other family members*) What's wrong with Anna? (*The therapist holds out the receiver towards the others*) Who wants to answer first?

Again, each one replied to the therapist's question, while Anna listened. Then the therapist asked Anna the same question while the others listened to her reply.

In the delicate situation created by the absence of the identified patient, the therapist gave the paradoxical prescription of directing the family not to communicate with Anna, and simultaneously directing them to communicate with her; and similarly, in telling Anna not to participate in the session, and yet asking her to participate. The therapist gave a directive and at the same time denied that he was giving it. In this way he forced the family members to do exactly what they had indicated that they did not want to do, and at the same time he denied that this was what was happening. Moreover, by using a series of double messages, the therapist paradoxically encouraged Anna to come to the next session, by accepting and encouraging her absence from this session.

One of the homeostatic mechanisms used by the family was circumvented by a paradoxical technique. All members of the family participated in the session by denying their participation and messages were allowed to be transmitted by denying the communicational value of these messages. Anna did come to the following session and took an active part in the therapeutic process. Through the strategy of prescribing its own dysfunctional rules to the family, the therapist stimulates the tendency to change present in the family system by provoking infractions of the rules that have led to the problem and that maintain it.

The therapist modulates the extent to which he advocates or pushes for homeostatic behavior by the family in accordance with the homeostatic learning of the family at the moment, and the particular stage to which the therapy has progressed. According to Stanton (1981), this strategy fits in a model of *relative contrasts*, in which the therapist tries to stay one step ahead of the family and, until later stages, almost invariably, pushes for more homeostasis than the family is comfortable with. In a sense he "one ups" them, and in their resistance to his directions, they start to change in an opposite direction.

If one reads the not very abundant literature on therapeutic paradox, it seems to be taken for granted that paradoxes are, and should be, unintelligible on all levels. Our experience leads us to believe that this is not true. Often, when an individual or a family group carries out a paradoxical task, or plans how to carry it out, they gain a more-or-less precise insight into the implicit meaning of the task. They can easily accept the *game of provocation* inherent in the paradoxical task, although they may discuss the details with great scrupulousness and earnestness. In this way, they in turn communicate how effective this mode of intervention is in activating change without causing family members to "lose face."

REFERENCES

Andolfi, M. A structural approach to a family with an encopretic child. *Journal of Marriage and Family Counseling*, 1978, 4, (1), 25-29.
Andolfi, M. *Family Therapy—An Interactional Approach*. New York: Plenum Press, 1979.
Andolfi, M., Menghi, P., Nicolò, A.M., & Saccu, C. A model of intervention in families with a schizophrenic patient. In Adolfi, M. & Zwerling, I. (Eds.) *Dimensions of Family Therapy*. New York: Guilford Press, 1980.
Haley, J. *Uncommon Therapy: The Psychiatric Techniques of Milton H. Erickson*. New York: Norton, 1973.
Selvini Palazzoli, M., Boscolo, L., Cecchin, C., & Prata, G. *Paradox and Counterparadox*. New York: Aronson, 1978.

Stanton, D. Strategic approaches to family therapy. In A.S. Gurman & D.P. Kniskern (Eds.), *Handbook of Family Therapy*. New York: Brunner/Mazel, 1981.

von Bertalanffy, L. *General System Theory*. New York: Braziller, 1968.

Watzlawick, P., Beavin, V., & Jackson, D. *Pragmatics of Human Communication*. New York: Norton, 1967.

Editor's Commentary: Notes on
Paradox and Absurdities

By definition a paradox is a statement that is seemingly self-contradictory but in reality expresses a possible truth. How strange, even absurd, that the use of paradox has flourished in the context of family therapy—a field with a tap-root in communication theory which posits the importance of clear, congruent verbal and nonverbal messages. The field's early pioneers revealed that frequent double bind messages which serve to confuse the receiver may be conduits to the cognitive distortions which became expressed in schizophrenic symptomatology. Thus, therapists should model unambiguous, consistent communication and metacommunication.

Yet, barely 30 years after the early revelations by Satir, Jackson, and Bateson, a well respected, diverse and much imitated band of ingenious therapists like Haley, Whitaker, Erickson, Selvini Palazzoli, and Goolishian have elevated the judicious use of paradox and counterparadox to a therapeutic art form. It seems a diametrically opposite stance! Skillfully prescribing the symptom and thereby exacerbating it to absurdium until it loses its potency requires correct formulation of the "systemic hypothesis," the au courant term for accurate differential diagnosis of the core problematic issues within the family system.

In this article, Andolfi, who calls his own mystical brand of intervention "provocative therapy," demystifies the technique; still, he elevates it to an art form that only the gifted can intuitively utilize. Explanation and understanding of how and why such confusion provocations work are the necessary but not sufficient secret for framing the right, harmonic paradox with precision and cadence. Overuse of paradoxical statements and injunctions is their death knell, freshness their vital energy source.

It can provide the strong leverage to unfreeze a rigidified system so that enough fluidity results for change to ensue. It is almost as difficult to teach as it is to learn. For therapists to utilize paradox strategically, they must be able to listen with the third ear (Reek, 1948) to the discordant nuances.

REFERENCE

Reek, T. *Listening With the Third Ear*. New York: Grove Press, 1948.

Chapter 12

Draw a Dream: An Intervention Promoting Change in Families in Conflict

By Bruce J. Tonge

The relationship of marital conflict with emotional disorder in children is well-known. The disturbed behavior of these children is a reaction to, and at times may be the only manifestation of, the parents' conflict. The author has developed an interview technique, based on drawing a dream, which enables children to effectively communicate their understanding of the stressful events in their lives that contribute to their emotional disorder. These drawings and the child's perceptions of their parents' conflict are then discussed with the parents. This often sharply focuses the problem for the parents and may facilitate a resolution of the marital conflict, thereby allowing a more appropriate realignment of family relationships, with a subsequent improvement of the child's emotional disorder.

Unresolved parental conflict is well-known to be associated with an increased risk of psychiatric disorder in children (Tonge, James, & Hillam, 1975). For example, Rutter, Graham, Chadwick, & Yule (1976) found in their Isle of Wight study that 30% of the adolescents with a persistent psychiatric disorder came from homes where there was a poor

This chapter is a revision of a paper which orginally appeared under the title "We Thought It Was a Secret", in the *Australian Journal of Family Therapy*, January 1980, *1*, (2), 50-56.

Bruce J. Tonge, M.B.,B.S., D.P.M., M.R.C. Psych., F.R.A.N.Z.C.P. is Director, Department of Child and Adolescent Psychiatry, Austin Hospital, Heidelberg, Victoria, Australia.

marriage relationship between the parents, compared with only 6½% of the control adolescents who did not have a psychiatric disorder. West and Farrington (1973) found that delinquency was twice as common in boys from families where relationships were strained and where there was marital conflict as in boys from families where relationships were generally harmonious. Other studies have also revealed a significant relationship between marital conflict and antisocial behavior in children (Rutter, 1971).

It has been demonstrated that when parents divorce or separate it is not the separation itself that disturbs the child; rather, the presence of parental conflict and disharmony leads to psychiatric disorders in the children (Douglas, Ross, & Simpson, 1968; Gibson, 1969; Gregory, 1965). Open hostility and quarreling in the family, particularly when the child is involved in the parental conflict, are most likely to be damaging to the child (Rutter, 1971; 1976). The stress on the child is further aggravated when there is a lack of warmth and affection shown towards the child and when the conflicts are prolonged over many years.

It follows that marital conflicts should be resolved as soon as possible so that the child may experience relatively stable, predictable, and warm family relationships, which are predictive of satisfactory psychosocial development. For example, Wallerstein (1977) reports from her research on children of parents who divorce that the reestablishment of stable caretaking and predictable routines, adequate care and parenting by the custodial parent, an absence of involvement of the child in any ongoing parental dispute, and a good relationship between the stepparent or partner (if there is one) and the custodial parent predict satisfactory developmental progress after the disruption of the marriage. These factors differentiate those children who cope well with the separation from those who remain disturbed.

What is less certain is the role the child's behavior or emotional disorder may play in maintaining, aggravating or modifying parental conflict. Minuchin, Baker, Rosman, Liebman, Milman, & Todd (1975) have suggested that psychosomatic disorders in children are complicated by a style of transactions and by chronic unresolved family conflicts, particularly between the parents. The child's symptoms and illness behavior are reinforced because they play a central role in family conflict avoidance. Awareness and understanding of the importance of the relationship of parental conflict to psychiatric disorder in children are essential in the assessment and management of these disorders.

DRAW A DREAM—A METHOD OF INTERVENTION

If a child is able to communicate his or her distress during the course of a psychiatric interview, then the consultation is likely to be therapeutic (Winnicott, 1971). The use of play materials and drawing often helps the child to relax and establish a meaningful contact with the therapist.

The assessment of the play, dreams, and fantasies of children must be done within the context of their age, sex, developmental level and previous and current life experiences. The content of a child's dreams, fantasies, and play often represents stressful life experiences that have contributed to the child's emotional disorder. It is often helpful and therapeutic to put into words for the child the link between the fantasies and the stressful reality of his or her life.

Winnicott (1971) gives an account of two children, a boy and a girl, who both had nightmares. Both children, after doing some squiggle game drawings, did drawings of themselves in bed having the nightmare. Reading this gave me an idea which led to the development of the projective technique of *Draw a Dream*. I make a simple drawing of someone in bed with an associated large cartoon baloon (Figure 1). If the child's name is Bill, I will say as I draw the dream balloon, "Here

Figure 1

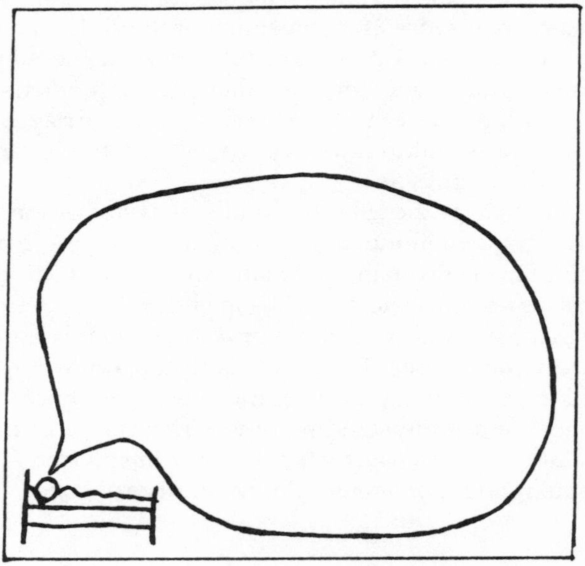

is a boy named Bill having a bad dream—perhaps it is even you. I wonder if you could draw that dream for me." Many children of parents in conflict, whom I have seen, have been enabled by the Draw a Dream technique to effectively communicate their distress and their perception of the family problem. Linking their dream drawing to real life events, such as their parents' quarreling, may help the child understand the meaning of their distressing feelings and behavior. This understanding often brings immediate relief. I then suggest, with the child's consent, that I show the dream drawing to the parents, as it may enable them to understand their child's feelings and problems. I give the child the choice of staying with me when I discuss the drawing and its links with family problems with the parents. This discussion may have a profound effect on the parents and has often acted to facilitate a change for the better in family life and relationships.

Following are some examples of how children of parents in conflict and their families have been able to use the insights derived from the child's drawings of a dream.

Angela—9 Years

Angela was in the hospital with a respiratory tract infection that was not too serious. She needed some physiotherapy and was only expected to be an inpatient for several days but she did not improve. She became withdrawn, lost her appetite, kept herself in bed, was calling out in her sleep at night, and remained physically ill. Her parents visited frequently and were increasingly concerned. Angela tended to ignore her parents when they were with her but became fearful and agitated when they left. When I met her, she was unable to talk with me and showed no interest in toys or drawing. I said that I had heard from her nurse that she was not sleeping well at night and I wondered if she was having some bad dreams. I then drew the dream cartoon and commented, "Here is a girl named Angela asleep in bed—maybe it is even you. She is having a bad dream. I wonder if you could draw me that dream."

Angela became quite animated, worked quickly and produced a drawing about two people (Figure 2). She said it was two people fighting "a terrible fight." When I asked who they were she went on to draw the second pair of people, saying it was a man and a woman, and the man had a "saw knife." I asked her what was the worst part of the dream for her and she said "that someone might get hurt" and she was "trapped in bed and couldn't stop them fighting." She appeared anxious and fearful. I asked her if she knew two people, a man and a woman,

Figure 2

who had "terrible fights." She whispered that her father and mother had terrible fights. I suggested to her that perhaps she was really afraid that her mother and father might have a terrible fight and get hurt while she was trapped in bed in hospital. She started to cry and admitted that she was very worried about that.

She told me that whenever she heard her parents fighting, she would go to them and "their fighting always stopped." I suggested that I show her dream to her parents and talk to them about their arguments. She was greatly relieved and decided that she did not need to be there when I talked to her parents.

When I showed the dream drawing to her parents and discussed its meaning, they were initially speechless. The father then moved his chair over to be beside his wife and took her hand. He explained how they had been experiencing increasing marital tension over the last six months. The mother, near tears, added "But we thought it was a secret." They claimed that they tried not to argue in front of their children and tried to behave "as if nothing were wrong." With relief they commented that they now knew that they must do something positive to solve their problems rather than just "hope they would go away."

Angela recovered rapidly and went home two days later. Her parents went to see a marriage counselor and in several sessions resolved their fairly straightforward relationship problems. Six months later the parents reported that Angela continued to be well, was more confident and progressing better at school. They spoke positively of their own "new relationship."

Marcus—8 Years

Marcus was referred by his school because he was increasingly aggressive towards other children and defiant and disobedient towards the teachers. He was failing with his educational progress. At our first meeting Marcus and his parents were resentful about the referral. The father said Marcus was timid and withdrawn at home, not listening to what he was told, which made the father angry. Later the mother tentatively alluded to marital arguments over her husband's drinking, but this subject was soon closed off as both the father and the mother turned the conversation back to Marcus.

I interviewed Marcus separately. He was surly, sullen and resentful but also appeared downcast. He played in an aimless way with a few cars and was not interested in drawing. I commented that some boys I knew who felt cross and a bit sad sometimes had bad dreams. As I drew the dream balloon I commented that it was a boy called Marcus, maybe even him, who was having a bad dream. He hesitated, then started to roughly draw a "home" that was being "broken up by an angry giant man" who was then going to leave (Figure 3). The worst part of the dream for him was when the giant man grabbed Marcus and shook him. When I asked how he felt when that happened he added another drawing of himself and described himself as "very sad" because he couldn't "stop the giant." I asked if there was any way to stop the giant man and he furtively said, "A bomb could." He drew in the bomb and made a mark over the giant man's face to indicate where the bomb would explode.

I then suggested to him that maybe things happen at home like in the dream and perhaps his father was like the giant sometimes. He told me that sometimes his father "got wild with everybody." I said that maybe father got wild with Marcus and shook him but also got wild with mother and broke things in the home and threatened to leave. Marcus looked very sad and started to cry. He said that his parents had "wild fights" and "broke things" and that his father had left home for two days after one of these fights.

I suggested that I show his dream to his parents and maybe this would

Figure 3

help them understand what worried him. He agreed eagerly and decided to stay while I talked to his parents. The parents were uneasy while I explained the dream drawing, linking it to events at home. The father put his hand on Marcus's shoulder and admitted that over the past year relationships at home were as Marcus described. Mother wasn't coping and was depressed and emotionally unavailable to her family and father was irritable and drinking heavily.

The father asserted that he didn't want his home to break up and asked for help. Subsequently, Marcus's behavior improved and he began to catch up on his education. The parents attended conjoint marital therapy and were quite motivated. It proved successful for their ongoing relationship.

By chance I met Marcus and his parents in a shopping center about a year later, Marcus greeted me warmly and told me that he didn't have "any of those giant men dreams anymore" and added that he now had "fun with Dad, we have friendly wrestles and fights."

Jane—6 Years

Jane was referred by a Child Protection Agency because there was a strong likelihood that she had been physically injured by her mother. Her mother had taken Jane to a hospital with strap bruises on her shoulders, finger-mark bruises on her neck and a bleeding wound on her forehead. The mother maintained these injuries had occurred when Jane hurt herself falling down some garden steps.

I invited all of the family to attend the first interview. Mother came with Jane, saying that the father was at home to look after their three-year-old son. She was resentful about coming and evasive in many answers she gave to my questions. She described Jane as an active, aggressive, oppositional child, who slept poorly at night. The school report confirmed that Jane was restless and distractible, and was making no educational progress. The mother admitted that she felt hopeless and overwhelmed by her daughter's behavior. Jane constantly interrupted our conversation with noisy, aimless play, which clearly irritated her mother.

I decided to see Jane alone briefly. Her activity increased when her mother left the room. Her play was aimless, noisy, and somewhat destructive. She moved away whenever I came near to her. She answered some of my questions but offered no conversation. With a low table between us, I started to draw the dream balloon, saying that here was a girl called Jane in bed. Jane had some trouble sleeping and had some bad dreams. I suggested that she draw me a picture story of Jane's bad dream. I then moved a little distance away and sat down, indicating again that Jane might draw me a picture of the bad dream. Jane had become still and watchful and she then tentatively approached the table and began to draw with increasing concentration and absorption. I slowly moved to kneel next to her and asked gently about the story of the dream (Figure 4).

Jane said it was a really bad dream of a "monster lady" who bashed Jane on the head until "blood came down all over my face." The monster lady was doing this because "she didn't like me because I came to a strange mother's place." The strange mother was the monster lady. Jane apprehensively told me that the worst part of the dream was when Jane "wanted to hit her back, and did, and the mother cried." She emphasized this by scribbling red crayon for blood all over the mother's face and added large blue tears. I suggested to Jane that the story of her dream may be what it was like between herself and her mother lately. Perhaps her mother had become a strange mother, who hit Jane on the head and made it bleed and who cried. Jane nodded her downcast head and bit her lower lip. I asked if Daddy was anywhere in the dream while all this was happening. She immediately drew in a red bed saying that her

Figure 4

father was "in bed and he doesn't care." Jane agreed to let me discuss her dream drawing with her mother and father and then spent some time playing happily with me at the doll's house.

Although the father was late, both parents came for the next appointment. The mother was again defensive and the father was indifferent. I recounted my conversation with Jane and showed them the drawing. The mother suddenly started to cry and admitted that she had lost control and hit Jane with a belt and thrown her by the neck to the ground where she had cut her head on a step. She then became more composed and said how amazing it was that Jane's picture "said it all." She angrily turned to her husband and told him how he didn't care about the family and when he was home, which was rare, all he did was sleep or watch TV. Father remained unmoved and retorted that she should not complain because he gave her "enough money."

The mother was keen to try and resolve the marital impasse one way or another but the father failed to keep any further appointments. He separated from his wife and family two weeks later "without warning." The mother continued to attend therapy regularly for several months with her children to talk about her adaptation to the new family structure and her parenting of the children. She admitted that she had been denying that their marriage had been empty and was finished, until her daughter's drawing made her "face the real situation." Jane's behavior is now socially adaptive and the "new family" is not troubled by the father's infrequent and undemanding access visits. In this case a separation allowed for a resolution of the marital conflict and the previously disturbed mother-child relationship.

Warren—9½ Years

Warren was referred by the school and the family doctor. He had outbursts of aggressive offensive behavior, alternating with periods of isolated, uncommunicative withdrawal at school. His parents had been separated for several years and divorce proceedings were in progress. Warren lived with his mother, seven-year-old brother, and mother's inconsistent male friend, Ross. The boys visited their father and his "fiancée" every second weekend.

The mother was anxious about the interview, fearing that their attendance might be held against her in custody proceedings that father had instituted. She was bitter about the separation and was depressed about the present situation, blaming the father, in front of Warren, for causing any problems that Warren may have. She gave, as examples, the fact that Warren was now disobedient towards her and had begun to wet the bed again.

When I saw Warren by himself he was a sullen, closed-in boy who avoided eye contact and had no spontaneous play or conversation. I sat beside him and drew a dream cartoon, commenting that I knew some boys his age who were also having troubles at night and who had bad dreams. I suggested that he might draw me a picture of the dream Warren was having (Figure 5). He selected a black pen and looked at the paper for several minutes clenching his jaw. He made some lines, then scribbled them over. I said that he seemed to have something in his mind, perhaps it was the sort of dream that made you clench your teeth. He then silently filled the page with his dream drawing. It was a "great big war" where "they fought duels in pairs, one against the other." I said that perhaps this was like some people he knew, maybe even mum and dad. He agreed and pointed out which airplane or tank was mum and which ones were dad. I asked how he felt about this and he added a picture of himself in the corner, shedding tears.

I suggested that it might be helpful to his parents if I showed them the dream drawing. He agreed, and added that he blamed mother's friend Ross for "taking" his mother away from his father and expressed

Figure 5

many uncertainties about his relationship with Ross.

Warren decided to stay with his mother while I discussed his dream drawing. After explaining about the "great war" between his parents, I pointed to the drawing of Warren feeling sad and crying and being helpless, unable to stop the fighting. At this Warren burst into tears of great distress. His mother cuddled him and rocked him in her arms as if he were a baby for the next few minutes. As Warren became more peaceful, she spoke tearfully of the bitterness in the continuing dispute with her ex-husband. She also resolved that she and Ross must make up their minds about either having a relationship or not, so that her sons could know "where they stood with Ross."

When I met the father and his "fiancée" he initially blamed his wife for any problems in Warren. I then showed them Warren's dream drawing and emphasized that Warren experienced his parents' ongoing conflict as a great war that left him feeling hopelessly sad and helpless. The father reflected that he had not realized that it "had got to Warren in that way."

Both parents independently came on several occasions to discuss the conduct of access and handover time and constructively used the time to resolve some disputes. Father decided to withdraw his custody petition and the mother and Ross decided to live together and create a new family structure. Warren made a rapid adaptation to these more stable arrangements and his behavior improved.

A META PERSPECTIVE OF THE INTERVENTION

The use of the technique Draw a Dream to elicit from the child a graphic picture and statement of *what* for him is really happening, and the sharing of this evocative communication with the parents may produce change in the family system. It is a relatively simple task to describe the technique; it is much more complex to postulate what events, interactions and maneuvers in the sequence are essential to the change induced. It may be irrelevant to attempt to explain why change occurred, as many explanations could be offered using a variety of theoretical models.

I am attracted to the conceptualization of change advanced by Watzlawick, Weakland, and Fisch (1974) as a useful framework to examine change following the use of Draw a Dream as described. The child is presented as the patient having the symptoms; the parents have tried various solutions directed at the child's behavior and they seek help from the therapist, asking the therapist to also focus on the child's behavior and attempt to change it. By using the Draw a Dream technique, the therapist steps outside the parent-child-problem perspective and provides the child with a means of expressing *what is really happening* in their world in a graphic and concrete manner. The child's dream drawing acts to reframe the conceptual understanding of what is happening in the family. The problem is redefined by the child in concrete terms and the covert problem is made overt. This reframing of the problem is made even more effective because it is the child's reframing and imagery that is presented to the parents.

The child's dream or fantasy may appear weird and unexpected, but the effect of the dream image on the family is to move the emphasis away from the focus on the symptom. In this new context a second order change becomes possible (Watzlawick, Weakland, & Fisch, 1974).

The Draw a Dream technique might also be further understood within the framework provided by Minuchin (1974) and Minuchin and Fishman (1981). The symptomatic child is the identified patient and the task of the therapist is to gather information that the family members may not consider relevant or do not have available. The child's dream drawing provides a metaphor which can be used as a concrete statement of issues that are relevant to the family but have been previously hidden. This enables a reframing of family myths and conflicts. The child is given some safety and security because it is only a dream, but the directness of the message and the dream imagery confronts the family with an unavoidable and new understanding of their conflicts which may circumvent previous patterns of conflict avoidance.

The role of the therapist in the application of this technique must also be considered. Some capacity to relate to and join with the child is necessary to enable the child to be able to produce, hesitatingly at times, a dream picture account of what is happening in the family. The use of the child's drawing and dream metaphor also provides the therapist with a means to get family members involved with one another but allows the therapist to maintain therapeutic maneuverability and distance (Minuchin & Fishman, 1981). It is the child's reframing statement that provokes change in the family.

In this context the therapist might be considered to be involved as the go-between in a go-between process (Zuk, 1966). The family first introduces a problem focused on the child. The child is then enabled by the Draw a Dream technique to define the hidden conflict that exists between at least two identifiable persons in the family. The therapist then acts as the go-between by presenting the child's representation of this hidden conflict to the family. This prompts the parents to further define their roles and positions. With this consequent redefinition of the conflict, change becomes possible. The child-therapist alliance may also act to cross a rigid generation boundary, particularly in a disengaged family.

It could be argued that the therapist, by aligning himself with the child, may be inappropriately undermining the power of the parents in the family. This entrapment of the therapist into the family system is avoided if the therapist simply conveys the child's drawing and message to the parents as a go-between, emphasizing that it is their child's message to them as parents which therefore pushes the parents to take the responsibility for the implications of that message. The child's dream drawing may appear deceptively simple, but has a complexity and power that may transcend the limits of verbal comprehension and communications. There are likely to be a series of meta-messages specific to the family, as well as some universal images, within the child's dream drawing, which the therapist and the family only dimly perceive, but which, nevertheless, have a powerful effect on the family system.

CONCLUSION

The preceding examples were of four children who suffered psychiatric disorders as a reaction to conflict between their parents. With each child, as part of the family assessment, the technique of Draw a Dream was used to enable the child to express disturbing thoughts which could then be related to real stress in their family life. The child's drawings and communications were then discussed with the parents. This acted to sharply focus on the problem of their marital conflict. The parents, when confronted with their child's dream picture, were provided with a powerful metaphor or representation of the parental conflict and its impact on the family. This was an experience that the parents could not easily ignore; it therefore acted to provoke a response towards change. In this way, the child's drawing-communication was used to challenge the family's pattern of conflict avoidance and therefore help the parents to correctly identify the problems with their relationship. Being able to correctly identify *what* is the problem, and to communicate and share that understanding with others involved in the conflict, is the essence of problem solving and adaptive change within the family (Epststein, Sigal, & Rakoff, 1968). Therefore, the communication from their child, contained in the drawing of a dream, may act as a new and different confrontation with reality that the parents cannot avoid, and may, therefore, provoke change and facilitate a resolution of the parental conflict.

REFERENCES

Douglas, J.W.B., Ross, J.J., & Simpson, H.R. *All Our Future*, London: Peter Davies, 1968.

Epstein, N.B., Sigal, J.J., & Rakoff, V. *Family Categories Schema*. Montreal: McGill University Human Development Study, 1968. Available from the authors.

Gibson, H.B. Early delinquency in relationship to broken homes. *Journal of Child Psychology and Psychiatry*, 1969, *10*, 195-204.

Gregory, I. Anterospective data following childhood loss of a parent. *Archives of General Psychiatry*, 1965, *13*, 110-120.

Minuchin, S. *Families and Family Therapy*, Cambridge: Harvard University Press, 1974.

Minuchin, S., Baker, L., Rosman, B., Liebman, R., Milman, L., & Todd, T. A conceptual model of psychosomatic illness in children. *Archives of General Psychiatry*, 1975, *32*, 1031-1038.

Minuchin, S. & Fishman, H.C. *Family Therapy Techniques*, Cambridge: Harvard University Press, 1981.

Rutter, M. Parent child separation. Psychological effects on the children. *Journal of Child Psychology and Psychiatry*, 1971, *12*, 233-260.

Rutter, M. Separation, loss and family relationships. In M. Rutter & L. Hersov (Eds.), *Child Psychiatry—Modern Approaches*. Oxford: Blackwell Scientific, 1976.

Rutter, M., Graham, P., Chadwick, O., & Yule, W. Adolescent turmoil—Fact or fiction? *Journal of Child Psychology and Psychiatry*, 1976, *17*, 35-36.

Tonge, W.L., James, D.S., & Hillam, S.M., Families without hope: A controlled study of 33 problem families. *British Journal of Psychiatry*, Special Publication, No. 11, 1975.

Wallerstein, J.S. Responses of the pre-school child to divorce: Those who cope. In M.F.

McMillan & S. Henao (Eds.), *Child Psychiatry: Treatment and Research*, New York: Brunner/Mazel, 1977.

Watzlawick, P., Weakland, J., & Fisch, R., *Change*. New York: Norton, 1974.

West, D.J. & Farrington, D.P. *Who Becomes Delinquent?* London: Heinemann, 1973.

Winnicott, D.W., *Therapeutic Consultations in Child Psychiatry*. New York: Basic Books, 1971.

Zuk, G.H., The go-between process in family therapy. *Family Process*, 1966, 2, 162-178.

Editor's Commentary: Dream Balloons— Sailing a New Metaphor

In discussing the Draw a Dream technique he uses with children evincing psychosomatic or psychological disorders, Tonge describes what for me is a captivating and innovative approach. His crystal clear description of his methodology seems to flow from an emphatic, intuitive, and sensitive tuning in to the forlorn, unarticulated pathos being experienced by his young, distressed patients. In seeking to fashion a more truly expressive channel through which his child patients, presented as identified patients or core problems in the family, could convey what was really troubling them, Tonge evolved the dream balloon. He gives the fantasized possessor the same name as the child he is treating; the children seem to quickly identify and go on to draw out and verbally reveal their traumatic story. In the four colorful case illustrations he utilizes to illuminate the implementation of his approach, the Draw a Dream technique is part of the family assessment. He utilizes it skillfully while seeing the child alone and then wisely offers the child the opportunity to be present when he shows and interprets the child's graphic depiction of the underlying disturbing problem to the parent(s). Evidently, most children choose to be present. This variation on the utilization of art therapy as an expressive medium for assessment and release of pent-up feelings is creative and engaging. It enables the child to use his/her own graphic and verbal language to disclose what is really happening in his/her world as he/she perceives and experiences it.

The nightmarish content is converted into dream material used as metaphor. The child's redefinition and reframing of the troubling interpersonal relationships and events become a statement of the critical issues which is shared with the parents. The interpretation, relayed by the therapist, may provide the parents with a startling realization that their child is aware of and disturbed by their marital troubles. The child's compelling reframing of the problem from his/her symptomatic behavior to the parental conflict issues is usually unexpected; it disrupts the rigidly held rationale about what the problem is, forces parents to redefine their version of the problem, and increases the possibility of triggering second order change. It appears as if the meta-messages conveyed in the drawings have a powerful impact and provide the impetus to replace efforts at conflict avoidance with efforts toward conflict resolution.

Tonge draws from and builds upon the writings of Minuchin on psychosomatic families, of Watzlawick, Weakland and Fisch on what makes the process of change occur, and of Zuk on the therapist as the "go-between" who presents the child's dream representation to the parents yet avoids becoming the child's ally and thereby averts becoming entrapped in the family. Here again we see the universal applicability of therapeutic principles and the similarity of types of family problems which surface in various countries.

It is our good fortune that Tonge's description is so lucid that we can embody his approach in our own clinical practice. My few attempts to utilize it recently have proved equally freeing for the children and informative and motivating for the parents. Usually balloons conjure up happy, evanescent images; perhaps used to stimulate dream drawings these can help transport more children from despair to valid hope.

Chapter 13

The Family as
Background to Obesity

By Hilde Bruch

In this chapter, the family roots of obesity are explored. Ways in which
the family heritage and dynamics contribute to perpetuating this eating
disorder are considered. Treatment strategies also receive attention with
emphasis on the fact that the "obese patient needs to learn to experience
himself or herself as self-directed" and "capable of coping with problems
without retreating to excessive food intake."

Obesity runs in families. This is old clinical and popular knowledge,
which is often cited as evidence that obesity is an inherited condition.
Others argue that families' eating habits account for the high incidence
of overweight in the children of fat parents. Although many fat people
do have overweight relatives, others, often those who are most severely
handicapped by the obesity, come from slender families. Each individual
acquires his or her obesity in his or her own way. The psychological
experiences of the obese individual within the family play an important
role in his or her becoming obese, and not only in the transmission of
eating habits.

Obesity continues to be looked upon as if it were a uniform condition,
which it is not. There are many different forms of obesity with different

This is a slightly revised version of an article orginally published in the *International
Journal of Family Psychistry*, 1980, *1*, (1), 77-94.
Hilde Bruch, M.D., is Professor Emeritus at Baylor College of Medicine, Houston, Texas.

physiological and psychological functioning (Bruch, 1973b). Obese people show a wide range of emotional and psychological reactions, which may or may not be related to their obese state. The incidence of obesity increases with age, but this malady also occurs in children and adolescents. In addition to an abnormally high weight, youngsters suffering from *developmental obesity* show maturational deviations and signs of poor emotional and social adjustment. The first study of the importance of the family background in obesity was carried out in a group of fat children.

EARLY OBSERVATIONS

In an endocrine pediatric study of obesity in childhood conducted at the Vanderbilt Clinic in New York City during the late 1930s, it was recognized that abnormal body configuration, inactivity, passivity, and social isolation of the obese children in the study could not be explained as a result of endocrine dysfunction. The negative evidence rested on the simple, but at that time startling, finding that obese children were taller and more advanced in skeletal maturation, not only as compared to hypothyroid children but also to children of normal development. Obese children were bright and intelligent and large in every respect, and they underwent normal or early puberty. Though they were physically well developed, many of the obese children were extremely immature and clingingly dependent on their mothers who fostered the dependency. The manifestations of dependency were not particularly dramatic but they occurred with great regularity (Bruch, 1973c).

Detailed inquiry into the children's living habits revealed that their inability to do things for themselves extended to practically every aspect of their daily lives. They were unskilled and inactive in games, avoided athletics, and preferred sedentary activities. Their food intake was often found to be astonishingly large. When the seemingly simple prescription was given to reduce a child's food intake and to encourage more activity, many of the mothers of the obese children showed signs of anxiety and acute disturbance. The mothers reacted as if a precarious balance in their life-style was being threatened. All of this pointed to disturbances in the emotional climate of the child's family.

When I turned to psychiatry for help in my effort to study these families I learned to my surprise that the psychiatric literature of the 1930s did not contain any family studies that might have served as a model or offered a basis for comparison. What little information there was came from child guidance clinics and seemed to be limited to applying descriptive labels, such as "overprotective," "hostile," or "rejecting," to certain features of maternal behavior that were considered the causal explanation of a child's obesity. References to the father's role or to the interaction of both parents in the marriage were practically nonexistent. A systematic study of the families of 40 fat children (representing 25% of the group then under observation) was undertaken. The children ranged in age from 3 to 15 years and had been overweight for some time. The study was carried out during the depression years and some families had attained a certain level of economic comfort but then were economically wiped out. In several cases the child had become obese, and in some cases so had a parent, after the family's financial reverses.

The purpose of the inquiry was to understand and appraise the influences that had molded the parents' development, their attitudes to their life experiences, and their adjustment to the marriage and the present life situation, and how this in turn had determined the way they reacted to their children. A great effort was made to include the fathers in the study but many of them were reluctant to give information; some fathers objected to any personal questions as "violating the sanctity of their homes."

The mothers, on the other hand, were eager to talk about themselves and used the interviews to express endless complaints and to reveal their unfulfilled aspirations. Many had suffered as children from poverty, hunger, and insecurity and felt that they had been thrown upon their own resources too early in their lives. Many had reacted to their experiences with self-pity and resentment and were overinvolved with their children. The parents showed great differences in temperament and this disharmony expressed itself in their marital relationship in open fighting and mutual contempt. The fathers were described as weak and unassertive with little drive or ambition. The mothers were dominant in the lives of these families and expressed their dissatisfaction without restraint.

The families were conspicuous by their small size. The average obese family had only 2.1 children and the sibling position of the fat child also appeared unusual. Thirty-five percent were only children and 35% were the youngest child in the family. Even at the time of the early study, the child's position in the family was not conceived of as an explanation for the development of obesity but rather as providing the setting for the overindulgent feeding.

A composite picture was constructed from information obtained from diverse families. A mother who is insecure in her fundamental attitude toward her child tends to compensate for this by excessive feeding and overprotective measures; at times the father will play this role. To many mothers, the offering of food was a way of expressing their affection and devotion and of appeasing their anxiety and guilt about the child. Under such conditions the food is endowed with an exaggerated emotional value and serves as a substitute for love, security, and satisfaction.

The mothers were preoccupied with the physical safety of their children. Some would go to fantastic lengths to keep control over their child and judged other children as undesirable or even dangerous playmates. An element of danger and threat clung to all activities that were not under their immediate supervision. All of these measures resulted not only in marked inactivity but also in poor social adjustment and emotional immaturity in their children.

This study was published in 1940 under the title, "The Family Frame of Obese Children" (Bruch and Touraine, 1940). The title was chosen to indicate that the family provides only the dynamic field in which a child grows up but does not explain in and of itself the abnormal weight and the serious adjustment problems of these children. The obese child may respond in many different ways to contradictory handling; his or her developing obesity is one form of such a response. As his or her need for gratification and security in other areas remains unfulfilled, the child will increase demands for food and indulgences. In such an emotional climate, it is difficult if not impossible for a child to develop proper self-esteem and a concept of inner security.

Emotional and personality difficulties of various intensity were observed, but few families were accessible to the recommendation of psychiatric help. The subsequent development of these children thus represents their natural history and many were seriously disturbed later in life. In a significant number of cases, there had been evidence of potential schizophrenic development and follow-up observations confirmed this suspicion (Bruch, 1961). Many similarities can be recognized between the family constellation of the obese child and that which has been described as conducive to the development of schizophrenia (Lidz, 1969). Both have in common that the severe intrafamilial disturbances fail to equip a child with conceptual tools and symbols for coping with life in realistic terms. The development of obesity in a child may be conceived of as an active process, as expressing the child's efforts to achieve growth and self-realization, though in a distorted way.

SUBSEQUENT OBSERVATIONS

This early report on the family frame was widely read and quoted, although there were few subsequent systematic studies (Raskovsky et al., 1950). Unfortunately, the report was also often misquoted as describing one fixed family constellation that would produce "psychogenic" obesity. The need for differentiation between accidental, external features and more general underlying aspects was vividly illustrated by a study in Denmark conducted during the late 1940s by five investigators who compared their findings to the observations reported in the family frame (Iversen et al., 1952). Each of the Danish investigators independently studied a different group of fat children. Their findings differ from each other as much as, if not more than, those made during the late 1930s in New York City. Only one investigator, a psychologist, recognized that disturbances might manifest themselves differently in a different cultural setting (Ostergaard, 1954). By focusing on dynamic configurations this investigator was able to observe comparable psychological injuries in many of the observed families. Three of the investigators found various manifestations of psychological disturbances and contrasted them to the New York picture. One investigator limited his observations to school children whose weight was outside the standard deviation, with only very few children having true weight excess. This investigator failed to observe psychological abnormalities in either the children or their families.

It was soon recognized that the findings from the clinic group needed to be supplemented by a study of obese children coming from a higher educational and economic background. The obesity in a young child was rarely a matter of concern to the clinic mothers; on the contrary, to them it meant health and abundance of food and they would object to changing anything in the way they cared for their children. However, as their children grew older the mothers would resent their demands and they would attack and berate their children for being awkward, shy, and greedy. In the middle and upper classes, obesity in a child is rated as undesirable at a much earlier age and at lesser degrees of overweight than among the lower classes. As to the essential problems, there were fewer differences in the emotional interactions than had been anticipated (Bruch, 1973a). As in the clinic group, these parents would also use their children as compensation for frustrations and disappointments in their own lives. Usually the mothers had a close hold on the potentially obese child, attempting to live out their own hopes and ambitions through the child. These mothers failed to conceive of their children as individuals who needed respect for their own development and independence. Quite often the child was looked upon as a precious possession to whom the very best of care was given.

In these monetarily successful families, the father's position was less inconspicuous, but a lack of real closeness of the fathers with the children, particularly the obese child, was frequently encountered. Many adolescents felt that they were just a possession to their fathers whose interest was in how well they performed and how beautiful they looked, but who showed no interest in them as individuals (Bruch, 1973d). There were fathers who took an acute, even grotesque, interest in the fatness of their daughters, who in turn seemed to be influenced in a negative way by their father's obsession with their obesity.

The husband's financial success did not always mean that he would gain more respect and admiration from his wife. The following observation was made during the analysis of a woman who was preoccupied with doing everything "right" and arranging everybody's life in the "best" way possible. This applied to her very successful husband who did not live up to her idea of the perfect man. She also dominated every detail of her children's lives. Her eternal concern was for her oldest daughter who was nervous and too thin. The two younger girls were more robust and demonstrated that they received the very best. They both became somewhat plump; this had been a point of pride as long as they were small—"such sturdy and beautiful children"—but it aroused great concern as they grew older. The second daughter became so obsessed with being too fat that she put herself on a diet when she was only nine years old and rigidly clung to it. She complained: "All the time she says, 'Eat, eat, eat,' and now she is angry that I am too fat." When the youngest child also became heavy the mother was at last willing to consider that her "best" may have been too much for her children.

The following example illustrates a successful father's morbid preoccupation with his daughter's obesity. This girl at the age of 18 was short and quite heavy and so slow moving and inhibited that on first impression she appeared to be retarded. She was the first child and the first grandchild in a large family and everybody agreed that there had never been a more beloved and better cared for little girl; her father in particular had been most devoted to her. An expression of the father's unfaltering love and devotion for his daughter was his talking about committing suicide because he could not stand the shame and humiliation of having a fat daughter. He brought her for psychotherapy so that she could be turned into a girl of whom he could be proud. The daughter said much later, when she had become capable of expressing herself: "Father thinks that a personality change is something like a facelift. If you go to the doctor then it is his job to change you into what he has ordered." The father was indignant at the mere notion that there might have been something in the emotional atmosphere of the home that had contributed to his daughter's obesity. The mother's reaction to the girl's increasing obesity was genuine compassion for the girl, but also a growing resentment that she, the mother, was being blamed for permitting her daughter to get so fat. The mother was expected to change this; in everything else she felt competent and capable, but here she was completely helpless. Like the father, the mother was extremely reluctant to recognize her own emotional involvement and the need to relax her excessive control over her daughter.

RECENT FORMULATIONS

Since these early reports, family studies have flourished, although little attention has been paid to obesity. With an increasing understanding, significant changes have occurred in the style, focus, and conceptual frame of the family study. It is no longer considered sufficient to give the family history in biographical or anecdotal detail. The essential aspects of family transactions must be formulated and generalized, even to abstract concepts, which might then serve as a basis of comparison from family to family and in different cultural settings (Bruch, 1966).

Follow-up observation has modified the picture as it was developed in 1940 in many ways. A few of the obese children had a fairly normal development with or without continued obesity. This happened when the family had been accepting of the child and was not overly concerned with his or her size and body build. In contrast fat children who had not "outgrown" their childhood plumpness, either physically or psychologically, suffered from severe deficits in the process of self-differentiation. The specific deficit in obesity is confusion about the eating function.

When food has been offered in early life as the unsepcific means of appeasing any discomfort, the eating function develops in a disordered way. The child fails to become discriminately aware of his or her own sensations and feelings. The fat person's indiscriminate desire for food, his or her "feeling hungry," whenever there is a disturbance in the interpersonal or intrapsychic equilibrium is an expression of this. The abnormal eating carries an enormous range of motivational and symbolic meanings. This diversity itself suggested new questions. How is it possible for a body function as basic and essential as food intake to develop in such a way that it can be misused in the service of such a multitude of nonnutritional needs, with the brain continuously making mistakes in not differentiating between bodily need and psychological tension?

The search for an answer to this question led to the deduction that awareness of hunger is not innate knowledge but that an individual needs to learn how to differentiate "hunger," the need to eat, from other signals of bodily discomfort and emotional tension states (Bruch, 1961, 1969). A simplified conceptual model of personality development was constructed. Behavior from birth on needs to be differentiated as behavior *initiated* in the infant and behavior *in response* to stimuli from the outside, relating to both the biological and the social-emotional field. The mother's behavior toward the child is either *responsive* or *stimulating*. The interaction with the infant can be rated as *appropriate* or *inappropriate*, depending on whether it fulfills the need that the signal indicates or disregards or distorts it. These elemental distinctions permit the dynamic analysis, irrespective of the specific area or content of the problem, of an amazingly large variety of clinical situations, and they avoid the traditional dichotomies, contrasting the somatic and psychological aspects of development or inherited potential and experiential events.

For healthy development, experiences in both modalities are essential: confirmation of clues originating in the child and stimulation from the outside to which he or she learns to respond. *Insufficient regular* and *appropriate* responses to his or her needs deprive the developing child of essential groundwork for "body identity" and perceptual and conceptual awarensss. The overanxious stuffing to which many obese children are exposed would be an example of such inappropriate early experiences. Not all children whose early feeding contained such inappropriate elements become obese as children; it is, however, often the background for obesity in adolescence or later in life. Excessive anxiety about control over eating is an essential feature of anorexia nervosa, which seems to have a similar background.

Abnormal hunger awareness is not an isolated symptom but occurs together with other disturbances in active self-awareness. It is also observed in schizophrenics and other psychiatric patients whose weight does not appear abnormal. Passivity has always been considered a characteristic of obese people. A common deficit was recognized in the background of such patients, namely, the absence or paucity of accurate responses to a child's expressions of his or her needs.

In an extensive study of mother-child interaction in the first three months of life, which corroborates this viewpoint, Ainsworth and Bell focused on the feeding situation since most of this interaction occurs during feeding (Ainsworth and Bell, 1969). The babies were under the care of pediatricians in private practice and were observed in their home setting. It was soon recognized that the factor of greatest importance was the *mother's response to the baby's signals*, whether she allowed the baby to determine the amount of food and whether the feeding was geared to the child's own rate. The mothers at the top of their list showed themselves highly sensitive to the signals of their babies who actively participated, thrived, and were happy. The primary emphasis was on gratifying the baby. In contrast, the mothers toward the bottom of their list were more dominant in their transactions and disregarded the baby's signals. The babies in turn were poorly nourished and unhappy.

Next to the sensitive mothers came those who tended to overfeed their babies in an attempt to gratify them. In another pattern, low in the grouping, the mothers overstuffed their babies with the intent of making them sleep a long time and thus demand little attention from them. The investigators felt that this distinction in intent was important. The mothers who would overfeed to gratify their babies tended to treat too broad a spectrum of clues and signals as if they indicated hunger. The deliberately overstuffed babies were not permitted to be active participants in the feeding situation nor were they well regulated in their rhythms. These mothers were often disturbed, detached, and insensitive to their babies signals.

Only a few of the mothers who tended to overfeed their babies had weight problems themselves. The babies who were most overweight had mothers who were not plump. The babies maintained their overweight, and their mothers persisted in stuffing them. This subdivision is in agreement with clinical observations on obese children, in which one finds mothers who are loving and accepting of their children though they continuously overfeed them, and others who basically reject their children for which they try to compensate by stuffing them with food although they are impervious to the children's needs and efforts at self-expression.

When tested at the age of 12 months in a strange environment, the infants with the most appropriate feeding interaction showed the strongest attachment to their mothers and made active efforts to gain and maintain contact with them. In contrast, babies with inappropriate feeding experiences showed little or no tendency to seek proximity, interaction, or contact with their mothers. In the group with superimposed overfeeding, the children were distressed by separation but showed less ability to use their mothers as a secure basis from which they would enjoy exploring the strange environment. The children generally displayed more maladaptive behavior in relation to new and strange situations. This observation is in good agreement with the accounts of the early behavior of the emotionally disturbed obese children, namely that of anxious clinging to the mother, extreme shyness, and fear of new situations and contacts.

The history of a 14-year-old boy who weighed nearly 300 pounds at a height of 5'5" serves as an illustration of a mother's inappropriate response to his needs. According to the first information he had "always" been an insatiable eater. Actually he had weighed only five pounds at birth and was difficult to feed. The father was more patient than the mother who had only reluctantly consented to have another baby, and he would get up at night and hold the baby and feed him. At two and a half months he weighed seven and a half pounds and still needed to be coaxed while eating. The mother had developed a backache, which made it impossible for her to lift the baby. When the child was able to sit in a high chair the mother still could not lift him and so he sat for long stretches and would become restless and cry. The mother discovered that she could keep him quiet by sticking a cookie into his mouth. This would not keep him quiet for long and the rate at which she would feed him increased. By the time he was 10 months old, he was decidedly chubby. At two years of age he weighed 65 pounds and was taken to a renowned medical center for study, where he was placed on a 500-calorie diet and lost some weight. However, the family felt he was becoming too weak and so he was again permitted unlimited food intake, with a resulting steady increase in weight.

The story of this boy gives evidence of a grotesquely inappropriate learning experience. Food was offered as appeasement for whatever discomfort the baby's crying expressed. The mother had felt at all times that this child was "too much" for her and paid very little attention to him, except for keeping him quiet by stuffing him with food. This early "programming" of his regulatory centers became his permanent pattern; it occurred at the time when an infant begins to show differentiated perception, cognition, and outward-directed explorative behavior, to which no confirming response was given. Thus, other modalities of his developmental needs were disregarded; there was no encouragement toward any physical activity or expression of initiative and autonomy.

Situations are occasionally encountered in which outer circumstances, not inner psychological problems, lead to overfeeding. An example is the history of a boy who was obese when he was two years old. He was a child of the depression years and his parents worked as a couple in another household. His parents were afraid of losing their jobs if the child was noisy, so they kept him quiet by giving him food. By the time the parents came for a consultation, they had reestablished their own home and the child's food intake was no longer excessive. The parents were open to reassurance that the child did not suffer from a glandular disease. The father took an active interest in his son and encouraged his participation in athletics. The mother refused to restrict his diet but she did not urge food on him either. The child did well and by the time he was ready for first grade he was only mildly overweight. He was outgoing and popular and enjoyed athletics. He did well in school, with real eagerness to share the activities of other children, something his parents encouraged. When he was last seen he was 18½ years old, tall, slim, and athletic. He remembered having been shown photos of himself as a fat boy, but he had no memory of being concerned about how much to eat or of having been handicapped by being obese.

OBESITY IN ADULTS

Thus far I have emphasized the importance of the family background for obesity in childhood and adolescence. This was not intended to imply that interaction with the family is not of importance in later years. In many heavy adults the obesity represents a continuation of a weight problem that had its onset in childhood or adolescence. The obese adults may have had periods of seemingly successful weight control but relapsed after they settled down. They had slimmed down for their wedding but then reenacted their dependency needs with the spouse, or stayed excessively close to their family of origin.

Other adults who become obese have no previous history of weight excess. In many of them the weight gain seems to be a sign of more sedentary living habits with increasing age and greater prosperity. In others, a relationship to upsetting life events can be recognized, such as the loss of a significant person through death, separation, or abandonment, or a serious illness or accident. In this *reactive obesity*, the overeating seems to have a definite function, namely that of warding off severe anxiety and depressive feelings. Such people find temporary relief from such unpleasant feelings that mistakenly are experienced as a "need to eat," but this relief is short lived and the cycle of "not feeling right" and unsatisfying eating is endlessly repeated. Like those with developmental obesity, those with reactive obesity are not clearly aware of their bodily sensations and psychological experiences.

In each case of obesity, we are dealing with at least three elements: the constitutional endowment, the conditioning life experiences, and the precipitating traumatic event; one of these is the hostile response to obesity of our society. Even more traumatic is the derogatory rejection from the family. As a result, many obese people suffer from self-contempt and continuous repetition of traumatic experiences.

It seems that the obesity which develops during or after pregnancy belongs to this group. Gaining weight sometimes follows each pregnancy, and sometimes it follows only the birth of one particular child. Several psychodynamic factors can be recognized: disappointment in the marriage, unfulfilled fantasies of what the child would do for the mother, or frank envy about the care the child receives and resentment about the demands he or she makes on the mother. Much has been said about obesity indicating a desire for pregnancy, although I have not been able to convince myself that this is a frequent cause of obesity. What I have observed in some cases is a definite rejection of pregnancy and of the maternal role, with a desire of the woman herself to stay a child. When some women become pregnant, they may develop a fear of being drained by the baby and they stuff themselves with food in an effort to compensate for this. Some women experience the delivery of the baby as losing a part of themselves; they feel empty and try to make up for it by eating.

Occasionally a father becomes fat after the birth of a child. In my experience this occurs in extremely dependent men who even before the baby was born felt that they never got enough. They will resort to overeating to compensate themselves for what they feel they are missing, and thereby thus combatting their anger and jealousy.

TREATMENT

The importance of the family's attitude is most apparent in connection with efforts to lose weight. Evaluation of the therapeutic results in the clinic group of obese children revealed an embarrassing contrast. The poorest outcome was observed in those who had been taken from doctor to doctor and had been exposed to a variety of reducing programs and endocrine and other medication. The damaging factor appeared to be the aggressive dissatisfaction of the parents who wanted their child changed at any cost. Serious psychiatric problems and disturbed family interaction had been recognized early but the recommended treatment was not carried out. Surprisingly, counseling that focused on particular problems within a family had a more lasting favorable effect than had been anticipated. On the other hand, the obese children who "outgrew" their obesity came from families who had been supportive of them and had not intruded when the patient decided on a weight-reduction program.

A family's attitude may interfere with reducing efforts in many different ways (Bruch, 1973e). Prescription of a diet for one member is occasionally reacted to as if it were a deprivation inflicted on the whole family. A punitive attitude toward an obese person and his or her greedy eating is common, particularly in relation to children and adolescents. The parents' intrusion on the life of such a youngster may involve every activity of the child and provoke extreme resentment. When the responsibility for reducing is completely taken over by the parents, the only way of self-assertion for a youngster is to react in a paradoxical way; he or she will use weight and food to defy the parents and refuse to engage in any activity just to show that nobody can tell him or her what to do. This type of overcontrol is common in the younger age group. It is often reinforced through medical advice, namely, when it focuses on symptom change only. Without this overcontrol, many youngsters would never have become quite so obese originally.

Not only parents and children are involved with each other in such intense struggles about reducing. The struggle occurs just as often with other family members, in particular between husband and wife, and may become just as destructive as that between parent and child. A husband on a diet is at the mercy of his wife. Her solicitous concern for him may provoke the same rebelliousness against being told what to do as it does in adolescents. Other husbands will complain that their wives are not concerned enough about their weight. For example, a man in his thirties, competent in his profession, felt quite helpless about controlling his weight. He left the responsibility to his wife and insisted that she check his weight every day. If she forgot to do so, he became so enraged that he would go on an eating spree, putting the blame on her. Husbands, too, can interfere with their wives' reducing efforts by making fun of all the fuss and foolishness of their wives' efforts, by supervising every detail, or by making tactless remarks about their not having the willpower to lose weight.

Dietary treatment in particular for an obese child and adolescent, should be instituted only after a preparatory conference with the significant family members. In cases with manifest psychiatric problems it is essential to clarify the disturbed transactional patterns of the family so that the patient can feel free to get involved in psychotherapy, and can develop controls from within and the conviction of owning his or her own body. The obese patient needs to learn to experience himself or herself as self-directed. When faulty self-awareness dominates the picture, therapy needs to help an obese fat person learn to differentiate between different needs and assist him or her in becoming capable of coping with problems without retreating to excessive food intake.

REFERENCES

Ainsworth, M.D.S. & Bell, S.M. Some contemporary patterns of mother-infant interaction in the feeding situation. In *Stimulation in Early Infancy*. New York: Academic Press, 1969, pp. 133-170.

Bruch, H. Developmental obesity and schizophrenia. *Psychiatry: Journal for the Study of Interpersonal Processes*, 1940, 21, 56.

Bruch, H. Transformation of oral impulses in eating disorders: A conceptual approach. *Psychiatric Quarterly*, 1961, 35, 458.

Bruch, H. Changing approaches to the study of the family. *Psychiatric Research Report 20*, Washington, D.C.: American Psychiatric Association, 1966, 1-7.

Bruch, H. Hunger and instinct. *Journal of Nervous and Mental Diseases*, 1969, 149, 91.

Bruch, H. Family frame and transactions. In *Eating Disorders: Obesity, Anorexia Nervosa and the Person Within*. New York: Basic Books, 1973a, pp. 66-86.

Bruch, H. Diversity of clinical pictures. In *Eating Disorders: Obesity, Anorexia Nervosa and the Person Within*. New York: Basic Books, 1973b, pp. 109-133.

Bruch, H. Obesity in childhood. In *Eating Disorders: Obesity, Anorexia Nervosa and the Person Within*. New York: Basic Books, 1973c, pp. 134-150.

Bruch, H. Obesity in adolescence. In *Eating Disorders: Obesity, Anorexia Nervosa and the Person Within*. New York: Basic Books, 1973d, pp. 151-174.

Bruch, H. The practical and psychological aspects of weight change. In *Eating Disorders: Obesity, Anorexia Nervosa and the Person Within*. New York: Basic Books, 1973e, pp. 309-333.

Bruch, H. & Touraine, G. Obesity in childhood. V. The family frame of obese children. *Psychosomatic Medicine*, 1940, 2, 141.

Iversen, T. et al. Psychogenic obesity in children with special reference to Hilde Bruch's theory. *Acta Paedeatrica*, 1952, 41, 574.

Lidz, T. Family settings that produce schizophrenic offspring. In *Problems of Psychosis*, International Colloquium on Psychosis, Excerpta Medica International Congress Series, No. 194, 1969, 196-210.

Ostergaard, L. On psychogenic obesity in childhood. *Acta Paedeatrica*, 1954, 43, 507.

Raskovsky, A. et al. Basic psychic structure of the obese. *International Journal of Psychoanalysis*, 1950, 31, 144.

Editor's Commentary: On Family Dynamics in Eating Disorders

Although the study which Bruch reports on in this article was originally undertaken in the 1930s, the manuscript provides some longitudinal study data, interesting illustrative case material, and pertinent literature which appeared into the 1970s. It is included here as a paper with important historical and therapeutic significance in that as early as the 1930s, decades before the advent of the field of family therapy, Bruch was conceptualizing the etiology of obesity in terms of its interactive meaning and formulating treatment in terms anticipatory of the family systems approach. She early recognized the confusion of body sensations which represent true food hunger with those which signal emotional hunger and describes how the obese person mistakenly tries to fill the emotional craving by resorting to overeating. She points up the vital connections between brain messages and body behavior and how erroneous decoding, learned from parental overstuffing, contributes to eating disorders.

Inherent is the role of the symptom in maintaining the family homeostasis, fostering dependency to keep individuals overly attached —often to justify the importance of the mother long beyond the normal developmental period that requires this much symbiosis. In discussing treatment, she indicates that the best results are obtained when the young person decides on his/her own weight reduction program and takes responsibility for carrying it through. The parents can be most helpful by supporting their youngster's program and by avoiding intruding upon it by sabotage, taking over control, or becoming overly invested in what is transpiring. The same can be said in terms of the family dynamics and course of treatment of the other major eating disorder—anorexia nervosa. Both compulsive undereating and overeating are life-threatening disorders with precipitating roots emanating from deep in the family's transactional pattern. Thus, Bruch, like Minuchin,

Rosman, and Baker (1978) and Selvini Palazzoli (1974) and Selvini Palazzoli, Boscolo, Cecchin, and Prata (1978), believes the treatment of choice lies in family therapy.

Bruch also alludes to the interactive, control issues which surface in an embattled married couple around weight control issues. (This constitutes yet another neurotic dyad combination.) Weight Watchers —harken! Consider bringing in the spouse too—so his or her investment in the accumulation of fat can be reduced.

The differentiation between developmental and reactive obesity is an important one—perhaps too often overlooked in treatment endeavors.

REFERENCES

Minuchin, S., Rosman, B.L., & Baker, L. *Psychosomatic Families: Anorexia Nervosa in Context* Cambridge: Harvard University Press, 1978.
Selvini Palazzoli, M. *Self-Starvation*. London: Chaucer, 1974.
Selvini Palazzoli, M., Boscolo, L., Cecchin, G., & Prata, G. *Paradox and Counterparadox.* New York: Jason Aronson, 1978.

Chapter 14

Adequate Joint Authority of Parents: A Crucial Issue for the Outcome of Family Therapy

By Theo Compernolle

At the Child and Youth Psychiatry Outpatient Departments of the Catholic University of Leuven (Belgium), structural family therapy has become the framework of the therapeutic interventions. While preparing a follow-up study to assess the outcome of therapy, we were puzzled by the fact that the outcome of therapy did not correlate well with issues such as diagnosis, chronicity of the problem, and prior psychotherapy. Therefore, 25 videotapes of initial interviews were reviewed to find out which factors were of better prognostic value. As we reviewed these videotapes, it became evident that a developmental issue was crucial for the outcome of family therapy: the fast restoration of adequate joint parental authority. This issue was further elaborated through the analysis of case folders, staff discussions and therapeutic experiments under live supervision. It became evident that a lack of consensus between parents about important child-rearing issues results at a minimum in an unpredictable environment for the child. Frequently, it results in a damaging triangulation which is often hidden behind rationalizations about democracy and children's rights.

This research was done in 1980 at the Child and Youth Psychiatry Departments of the University of Leuven (Belgium). This is a revised version of a paper presented at the International Confernce on Family Therapy and Network Interventions, Brussels, March 26-28, 1981.

Theo Compernolle, M.D., is a child psychiatrist who is currently the Director of the Child and Youth Psychiatry Outpatient Departments at the Catholic University of Louvain (Belgium). He is Director of Clinical Training at the University of Paris and Director of the Louvain Institute for Systemic Therapies.

Although a balance needs to be reached between autonomy and authority, the most efficient therapeutic approach seems to be first to restore parental authority as this facilitates the resolution of a child's major psychological problems, especially depression, and the development of the child's autonomy.

The use of the family environment as an alternative to institutionalization of the mentally ill started in Belgium as early as the 17th century in Geel. The introduction of family therapy as a modern psychotherapeutic method, however, happened only about a decade ago (Compernolle, 1980a) in Belgium.

At the Child and Youth Psychiatry Outpatient Departments of the Catholic University of Leuven (Belgium), structural family therapy (Minuchin, Montalvo, Rosman, & Schumer, 1967; Minuchin, 1974, Minuchin, Baker, Rosman, Liebman, Milman, & Todd, 1975; Minuchin, Rosman, & Baker, 1978) became the overall framework for a systems-oriented therapeutic approach (Compernolle, 1978, 1980b, 1981a, 1981b) which often includes, in addition, social learning interventions (Patterson, 1976; Patterson, Reid, Jones, & Conger 1975; Compernolle, 1981c) and problem solving interventions (Haley, 1963; 1967; 1973; 1976; 1980; Watzlawick, Beavin, & Jackson 1967; Watzlawick, Weakland, & Fisch, 1974).

While preparing a follow-up study to assess the outcome of therapy, we became puzzled by the fact that the outcome of therapy did not correlate well with issues such as diagnosis, chronicity of the problem, and prior psychotherapy. Problems such as anorexia nervosa, complicated phobic and obsessive behaviors, and encopresis, which had existed for four or five years and which had deteriorated in spite of intense long-term individual therapy, were resolved in three to five sessions; other in many ways very similar cases or seemingly minor behavior problems required much longer treatment—and some were failures. To conduct a regular follow-up study did not seem a very useful way to find information about more specific factors determining success or failure. The information available in the folders about issues such as diagnosis, chronicity, prior therapy, even severity of family dysfunction, problems with the family of origin, profession of the therapist did not answer our question. Whenever we thought we found a prognostic rule, we also found many exceptions. This information leading nowhere, we considered the possibility that instead of certain features of the cases, qualities of the therapeutic process might be of better prognostic value. Therefore, we decided to analyze 25 videotapes of of initial interviews of cases with both unsuccessful and successful outcomes.

COMPARING SUCCESSES AND FAILURES

We analyzed 25 videotapes to compare the quality of initial sessions with the results upon follow-up. The cases studied were behavioral problems ranging from mild child-rearing difficulties (four cases) to severe delinquency (two cases). Others concerned referral diagnoses such as anorexia nervosa in girls (six cases), anorexia nervosa in boys (two cases), schizophrenia (two cases), encopresis (two cases), anxiety attacks (one case), obsessive behaviors (two cases), school phobias (two cases), chronic nausea and vomiting (one case), and severe child abuse (one case). The ages of the identified patients ranged from three to 19 years; the length of family therapy ranged from one session to more than one year, with an average of six months. The therapies were executed by staff members of the department: one child psychiatrist with two years training at the Philadelphia Child Guidance Clinic (the author), two psychologists, and one social worker. The basic orientation of therapy was structural family therapy, albeit with frequent use of social learning interventions as developed by Patterson and occasionally a problem solving intervention, such as a paradox or a benevolent ordeal. The follow-up took place six months to one year after the closing session.

In analyzing the tapes we concentrated upon issues such as the therapist's ability to join and to take leadership, the extent to which he/she was able to introduce a new reality and make the family accept it, the intensity of his or her interventions, and the sex of the therapist (Kruth, 1981). We tried to analyze the style of the therapists (for example, one therapist having more feeling for little children, while another one worked more efficiently with adolescents) and the possibilities of a therapist-family match or mismatch. We had the impression that this latter factor influenced the duration of therapy, but not the final outcome. At the end of the study, not a single one of these aspects correlated satisfactorily with the outcome of treatment. *We then discovered by coincidence that all cases with a swift success had something in common that was missing in all failures: a rapid reestablishment of adequate joint parental authority.* By "joint" we mean that there was a basic agreement between the parents about child-rearing issues. "Adequate" refers to the balance of control and autonomy proper for the age of the child.

THE IMPORTANCE OF JOINT PARENTAL AUTHORITY

When we reviewed our videotapes, it became obvious that parents were able to resolve problems, even major ones which could not be resolved with long individual treatment, if they were able to make and implement joint decisions about what they expected from their child. We observed that many of our cases centered around the restoration of the adequate authority of the parents as a unit. Adequate leadership seems a necessary condition for the development of the child's autonomy and the child's self-confidence, which in turn creates room for a mutually respectful and loving relationship.

In our clinical practice parents often explain how they run their families as a democracy. Often this story turns out to be a rationalization hiding a fundamental lack of agreement between the parents. Too often in these situations one quickly discovers that when father says "do" mother says "don't." The parents are unable to resolve their disagreement and then *leave the child to its rights!* The child is triangulated and the choices left are largely dysfunctional ones.

Once these kinds of patterns of interactions are established, it becomes irrelevant to ask whether the parental conflict or the child's problem behavior came first. The child's behavior at that point plays a major role in the lack of conflict resolution by, for example, dividing the parents, diverting the conflict before it is resolved, or siding with one parent (see Minuchin, 1974; Minuchin et al., 1967; 1975; 1978).

Adequate joint parental authority does not mean that parents always have to agree about every single issue. There is a continuous shift of coalitions and alliances in all healthy, flexible families. The structure of a family changes when the issues change. About important family matters, however, and certainly about important child-rearing issues, there needs to be a basic agreement between the parents about what they want and about how they will implement it.

An adolescent will often be able to integrate differing child-rearing views and approaches of two parents. A young child, however, generally cannot do this, especially if there are significant differences in relation to important issues. In the latter situation, even an adolescent might have trouble.

On this issue of parental control we disagree with some of the statements of Gordon (1970). Although the approach by Gordon might be useful to improve an already good relationship between parents and children, we think it is unwise to follow this kind of advice with serious problems. Weekly we see parents who become even more inefficient and confused in dealing with their problem children after reading Gordon or after attending a Parent Effectiveness Training group. One major reason for this deterioration seems to us to be not only the lack of emphasis given in this approach to the importance of adequate joint parental authority, but also the frequent undermining of the latter.

THE BALANCE BETWEEN AUTONOMY AND AUTHORITY

As a child grows older, his or her autonomy increases, while the parents' control decreases. Adults do not start arguing with a 18-month-old child who starts climbing a steep open staircase. The parent lifts the child up, disregarding the child's opinion on the issue of climbing dangerous stairs, says "no, no" with a firm voice and puts the child in a safer place. A little later the parent will start teaching the child how to climb those stairs in a safe way. Once the child has mastered this skill, the control by the parents decreases and the freedom and autonomy of the child and the parents increase; the child can use the stairs safely and the parents do not have to run after him all the time.

Adolescence can be seen as the crucial period when the autonomy of the child becomes more important than the parental control (Figure 1). Problems arise when the control by the parents is inadequate for the developmental stage of the child. There can be relatively too much control combined with a lack of autonomy or there can be a relative lack of authority with too much freedom. In the population of our outpatient Child and Youth Psychiatry Department at the University of Leuven, often the problem seems to be too much freedom. We are often confronted with a particular combination of both, that is, families where a lack of authority of the parents goes hand in hand with a lack of autonomy of the child. Left to their own resources to make a perilous choice between two alternatives set by the parents, children often avoid an age-appropriate choice and the conflict likely with the parent whose alternative they do not choose, by functioning at a much more infantile level.

THE REESTABLISHMENT OF PARENTAL AUTHORITY:
A PRIORITY IN FAMILY THERAPY

Figure 1 could be a guideline for therapy. If the identified patient is a young child, the therapist could stress parental control. The older the identified patient is, the more the therapist could emphasize the development of autonomy.

In trying to put this into practice we ran into trouble, especially when the identified patient was an adolescent causing major problems. Whenever we focused upon the development of autonomy, rather than upon

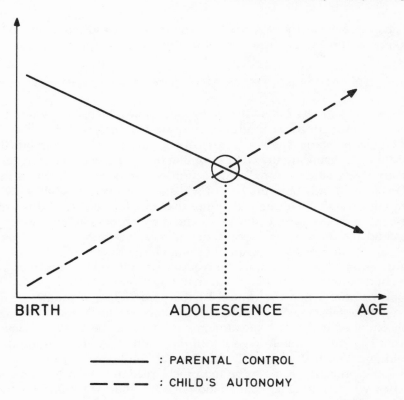

BIRTH   ADOLESCENCE   AGE

——————— : PARENTAL CONTROL

— — — : CHILD'S AUTONOMY

FIG. 1

the parental authority, from the beginning of therapy the family therapy became long and laborious. After a few failures it became obvious that many parents could give the necessary autonomy and freedom to their children only after having (re)gained control! Many of these parents needed to have a proper experience of taking command to enable them to feel safe to release their control.

After a long period of lack of authority, parents will often exaggerate their control once the therapist manages to put them in charge. Often, even without explicit therapeutic intervention, the family will soon find an adequate balance between authority and autonomy (see Figure 2). If not, once the parents' authority is restored, the family therapy will need to focus (arrow 2 in Figure 2) on the issues of autonomy and independence, for example, by facilitating negotiations between the

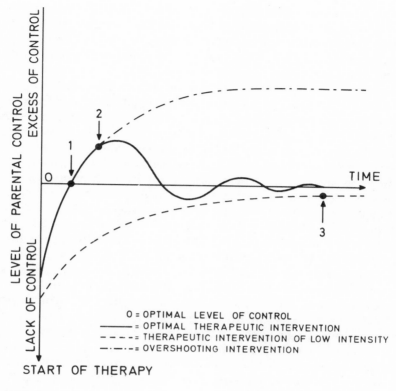

FIG. 2

united parental dyad and the child. Sometimes the therapist will be able to stimulate proper authority and adequate autonomy simultaneously. If, for the above mentioned reasons, this is not possible, we prefer to start with the establishment of appropriate authority. We do this not because we consider autonomy less important than authority, but for strategic reasons—in practice, it is easier to realize the development of a child's autonomy after proper authority is established rather than the other way round.

In our therapeutic approach we now prefer interventions of high intensity from the initial sessions on, to force the parents to reestablish the authority as quickly as possible (see Figure 2). This way the parents and children quickly experience what adequate joint authority stands for. This enables them to experience its effect on the family as well as upon the presenting problem. It is possible to reach the necessary level of authority by interventions of low intensity, but then the family will experience the difference in the interactions, as well as its results, much later (arrow 3 in Figure 2) and the difference between authority and lack of authority will be less obvious to them.

The authority of the parents is an aspect of the functioning of the family as a whole. The restoration of adequate joint authority of the parents always goes hand in hand with changes in the family as a whole, not just in the identified patient. The family as a unit has to change to allow the restoration of the authority. Stable coalitions of parents with their children, for example, undermine the parental authority and at the same time are fomented by a lack of authority. Breaking up such a coalition between one parent and a child might make it easier to establish joint parental authority, but this will also provoke a major change in the position of this child among his siblings. The latter change will have to be monitored and guided to make sure it becomes a productive one and to make it fit in a more functional overall pattern of interactions.

To reestablish parental authority it is necessary not only to change the patterns of interaction of the family as a whole, but also to undo previous psychiatric diagnostic labels such as anorexia nervosa, schizophrenia, character disorder, and neurosis. These labels set the problem out of the parents' reach. To give a child a "disease" label is to call for the authority of a specialist, a doctor, or a psychotherapist. This kind of view of the dysfunction is an unworkable one for the family, and most often paralyzing for the therapist as well. To enable the family to take charge of the problem, the therapist needs to create a workable view of the problem, preferably an interactional one. Families do not know how to deal with the "mysterious disease of anorexia nervosa," but they know most often very well how to deal with "a child who refuses to eat" or "a girl who will not eat unless she develops proper autonomy." Parents have few tools to deal with a boy behaving as a little Napoleon and labeled as "schizophrenic," but they know how to deal with "a boy who is extremely disrespectful towards his parents and who defeats them using the Napoleonic code and the Bible."

This issue of creating a workable reality for the family is an important one for many more reasons than the mere reestablishment of adequate parental authority. In the context of this paper, however, we only want to mention its importance without elaborating on its specifics.

There are two related exceptions to the rule that the restoration of adequate parental authority results in a good prognosis. The first exception is when the child is no longer emotionally or financially dependent on the parents, for example, in the case of a delinquent, promiscuous and drug-dealing 16-year-old girl who finds a support system in the underworld which hides her, supports her and defends her against her parents.

The other exception is when a person, a group, an institution, or an organization with greater authority than the parents sides with the child against the parents. In such a situation even a child who is still dependent on his or her parents can defeat their authority. Since the study was done, we have seen cases where children were able to defeat very adequate joint parental authority with the help of the juvenile court magistrate, the family physician, the parish priest, grandparents, or the school. The therapy failed when those other adults could not be motivated to support the authority of the parents.

THE INFLUENCE OF THE RESTORATION OF PARENTAL AUTHORITY UPON THE CHILD'S AFFECT

It is surprising to see how children react positively and with increased happiness to the restoration of parental authority, even if they have to give up a large part of their (inappropriately taken) territory and even during the transitional period when the parents exaggerate their control. We gained the impression that the restoration of clear, unanimous rules provides an important basic security. Rules can be followed or infringed; in both cases the rules provide a necessary guideline. Certainly they provide a more comfortable situation than triangulation does. Moreover, clear rules seem necessary for the child to make the necessary value judgments to develop adequate self-esteem.

This leads to a most puzzling observation of this study: Together with the chief complaint, many children showed signs of depression. Most often these—sometimes severe—depressive symptoms quickly and unexpectedly disappeared merely with the restoration of clear, consistent, and unanimous rules and limits. It is an intriguing finding that the mere restoration of parental authority sometimes cures depression in children. This seems in accordance with Seligman's (1975) speculations that early experience with uncontrollable events may predispose a person to depression.

Case Presentation

Upon referral, Cindy, a 16-year-old girl, had been suffering from obsessive behavior for four years. The rituals had become so elaborate that she was unable to carry out any regular daily tasks or chores, some of which were just plainly forbidden by voices in her head. Her marks in school dropped from straight A's to a level where she would fail the grade. Although she always had been a cheerful and sociable girl, she now avoided all contact with peers. She had been in play therapy and individual therapy along analytical lines. Her behavior had been labeled as neurotic, schizophrenic and even autistic.

The family consisted of her father, a busy technician, her mother, a housewife, and her sister Lora, age 21, a nurse. When the session started, the three women were seated together, with father a little farther away. In their discussions of their family life, as well as in their interactions in the sessions, it became evident that father took a peripheral position on most issues. Lora seemed to have taken over some of his parental functions. Mother tended to discuss many parental issues related to Cindy's behavior with Lora rather than with father. The therapist joined first strongly with father, making him more central by gradually giving his opinion about the problem more emphasis and by later using one of his statements " . . . Once in a while, albeit very seldom, I have the impression she pulls my leg . . ." as a first building block to gradually introducing the idea of the importance of joint decisions. A major break-through was achieved by asking the parents to make their daughter execute a few tasks in the session. The parents decided to ask the girl to clean the blackboard. First mother implored—much to father's disdain—many times talking about her love for Cindy and how she did this for Cindy's well-being. The girl did not move. Then father, in a firm tone of voice, ordered her to do what mother asked her to do, while mother did not hide her condemnation for this brutal approach. The parents then were told to discuss the issue with each other to find a mutually acceptable approach. Lora was asked to discuss with Cindy how she could help her as a sister, not as a pseudo-mother. When the parents then asked Cindy again to clean the blackboard, she first tried to split the parental unit by complaining to mother about father's brutality and by asking mother for a handkerchief to dry her tears. The therapist had to intervene a few times to keep the parents united and to prevent Lora from being pulled into a parental position. The parents then repeated their request a second time, and the girl executed it smoothly, without rituals, and without the usual repetitions.

Upon the conclusion of this little drama, the parents came to the conclusion that their daughter was neither crazy nor sick and that they really could help her over the threshold when they worked together.

Two weeks later, the day before the next appointment, the parents called to say that what happened with Cindy looked like a miracle but that they preferred coming to the appointment without the children because they discovered that their major problem was that they had difficulties in reaching agreements as parents and as a couple.

In the next two sessions they came without children and the therapist helped them to discuss parental and marital issues. At the next family interview, six weeks after the first session, the therapist met a very different Cindy. She had undergone a real metamorphosis; the rather infantile, cranky, pale, unattractive little girl had become a little lady and the parents obviously had developed a very different kind of relationship. The case was closed. At follow-up nine months later this new situation had stabilized, Cindy had been able to pass her exams with some special help from a teacher, and she had resumed her social activities.

CONCLUSION

Although other factors certainly are involved in the outcome of family therapy with children as the identified patients, adequate joint authority of parents proved to be a crucial one. Authority of the parents separately is not sufficient. Joint authority is necessary for a fast resolution of major emotional and behavioral problems of children. Moreover, the parental authority needs to be rational in the sense that it should be flexible and in harmony with the child's level of development.

This issue of parental authority and the more general one of decision-making processes in families highlight the importance of child developmental issues for the outcome of family therapy and suggest fruitful leads for further investigation. The very beneficial influence of the restoration of adequate joint parental authority on the depression of children is so obvious that we think this issue should get priority for further research.

REFERENCES

Compernolle, T. The Systems View of Prevention in Mental Health. Paper presented at the conference on Prevention in the Field of Child and Youth Psychiatry. Leuven, Belgium, May 1978.

Compernolle, T. Family therapy in Belgium: A U.S. product on local assembly lines. *AAMFT Newsletter*, 1980a, *11*, (2), 7-10.

Compernolle, T. La thérapie familiale structurale: Approche systémique par excellence

(Structural family therapy: A preeminent systems approach). *Bulletin de Thérapie Familiale de Langue Française*, Jan. 1980b, 2, 9.

Compernolle, T. Het alcoholisme vanuit een systeemoptiek (Alcoholism from a systems point of view). *Tijdschrift voor Psychiatrie, 23*, 9, 1981a, 521-532.

Compernolle, T. Gezinstherapie als uiting van een fundamentele verandering van het wetenschappelijk denken (Family therapy as an expression of a fundamental change of paradigms in science). *Tijdschrift voor Relatieproblematiek*, 1981b, 3/4.

Compernolle, T. Eko-Psychosomatiek: De invloed van het gezin op het zieke kind en vice versa. *LIST-Werkschrift*, Leuven, 1981c, 4, 1-20.

Gordon, T. *Parent Effectiveness Training*. New York: David McKay, 1970.

Haley, J. *Strategies of Psychotherapy*. New York: Grune and Stratton, 1963.

Haley, J. *Advanced Techniques of Hypnosis and Therapy: Selected Papers of Milton H. Erickson*. New York: Grune and Stratton, 1967.

Haley, J. *Uncommon Therapy. The Psychiatric Techniques of Milton H. Erickson, M.D.* New York: Ballantine Books, 1973.

Haley, J. *Problem Solving Therapy*. San Francisco: Jossey-Bass, 1976.

Haley, J. *Leaving Home*. New York: McGraw-Hill, 1980.

Kruth, M. De rol van het geslacht van de therapeut op zijn positie in de gezinstherapie (The role of the therapist's gender upon his position in family therapy). In T. Compernolle (Ed.), *LIST-Syllabus*, 1981, 2, 3.

Minuchin, S. *Families and Family Therapy*. Cambridge: Harvard University Press, 1974.

Minuchin, S., Baker, L., Rosman, B., Liebman, R., Milman, L. & Todd, T. A conceptual model of psychosomatic illness in children: Family organization and family therapy. *Archives of General Psychiatry*, 1975, 32, 1031-1038.

Minuchin, S., Montalvo, B.G., Jr., Rosman, B.L., & Schumer, F. *Families of the Slums*. New York: Basic Books, 1967.

Minuchin, S., Rosman, B.L., & Baker, L. *Psychosomatic Families: Anorexia Nervosa in Context*. Cambridge: Harvard University Press, 1978.

Patterson, G.R. The aggressive child: Victim and architect of a coercive system. In E.J. Mash, L.A. Hamerlynck, & L.C. Handy (Eds.), *Behavior Modification and Families*. New York: Brunner/Mazel, 1976.

Patterson, G.R., Reid, J.B., Jones, R.R. & Conger, R.E. *A Social Learning Approach to Family Intervention (Vol. I): Families with Aggressive Children*, Eugene, OR: Castalia, 1975.

Seligman, M.E.P. *Helplessness: On Depression, Development, and Death*. San Francisco: Freeman, 1975.

Watzlawick, P., Weakland, J.H., & Fisch, R. *Change*. New York: Norton, 1974.

Watzlawick, P., Beavin, J.H., & Jackson, D.D. *Pragmatics of Human Communication*. New York: Norton, 1967.

Editor's Commentary: The Centrality of Parental Executive Authority

Compernolle's theme is a focused one: For family therapy to have a successful outcome when the presenting difficulty is an acting-out, depressed, or otherwise upset child or adolescent, the therapist must intervene swiftly and strongly to establish or reestablish adequate and clear joint parental authority. Only when the parents function in concert and reinforce each other's requests and actions can the child know what the expectations are. After a period of testing out his or her parents' new team decisions, the youngster will no doubt feel more secure and safe, even though initially some hostility toward the parents for "ganging up against me" may be expressed. These clearer expectations and the certainty that the parents cannot be played off against each other enable the child to settle down and function better as the emotional climate is less conflicted and the child is no longer triangulated. The case example given here provides an interesting illustration of brief family therapy utilizing the strategy of strengthening the parents' joint authority and extricating the child from being "the problem" by seeing the parents alone and shifting the context and focus.

The influence of the work of several Americans on Compernolle's thinking and treatment mode in Belgium is obvious; he acknowledges what he has derived particularly from Minuchin et al., Haley, and Watzlawick et al. One also senses shades of Bowen. Here again the universality of theory, of many syndromes, and of effective therapeutic approaches becomes visible. We in turn derive reinforcement from therapists in other lands about the applicability of our theories and techniques cross-culturally and benefit from their dialogue and elaborations.

257

Chapter 15

A Model for Evaluation in Child Custody Disputes

*By Richard Chasin
and Henry Grunebaum*

Over one million children in the United States were involved in child custody decisions in the past year (Glick, 1979). Mental health professionals have been increasingly employed in such decisions. In this paper, we will delineate a model for clinicians to use in evaluating the family with respect to custody and will describe the values which guide our methods and recommendations.

During the past decade, dramatic shifts in social attitudes and court practices have eroded many of the longstanding traditions which served to make custody decisions simple and automatic. For example, it is no longer true that mothers get custody unless they are morally or mentally unfit. Less weight is now being given to the grounds for divorce, such as adultery. Socially devalued ways of life, such as homosexuality, are becoming less significant in custody determinations. One result of these changes is that we are less commonly faced with situations in which one

This article was first published in *The American Jouranl of Family Therapy*, Fall 1981, *9*, (3), 43-49.

Richard Chasin, M.D., is Assistant Clincal Professor of Psychiatry, Boston University School of Medicine, and Harvard Medical School. He is on the Faculty of the Family Institute, Cambridge, MA. Henry Grunebaum, M.D., is Director, Group and Family Psychotherapy Training, Department of Psychiatry, Cambridge Hospital, and Associate Clinical Professor of Psychiatry, Harvard Medical School.

party is supposedly "unfit" and are increasingly faced with evolving the best custody and visitation arrangement given two "good enough" parents. Another result is that parenting ability is becoming the paramount criterion for custody. It is easy to see why mental health professionals are frequently called upon to participate in the custody decision process.

However, the nature of the clinician's involvement can take many shapes. One may have been as therapist to member(s) of a divorcing family. In such an instance, the clinician may be asked to provide information to an attorney, give a deposition, speak to a court-appointed *guardian ad litem*, or testify as an expert witness in court. In this paper, we will not deal with such involvements but rather treat only those situations in which the professional enters a case specifically to aid the custody decision process.

A variety of contributions have been made to assist professionals in this role. Watson (1977) describes a method whereby the clinician is an active participant in custody negotiations. McDermott et al. (1978) show how videotapes of families doing specific tasks can facilitate decision-making. Goldstein, Freud and Solnit (1973) propose that it is of value for professionals to move quickly and decisively toward a permanent "least detrimental alternative." Gardner (1977) offers a multiplicity of practical suggestions for both parents and clinicians. Our thinking has been much influenced by a publication of The Group for the Advancement of Psychiatry (GAP, 1980) which deals with the issue of custody in detail and in depth.

Most of the contributions aimed at assisting professionals who participate in the custody decision process have been concerned with the nature of the interaction between clinicians and other participants, the values that should guide custody decisions, or very specific procedures and devices one might use in performing custody evaluations. In our paper we will attempt to integrate all of these elements into a single model.

One major guideline in our model is that the mental health professional should strive to establish and maintain a neutral position equidistant from each parent. In general, we avoid providing an evaluation for only one party to a dispute. Doing so may invite a confusing and destructive battle of experts, each of whom draws conclusions from studying a fragment of the situation. Furthermore, it engages the child in a process which is predesigned to injure the interests of one of his/her parents. We prefer strongly to act only when both parties and their attorneys agree to hire us as impartial evaluators of the entire situation. Often a judge will ask us to perform an independent investigation by appointing us *guardian ad litem*. Even in these instances it is best that our selection for that task have the support of both parties and their lawyers. Even when the court does not appoint us as a *guardian ad litem*, we do not avoid testifying in court. We do so to minimize the likelihood that the parent dissatisfied with our results will call upon the court to provide a new evaluation, thus increasing the emotional and financial expense without providing necessarily any new findings or recommendations.

We ask both parties to sign an agreement which outlines the evaluation process and criteria that we use in making recommendations. In our financial agreement, we prefer to have the husband and wife share the expense of our work, except in cases where it would not be equitable to do so. We insist on payment in advance since it is tempting for parents not to pay for findings and recommendations which displease them.

Let us now turn to a description of the actual procedures we employ in carrying out an evaluation. First we negotiate and agree on a contract for the evaluation. We indicate to both parents that not only will we speak to them, but we are willing to read any material they might care to submit and talk with anyone whom they feel has information bearing on the question of custody. This offer is intended to make both parents know that they will have the opportunity to present their views in the way they want to. After agreeing on a contract, we interview the parents and the children. While we start by seeing each parent alone, eventually we always meet with all the children. There is no exact formula for the composition and sequencing of the parent and child interviews. We are guided only by what seems to be the most efficient and humane way to gather information and promote resolution. In a single case we might have the following sequence of interviews: each parent separately, all children together, each parent with all the children, then each parent separately again. More complicated situations may require more interviews.

In addition to these variations, we seek out conversations with significant others, such as grandparents, housekeepers, friends, teachers, physicians, neighbors and psychotherapists. Interviews may take place in our offices, on the phone or in home visits. Finally, if the situation is moving toward a negotiated settlement, we may have a series of meetings with the parents and their attorneys.

The essential problem in the parent interview is how to elicit valid information from an individual who may be motivated more to make his/her case than to be candid. The following are basic questions we pose to each parent separately: 1) What is the ideal custody arrangement for your family? Why? 2) How would it affect you if the other parent got custody? 3) Joint custody involves equally shared decision-making and may or may not involve equally shared child care. What would be its benefits and drawbacks for your family? 4) What aspects of your ideal arrangement would you be willing to negotiate? 5) For each child, describe his/her daily routine, friends, teachers, likes, dislikes, interests, fears, skills and problems. For each problem, describe the remedy you feel would be most effective. 6) What are your strongest assets as a parent? What are your weaknesses? 7) What are the strengths and weaknesses of the other parent? Our further lines of inquiry are guided by the answers to these questions and by the special issues of the case. Our attitude in the interviews is serious, concerned and empathic. In most cases we tell parents that a decision made by them will be superior to one imposed by the courts, and that we support the idea of a negotiated settlement.

Before discussing the conduct of the child's interview, it is important to state both the benefits and hazards of the child's direct participation in the custody investigation. In custody cases, even more than in clinical situations, we cannot rely on second-hand information about children. Thus, for the purpose of getting objective information alone, we must see the children ourselves. However, there are other reasons to include them in the process. It gives children an opportunity to have some impact on their future, and it makes it easier for parents to shift their focus from their own wishes to the needs of the children. While, in our experience, most children do not want to express an opinion which will be decisive in determining custody, some do. And almost all children want the decision makers to know them as distinctive human beings and to know their opinions and feelings concerning custody. Often they want to make statements "for the record": A child may want to avoid guilt by declaring that he or she has no opinion about custody or that he or she opposes any arrangement except joint custody.

There are also hazards in the child's active participation in the custody decision process. Many young children feel responsible for the divorce. If the decision injures one of the parents, such a child may feel an increased sense of guilt. When a parent has abused a child, that child is in a position to betray his/her parent and yet may be most fearful of doing so. We know of children who have testified "against" one parent in court and who have never been able to reestablish a relationship with that parent, even though the parent sought to do so. The child's guilt was too great. Children's feelings of love and attachment can also be a problem. Often children will seek to live with the parent who they feel needs them the most; occasionally even a psychotic parent. A final hazard is that indelicate or dishonest handling of a child by professionals may result in the child's future mistrust of legal and therapeutic processes.

We are convinced that all these hazards are aggravated when the dispute is long and bitter. In an extended dispute, the child's sense of security and stability is disrupted. What is a long time for adults may be experienced as "forever" by a child. Thus, a timely and good decision is generally better than a "best" decision that takes years to make.

Our interviews with each child include several key steps.

1) We tell the parents exactly what we want them to say to the child about the interview. For example, "You are going to see someone who will help us decide the best way for us to take care of you after the divorce. He won't hurt you or give you tests. He wants to play with you. He wants to understand you." We tell the parent that our first question to the child will be, "What did your parent tell you about your visit to me?" Thus, after a brief introduction we would open the child interview by asking, "What did your parent say this visit was about?"

2) We explain, "Your parents do not now agree about how much each of them should take care of you after the divorce. I hope I can help them come to an agreement about it. If I can't, I will have to tell a judge what I learn from you and others. When I talk to the judge, your parents will hear what I have to say. The judge will listen to me, to your parents, and to other people who care about you. The judge then will decide the best way for your parents to take care of you."

3) We tell the child, "My job is to help you get what is best for you. I will try to answer any question you have. I shall ask you to tell me or play out things about you and your family, but you do not have to reply when you don't know the answer or when you do not feel ready to talk about the question I am asking."

Younger children may not understand much or may need us to repeat, to paraphrase, to tell stories about, or play out what we say in order to grasp it.

We believe that in most instances each child should be seen alone and then together with his/her siblings before being seen with the parents. In the individual interview one has the best opportunity to establish rapport, to use age-appropriate play materials and to learn about matters which the child may be reluctant to reveal in front of others, particularly about his/her custody preference. It is often useful to approach the custody issue indirectly by asking a question such as, "What do you imagine it would be like if you spent weekdays with mother and weekends with father?" Such an approach permits the child to avoid asserting directly a preference thereby reducing his/her sense of responsibility and guilt for the final decision. In addition, the child's stated preference is frequently less useful than his/her reflections on each plausible alternative arrangement. Sometimes children override this careful approach and state, "But you haven't asked *me* what I want."

In the meeting with all the children together, we learn a great deal about the quality of family life and about each parent. A child in the presence of siblings is stimulated to be more candid than when seen alone by a strange adult. Furthermore, the sibling meeting may reveal patterns of alliance and antagonism among siblings—a crucial factor if one is considering split custody.

The meetings with the children together with one parent are structured around specific tasks. An evaluator will learn very little if he/she just sits back and expects the family to interact in a natural and informal way. Tasks should be so designed as to elucidate the nature of the parent-child relationship. A parent might be asked to guide a three-year-old in play to build a structure of blocks, or to make up a puppet play, or plan a vacation with older children. Mostly we learn by directly observing the parents' attentiveness, understanding, empathy, capacity to talk and play with a child on the child's level, and the capacity to allow spontaneity and maintain discipline.

When our investigation is over, we prepare a report which includes our findings, the plausible alternatives and our recommendations. The following principles guide our thinking:

1) Studies of children of divorce convince us that the child should experience as little loss as possible. Therefore, we prefer that both parents—if competent—continue to share substantially in decision making and child care since this makes detachment of a parent less likely. If the intensity of active conflict between parents precludes mature cooperation, most decision making and child care must begin to rest with one parent. We disagree with Goldstein, Freud and Solnit (1973) that the custodial parent should determine visitation. Visitation is not a right of the noncustodial parent to see the child, but rather a right of the child to not lose access to either parent.

2) In recommending custody for one parent, we favor the parent who: (a) Is most likely to foster visitation and who shows the most objective and respectful attitude toward the other parent. This principle is an update of King Solomon's rule that the better parent is the one who would rather give up the child than see it destroyed. (b) The parent who

will maintain the greater continuity of child contact with relatives, friends, neighborhood, school, etc. (c) The parent who has the best skill in dealing with the child. Skill includes empathy, detailed knowledge of the child's life, ability to talk at the child's level, appreciation of the child's developmental needs, and competence at guidance, discipline and problem solving. (d) The parent who shows humanity, consistency and flexibility in handling the child. (e) The parent to whom the child is most deeply attached. This principle should not be applied when the basis for the attachment is grounded in the wish to take care of the parent. We do attempt to find safe ways for a child to maintain contact with unfit or abusive parents.

We should include a note about age. Ordinarily, very young children should have frequent short visitation, even if such visits need to take place in the home of the custodial parent. The risk of detachment increases with every week that goes by without contact between an infant and a visiting parent. Older children can manage longer intervals between visits better. The wishes of adolescents should be a key determining factor in choosing custody. It is common for adolescents to choose to remain with the parent of the same sex. This choice often is the outcome of good parenting on the part of the parent who is being left, even though it often feels cruel to a mother that her son wishes to leave her just when he is becoming interesting company. Sometimes the child's wish should not be granted, as in cases where a girl is avoiding normal struggles with mother in order to live with previously distant, attractive, less competent father.

Siblings, particularly before adolescence, should remain together unless they are markedly disinterested in or chronically destructive to one another. If they are separated, they should have ample opportunity to visit each other.

Recommendations should not only provide for current custody, but should look to the future and allow for modifications as the children get older.

Divorce is a family crisis, and a divorce with a custody dispute is a particularly dangerous family crisis. All professionals involved in such disputes should appreciate the potential damage of the dispute itself. They should do everything possible to help the family make the dispute a situation in which they use professionals as aids in resolving crises rather than a situation in which professionals join forces with destructive elements in the family, deepen rigidities, aggravate hostilities, stimulate betrayals, and prolong an embattled atmosphere.

BASIC CONTRACT

Dear ....:

You have requested that I make an evaluation and a written report with respect to the determination of appropriate custody and visitation arrangements concerning your minor children.

My evaluation and report are to be prepared in connection with the case now pending in the .... Probate Court, involving these issues.

I have carried out such professional services in the past, and my experience has been that, because of the highly emotional and important nature of the questions involved, the parents react to my evaluation and report according to whether or not they are pleased with my conclusions. I have also found that, although one or both parties have agreed to be responsible for the payment of my professional fees, I have often had difficulty in being paid because of one party or another's displeasure with the outcome of my evaluation.

Rather than beginning the work in an evaluation without making certain things clear, I have decided that it is better to have various matters understood in advance.

I am willing to be retained by both of you to perform the evaluation and furnish a report in connection with the Probate proceedings but only upon the following express conditions, which must be accepted and approved by you:

1. Although you, ..., as the parents of minor children have retained me, my sole responsibility is to evaluate and report what in my professional opinion is in the best interest of the minor children under the family circumstances as to custody, visitation and matters pertaining thereto.

2. My usual procedure in performing my evaluation and in the preparing of a report is as follows below. By your acceptance and approval of this letter, each of you agree that such procedure is appropriate and is accepted by you in connection with my performing the evaluation that you requested.

   (a) It is my usual procedure to talk with both parents separately; and to talk with their children separately, as well. Sometimes I will interview the children with one or both parents—or, depending upon age, will visit in their home. Not infrequently, it is necessary to see some of the members of the family a second time as well to discuss the situation with knowledgeable outsiders, such as: family service officers attached to the Court; professionals such as psychiatrists, and teachers; relatives who may have useful information; and, on rare occasions, others. No interview will be held with any individual who is not a member of the immediate family without your knowledge.

(b) In addition, supplementary materials in written form are useful (reports from social services and from other consultants). Often, one or both parents wish to submit their personal views in writing in addition to discussing them in person. Finally, psychological testing of one or both parents and/or children is often part of an evaluation.

(c) Making a recommendation for custody and visitation is difficult, for there are no clear-cut guidelines. However, I think it appropriate that you should know the guidelines I follow. In general, I try to make a determination in the best interest of the whole family unit, which I view as continuing even though under the different circumstances. The husband/wife relationship has ended but the father/mother relationship continues. I try to have the child remain in continuing contact with both parents and their extended families. Placement with a specific parent will not be determined by the sex of that parent, religion, race, political or ideological belief or psychological health even though each of these is a consideration. Similarly, continuity of school, neighborhood and friendship are significant, but not determining factors.

(d) This outline of procedure is meant to be viewed as an outline. It is by no means intended to cover all of the factors that I will try to give consideration, but rather to give you some idea of my procedure and views in helping you with this difficult decision.

3. I shall be compensated for all services, other than Court appearances at the rate of .... per hour. This rate is applicable to all time spent in evaluation: interviewing of children, parents, siblings, and any other person I feel may have information which may be helpful to me; as well as time spent in preparation of the report and in discussing the same with the parents or their attorneys. The time spent in psychological testing performed by me or others will also

be at the rate of .... per hour, or the flat fee the consultant charges.

4. Before I do any work, I will receive a retainer of .... to be applied against payment for services as performed. Should my services and those of others result in charges equal to the amount of the retainer, then I will be paid an additional retainer in the same amount immediately; and until I receive same, I need not go forward with any further work or services.

5. Each of you shall be jointly, and singularly, responsible for the payment of all my fees and those of any consultants and agree to pay such bills as they are rendered.

6. I will not be called upon to furnish my report to any person nor to file the same in Court or discuss its contents in any way until all of my fees for services and the services of any consultants I may have retained shall have been paid in full.

7. In connection with any Court appearance, I request that I not be called upon as a witness, nor that you or either of your counsel issue a subpoena requiring my attendance on less than seven days prior notice. I must request this as a condition so that I will have sufficient time to reschedule patients who are in treatment with me on a regularly scheduled basis.

8. In connection with my attendance in Court, I am to be compensated at the rate of .... for being present at Court either the morning or the afternoon session.

9. It is understood that I will make every effort to cooperate and to be available if called upon to testify, I will still be compensated according to the rates in Paragraph 8 above.

10. Each of you agree that under no circumstances shall I be required to attend any Court session, or give any testimony in any hearing if, at that time, I have not been paid in full for all services and all consultants' bills have been paid in full as well. You agree to instruct your respective attorneys to abide by this requirement.

In order that each of you has some idea of my qualifications and to enable you to review them, and be satisfied with them, before I begin to perform any services, I have attached a resume of education and experience hereto.

AS EVIDENCE OF YOUR AGREEMENT THAT THE FOREGOING ARE THE TERMS AND CONDITIONS UNDER WHICH I HAVE BEEN

RETAINED, PLEASE SIGN A COPY OF THIS LETTER, AS BELOW
PROVIDED:

Very truly yours,

....

HENRY GRUNEBAUM, M.D.

ACCEPTED & APPROVED BY:

....

(MOTHER)

....

DATE

....

(FATHER)

....

DATE

THE PROVISIONS OF THE FOREGOING LETTER ARE ACCEPTED
INSOFAR AS THEY CONCERN DR. GRUNEBAUM'S ATTENDANCE
AT ANY PROCEEDINGS AS A WITNESS OR THE RELEASE OF ANY
REPORT OR OTHER MATERIAL DEVELOPED IN THE COURSE OF
HIS EVALUATION.

....

(ATTORNEY FOR MOTHER)

....

DATE

....

(ATTORNEY FOR FATHER)

....

DATE

REFERENCES

GAP Committee on the Family. *Divorce, Child Custody, and the Family.* New York: Group for the Advancement of Psychiatry, CL#443, 1980.

Gardner, R. *Parents' Book About Divorce.* New York: Doubleday, 1977.

Glick, P. C. Children of divorced parents in demographic perspective. *Journal of Social Issues*, 1979, *35*, (4).

Goldstein, J., Freud, A., & Solnit, A. *Beyond the Best Interests of the Child.* New York: The Free Press, 1973.

McDermott, J. F. Jr., Wen-Shing Tseng, Char, W.F. and Fukunaga, C. S. Child custody decision making: The search for improvement. *American Academy of Child Psychiatry*, 1978, *17*, (1).

Watson, A.S. Child custody problems during divorce. *Weekly Psychiatry Update Series*, 1977, *2*, (2).

Editor's Commentary: Whither the Children of Divorce?

No "International Book of Family Therapy" would be sufficiently comprehensive and representative in the 1980s if it did not include a treatise on children, particularly those affected by divorce and child custody disputes. Given that the divorce rate continues to spiral upward in numerous countries around the world, family therapists almost everywhere are concerned about the rapidly escalating number of children whose parents decide to dissolve their marriage, thereby severely altering the structure and dynamics of the family and placing the child in a turbulent and trying situation.

In this pithy article Chasin and Grunebaum convey their procedures for doing child custody evaluations. Since this has been an area of particular interest in my own work (see, for example, Kaslow, 1979; 1980; 1981), I resonate to the soundness and clarity of much that they are saying. Particularly valuable is their clear contracting, including asking that both parents share in paying the cost of the evaluation, that payment be made in advance of service so as not to be contingent on receiving a report favorably disposed to the recommendation they desire, and their pointing out the advantages of a negotiated settlement (over, we can assume, a courtroom custody battle) and joint custody, whenever feasible. I also agree with the general sequence of the various interviews, the key questions they are likely to pose, and the room allowed for flexibility and tailoring the queries to the particular people and situation. It is refreshing to receive nonrigid guidelines. Also to be emulated is their predilection for being appointed the child's guardian ad litem so that it is apparent they are seeking to determine what is in the best interest of the child and not to be in either an adversary or advocacy position for or against either parent. Their suggestions for involving the child in the evaluation alone, with siblings, and with each parent is a sound one. So is the statement that children should not be asked to state their preference for a custodial parent but rather to describe relationships and possible future situations, as an indirect way to glean their wishes, thereby avoiding placing them in a loyalty bind.

I take issue with these authors on one statement. They indicate that when children are prepared for their visit with the evaluator they should be told there is no testing and then that none will be done. In some instances I have not found the use of straight and indirect questions, play sessions, interactive tasks and role playing sufficient to acquire an understanding of some of the in-depth feelings and intrapsychic dynamics in a complex case where the youngster has become skilled at masking feelings and camouflaging thoughts for self-protection and in order not to further hurt parents. Here, and when a dynamic formulation about what really constitutes the best interest of the child is at issue, I think that a good battery of judiciously selected psychological tests is very much in order. Judges tend to respect results from standardized tests when one is called as an expert witness. Rather than just giving one's clinical opinion, one can back this up with objective test data checked for reliability and validity against a large body of documented research data. Of course, the therapist would need to be competent in psychodiagnosis and test interpretation or refer to another colleague who is.

For some clients being evaluated, the authors' model contract might prove wordier than necessary. It could be streamlined, avoiding such phrases as "my usual procedure" and just outlining the process. Also, passive rather than active voice could be used to make a less personal and more objective sounding document. This should minimize inducing possible negative transference phenomena which are more likely when the evaluator talks about "I."

There are some salient points that are not included, no doubt because of the shortness of the original article. I think it important to mention that there are child advocates (O'Shea & Connery, 1980) who perceive their role as very similar to that described herein. Also, there are an increasing number of mental-health-trained as well as law-trained family and divorce mediators who specialize in child custody settlements. The latter group also often handles support payment and visitation negotiations, with a respectful awareness of the tax implications which surround financial stipulations. There is much that the psychiatrist, psychologist, family therapist, or social worker engaging in custody evaluations can learn and borrow from these other professionals to enrich his or her own practice.

REFERENCES

O'Shea, A.T. & Connery, M.G. The child advocate attorney—The mental health professional: A current courtship. *Journal of Marital and Family Therapy*, July 1980, *6*, (3), 277-284.

Kaslow, F.W. Divorce and divorce therapy. In A.S. Gurman & D.P. Kniskern (Eds.), *Handbood of Family Therapy*. New York: Brunner/Mazel, 1981.

Kaslow, F.W. Stages of divorce: A psychological perspective. *Villanova Law Review*, 1979-1980, *25*, 4-5, 718-751.

Part III

*Family Therapy within
the Institutional and
Societal Context*

Chapter 16

The Inpatient Care
of Families at Vikersund

By Ingerid S. Ravnsborg

This article describes a unique and interesting family inpatient treatment program situated in a tranquil rural community 50 miles outside of Oslo. Screening of families is rigorous and families consider themselves fortunate to be accepted there. A variety of treatment modalities are utilized selectively. Progress seems good and the modality appears to yield lasting benefits.

The family department at Modum Bads Nervesanatorium, Vikersund, is one of the very few hospital units in the world where whole families can be admitted for family treatment and live in houses of their own.

The initiative to build this hospital came from a group of practicing Christians, both doctors and laymen. The central force was Gordon Johnsen, a psychiatrist. After some years of preparation, the group bought an old place that had been a spa from 1858. This resort had contained many small, wooden, Swiss-style bungalows, and a few large ones. Some of these still existed when the new hospital, Modum Bads Nervesanatorium, was built from 1955 to 1957. The hospital is situated in the country, some 50 miles west of Oslo.

The hospital admits patients from all over Norway. During the first

This is a slightly revised version of an article which originally appeared in the *International Journal of Family Psychiatry*, 1980, *1*, 3, 373-392.

Ingerid S. Ravnsborg, M.D., is Clinical Director of the Family Department at Modum Bads Nervesanatorium, Vikersund, Norway.

six to eight years, only individual patients were admitted, but later this pattern changed. Often it was helpful to see the close relatives of the patient and readjust the pattern of interaction within the family. The old wooden bungalows made this possible. The relatives were invited to come and stay in one of the bungalows for some days or weeks as guests of the hospital. The patient moved out of the ward and stayed with the family; the psychiatrist could see the whole family together and get a feeling of its life style. This was felt to be very useful, and gradually plans for a continuous family department materialized. This meant investment in buildings, staff, philosophy, treatment—and finances.

FACILITIES

The original wooden bungalows, constructed for summer use only, were rebuilt and modernized for use all the year round. Gradually eight houses were completed, five for families (one family in each) and three for married couples (two couples in each). Each house has a kitchen, a sitting room, two to three bedrooms, and one to two bathrooms. The family department is like a small village.

The village also has a building that contains a kindergarten for children under school age (that is, under seven) on the ground floor and a center that provides occupational therapy for the grown-ups on the first floor. This center is also open for use in the families' spare time and has a TV for evening use. For the school children (seven to sixteen years old), there is a school with five or six small rooms in an older building. The hospital's church is also situated in the village, but of course serves more than the family department. One new building was built in 1974, connected with the main hospital. It contains a large sitting room, offices for doctors and for nurses, an observation room for the child psychiatrist, a medical library, and a video studio, among other facilities. The patients have access to the hospital's dining room, library, table-tennis room, sports grounds, swimming pool, etc. The hospital keeps three ponies for riding, two Icelandic horses and one Shetland pony, and these are an integrated part of the week's program for the families.

The staff of the department consists of the clinical director, who is a psychiatrist, one child psychiatrist, one psychologist, one family therapist, one trainee psychiatrist, six milieu therapists (of these five are psychiatric nurses and one is a preschool teacher), two occupational therapists, one trainee in occupational therapy, one leader of the kindergarten, and two and a half school teachers. The teachers are paid by the local borough council (the only ones paid in this way) but work in the department as closely as the others.

Regarding finances, the hospital's and the patient's rights are now the same as for other hospital patients in Norway. In the beginning, the relatives of the individual patients were just guests. Later the hospital got a 40 percent contribution for their care from the National Health Service. After the hospital managed to convince the authorities that it was clinically effective to have all the members of the family there and that such treatment paid in the long run, the hospital got full allowance for all family members as if they all were individual patients. The patients themselves get full rights regarding salaries and side pay, just as if they were in a hospital for other reasons. The patients themselves pay nothing to the hospital. The hospital is privately owned, which makes flexible administration possible. The administration is responsible to a board and to the state's health department.

ADMISSIONS POLICY

Admissions are based on written applications from professionals treating people all over the country. These are general practitioners, family counselors, psychiatrists, school psychologists, and ministers. As we get more applicatants than we can admit, a selection must be undertaken. Two main factors influence our admissions policy. The first is geographical. If the distance to reach any qualified family treatment is so great that this is virtually impossible, we can admit a family on the grounds that this is their only chance. Since this is the case for a number of families, we get a variety of problems. The problems may be presented by the parents or the children, or by both. Among the children, symptoms have included anxiety, symbiosis, encopresis, school phobia, maladaptation, and so on; among the parents, all kinds of emotional conflict, including aggressive behavior, drug and alcohol abuse, and sexual malfunction. In some families admitted, the question of divorce is being discussed, but this is more often so with married couples without children.

The other factor affecting admission is a specific clinical indication: where inpatient therapy would provide more advantages than an ambulant therapy. As we claim that *all* family members must be willing to join in the therapy as long as the stay lasts, we have the advantage over other therapies that every family member is present and gets involved. Thus, if a local ambulant therapy proves ineffective but the therapist and patients are still motivated for further, closer, more concentrated and coordinated work, we can accept such a family. An example is a multiproblem family in which the therapy needs to be concentrated and administered by a single team. Behavior disorders, such as aggression, fits, and withdrawal among the children or parents are accepted on this basis. Persistent school phobia has proved amenable to our therapy. If individual treatment has failed with a patient in a severe state of anxiety, or a patient does not dare to leave his or her partner, this can be a valid reason for admission where maintaining the marriage seems an important goal. Sexual malfunctioning may be grounds, if other factors have been solved or are nonexistent.

What we do not admit are psychotic families or families with a psychotic member. Drug addiction or alcoholism must be under control before admission. This form of inpatient treatment demands some emotional stability, intellectual resources, and motivation. When these qualities are lacking, we have sometimes failed. If each partner in a marriage just wants the therapist to understand that all problems are related to the other partner, it is hard to get anywhere. We feel that social problems mainly related to housing, neighbors, or the economy are not valid reasons for admission.

Before we decide to admit, correspondence with the local doctor or with the family itself may be necessary. Sometimes the family is seen at the hospital or in their own home before a final decision is made. The families accepted for admission are put on a waiting list.

INVESTIGATION

When a family is admitted, investigation is started gradually. The main therapist and the milieu therapist act as therapist and cotherapist respectively. There are one or two initial interviews about the present problems, then background, life history, and a clinical record for each adult is taken by the therapist. A somatic examination is carried out. Further tests often administered are the Wheelwright test for couples, Kvebaeks' Sculpture Test, and the Rorschach for couples.

The milieu therapist takes a clinical record for each child in talks with the child and its parents. The somatic examination of the children is carried out by the child psychiatrist, who happens to be a pediatrician as well. If any emotional symptoms are observed in the children, the child psychiatrist expands her work to more detailed interviews, tests, and drawing and play observation. The Children's Apperception Test (CAT) is the most common test utilized.

The parents start immediately in occupational therapy. Here the staff observes how they work and adapt, how they occupy themselves, and how they relate to each other and to other patients.

The children attend school and the teachers see them during lessons and breaks. They observe their intellectual capacity and their emotional reactions. In the small school, which covers nine grades, the pupils are divided into two to three groups. This often provides an opportunity to see siblings' reactions to one another at school. In the kindergarten, the staff see the small children and make their observations while caring for them.

After about two weeks in the family department, all information is brought together at a staff evaluation meeting. An assessment of the family is formulated and a plan made about what kind of treatment shall be carried out and about *who* is to do *what*. Later the same day these thoughts and plans are discussed with the family itself. The date for discharge is sometimes fixed at the staff meeting, sometimes not until after a second follow-up discussion.

An example can be given of the investigation in an uncomplicated small family. A father, thirty-six years old, a mother, twenty-nine years old, and their four-year-old daughter have been admitted after application from their local doctor and a local psychologist. The main symptom presented is the mother's state of anxiety. In addition to or connected with this is the daughter's restlessness, day-wetting, and anxiety. Lastly, there is the father's dissatisfaction with his job as a cook in a small restaurant—a job that involves working late nights.

The investigation starts with the taking of a detailed case history about the present symptoms, problems, and family situation. Two case history sessions are held in their house, with all three family members present, plus the cotherapist and the psychiatrist. They are asked about their own needs and what changes each of them hopes to gain during the stay.

Later we take individual case histories for all three family members, their background, family of origin, relation to parents and peers, school, work, etc. With the two adults together, we take the marriage history: how they met, what attracted them to each other, and how it all has developed through the years. The years they have been together we want to hear about when both are present.

A physical examination is carried out on each of the three.

The adults go to occupational therapy, and the occupational therapist observes their relation to work, to the other patients, and to each other. Later in the stay they are also given a cooperation test; they must produce a collage from pictures cut out of magazines. We observe the topics each of them chooses and how they put it all together on one large sheet of cardboard.

To see more of both their personalities, they are given a Wheelwright. This they take in a group of the patient population. The scores are discussed generally in the group and in more detail with the couple, to see how the two personalities relate to each other.

A visiting psychologist who comes once a week administers the Rorschach for couples test. This psychologist has developed a special technique and is experienced with couples. Each couple is given this test and the scores and written evaluation brought back to them.

The daughter is seen by the child psychiatrist both for the physical examination and for psychiatric evaluation. A CAT is given and there are two play observation tests.

TREATMENT

Treatment goes on all day. In the morning from 7:45 A.M. to 8:15 A.M. the milieu therapist pays a visit to the house and sees the family. At 8:30 A.M. the school children go to school, which lasts till 1:00 P.M. The small children are taken to the kindergarten just before 9:00 A.M. and collected at 1:30 P.M. at the latest. From 9:00 A.M. till 1 P.M., the adults are in occupational therapy, interrupted by a coffee break from 11:00 A.M. to 11:30 A.M. and by sessions with the other therapists.

At 1:30 P.M., one member from each family collects a ready-made hot dinner from the main kitchen. They take this back to their house and the family eats together. Sometimes the milieu therapist eats with the family. During the rest of the day there is nothing compulsory, but several things have to be done. For example, food needs to be brought in for the morning and evening meals and clothes need washing. There are also possibilities for sports, cycling, swimming, discussion group with the pastor, TV, and country dance group. Each child can go riding twice a week, the parents being responsible for saddling and leading ponies which belong to the hospital.

Each family and couple have three to five psychotherapy sessions every week, each lasting one hour. The sessions include the whole family or just the couple, depending on the nature of the problem. We may also alternate, sometimes including the children, sometimes leaving them out. Both the therapist and the cotherapist take part. The cotherapist also sees the family in the house later in the day and may hear their reactions to the session and answer questions. The cotherapist can also plan practical training with members of the family. She or he can discuss and make agreements about changes in the family regarding attitudes and about practical tasks for the different members. An important part of this session is discussion with the family members to make clear what each member shall be responsible for, such as, children getting to bed at an agreed time. Sometimes contracts are written for training projects or distribution of tasks in the family. The milieu therapist checks how these are working.

The work done at occupational therapy is not industrial, but includes various forms of handwork—weaving, painting, sewing, & carpentry. In summer, sometimes there is out-of-doors work instead, on the grounds, like picking berries. The goal is activity and self-confidence, together with the joy of doing things never tried before. The patients usually choose themselves what they want to do, but sometimes suggestions are made. Sex roles can be expressed and also moderated through this work; men often like to learn how to handle a sewing machine so they can sew a pair of trousers or a shirt for themselves. Sometimes we utilize collaboration work, using the occupational therapist and the milieu therapist. Each member of the couple gets, for example, the task of cutting out the pictures they like from old magazines. After thirty minutes, they have to put a collage together on one large sheet. At a later session they may pick a topic for their cutting, for example, what each wants from the other, and what each wants to give him or her. After the collaboration exercise, they talk about their feelings related to it.

If there are difficulties, such as quarreling in the family, the milieu therapist, being closest to them, will try to help them understand the problem.

At 4 P.M. the staff leave; what happens after this the family members have to clear up themselves. They can ring for a nurse on duty in another department, but as the evening's possible difficulties have been anticipated and discussed earlier in the day, assistance from outside is rarely necessary.

Psychotherapy sessions deal with current problems seen in the light of an individual's upbringing, early relationships to parents, and experiences in later life. The theory behind our practice is eclectic. Although the therapists on the staff are all psychoanalytically oriented, as is the hospital in general, communication models, system theories, three-generation thinking, and behavior therapy are all employed to varying degrees. The department is necessarily organized as a therapeutic community, with quite a lot of responsibility given to the patients as a group and to the family unit.

When sexual problems are seen as important and therapy is indicated and possible, we employ a concentrated period of work based on techniques derived from Masters and Johnson. This therapy may last from two to four weeks, and we ask the couple to leave the children behind for this period.

As part of our therapy, there are also group sessions. Patients are offered two weekly lectures, with discussions following. One is about marriage; the other, about child development and the relationships between children and parents. Information from these groups often activates a couple, and they bring the information and their reactions to it into the sessions with their own therapists.

Information on, and models for, cooperation are also provided through the weekly "playing hour." Parents are invited to take part in the kindergarten one hour a week, together with all the kindergarten children, parents, and kindergarten staff. The parents also meet the leader of the kindergarten separately and can discuss their own children and the resources and problems observed.

The school teachers see the parents once a week, sometimes less frequently, to discuss the parents' relationship to the pupil and his or her school work. The first stay for a family with children is often ten to twelve weeks. Readmissions are accepted. In some cases this possibility is mentioned when a family is discharged. If, when they return home, it is apparent that some improvement has taken place but that further treatment is needed, a readmission may occur. Readmissions after several years also occur, but usually a limited, specific goal is identified before this takes place. Stays for readmission, like those for observation, normally last for from one to three weeks. The average stay is for forty-one days.

During the last weeks of a stay, we begin to discuss what kind of aftercare will be necessary, and how it can best be carried out. If the family does not live too far away, the hospital staff can continue as therapists. In most cases, however, a contact close to home is the most practical, and correspondence with, or visits to or from, local professionals take place during the stay.

STAFF TRAINING

Working with families requires experience and wisdom. We prefer staff with some maturity and some clinical experience previous to starting in our department, but training is continued once they are employed. We like about equal members of each sex on the staff and find that the experience of married life is also useful. Neither of these goals is totally met. At present we have more women than men, some of whom are unmarried.

The trainee psychiatrist has usually first been three to four years in another department in our own hospital, or elsewhere. The psychologist is expected to be a specialist in clinical psychology and to have experience with children, young people, and family work. This is even more important in regard to the child psychiatrist. The rules for becoming a specialist in clinical psychology or child psychiatry are quite strict in Norway, and include supervision over several years. The six milieu personnel are usually trained nurses. Some have the one to two years' additional psychiatric nurse's training. Some have been trained as district nurses and have experience from working in social care with families.

In our department, supplementary training is given both to the staff as a whole and to groups divided up by profession.

The case presentations and discussions at the evaluation meetings are good training and education for all present. They are also attended by visitors and trainees attached to the hospital for shorter periods, who are free to offer additional ideas and suggestions. The evaluation meetings play an important role in conveying common thinking and style to new co-workers, so that the department can work as a unit with the same goals and ideals. (Openness, for example, is one of the department's main ideals.)

Some training is given to the therapists along with staff from other departments. The hospital is equipped with video studios and a one-way mirror. Our department uses this equipment for two weekly supervision groups for the therapists, each lasting one and one-half hours. Each group consists of five to seven staff, including at least one senior person who is a qualified supervisor. The senior therapists have irregular ad hoc individual supervision, but they are also supervised by the team at the evaluation meetings and by their colleagues. The milieu therapists have one hour a week of individual supervision by the head nurse. The trainee psychiatrist is supervised by the child psychiatrist. The school and kindergarten staff have supervision in groups, also led by the child psychiatrist. More specific training is given during a one hour a week study group for the milieu therapists and kindergarten staff. Here literature is studied and discussed. Virginia Satir's work has been utilized in this connection.

Four or five bigger seminars are held each year at the hospital; two of these are on family therapy. The staff attend these seminars and often have the task of presenting papers.

CASE REPORTS

The problems and the families are never alike. It is not possible to say that one special constellation is typical. Two different cases are presented as illustrations: one couple and one family.

Case 1

A married couple presented to us, with the wife suffering from anxiety and with the problem that during seven years of marriage there had yet been no sexual intercourse. The marriage was said to be stable and good. They were admitted for observation, with the possibility of sex therapy, if indicated.

The wife was twenty-seven, the husband twenty-nine. The husband was an only son, with one sister. He lived a sheltered life close to both parents. He had a handicap from birth, a clubfoot, which prevented him from taking part fully in sports. He was a shy, kind boy, and was active in the church to which his parents belonged. Both parents had died in an accident when he was eighteen. He then left school and started work on the railway, the same work his father had done. Sexually he was slow and shy.

The wife was the second of four sisters. She had a poor relationship with a nagging mother to whom she never felt close. The relationship with her father was somewhat better, but he had been an alcoholic, noisy when drunk, dissatisfied with life and his job.

The daughter, our patient, suffered from anxiety early in her life. She feared animals, illnesses, strangers, and buses. Her mother found this impossible to understand and gave her little support. The girl was bright at school. Her anxiety decreased gradually up to the age of thirteen. Then it suddenly worsened again when she fell in love with a boy in her class. Her love lasted for three or four years, but the boy did not feel as fond of her as she was of him. She completed secondary school and went on to a secretarial college. In her work as a bookkeeper she did well.

Our couple had met at a party. He had a kind, peaceful way that she liked, and she had a vivid, active way that appealed to him. After a year and a half they married. They have always enjoyed each other's company, but after marriage they found that attempts at sexual intercourse caused her pain and could not take place. She became anxious when he tried, and he gave up.

After three years, she went to a doctor who gave her some lubricating cream without examining her. After two more years, she was examined and a thick hymen was revealed. This was operated upon, and they were told that her anatomical condition was now quite normal. Nevertheless, her anxiety and pain persisted. Her anxiety increased; she got dizziness and diarrhea when she went out, and this kept her at home. She felt uneasy about comments on their childlessness.

When they arrived at the hospital, we could confirm that many sides of the marriage functioned well. A Rorschach for couples was administered. It confirmed the matching of the two personalities and showed that she feared masculine activity, while he partly denied masculine aggression in himself. The test gave us resources for therapy. One problem was that the husband was easily offended and this made him silent. His silence aroused her irritation and this made him even more taciturn. This problem was elucidated and dealt with.

Sexually they had found their own way. She was quite active in caring for his sexual needs, but suffered with intense vaginismus and fear of penetration. When good contact had been established and a vaginal examination conducted, I prescribed a detailed training program for her alone, starting with her insertion of the smallest Hegar dilator twice a day. With such programs we like a report at the session each day. The size of the Hegar was gradually increased. After a while, some limited physical contact with the husband was to accompany the Hegar. Later penis intrusion was programmed, with a clear contract about "nothing more." After four weeks they wanted to try the "natural way." To their great surprise, they succeeded. Intercourse was not at all as complicated as they had expected. During the following weeks, I placed some restrictions on intercourse frequency, and warned that difficulties could still come.

The wife's anxiety was almost entirely absent in the hospital. We had also given her training in walking and traveling (travel by bus had been a problem). After she returned home, her anxiety was almost gone. She felt her husband to be more active and helpful in the house. Sex is quite satisfactory for both.

In this therapy, the contact and sessions with the therapist and the report program were central. The milieu therapist worked with those interactions she could see directly.

The occupational therapy proved a good milieu. Both were well accepted there. At first, the wife felt insecure, despite her high tempo and activity, but she gained some self-confidence by sewing a pair of trousers for the first time. After a pair for herself, she sewed another for her husband.

Medication was not a great factor. She had previously used a small amount of tranquilizers. This was reduced and reserved only for "great occasions."

What made this therapy a success was a combination of several factors. The couple cared for each other, had a sense of humor, and were motivated for therapy. Both personalities could be understood against the background of their family histories, and they could work with this material. The anatomical hindrances had been totally removed; what had to be loosened was a conditioned reaction. The wife's anxiety was related to her fear of men's sexual needs and aggressiveness. Her husband's cautious style and her own need for closeness helped her overcome some of this. Some of her anxiety had also to do with her feeling shame for staying childless without being sterile. She felt she misled people around her.

Case 2

This family consisted of a curate of thirty-seven married to a teacher of thirty-five, with two children of eight and five.

The first letter to the hospital came from a doctor who had been contacted by their vicar. The problem presented was the father's being harsh and dominating toward the children. The children were nervous. The wife disagreed with the husband about the children, but got nowhere. The father saw no reason for therapy or change, but the mother did. She was the one who had talked to the vicar about the situation.

After some correspondence reassuring them that we had an open village situation, a good milieu, and had had similar professional people as clients, the family elected to come. The father had expressed dislike for such words as "patient" and "admission," preferring to use instead "client" and "get a house."

At admission we found him active, preoccupied with details, trying to be positive and correct. His eyes showed distance, uncertainty. His main topic was the rhythm in the home and his wife's lack of such. She was somewhat slower and dysphoric. She stressed his dominant, authoritarian way and his strictness and brutality toward the children and herself.

The son of eight was quite tall, active, and restless; he showed anxiety. The daughter of five was a bit shy and quiet and seemed less disturbed.

The father's own father was a strict, authoritarian man. His mother was caring, but strict. They lived on a small farm. The duties on the farm had to be performed; objections were nonexistent. Three of the seven siblings had had psychological problems in their youth. He was number six. He had been quiet and shy as a boy, mediocre as a scholar, and immature. He worked as a teacher for some years before training to be a minister and had worked as such for four years. He had wanted to work for the Seaman's Mission abroad, but the organization would not accept him.

The mother's father had been a clerk. He was strict but fair and caring. Her mother was withdrawn and insecure, but a good mother. The daughter, our patient, had good contact with both. She was the eldest of four and there had been no special problems with these. There had been some indecision regarding her choice of career; finally, she decided to be a teacher. She was now working part-time.

The couple had become acquainted via an advertisement, which is unusual but not quite unknown. After three years of acquaintance, they were married in 1967. His needs had been for a partner to help him out of a lonely bed-sitter existence. Her expectations were more for companionship and equality.

In the marriage she had quickly found him to be rigid and dominating, and had reacted with passivity and submerged protest. The two children were planned, but she felt her views were unlike his and that they could not agree. He was easily irritated, brutal to her with the children present, and also brutal to the children. She felt she should continue as a teacher and did so, sometimes part-time, sometimes full-time. This meant that he had to take over the children and adapt his working hours to hers.

After contacts with her own family and the vicar, steps were taken for admission.

Once they were in the hospital, in their bungalow, we saw how he dominated the family: there were many rules about the table manners, what they ate, economy, and sleeping hours. We also saw that she was very interested in handwork at occupational therapy and enjoyed being there in her spare time during the afternoons and evenings.

The son had a shouting voice and seemed unhappy. He was left-handed, which the father disliked and punished. In the CAT test we found great anxiety, especially fear of being destroyed. In standardized play observation, he used signs and boundaries, but also chose aggressive toys. Initially he showed inhibition. The Bender Gestalt test result was poor and suggested organic brain damage, as did an EEG. At school, he gradually came into contact with the other pupils. Toward his father, he was on the alert.

The daughter of five also showed some anxiety, but less than her brother. The same tests were taken, and there were no signs of brain damage. At the kindergarten, she gradually made good contacts. But her insecurity was shown when the leader was ill one day. A new one came, and she ran out.

Individual Rorschach tests were taken of the adults. The husband was described as having psychopathic traits; his rigid rules worked as controls for primitive, poorly integrated sexual and aggressive forces. According to the test, the wife felt inferior to men, was indecisive, and sought authority. She had control of her impulses and good ego functions. Romanticizing and repression were her defenses.

In the therapy we worked on his rules and their effects on the family, but also on his need for more active, responsible behavior from her side. He said that he was willing to withdraw from so much intervention with the children, if she took a greater part. But neither of these two things happened.

After six weeks, she decided to leave him. She was supported by her relatives in this, and was invited to stay with some of them. Her plan was to live alone, with the children. He went back home to work. They were all discharged.

Eight weeks later, we got a letter from the relatives where she was staying. They found her surprisingly indifferent to the children, being more interested in her own hobbies and work. She was also now more interested in living with her husband than before.

Five months after they had been discharged, they came back for a stay—to reunite. She was more motivated for working on her lack of system—late nights and late getting ups. The relation to her own father was taken up and her fear of men grew less pronounced. As a result of this, the husband was less provoked and became calmer and less restricting. This stay lasted seven weeks.

A follow-up two years later showed that the situation was much better. The husband still disliked being regarded as having been a patient, but accepted our interest in the family as a whole. He considered he had gained the following things from their stays: a more relaxed relation to money and more openness about himself having an irritable temper. The wife felt stronger, more secure, and accepted his ways to a greater extent.

They have invited a young relative of his, a girl, to live with them. She does some housework and relates well to the children. The wife gets up in due time in the morning, which gives the husband a more relaxed feeling for the practical tasks. He feels freer from home duties and can plan his own work more satisfactorily. She still has her hobbies, artistic ones, and she also works part-time as a teacher. The children are less anxious and are developing normally.

Our theories about this case were that we had a father who, from his own background, had special character traits that made him not easy to live with. He was provoked by a wife who left to him too many unstructured tasks concerning the children. Her own lack of structure and irregular hours put pressure on him, while his irritation and brutality made her passive.

The wife, being more flexible as a personality, was led to see her provoking effect and could thus change some of her ways. He gained some insight about the children's reactions through supportive intellectual sessions. Bringing in the young relative was an aspect of vector therapy, having a compensatory effect.

CONCLUSIONS

Family work in a therapeutic village permits a concentrated, multidirectional treatment that is appropriate when problems are complicated and when continuous therapy is required. It also is of value when geographic isolation makes other forms of therapy impossible.

It is certainly an expensive form of therapy and needs a team of trained staff; however, the facilities and program can also work as a training center for professionals who intend to do family therapy on a polyclinic basis.

Evaluating results is difficult. Almost all patients are thankful and feel they have learned a lot during their stay. The reaction is the same just after the stay, as well as later. Even if a couple later divorce, they feel that the stay made things clearer.

Motivation for change, together with intellectual and emotional capacities, is necessary for the best results. Results have been poor when the stay was just to "show willingness" before a divorce that is already decided upon is carried through. When social problems dominate, our therapy can be of little value.

It is essential that the hospital staff make a good evaluation of the problems to be solved, before admission. We try to avoid admitting patients we consider that we have little or no chance of helping or those whom we consider could obtain adequate therapy elsewhere.

Editor's Commentary: A Model for Family Inpatient Care from Norway

Modum Bads Nervesanatorium is set in a beautiful, spacious wooded area. It looks more like an attractive resort than like a mental hospital. The atmosphere is comfortable and soothing, yet there is an air of efficiency and important work being done.

In the summer of 1981 I was invited to Modum Bads to conduct a family therapy workshop for several days. We spent almost a week living on the premises. Like most of the patients and trainees, we quickly settled in and felt cared about and welcome.

We came to realize that Modum Bads is well respected as a training facility throughout Norway. Interns and residents in many disciplines go there for long blocks of time. In addition, special guests come there from many parts of the world to lead symposia or conduct workshops. These latter events are open to all clinicians and attending them is an event that seems eagerly anticipated and highly valued.

The staff remain abreast of the literature and current developments in the field; they also actively contribute from their expertise. The staff are extremely invested in their work and very proud of Modum Bads. Many live in staff homes on the premises; others live within a 10-mile radius of the facility. A good deal of the staff's social and recreational life takes place at the institution. For example, one evening while we were there, two of Norway's finest musicians gave a concert in the beautiful formal auditorium. They played to a full house as the concert was attended by patients, staff and workshop participants. Such informal contact of staff with patients after hours adds to the sense of shared community; it facilitates realization of the highest goals of a total therapeutic milieu.

The actual treatment of families is vividly described by Ravnsborg. Among the many aspects of this assessment and treatment process which bear highlighting are 1) the very careful and realistic selection

291

process which is conducive to choosing the kinds of families they are best equipped to treat and minimizing the frustration which comes from a low success record; 2) the multidimensional, multidisciplinary assessment which routinely includes psychological and physical examinations and educational, neurological and occupational therapy evaluations as needed; 3) a well integrated collaborative team treatment effort supplemented by recreation therapy; 4) planned post discharge follow-up; and 5) the possibility of a return stay if need be.

Modum Bads grappled with the Norwegian government and succeeded in having the cost of inpatient family care paid on a par with other hospitalization. In addition, they were able to insure that wage earners would continue to receive their salaries while at Modum Bads. Thus, patients are not faced with fears of mounting financial debts and can concentrate their energies on the therapeutic task at hand. Services are therefore equally available to families at all levels of the socioeconomic scale.

Here we see a vivid example of the political process that mental health professionals in one country have engaged in successfully, heralding a compelling commitment to the improvement and enrichment of their patients' lives. No doubt in every country there are some families for whom inpatient care might constitute the treatment of choice. Perhaps this chapter will serve as a stimulus to endeavors to make it an actuality.

Chapter 17

The Family as the Real Context of All Psychotherapeutic Processes

By Jorge E. García Badaracco

The history of psychotherapy is linked to the idea of a technique. Clinical experience shows, however, that we need to be able to visualize, over and above the different therapeutic techniques available to us, the psycho-therapeutic process. The author takes the view that, regardless of the technique used, any true psychotherapeutic process is similar to the normal process of growth and development within the family, and constitutes a sort of redevelopment in a real or "virtual" family context. In individual psychotherapy the presence of the family is only virtual. The more ill the patient is, the more real will the participation of his family or the presence of the family dimension in treatment have to be in order to make the psychotherapeutic experience possible.

The history of psychotherapy is linked to the idea of a technique, but clinical experience has taught us that, beyond the different techniques available, it is necessary to be able to visualize the psychotherapeutic process. Like the normal process of growth and development in the family, any true psychotherapeutic process, whatever the technique or treatment used, constitutes a sort of redevelopment in a real or "virtual" family context. In this paper I shall attempt to elaborate on this concep-

This is a revision and extension of an article which originally appeared in the *Revista Argentina de Terapia Familiar*, March 1978, 1.

Jorge E. García Badaracco, M.D., is an Associate Professor of Psychiatry at the National University of Buenos Aires, and a Psychiatrist at the Clinica Psiquiatrica, Buenos Aires, Argentina.

tion which, although it has been based principally on clinical experience with psychotic patients, in the author's view may be extended to every kind of patient. Going beyond family psychotherapy as a primary modality for use in treating individual and group mental pathology, then, we believe that the family constitutes, in one way or another, the real context for all psychotherapeutic experience, and directly or indirectly plays a fundamental role in every psychotherapeutic process.

After working with hypnotism, Freud developed psychoanalysis on a firm footing in the treatment of neurosis. This became a valuable tool in the investigation of the unconscious, resistances, the notion of conflict and defense, the mechanisms that operate in the psyche, and the changes that may be brought about through transference and insight. Freud developed the concept of infantile sexuality. By means of self-analysis he discovered the Oedipus complex and saw how, through identification with parental figures, the definitive threefold structure of the psyche, the familiar id, ego, and superego, is built up. During psychoanalytic treatment the patient repeats patterns of behavior and relives desires and emotions he has experienced in relation to his parents. It is through working out, transferentially, these primitive conflicts that the possibility of a truly therapeutic change comes into play. In other words, the family dimension was present in Freud's work from the very beginning.

The psychoanalytic technique was applied to neurosis and then to other syndromes. But the hopes placed in psychoanalysis were not fulfilled in a variety of ways. Not all patients could be cured; treatment became gradually longer and longer, without yielding the expected results; and psychotic patients continued to be largely untreatable by psychoanalysts.

Freud's attempts to treat psychotic patients by means of psychoanalytic techniques made him go through periods of enthusiasm and also of pessimism, and led him to make apparently contradictory remarks and statements. Nevertheless, a close reading of Freud's work proves that he was always interested in psychosis. This concern is in evidence from the beginning to the end of his writings. The study of psychoses went hand in hand with the study of neuroses, and was its indispensable complement. It not only formed part of the general psychoanalytic knowledge base, but also made it possible to deepen one's understanding of neuroses by comparison with knowledge of psychoses. Moreover, while it is true that Freud did not devote himself to treating clearly psychotic patients, he did have occasion to treat very ill patients, as can be seen in the published accounts about patients whose personalities had clearly psychotic elements. Both Anna O. and Wolf Man were patients we would today consider psychotic rather than neurotic.

For a long time discussion concentrated on the problem of technique. Within the psychoanalytic movement some suggested changes in this technique and others defended the so-called classic technique. Some psychoanalysts saw psychosis as a regression to a state of oral fixation of the libido, that is to say, a pregenital structure. Following the work of Abraham, Melanie Klein studied primitive object relationships in the formative state of the ego, and discovered the existence of primary anxieties of a paranoid-schizoid and depressive type which set in motion the primitive mechanisms of ego defense before the appearance of anxiety as an alarm mechanism, which is what Freud studied. If we accept this interpretation of things, the distinction between neurosis and psychosis disappears, so that in both neurotic and psychotic pathology there is a basic psychotic core. The technical implication of this point of view is that psychosis should be approached with the same techniques as neurosis, and that if psychoanalytic theory and practice as regards psychosis are still uncertain, that is because we still have inadequate knowledge about the phase in which object relationships come into being and about the formation of the ego.

Other analysts see an important difference between the structure of neurosis and that of psychosis, even though there may be analogies, and therefore say that psychotherapy must be differentiated from classic psychoanalysis, which is applicable only in the case of neuroses. The work of Federn, Sullivan, Frieda Fromm-Reichmann and others, and in the United States the school of ego psychology, fit into this school of thought. These writers emphasize that the problem lies in the formation of the ego and in its synthetic function. Attempts to apply psychoanalysis to children presented similar problems in that they made it necessary to introduce modifications to the technique, and in this way the technique of psychoanalyzing children was born in the pioneer work of Melanie Klein and Anna Freud.

The first experiments in group and family psychotherapy began in the 1930s. After that, several additional forms of psychotherapy appeared, including: existential, behavioral, occupational, bodily expression, musicotherapy, and psychodrama. In the 1950s, the discovery of psychotropic medication led to a great advance in the possibility of approaching psychotics through a combination of pharmacotherapy and psychotherapy. Simultaneously, in the social dimension, the notion of sociotherapy and the therapeutic community were also introduced as new techniques for approaching mental illness. While the incorporation and development of new techniques were enriching the therapist's stock of resources and allowing him to choose the best way of approaching the patient according to his psychopathology, this trend accentuated the tendency toward hermetic compartmentalization, with practitioners of the different psychotherapeutic techniques competing for good results without properly investigating the reasons for their failures.

In attempting to study the reasons why different techniques fail, and in searching for the way to make these techniques available to patients who are practically unapproachable, we discovered that in many cases the failure is not attributable to the psychopathological condition itself, but rather to the fact that we put the patient into a situation which does not take his real needs into account. In this situation it is impossible for him to travel down the road towards a cure. There may be difficulties in the relationship between the patient and his therapist, such as when a psychotic patient cannot tolerate a very strict setting. We may also encounter negative influences exerted by the family on the patient that are strong enough to paralyze the therapeutic process itself. These are referred to later.

THE PATIENT-THERAPIST RELATIONSHIP
AND THE THERAPEUTIC EXPERIENCE

Psychotherapy has generally been studied as the patient-therapist relationship without taking into account sufficiently the set of conditions, factors and circumstances that surround the patient (and the therapeutic relationship). Most important among these are the family and the social environment, which constitute what we have called the real context (García Badaracco, 1978) of the psychotherapeutic experience. Psychotherapy, generally understood as the relationship maintained by patient and therapist via a series of interviews, requires that the subject be capable of expressing himself and demonstrating receptivity and emotional reactivity. If he is completely prostrate or very excited, or if he is suffering from disturbances which are openly psychotic, then the patient is not thought to be in a fit state to benefit from any sort of psychotherapy. Freud indicated that the patient, in order to be analyzed, must be capable of establishing a sort of therapeutic alliance with his analyst as a necessary condition for any psychoanalytic approach. The psychotic patient often appears incapable of forming a liaison of this nature, but our experience over a number of years has shown us that the ego's ability to establish a "therapeutic relationship" is not determined solely by the psychopathological condition or by the changes or disturbances in the patient's ego, but depends to a great extent on the ability of the analyst and the "real context" of the therapeutic experience (García Badaracco, 1975; García Badaracco & Zemborain, 1975).

This notion of context should not be confused with the "setting" of the treatment, which consists of the rules followed in treatment. Many psychoanalysts have postulated the need for a strict setting that excluded the family, as a way of preserving the purity of the therapeutic experience when it is maintained as a bipersonal analyst-analysand relationship. Bit by bit it has become clear that this purity is often a fiction kept up by the analyst. The reality is that the patient under analysis is caught up in a network of situations and factors that act directly or indirectly upon the psychological field of the analytical relationship.

For a psychotic patient in particular, external factors are very powerful. In the first place, he is affected by economic dependence and rarely pays for his treatment because of his inability to have an income of his own. To this economic dependence are added other forms of dependence caused by his pathological condition, which are intimately linked to the incapacity of the ego to cope with everyday reality. One of the most important is dependence on certain members of the family. The patient is trapped in a family net of symbiotic-type relationships. Psychoanalytic treatment may produce changes in the intrafamily links and in the form of object relationships within the family by affective mobilization of the transferential relationship, and by means of the psychic changes this produces.

These modifications generate a series of reactions and counterreactions that tend to return things to their previous state, in what we may call a homeostatic mechanism. Such mechanisms sometimes act on the individual undergoing analysis in a powerful way. Freud pointed out that it is very difficult to analyze a patient when the field is subjected to a series of attacks, and compared this to what a surgeon would experience if the operating area were being contaminated from outside. A negative therapeutic reaction is often profoundly influenced by a relation who causes the patient to experience an intense feeling of guilt for some improvement. Again, a severe relapse may be triggered by the rigid and castrating attitude of a father or mother who will not tolerate signs that the sick child is growing up. Finally, many times the family will oblige the patient to interrupt treatment on different pretexts just when a sustained period of treatment is beginning to pay off. It also happens frequently that the family will cut off treatment when the patient undergoes a severe regression that may be an inseparable part of the necessary therapeutic process, on the grounds that the patient is worse and that the treatment must be aggravating the illness, when in reality it is they who cannot tolerate the kind of regression the patient is going through, even though it is necessary to alter certain basic structures and effect a cure. In these cases it is clear that there is a real context for the psychoanalytic experience that is not just the treatment setting, but also includes a set of factors that form a network around the treatment and must not be ignored.

The way to take these factors into account is to include the family in the therapeutic process by getting it to take part in treatment through family therapy. Sometimes doing so is difficult. Nonetheless, the use of simultaneous family therapy and individual psychoanalysis does not in itself cause problems; rather it enriches treatment, provided both techniques can be mixed without leading to insoluble conflicts between therapists.

THE CONCEPT OF THE THERAPEUTIC PROCESS

Clinical experience has led us to differentiate between the concept of treatment, understood as a technique, and that of a therapeutic process. Treatment may be said to include everything that occurs in the sessions, from the first encounter between patient and therapist to the last. It may be described or registered in a variety of ways, but it begins and ends with the sessions. The therapeutic process, on the other hand, may be defined as the series of transformations experienced by an individual during the course of treatment. The concept of a process implies a succession of changes that may become apparent in a variety of ways but are internally consistent and progress towards a human condition which we attempt to define as integrating the personality and producing greater maturity and better emotional equilibrium. We can speak about objectively verifiable changes in the individual's behavior (in his interpersonal relationships and in what he actually achieves) or about changes in his subjective experience, but in our view these changes must be an expression of a profound internal transformation which could be described as a change in personality structure, in object relationships, and in the very nature of the patient's internal objects or the way he manages his dialectic relationship with reality. The therapeutic process is thus an internal change, often hidden within the individual, and it may even take place without producing any visible signs, only to reveal itself unexpectedly in the shape of a change at a given moment during treatment or even after. So a real therapeutic process can commence before or quite a long time after the beginning of treatment, and end after the termination of treatment, or never. The psychotherapeutic process means restarting the individual's normal process of growth and psychic and emotional development, which for different reasons was interrupted and remained arrested or waylaid on the path which is constituted by a fulfilled life.

The distinction that has been made between treatment and therapeutic process shows that there may be different types of treatment as regards techniques and therapeutic resources, but that the "therapeutic process" is a unity that depends on the individual's capacity for internal growth. If interpreted in this way, the concept of therapeutic process is relatively new in the scientific literature on psychotherapy.

The definition of the therapeutic process depends on the way the personality is viewed and the terms that are used. Psychoanalysis talks in terms of instinctive drives or object relationships. The existential point of view is expressed in phenomenological language. Behaviorist theory talks about behavior and adapting to the environment. Rogers talks in terms of "organisms." One way or another, psychotherapy is always about an external process of interaction and an internal process of change. As has been said above, the external process of interaction is what has been described as treatment, and the internal process of change is the therapeutic process proper.

FAMILY THERAPY

Within the context of the therapeutic process, one of the most important factors is the patient's links with his family. The kind of neurotic or psychotic link that the patient has with his family reveals his psychopathological structure, as well as the character of the object relationships which make up his personality. When these structures begin to change during the course of the therapeutic process, the members of the patient's family, consciously or unconsciously, exercise a series of influences aimed at avoiding, slowing down, or immobilizing the very changes that the psychotherapy is trying to put in motion. Under these circumstances, transference—one of the most important forces in the process—is quite often blocked by the force of the real links that the patient maintains with the members of his family, who by means of all sorts of complicities (García Badaracco & Proverbio, 1970) act openly or secretly against the very possibility of a genuine therapeutic process. Including the family is not an easy task, and experience has shown us that when we see the patient together with his family, profound anxieties result, not just in the former but also in the latter, whose control or regulation is not always easy. To understand better the nature of the anxieties and difficulties that we have encountered, we have formulated certain ideas that we have collected under the titles "The Pathology of Family Narcissism" and "The Family's Influence on the So-called Negative Therapeutic Reaction" (García Badaracco & Canevaro, 1970).

Psychotic pathology corresponds in large measure to a family syndrome in which the patient has never been able to have a really full psychological life of his own, having only been allowed to express certain aspects of a personality corresponding to different parental identifications. In the patient's interpersonal relationships, we encounter primitive or narcissistic object relationships in which omnipotence still plays a predominant role. The members of these family groups treat one another as partial objects and try to manipulate each other as if the others were merely parts of the individual. Parts of the self considered to be undesirable because they produce pain and anxiety are projected in an omnipotent manner onto others, who are thus used as depositories. It is usually the mental patient who assumes this role, and his psychotic crisis marks his transformation into a sort of stabilizer of the sick family structure. In narcissistic family structures, the members cannot accept the separation of the self from the object, that is, the process of individuation, but try to maintain agglutination and symbiosis as the ideal in family relationships. This results in the impoverishment of exchanges. Any attempt at individuation on the part of one of the members brings out the feelings of pathological dependency which have been hidden and disguised by omnipotence, not just in the person who is trying to individualize himself, but in the others as well. In this dramatic situation, deep feelings of aggression, envy, and pain come into play, making the psychological climate necessary for such individuation impossible. Individuation under these circumstances becomes very difficult, particularly in regard to working through the pain of separation. In this context the psychotic patient can be viewed as the member of a family whose structure is narcissistic, who tries to become an individual but, finding the process of change intolerable and the separation from symbiosis impossible, fails and becomes psychotic. When the sick member becomes "crazy," the difficulties inherent in the psychotic illness itself are multiplied by the difficulties in the family group, which unconsciously forces madness on the patient.

Under these conditions psychotherapy which aims at working through the psychotic nuclei and reconstructing the total personality is greatly benefited by the inclusion of the family in the therapeutic process in order that the patient may detach himself from his unhealthy internal objects by working through his object relations with real external objects (García Badaracco, Proverbio, & Canevaro, 1972).

It is in psychotherapy with a psychotic patient that the importance of the context he is in becomes clearest, for, since he is unable to establish and maintain with any ease a therapeutic relationship, he needs treatment to take place under conditions of psychological security that constitute a valid "container" and a genuine ego support. Thus, he can put up with the transferential reactivation of his conflicts and the intolerable intensity of the emotions which are awakened and endure the corrective experiences necessary for the growth of his ego.

INSTITUTIONAL THERAPY:
THE PSYCHOANALYTIC THERAPEUTIC COMMUNITY

We work mainly with patients who suffer from severe neuroses, openly psychotic states, or narcissistic personalities; in other words, with patients who in many cases need to be hospitalized or to undergo some sort of treatment in an institution. Experience has shown that the ability of the ego to form a therapeutic relationship is not determined only by the patient's psychopathological condition, but that it depends to a great extent on the real context of the therapeutic experience. In many cases institutional therapy is necessary so that the patient can regress in a way necessary to allow him to recover the healthy parts of his personality and redevelop. The institution must have the necessary facilities and therapeutic resources for such cases. The organization we use is what we have christened the "Psychoanalytic Therapeutic Community" (García Badaracco, 1969).

If we consider the community as the context for the therapeutic experience, we may say that it behaves as a substitute family that can constitute a valid "container" for the most psychotic elements in patients, or for their more regressive moments. In this sense, the patient can take advantage of the climate of emotional security offered by the institution to express the sickest parts of his personality, and through an operative regression, develop the healthy aspects of childhood that were stymied during his development within the family nucleus. Such development involves the need to recover spontaneity and the ability to play, the development of a genuine ego, and the sense of a proper identity, meaning a process of de-symbioticization that is usually extremely painful. The family must learn to tolerate regression, participate in the de-symbioticization process, and promote individuation. The family frequently becomes the "patient" or several of its members in turn require special attention. The community as a substitute family may behave more suitably than the real family, permitting a series of developmental experiences that the patient was unable to have before.

The need to take responsibility for the patient and his family must be shared by the therapeutic team, which in turn has to work in an integrated way in order to assure maximum coherence in the treatment. Such coherence is generally threatened by the tendency on the part of the patient as well as the family to divide us. But beyond this, the therapeutic team necessarily participates in the psychological working-through of conflicts, because the therapeutic process of the psychotic patient is not carried out just in the transferential dimension with the individual analyst. The intense mechanisms of splitting, transferences that are displaced on other team members, and the frequent acting-out in which the most intense psychotic conflicts are often expressed enrich the process of psychoanalytic working-through enormously when it is complemented by group therapy, family group, and community group. In this context, the work of interpretation can focus more on external reality and the confrontation between the inner world and the outer world.

INTEGRATION OF THERAPEUTIC RESOURCES

In the field of work where we have been doing research over the last 15 years, we have had the opportunity to integrate various therapeutic techniques, work in a team, combine different types of assistance, and above all, recoup the failures, that is, transform them into successes by reviewing the errors that were made. In order to explain more fully the different techniques and therapeutic resources used in the community, a description of how it works follows.

The clinic, which has facilities for 40 inpatients, works as a therapeutic community. While every patient has individual psychotherapy with a therapist who is not his family therapist, great importance is attached to family and group treatment. This takes place in different groups (microgroups) into which the patients are split up so that, because of the smaller size of these groups, the tasks carried out by the patients can be better and more systematically supervised. The microgroups meet three times a week in total; once a week members of the patients' families are included (family microgroups).

All these microgroup meetings are coordinated by a Director or Assistant-Director and some resident doctors. Their task is to supervise patients in the day-to-day activities of the clinic. For instance, they administer medication, decide if the patient is fit to go outside the clinic, and accompany him within it. They also have team meetings with the patient, his individual therapist, members of his family, his family therapist, and the group coordinator, in order to pool information, to decide what stage of the therapeutic process the patient has reached, and to suggest what changes need to be made in the treatment and what strategies adopted.

There is also a daily general meeting with all the patients (macrogroup) and once a week there is a meeting with all the patients and members of their families (multi-family group), which also may be attended by any ex-patients and members of their families who wish to come. This group is coordinated by various therapists. Those present recreate situations they are going through. Anyone is free to take part as far as he can, contributing his experience, his questions, and his worries, so as to learn from this shared experience.

The therapeutic process is aided, apart from all these meetings, by means of various resources and techniques. We incorporate the use of psychopharmacological and biological elements as necessary, depending on the patient's clinical state.

In addition to group therapy activities, the patients also have the benefit of other activities, such as occupational therapy, music therapy, games, and bodily expression. All these modalities enable us to look after patients with different pathologies and different needs who come from different economic and cultural backgrounds. In this way, we deal with patients who are psychotic, others who are going through a crisis, neurotic patients, alcoholics, depressives, women suffering from postpartum psychosis, and so on.

Seeing the patient simultaneously and systematically in his daily life, in individual psychoanalysis, group therapy, community, nuclear, family and multiple-family therapy, occupational therapy, bodily expression, etc., on the one hand, constitutes a therapeutic network for the patient and, on the other, provides data for research by the therapists which have allowed us to make significant correlations of all kinds — technical, clinical, and theoretical. The enrichment and strengthening of the therapeutic experience for both the patient and the analyst gave us the chance to gain a multidimensional vision of the phenomena and permitted us to share many of the experiences. Since these therapeutic experiences were approached largely through various forms of co-therapy, with the participation of different members of the therapeutic team, the interpretation of the data and the working-out of the therapeutic process were also shared. This made for much greater objectivity, based on a reciprocal control of the interpretations involving the exchange of experiences.

Working in this context brought home to us that the attitude of classical psychiatry, which has pessimistically condemned psychosis as an incurable condition, is similar to that of the patient's family, which is also incapable in most cases of coming to grips with the profound anxieties of the patients, who are immature beings in need of great support. The problem of treatment and cure for these patients, then, is linked to the question of who is willing to take responsibility for this person who must now grow and travel down a road he missed earlier, a person who is burdened by frustration and deprivation, profound insecurities and mistrust, whom personal experience has led to believe that nothing and no one can pull him out of his failure and who is, moreover, often unwilling to accept new illusions without adequate guarantees. Seeing things in this light makes it easier to understand what we have been gradually discovering and systematically verifying over the years—the existence of an unconscious complicity among patients, their families, doctors, and institutions in accepting the incurability of mental illness as definitively established and demonstrated.

On the contrary, when mental illness is viewed as arrested or distorted development in the family nucleus which may be cured through a process of redevelopment, the psychoanalytic therapeutic community becomes the most valid "container" for the psychotic patient (especially the schizophrenic) because it provides the most suitable conditions for the therapeutic process which will require that the family accompany the patient in his redevelopment, learning to do now what had not been learned or was not possible at the proper time. The family must be taught to tolerate the regressions and favor the advances, and this implies that its members will also need to undergo a therapeutic process of redevelopment. Each as an individual and the family as a whole will have to discover and develop more mature interpersonal relationships as well.

The ways in which the family and the family structure are constantly present in our psychoanalytic work in the therapeutic community are many and varied. First of all, families form part of the community in the sense that each patient brings within himself his own family history. In other words, within the structure of his personality there are identifications and internal objects representative of his family, as well as object relationships that are representative of his childhood relationships with the members of his family. In the functioning of the community, these internal objects rapidly find real external personages in which to materialize, in such a way that doctors, nurses, other patients, or other family members may represent parental figures, siblings, or children. In the community, thus, the patient lives out in a transferential way the internal conflicts of childhood that he was not able to work through before. These situations are extensively used to demonstrate and explain how many conflicts that are experienced in the community clearly represent the repetition or reproduction of internal conflicts or family conflicts, and offer opportunities and valuable material with which to work through these conflicts and overcome the deprivations. Psychotic patients in particular form projective identifications quite rapidly, acting out psychopathically in the interpersonal relationship their conflicts with internal objects. It is by interpreting this external behavior that these conflicts with internal objects may be worked through. Another eventuality is that the patient is maintaining sick relationships with his family members in complementary roles, whether because he is in one way or another a product of the sick family structure or because in some way he chose a sick partner in order to deposit in the latter some of his own illness.

The most difficult part for family members to tolerate is when the patient is halfway on the road to recovery. They must then carry the burden of certain still unsolved aspects, collaborating with the necessary patience until the patient is finally able to hold his own. In order to achieve this, it has been our experience that the family *must* participate in the patient's therapeutic process. This in turn brings out the sick aspects of other members, who generally come to realize that they too need some form of treatment. Perhaps the most important part of the whole process is the development of family insight and the capacity to tolerate anxiety and accompany the most needy member in turn. Under these conditions it is possible to maintain a better attitude vis-à-vis the vicissitudes of treatment and the relapses, which should not necessarily be seen as therapeutic failures, but rather as forms and changes within the curative process, as the trial-and-error by which the patient acquires internal stability and security. Quite often the family members are testing the possibility of future treatment and cure for themselves through the treatment of the patient. Secretly they are measuring such aspects as the doctor's ability to handle difficult situations, his aggressivity, his tolerance of anxiety, and his confidence of success. In these cases, the doctor or therapeutic team must be prepared to take charge of the whole family.

The family may participate in the therapeutic community in several ways. We have tried having meetings with the nuclear family of the patient with and without the latter's presence. We have brought together all the family relations of the patients in the community to discuss and work out common problems. We have included families in the daily meetings of the patients' therapeutic community, and we have formed large groups of patients and family members to participate in a community meeting that we call the multiple family group (García Badaracco et al., 1970). This entire focus involves conceiving of the psychoanalytic therapeutic community as a psychological field with a multi-family structure, and of the therapeutic process as a set of changes that take place in the individual, in the members of his family, and in the family group as a whole, in the sense of a greater maturing on the part of each, with more individuation and personalization of the members within the group, and as a consequence, more mature interpersonal relationships among them.

In conclusion, I would like to point out that even though the ideas developed in this article refer particularly to the psychotherapy of psychotics, the author believes they are equally valid for the psychotherapy of any patient. The problems of children and adolescents are quite similar to those of psychotic patients. The same may be said for neurotic patients, although a more extensive groundwork should be laid.

SUMMARY

In this article I have developed the idea that the family constitutes the real context for every psychotherapeutic process. The need to distinguish between the concept of treatment, which is associated with the idea of a particular technique, and the concept of the therapeutic process, has been stressed. There are various psychotherapeutic techniques, but it is necessary to aim beyond them towards a growing integration of resources around the unity of the true therapeutic process.

Psychotherapy has generally been studied as a relationship between patient and therapist, without sufficient attention having been paid to the real context that surrounds the patient and the therapeutic relationship. After a brief history of psychotherapeutic techniques, it is suggested that the reason for failures has not been properly investigated. Based on my clinical experience and research in this area, I have postulated that the family's inclusion is fundamental if a psychotherapeutic approach to the psychotic patient is to be made possible. When the patient requires hospitalization, the institution should behave as a substitute family so that the patient can tolerate the vicissitudes of treatment with respect to regressions, advances, and emotional mobilization through transference. Although difficulties arise in family therapy when the aim is to guide these patients in a profound working-through of their problems, it is argued here that the possibility of cure exists, provided that the special characteristics of the psychotic patient vis-à-vis the therapist, and the real context he requires in order to carry out the corrective experiences necessary for his ego to grow are borne in mind.

REFERENCES

Ackerman, N.W. *The Psychodynamics of Family Life*. New York: Basic Books, 1958.

Bateson, G., Jackson, D.D., Haley, J., & Weakland, J.A. Hacia una teoría de la esquizofrenia. In *Interacción Familiar*. Buenos Aires: Tiempo Contemporáneo, 1971.

Boszormenyi-Nagy, I. & Framo, J.L. (Eds.) *Intensive Family Therapy: Theoretical and Practical Aspects*. New York: Harper and Row, 1965.

Bowen, M. Family psychotherapy with schizophrenia in the hospital and in private practice. In I. Boszormenyi-Nagy & J.L. Framo (Eds.), *Intensive Family Therapy*. New York: Harper and Row, 1965.

Fleck, S. *Psychotherapy of Families of Hospitalized Patients*. In Masserman, J.H. (Ed.), *Current Psychiatric Therapies*. New York: Grune and Stratton, 1963.

García Badaracco, J.E. Official Paper on Community Therapy. IV World Congress on Psychodrama; 1st Panamerican Symposium on Group Psychotherapy. Buenos Aires, 1969.

García Badaracco, J.E. Avances en psicoanalisis de neurosis y psicosis. Paper presented to the Latin American Psychoanalytic Congress. Buenos Aires, 1975.

García Badaracco, J.E. Le processus psychothérapeutique et sa relation avec le contexte réel de l'expérience psychothérapeutique. 1978.

García Badaracco, J.E. & Canevaro, A. La reacción terapéutica negativa y la influencia familiar. In *Patología y Terapéutica del Grupo Familiar*. Buenos Aires: Fundación Acta, 1970, 221-225.

García Badaracco, J.E., Canevaro, A., & Czertock, O. Coterapia y grupo familiar. In *Patología y terapéutica del grupo familiar*, Buenos Aires: Fundación Acta, 1970, 226-229.

García Badaracco, J.E., Canevaro, A., Czertock, O., Sicardi, A., & Zemborain, E.J. El grupo familiar múltiple para el tratamiento de pacientes psicóticos en comunidad terapéutica psicoanalítica. VIIth Latin American Psychiatric Congress. Punta del Este, 1972.

García Badaracco, J.E., & Proverbio, N. Las alianzas en la terapia de familias de psicóticos. In *Patología y terapéutica del grupo familiar*, Buenos Aires: Fundación Acta. 1970, 230-231.

García Badaracco, J.E., Proverbio, N., & Canevaro, A. La terapia familiar en comunidad terapéutica psicoanalítica de pacientes psicóticos (grupo familiar múltiple y grupo familiar nuclear). In *Patología y Terapéutica del Grupo Familiar*. Buenos Aires: Fundación Acta, 1970, 150-152.

García Badaracco, J.E., Proverbio, N., & Canevaro, A. Tratamiento de pacientes psicóticos. *Acta Psiquiatrica Psicologia Am. Lat.*, 1972, *18*, 232-243.

García Badaracco, J.E. & Zemborain, E.J. La regresión en la comunidad terapéutica psicoanalítica. VIIth Latin American Psychiatric Congress. Punta del Este, 1972.

García Badaracco, J.E., & Zemborain, E.J. El narcisismo en pacientes psicóticos. Analizabilidad de las "neurosis narcisisticas" en función del comportamiento del analista como objeto externo. *Revista Psicoanalítica*, 1975, 3.

Haley, J. *Changing Families*. New York: Grune and Stratton, 1974.

Lidz, T., Cornelison, A., Carlson, D.T., & Fleck, S. El medio intra-familiar del paciente esquizofrénico: La transmisión de la irracionalidad. In *Interacción Familiar*. Buenos Aires: Tiempo Contemporáneo, 1971.

Pichon Riviere. Tratamiento de grupos familiares (1960). Previously unpublished work printed in *Del Psicoanalisis a la Psicología Social*. Buenos Aires: Galerna, 1971.

Rubinstein, D. Family therapy. In J.H. Masserman (Ed.), *Progress in Neurology and Psychiatry*. Vol. 18. New York: Grune and Stratton, 1963.

Wynne, L.C. Indicaciones y Contraindicaciones de la terapia familiar exploratoria. In *Interacción Familiar*. Buenos Aires: Tiempo Contemporáneo, 1971.

Zuk, G.H. & Rubinstein, D. A review of concepts in the study and treatment of families of schizophrenics. In I. Boszormenyi-Nagy & J.L. Framo (Eds.), *Intensive Family Therapy*. New York: Harper and Row, 1965.

Editor's Commentary: Going Crazy
and Becoming Sane
within the Family

García Badaracco, an Argentinian psychoanalyst, provides us with an excellent backdrop, rationale, and scenario for simultaneously offering individual psychoanalytic therapy and various forms of family therapy within an inpatient therapeutic milieu. Bringing these three approaches together in a compatible, congruent, and mutually reinforcing fashion is a difficult task and one that García Badaracco has succeeded in doing extremely well. In this field one frequently hears that an individual intrapsychic-analytic approach and a family systems approach are inherently contradictory; García Badaracco's research and experience offer important evidence to the contrary.

He writes from the vantage point of the medically trained psychoanalyst, recapitulating the importance of the initial growth and development process within the family and implying that psychoanalytic therapy, geared to restructuring the personality, provides a second chance for a healthier personality formation and integration. He deftly interweaves object relations theory, concepts of omnipotence and narcissism, and such defense mechanism of the ego as projection, splitting, repetition compulsion, and projective identification with transactional and interactional patterns in the family system. As in Bruch's chapter, there is concern here with symbiotic enmeshment and how to disentangle the psychotic member in this case, or the obese member in Bruch's article, from other family members. Like Pollack, Kaslow and Harvey, García Badaracco looks at the other person(s) in the complementary relationship who stabilizes and perpetuates the symptom in the identified patient. He engages the individual patient in deep regression so that he or she can then live through a healthier development process; concurrently he insists that the other family members be involved in ongoing treatment so that they can tolerate the regression and not disrupt the therapy, develop family insights, and perhaps realize the family's need for therapy for itself as a unit. He posits this can only be done when the therapist takes charge of the whole family.

I certainly concur with his statement that:

> Under these conditions psychotherapy which aims at working through the psychotic nuclei and reconstructing the total personality is greatly benefited by the inclusion of the family in the therapeutic process in order that the patient may detach himself from his unhealthy internal objects by working through his object relations with real external objects.

What I do not agree with, and prefer to attribute to differences in our cultural heritage, is the strong implication that medically trained analysts are the only ones well qualified to be primary therapists. This just is not the experience in the United States, Canada, Australia, and other countries.

García Badaracco provides an interesting distinction between the concept of treatment and the concept of therapeutic process. He holds that treatment deals with the external process of interaction while the internal process of change is what constitutes the arena of therapeutic process. By contrast, my clinical experience has been that in psychoanalytically oriented family therapy one deals, sometimes sequentially and sometimes almost simultaneously, with internal (intrapsychic) and external (interpersonal) processes. No doubt it will be years before we have the definitive answer on this controversial issue.

Notwithstanding García Badaracco's apparently traditional analytic training, he criticizes the attitude of classical psychiatry about psychotics being "incurable." In a provocative analogy, he likens this psychiatric posture to that of the despairing family that believes its "crazy" member is beyond repair. He decries the complicity of such families, psychiatrists, other physicians and institutions in what I will call the "pessimistic myth of incurability" and instead holds out an optimistic picture of what has been and can be done through a multimodal approach of judiciously combining individual, family, and institutional milieu therapies.

Paired together, Ravnsborg's article on inpatient care of neurotic families in Norway and García Badaracco's chapter on inpatient care of psychotics (in Argentina) accompanied by what appear to be mandatory family therapy sessions for (outpatient) family members present some challenging ideas about what good inpatient treatment can provide to a wide range of patients with diverse symptomatology and diagnoses. In an era when the validity of institutionalization in mental hospitals has been seriously questioned in some countries, such as the United States and Italy, and de-institutionalization almost held out as a sacred goal, the humane approaches and seemingly efficacious results described by these two authors who live in very different societies provide an important counterpoint for consideration in these deliberations.

Chapter 18

"The Back Is Gone": A Systems View of Work Injuries and Invalidism in Australian Migrant Families

By Brian Stagoll

Australia has a large non-English-speaking industrial workforce with a serious incidence of chronic invalidism following work accidents. Health services are relatively ineffective in preventing this and instead often seem only to amplify the problem. The accident victim and his family frequently get locked into a sequence of destructive interactions with health and legal services which ends in disablement and family collapse. A model of this malignant social process, termed "the accident victim syndrome," is proposed. Its effects on families are described, including how pain can become the major focus of family communication, and the phenomenon of maladie à deux (or symmetrical development of symptoms in spouses). The implications of this model for effective intervention, for family therapy and for general health care are discussed.

This chapter is a revised version of an article which originally appeared in the *Australian Journal of Family Therapy*, January, 1981, 2, (2), 63-75.

Parts of this paper were presented at the 39th Annual Conference and 1st International Meeting of the American Association of Marriage and Family Therapy, Toronto, Canada, November 1980, and at the First Australian Conference on Family Therapy, Melbourne, September 1980.

The author wishes to acknowledge the major contribution of Dr. John Lloyd in the formulation of these ideas, and the Staff of Melville Clinic, West Brunswick, Victoria, for their courage and persistence in carrying them out.

Brian Stagoll, MB.BS., D.P.M., F.R.A.N.Z.C.P., is a psychiatrist at the Williams Road Family Therapy Centre, Windsor, Victoria, Australia.

The following story is sadly familiar to health workers involved in ethnic health services in Australia.

Mr. T. is a 36-year-old Greek man, married, with two children age 10 and 6. He can understand, but not read English, and normally speaks Greek. He came to Australia in 1972 from a small farming village. Before this he had served in the Greek Army, obtaining officer rank. Australia offered better economic prospects and he moved here with his wife and daughter. After arrival he worked in a sink factory doing piecework, often for 12 hours a day, earning double wages. He saved to buy a house, and had a son.

Four years later he hurt his back lifting metal. He was taken to the hospital with acute back pain, diagnosed as ligamentous damage. He was given two months off from work, and told to rest and come to the hospital for various treatments. His back pain did not improve much, but after a period of time he attempted a return to work. "Light duties" had been prescribed, but these did not eventuate. Instead he went back to his old job, and was unable to work longer than half a day before he collapsed. After this he developed pains in his neck and left arm and began complaining of headaches, dizziness, and impotence.

Nine months after his accident his wife developed back pains after falling on her left arm at her job in a clothing factory. Visits to her local doctor and then to specialists brought no improvement. She did not return to work, but instead stayed at home to minister to her sick husband, whom she felt she couldn't leave alone, and to control the children, who irritated him. She also developed further symptoms, including headaches, asthma and abdominal (gynecologic?) pains.

Mr. T. first came to Melville Clinic, a Community Mental Health Centre in Melbourne, about two years after his injury. He never had a day free from pain and had been almost totally confined to his home. He had seen over 30 doctors for assessment, and had received multiple tablets without any relief. He was unable to play with his children, saying their "noise" disturbed him, and had frequent arguments with his wife, which could become violent. He felt a failure as a man and father and had lost contact with old friends. He did not believe that anybody, including his family, had any respect left for him.

Mrs. T.'s health was also deteriorating. However, she could still manage the housework with the help of her daughter. The daughter was mature for her age, spoke the best English in the family, and was doing well at school. However, she was still enuretic. The son had various animal phobias and stayed close to mother, often missing kindergarten.

Four years after the injury and after prolonged uncertainty, the compensation case was finally settled. Mrs. T.'s case is still pending. Mr. T. felt he was not awarded an amount which matched his degree of suffering and asserted that justice had not been done. His pain and symptoms have continued and his view of the future remains pessimistic. He is a broken man. When he says "The back is gone . . . ," he is alluding to much more than the status of his vertebral column.

In this paper a systems model is developed to comprehend the plight of Mr. and Mrs. T. We believe this model may be useful to health workers who often unwittingly get caught up in the social processes to be described, with resultant frustration and loss of morale and therapeutic influence. This can result in health and legal services designed to treat and protect an injured person instead having the opposite effect of generating more distress and disablement. These services become "part of the problem" instead of "part of the solution." In the months after an accident, a tyrannical chain of events can be set in motion, which will amplify the pain, powerlessness and passivity of the injured worker to a point of chronic and irreversible disablement. The injured person and his helping network appear to become "locked in" to an increasingly inflexible and stereotyped relationship which drives on inexorably through friction, frustration, and resentment to stand-off, resignation, and defeat for all involved. Such destructive interactions and their prevention and unlocking are the subject of this paper.

EXTENT

Reliable statistics are not available on the extent or course of occupational injuries in migrant groups, or, for that matter, for the general population of Australia. Widely quoted assertions such as "40% of all industrial accidents involve migrant workers" or that "overseas born workers have twice the rate of industrial accidents to locally born workers and almost twice the time rate of recovery" are shown by Morrissey and Jakubowicz (1980) to be without valid statistical foundation. However, anybody working with ethnic groups will attest to the fact that the chronically disabled migrant worker is a common problem and a significant drain on health services. Some reports suggest alarmingly high rates of work injuries and invalidism in some ethnic groups. Hackett (1979), studying Invalid Pension applications, claims that Greek-born citizens show three times the invalid rate of Australian-born, 15 times the rate of disability due to "vertebral disease" and 12 times the rate of "neurosis." Casey and Yaman (1980), studying a group of South American and Turkish immigrants living in a high-rise housing project, found that over half of the group had had work-related injuries, with delayed return to work for nearly 60% of those who had been injured. These two reports can be criticized on methodologic grounds but they still reinforce an increasing clinical suspicion among many health workers that work-related injuries and incapacitation are endemic in some Australian ethnic communities. More research is urgently called for in this area.

This paper focuses on a group afflicted with the most extreme outcomes of work injury. Such outcomes only occur in a minority (albeit a minority of undetermined size) but we believe that the interactions described have varying but significant effects on *all* individuals and families that are caught in potential "victim" situations. As such, we believe that understanding these social processes is of paramount importance if we are to overcome the unintended but disabling and invalidating "iatrogenic" effects of our health care system.

We have previously coined the term "accident victim syndrome" to describe the outcome of the social processes we are describing (Lloyd & Stagoll, 1979). This has come from a dissatisfaction with traditional (and linear) diagnostic categories such as "compensation neurosis," which ultimately explain the accident victim's behavior in terms of his own inner psychopathology and exclude a recognition of the crucial contexts and social processes in which this behavior is embedded.

CONTEXTS

The Migration Context

Migration is a complex, long-term and stressful process. Morag Loh (1978, 1980) has eloquently recaptured the feelings and struggles of migrants settling in Australia in her oral history interviews. In the preface of her latest book she quotes "the simple truth" of one of her subjects, Grazia: "Everyone who works for a living got problems I suppose. . . but us migrants have a few extra!" (Loh, 1980). Carlos Sluzki (1979) has recently proposed stages in this process. Although migration is a transition accompanied by few prescribed rituals, Sluzki suggests that, nevertheless, there are outstanding regularities shown in the completion of discrete stages. He suggests that each stage of migration "has distinctive characteristics, triggers different types of family coping mechanisms, and unchains different types of conflicts and symptoms" (p. 380). The stages are:

I. Preparatory stage.
II. Act of migration.
III. Period of overcompensation (in the months after migration . . ." a period of heightened task-oriented efficiency," and splitting between "instrumental" and "affective" roles in the family, as the family organizes for the new adaptation).
IV. Period of decompensation or crisis.
V. Transgenerational impact (where the second generation takes up any unresolved conflicts or previously avoided issues around migration).

Sluzki suggests that Stage IV is a crucial one, when the family reshapes and accommodates to the new reality and culture. This is a stormy period, when the family's need for continuity and identity is balanced with the demands of the new environment. The family rules and values need to change and to permit this; the group must also begin to activate "delicate and complex rules about changes of rules" (p. 384)—a daunting task. How the family copes with these redefinitions has cumulative effects, which express themselves over months and years.

One frequent coping mechanism is for a family to develop a split between instrumental and affective roles; here one member, usually male, deals with present and future-oriented activities outside the family, and another, usually female, centers on past and present affective activities within the family, as well as involvements with their former life and country. This can be adaptive in the first months, but has a potential for escalating into a major crisis in the relationship if the roles are rigidly maintained. Factionalization and polarization will occur with tension and overt conflict developing between spouses, and with offspring triangled into the conflict. In order to resolve and/or express the accumulated stress, tension, or conflict, Sluzki hypothesizes that family members may "activate the socially acceptable and interactionally powerful pattern of the somatic complaint or the psychiatric problem" (p. 386).

The disabled workers we have seen have been, almost without exception, hard workers before their accident, committed to succeeding in their new country, working long hours and shifts, and with little leisure time. They could clearly be seen as being fixed in a relatively rigid instrumental role in their family. The notions of an "accident waiting to happen" and of a worker sending out signals and "expecting" an accident (as proposed by Behan and Hirschfeld, 1963, 1966) may be relevant here: we have observed an association between marital conflict and depression prior to the accidents, but this needs further study. The C.U.R.A. Study of the rubber industry (1979) (see next section) indicated that accidents occurred with greatest frequency in the first and last hours of work, which suggests family worries or fatigue may be factors. Sluzki's model can be used to tie these observations together. In line with Sluzki we propose that the injured worker and his family may find that an accident is a way out of the tensions around the rigid role organization the family has gotten caught up in, as they attempt to cope with the stresses of migration. An accident is not just an isolated occurrence but an event happening in an interactive process which may have started even before the family migrated.

The Work Context ("Combat Zones"?)

Australia has the most diverse work force of any Western industrialized country outside Israel. Of a population of 14 million, 4 million are first or second generation immigrants. Since 1945, more than half of all the manual workers in Australia, and 60% of Australian working women were born outside the country. For many of the migrant groups the percentage at the bottom end of the work force is incredibly high. Of all the workers who came from Greece in the last 30 years, 83% are in semi- or unskilled occupations (Grassby, 1980). Work conditions for migrant workers vary but can be generally characterized as semi- or unskilled jobs, "with low pay, low promotion prospects, hazardous working conditions and shift work" (Casey & Yaman, 1980). The occupational context of the migrant worker has seldom been given much attention until recently, when some impressive (and dismal) reports have appeared (Casey & Yaman, 1980; C.U.R.A. 1975; 1979)

In a previous article (Lloyd & Stagoll, 1979), we compared the working conditions in the rubber industry, which has a high concentration of migrant workers, as "coming the closest to actual combat conditions found anywhere in civilian life." This assertion was based upon a study of this industry by the Centre for Urban Research and Action (C.U.R.A.)

(1979) in Melbourne. The C.U.R.A. report described working conditions of "arduous labour, deafening noise, everpresent fumes, extremes of temperature, and various hazardous machines." It reported that 75% of workers expected to develop permanent disability if they continued to work in these conditions. Fifty-eight percent had had accidents, most often back, shoulder, leg or arm injuries. Management acknowledged that 70% of the accidents were not due to workers' carelessness. Eighty-seven percent of workers were of non-English-speaking origin, nearly all from rural backgrounds with primary school education, and only a minority could speak English. Thirty-seven percent stated that they had received injuries which they had not reported, because of fear of losing bonus time, of upsetting workmates, or of the supervisor's reactions. The highest at-risk group were workers with less than six months' experience.

The rubber industry may represent one extreme of working conditions, but we believe it gives a true description of many of the industries involving migrant workers and that the "combat analogy" is not too far off the mark.

The Worker At Risk

Our examination of the contexts of migration and work provides a picture of the worker at risk. He is inexperienced on the factory floor, and believes his working conditions may cause permanent disability, yet is loath to seek medical treatment when accidents occur. He comes from a rural, traditional culture and his work is in a setting of novel industrial technologies and of a foreign language he struggles to understand. His identity is that of a worker with a "strong back"; he has few other skills. He has been forced into a rigid instrumental role in his family as a response to the stresses of migration, but tensions remain in his family in spite of (or because of?) how hard he works.

He may work in conditions of danger and stress approaching those usually reserved only for military combat zones. When (as is highly likely), he sustains a back or shoulder injury, it is not primarily related to his own carelessness, although family worries may be a predisposing factor.

These factors condition the workers' response to this injury. We can see how seeds are already sewn for the development of conflicts about returning to work, anger at management, guilt and depression about letting down his family, and anxiety and perplexity at the confusion of it all.

INJURY AND POST-INJURY

Treatment System Responses

The injured worker reports his injury and is referred for an initial medical examination. How this is managed is likely to be crucial in determining later outcome. This initial attendance "sets the program" for future doctor-patient transactions, and can determine whether the worker will return to work in a standard period of time.

If the physician makes a demonstrably thorough assessment, explains in clear detail what can be expected, including progress, treatment and further investigations, and makes sure, if necessary with the aid of an interpreter, that the injured worker understands his situation, then return to work within an optimal time is likely. It further helps if an attempt is made to recognize and explore the complex and conflicting feelings the worker may have about the accident and the difficulties, social and domestic, it is likely to cause.

Unfortunately, such therapeutic and confidence-building transactions seem to be exceptional. Instead, the accident victim is cursorily examined, given vague and pessimistic messages and may be sent to the nearest hospital, sometimes transported by ambulance, where he is first seen by a junior doctor, often under great stress himself. An interpreter with whom the doctor has not worked before is brought down, and the doctor hands over any work of explanation and support. A batch of X-rays and other tests are ordered, and the worker lies around anxiously in a busy casualty department. Eventually the worker is discharged with appointments ranging over several weeks to multiple hospital departments and different doctors, without logical explanation. He is also given a sick certificate to cover this period, along with an injunction to "take it easy."

Family Responses

On return home to the family "to rest," the accident which has been long feared has finally happened, resulting in urgent hospitalization and long sick leave. The family has seen it happen to others in their community and now it has happened to them. They cannot doubt the gravity of the situation. This is what the hospital referral, the tests, and the long sick certificate all mean.

This is a family crisis and there is a restructuring of family roles. The "disaster" affects all family members and the way they respond will significantly facilitate or impede the recovery process. They may react in different ways. We see three patterns:

1. Where the father has been in a dominant and instrumental role, the wife tends to become very involved in the pain of her husband. The family acts as a unit to maintain the father in the protective role, by withdrawing from outside contacts, and by members' sometimes developing symptoms themselves. In this way the father's picture of himself as provider is maintained, and the complex, hostile environment outside the family is much simplified. This pattern of enmeshment and withdrawal may escalate to extreme forms and the "maladie à deux" phenomenon which we shall describe later. It appears to be the most pathogenic.
2. A pattern with a firm cultural base in ethnic groups is for the eldest son to take over executive and provider roles, leaving father excluded and disengaged.
3. In more distant, "disengaged" families, angry distancing may occur, with hostility and expressions of anger at the breakdown of a financial contract (e.g., based on a proxy marriage) and doubts from the spouse about the pain and injury.

Incubation

Each of these patterns of family reorganization increases the isolation and loss of role of the accident victim.

A period of waiting and idleness follows, punctuated by visits to a complex net of treatment services, typically uncoordinated and anonymous. There is ambiguity and confusion, both for the patient and for family members who accompany him on his visits and often act as interpreters. There is enormous disruption of the previous family patterns. Financial difficulties or a drain on hard-earned savings proliferate. The worker is demoralized, anxious and, in most cases, impotent. He is pushed into positions of enforced inactivity and passivity. He is isolated from his workmates and may spend his time in ethnic clubs and coffee-bars. These places tend to reinforce his worst fears and resentments. Rumors abound about how injured workers are mistreated, and how investigators are out everywhere checking on such workers. Some injured workers tell unlikely stories of massive compensation settlements.

We regard the process up to now as an *incubation period*. The marriage between injury and chronic disability has not yet occurred. The probability of such an outcome is heavily influenced by suggestion and the system is heavily weighted in the direction of chronicity, but there is still time to reverse the process. What we call the "lock-in" occurs at the time the specter of litigation is raised. At this time the rules of the game change, and the outcome appears almost inevitable from this point on.

Up until this time the worker has been granted the sanctions that go along with the sick role. Indeed, the response of the system has been to totally reinforce this role in the ways outlined above. The worker is ambivalent about this role, but what else can he do? His customary family and social roles are being eroded by his withdrawal, inactivity, and pain. He is losing both income and self-esteem. He is told he is too sick to return to work. This is also how he feels.

THE LOCK-IN

The Doctor-Patient-Lawyer Triangle

The injured worker, demoralized and confused, is now referred by his union to a legal firm to begin compensation proceedings. It is an unfortunate fact that the worker does not usually understand what his options are. His levels of education, English and anxiety do not leave him well prepared to cope with complex legal matters. The worker could, in theory, return to work at some point without jeopardizing his right to compensation. However, his lawyer may advise that such a return to work could be used as evidence that his injury is not as severe as it might otherwise be. The worker is left feeling that a return to work would be unwise (even if he did feel well enough, and had a job to return to or could find a new one—all increasingly unlikely as time passes). In theory, his lawyer could encourage activity (and a return to work) but in practice this rarely happens. Such "rehabilitative" advice is not part of the legal repertoire—the point of the legal consultation is to establish severity of injury, not diminish its effects.

To establish the severity of injury the worker will be seen by "independent" physicians, referred by either his union law firm or the legal firm representing the insurance company of management. The "independence" is questionable, as revealed by the widely-known fact that legal firms keep unofficial lists of "friendly" and "unfriendly" specialists. The patient does not know this. He believes he is seeing another doctor for treatment, when actually something quite different is happening. The examining doctor is no longer acting on behalf of the patient, but for a third party. If the patient asks the doctor a question, the likely reply is that the doctor is unable to answer, and that the patient should ask his lawyer instead! The patient has been sent for judgment, not treatment. There has been an abrupt but covert transition from the system of therapeutic alliance of medicine (doctor and patient) to medical collusion with the adversary system of the law (doctor vs. patient). The worker is now placed in a situation where he must prove his injuries as "real." This is a step backwards from his previous dealings with health professionals, however unsatisfactory they may have been.

From here on, *no* attention is paid to rehabilitation. Medicine has been overtaken by the law. The traditional doctor-patient relationship is deformed beyond recognition and considerations of treatment are pushed aside. Instead the worker is left, caught in a crossfire between the union that wants to "get" management and management which believes the worker is "malingering." This is a war; the patient becomes a dispensable object, not so different from the front-line soldier. As Behan and Hirschfeld (1963, 1966) state: "Every time the patient enters the doctor's office, a segment of the (class) war also enters." Although this battle may be legitimate enough for the courtroom or political platform, it does not belong in the doctor's office. At the least its presence there should be acknowledged and explained, with the worker being told his options and their likely consequences. Instead it remains, "poisonously invisible" (Behan & Hirschfeld, 1963, 1966).

Effects

The effects of this process are clear enough. The patient is under great pressure, both covert and overt, to hang on to legally valuable symptoms. The doctor has to assess, or "give an independent opinion without the implication of treatment." The context in which this judgment must be made is one where there is a real degree of ambiguity about the extent of a soft tissue injury, where there is an adversary atmosphere between doctor and patient, and where the doctor is pressed to deliver a precise and unequivocal judgment of the degree of severity of the injury. In this milieu, treatment based upon a psychologically sensitive relationship, with a developing sense of alliance and a recognition of conflicts around the accident, is just not possible. Instead, there is a cautious clinging to a limited medical construction of events, with unspoken mutual feelings of holding back, distrust, and hostility between doctor and patient.

The patient is left feeling helpless and paranoid in a complicated and foreign system he does not understand, experiencing rejection and anger from a medical system which seems interested in discrediting but not treating him. He feels betrayed and his depression alternates with anger and impotent rage, as he hangs onto his symptoms as the only way out of his impasse.

The doctor is also caught in a difficult and alien situation. He is not practicing medicine as he knows it, but trying to evaluate the medical reality of the symptoms of an angry, non-English-speaking patient with a complicated story of previous treatment. He faces the prospect of being subjected to cross-examination about his judgment by an unfriendly and doubting barrister. Even if he is not the client of a third party, but an independent practitioner, he finds himself literally hunted down and importuned to give reports and pass judgment, which immediately tilts his relationship with his patient in the ways described.

The lawyer too is caught in an uncomfortable position. Many lawyers recognize the effects that the current compensation system and the adversary process have on their client, but there is little else they can do. In supporting their client in an attempt to return to work they might run the risk of being discredited as not acting in their client's best interest for compensation.

Who Is to Blame?

There is little point in assigning blame to participants in this triangle, although anger and cynicism are tempting. Such responses, which are common among doctors and solicitors, only serve to make a bad situation worse. In truth, all—patient, family, doctors and lawyers—are struggling with a difficult situation, and the harder they struggle the worse it becomes, the classical sign of the lock-in.

END POINTS

Multiple Assessments and Increasing Defeat

Accident victims are usually subjected to multiple assessments, with visits to between six to 50 doctors. The average is about 20, usually for multiple visits. Yet at the same time, the more doctors he sees and the more visits he makes, the less likely he is to get any kind of worthwhile treatment. In spite of this, he continually persists, with amazing tenacity, only to get more enraged. He attributes his bodily perceptions of helplessness, fear, and anger to the injury and untreated disease process and reports a tortured litany of his symptoms to anybody who will listen. His symptoms become his major point of communication. Relief of these symptoms can come to represent defeat in his mission to justify himself, and also a risk of loss of income. He is left holding onto his symptoms with fury and resentment, at the same time feeling helplessly trapped by them.

Family Withdrawal

Several months will have passed since the accident and the life of the family becomes hopelessly snarled. The more the medico-legal system argues over the validity of the injured worker's sickness, the more the family will support his self-definition of "being sick." In ever decreasing spirals the family system reorganizes into a more rigid homeostasis, closing over into stereotyped and repetitive patterns which further maintain the illness behavior. A feeling of powerlessness and defeat against a hostile and perplexing external environment pervades the family. The only way the injured worker can confirm his identity is as a pained and aggrieved person. Family anxiety and despair are kept within limits by somatic preoccupations and the denial of other family tensions. The family, especially the wife, increasingly accepts the reality of the father's symptoms and responds by assuming increasing responsibility for his care. This reinforces the hurt person's sense of powerlessness, passivity, and loss of role. In turn, the spouse feels trapped, unable to express her resentments. Pain, after all, is an excuse with honor, and hard to challenge, and therefore a powerful weapon of interpersonal control. Communication becomes more indirect as hostile-dependent interactions increase. Explosions of anger surface, only to be pushed down again, covered over by exacerbations of pain and a refusal to consider any social or psychological explanations. The family pulls back from previous social contacts, which they can no longer financially afford anyway. They are left spending excessive time together, waiting for protracted periods, feeling useless and disillusioned with life in their new country, and afraid of the future. Pain and symptoms become the main vehicle of transactions within the family and with the outside world. Bodily perceptions of distress are forcefully presented as due to the injury. The injured person strives to confirm and justify himself with his great suffering and unrelievable agonies, which he insists on everyone knowing about.

Maladie à Deux

This is an extreme but not uncommon pattern. In response to the husband's injury and increasing distress, the wife begins developing symptoms, usually following an accident at work. This particularly occurs in enmeshed families where the father has a dominant instrumental role. The wife develops symptoms as a way of protecting and maintaining the father in his role as provider and family leader. An element of competition and hostile withdrawal from the husband's demands can also be seen in the development of her symptoms. "Sympathy" pains in a spouse, as well as having the effect of maintaining the husband's picture of himself, also result in further family withdrawal from the hostile outside environment. Meaning is restructured for the family, with the rules regulating role expectations modified to the new restricted environment, but with the father still held in the dominant position, and the wife submissive; thereby an unacceptable role reversal is avoided. This pattern is very destructive, as the family withdraws further and further in response to external pressures. It frequently ends with a joint application of husband *and* wife for invalid pension. Family collapse or break-up is the typical outcome.

Wikler (1980), in a discussion of "folie à famille," or a commonly shared delusion permeating a family, points out how such phenomena represent extreme forms of the way all families share beliefs. "Folie à famille, family myths, incongruous shared concepts, and shared idiosyncratic reality are all points on a hypothetical continuum of family beliefs" (p. 266). These beliefs are based on the "complex emotional interdependency of family members that serves to buffer the family against the outside world, the establishing of a shared common reality that all families achieve and the drive towards homeostasis" (p. 259). Maladie à deux is similarly based on these factors and fits into Wikler's spectrum, towards the pathological end.

Chronic Stress Reactions

Injured workers at this point show the psychophysiologic manifestations of long-term stress. Grinker and Spiegel (1945), in their classic study of combat neuroses, describe a variety of reactions that are also commonly seen in the accident victim syndrome, including anxiety, nightmares, phobias, excessive startle responses, hyperacusis, cognitive impairments, fatigue, irritability, sensitivity to weather, muscle tension, headaches, gastrointestinal disturbance, impotence, dizziness, as well as the amplified original symptoms and pain.

These stress symptoms can be understood as a result of the failure to stabilize the accident victim in a defined social role. He can be seen as being forced to move from his role of worker, to another role with lower expectations and demands, and different but legitimate benefits. He struggles with the changes he perceives in his role, with much guilt, self-blame and doubt. Ultimately he might be able to undergo this role transition, but instead, soon after the health system has actively recruited him into a sick role, there is a mysterious change and an apparent attempt via the adversary processes of the law to disprove the legitimacy of his symptoms. He is left in limbo, waiting, seemingly endlessly, for a resolution. The present is ambiguous, the future uncertain; he has no outlet apart from his family for any effective expression of fear or rage. By this time any attempts to give up symptoms will almost certainly be opposed by the demands of his legal entanglements. He is in no man's land, neither a worker nor an invalid. His self-esteem is shattered and he suffers a severe and often irreversible disorganization of his sense of self. He plaintively repeats his wish to be a worker in his pre-injury state, interspersed with his demands that he is sick. He is not allowed to be either. He withdraws into a state of learned helplessness, and parasitic dependency, where the world is seen as an unbearably hostile and foreign place.

Modlin (1967) had likened the accident victim at the end of this process to "a hurt animal who withdraws to the safe seclusion of his cave to lick his wounds. If someone approaches he growls an uneasy warning."

Balla and Moraitis (1970) have spoken of these injured workers as "knights in armour," referring to the collars and crutches these men use as their badges of sick role status and their symbols of externalization of their pain, all started by a minor injury. They also demonstrated how badly these victims of the industrial wars do after the war is over and financial compensation (never in the amount expected) is finally settled. In their follow-up study they stress that the majority do not return to work or lose their symptoms.

TABLE I
THE ACCIDENT VICTIM SYNDROME
Interactional loops in the downward spiral into chronic disability/invalidism.

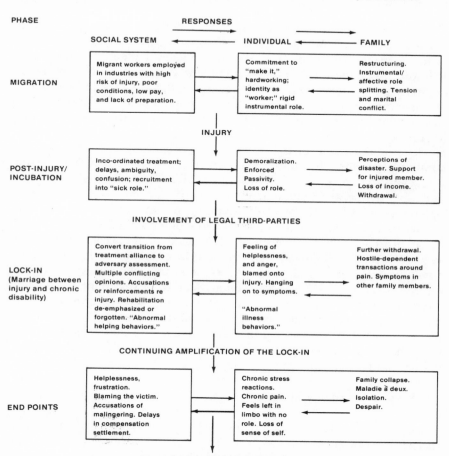

PHASE

RESPONSES

SOCIAL SYSTEM ⟷ INDIVIDUAL ⟷ FAMILY

MIGRATION

Migrant workers employed in industries with high risk of injury, poor conditions, low pay, and lack of preparation.

Commitment to "make it," hardworking; identity as "worker;" rigid instrumental role.

Restructuring. Instrumental/affective role splitting. Tension and marital conflict.

INJURY

POST-INJURY/ INCUBATION

Inco-ordinated treatment; delays, ambiguity, confusion; recruitment into "sick role."

Demoralization. Enforced Passivity. Loss of role.

Perceptions of disaster. Support for injured member. Loss of income. Withdrawal.

INVOLVEMENT OF LEGAL THIRD-PARTIES

LOCK-IN (Marriage between injury and chronic disability)

Convert transition from treatment alliance to adversary assessment. Multiple conflicting opinions. Accusations or reinforcements re injury. Rehabilitation de-emphasized or forgotten. "Abnormal helping behaviors."

Feeling of helplessness, and anger, blamed onto injury. Hanging on to symptoms.

"Abnormal illness behaviors."

Further withdrawal. Hostile-dependent transactions around pain. Symptoms in other family members.

CONTINUING AMPLIFICATION OF THE LOCK-IN

END POINTS

Helplessness, frustration. Blaming the victim. Accusations of malingering. Delays in compensation settlement.

Chronic stress reactions. Chronic pain. Feels left in limbo with no role. Loss of sense of self.

Family collapse. Maladie à deux. Isolation. Despair.

Three to four years before legal settlement.
This is only a further disillusion, and symptoms persist.
A chronic invalid has been created from a healthy worker.

INTERVENTIONS

Prevention

By the time the "end points" have been reached the accident victim presents an almost impossible rehabilitation problem. It is more realistic to focus on prevention of industrial accidents and adequate early intervention, involving a coordinated treatment approach, with a multidisciplinary and multilingual team (e.g., physiotherapists, ethnic workers and a community nurse) directed by an independent practitioner who can regulate and control all aspects of treatment. Such a team should ideally be community-based and available on a crisis basis, and intervene as close to the scene of the accident as possible. The analogies with combat psychiatry are close. The aim must be to return the injured worker to the work-role as soon as possible. This will often mean negotiating temporary limited work or "light duties" with the factory. Attention must be paid to helping employers understand the benefits of such an approach, not the least being the potential cost saving. Where these approaches have been used, they have been successful (Cooper 1980; Wyett, 1978). Only when they are in operation is it possible to develop an accurately defined and cooperative relationship with the injured worker, based on early contact, careful assessment and explanation, regulation of treatment procedures, and sensitivity to the conflicts and confusion of the injured worker and his family. Only then will recovery occur in the optimal time. Unfortunately, this does not often happen. Until it does we can expect the social processes surrounding the accident victim to remain malignant.

The Relevance of Family Therapy

The end-stage accident victim, locked into his symptoms and showing classic signs of chronic stress, presents an extremely difficult rehabilitation problem. Often the most that can be achieved is to avoid amplifying symptoms further. We have found that the following approaches are necessary if we are to accomplish this.

At the outset it is vital that the therapist establish his independence from medico-legal processes, and be explicitly clear about what he can and cannot offer. He must do this to avoid being caught in the position of either passing censure and judgment or offering facetious collusion. It is wise to be completely open about all communication with legal parties, giving the patient copies of written communications, and actively seeking his participation in their preparation.

Promises of "cure" should not be held out to an end-stage accident victim. There may be considerable pressure on the therapist to attempt major symptom removal, but this needs to be resisted. He is not a great deal more clever than the other experts. He is offering something else—sympathy, some comfort and a respect for the person's suffering. He must not disaffirm the patient's pain, but accept it, as a prelude to accepting the injured worker and his family as being more than a painful "object of study." It is useful to facilitate and validate expressions of rage or frustration. The injured worker can be told, honestly, that his anger is justified and his feelings of powerlessness are real. In this way new meanings can begin to be attached to the pain—as his protest and struggle against the hostile world. This more positive connotation of the pain can confirm the worker in his "strong man" role, as well as supporting his spouse and the sacrifices she is making to support her husband.

It is helpful to enter into detailed analyses of the transactions between the injured worker and the medico-legal system. A recounting of "assessment examinations" frequently reveals invalidating and destructive sequences of interaction. After the worker experiences such an event he usually responds with a flurry of chronic stress symptoms. It is crucial that his perceptions of what has happened be confirmed. Examination of his transactions with the larger system are grist to whatever therapeutic mill can be generated. As Rabkin (1964) has put it: "It is not disturbed communication, but disturbing transactions between communicating men that forms the basis" (of conversion) (p.355). Only when this is recognized and the worker's feeling of being blocked and made impotent is validated can he begin to regain any sense of himself as a person who can have some influence over events in his life. Such analyses of the transactions between the worker and the larger system are also important for the therapist. He learns how pervasive and powerful the processes of invalidation are. He is able to put his patient's symptoms into a larger frame and give them a new meaning. He can move beyond getting locked in himself to a painful and fruitless struggle with the injured family, a widespread phenomenon which may explain the avoidance behaviors, anger, and cynicism which many health professionals show towards industrial accident victims.

As the frame expands beyond the injured worker and his family, two further possibilities arise.

First, the therapist begins to see occasions where he can effectively advocate for his patient. He should not avoid this opportunity, yet at the same time he should be explicit with his patient about what he is doing. Appropriate advocacy interventions by the therapist can provide good modeling experiences for the patient for assertive behaviors and gaining control over the environment. An ethnic worker teaming carefully with the therapist can be very useful here; examples include going with the patient to assessments (as an "interpreter"), or working with him tracking down the inevitable bureaucratic tangles.

Secondly, more "traditional" interventions with the family become possible. Focusing on processes between the family and the medico-legal and treatment systems helps the therapist to "join" with the family and gain an entry as an ally. With this he can then direct more attention to family therapy per se. Structures maintaining the hostile-dependent interactions around symptoms can be modified. Focus can be directed to supporting relatively nonsymptomatic areas of function (for example, parenting). The injured worker can be reinforced in useful family roles other than "worker/provider." Enmeshment and controlling manipulations around pain can be blocked and replaced by more adaptive methods. We find the models of structural family therapy and behavioral approaches to chronic pain management to be very useful here (Hudgens, 1979; Minuchin, 1974).

These approaches do not become relevant or possible unless the larger frame is continually kept in mind. None of the above is easy. Rather it is simple to get locked in to a demoralizing battle with these families. The family has experienced other "experts" and it takes a long time and much struggling to convince them that their new therapist is more expert or more to be trusted. False starts are inevitable, and there will be recurrent setbacks as, yet again, the family gets snarled in adversary medico-legal tangles. At such times it is truly difficult not to add further insult to original injury (Watson, 1980). In any event the injured worker is unlikely to give up many of his symptoms until after settlement. Symptom removal should not be the main aim. The value of working with the accident victim and his family is that they can be helped to bear the symptoms with less pain and with less destructive effects on family life. After settlement, the accident victim's chances of adjusting to a new role will be greater if the therapist has been able to stay with the family. Compensation is never felt to be enough, nor what was expected, and symptoms are likely to be maintained after settlement, driven by further feelings of rage and injustice. Family therapy may promote a less destructive outcome for the worker and his family, and we believe this to be a worthwhile aim. However, finally, the answer lies elsewhere in the realms of legal reform and changes in compensation law, immigration policies, occupational health and industrial accident prevention.

THE T. FAMILY (CONTINUED)

When initially seen, Mr. T. only wanted relief for his forcefully presented multiple pains and was suspicious of any other inquiry about the rest of his life. His pain was acknowledged and validation given for his angry complaints about how he had been treated. Care was taken not to disavow the "real" nature of his pain or make any psychological explanations of it. In his own language (via an interpreter) he was offered help in sorting out his legal problems, a chance to see a doctor regularly and a sympathetic hearing without any promises of dramatic symptom relief. He was told he must be a "strong man" to be able to bear his pain, and he must have worries about his family. He alternately accepted and impatiently rejected these messages, but kept appointments, and eventually agreed to bring his wife along. She was pleased to be involved: Her husband's doctors had never consulted her before. There were a number of discussions centering on either Mr. T's legal entanglements or his pain symptoms. The connection was that the pains always flared up around the time of a medico-legal assessment, and it was also then that marital violence occurred. At such times it was important to focus on Mr. T.'s angry perceptions of how he was being judged and disbelieved by the examining doctor. The Greek interpreter who participated also accompanied Mr. T. on his medical visits and was able to give appropriate validation of Mr. T's perceptions. This helped Mr. and Mrs. T. understand that the anger Mr. T. expressed inside his family was connected to his anger at the events happening outside, anger which he could not effectively express. Understanding this reduced the levels of guilt felt by the couple, and was an important confirmation for them, which led to an opening up of intra-family issues. Mrs. T. was even more sensitive to her husband's pain than he was, always responding quickly in a protective and solicitous manner. Mr. T. was able to express some irritation at her constant concern. His wife agreed to try to let him manage more on his own, unless he directly asked for help. Mr. T. was encouraged to prepare charts of his variation in symptoms, and also in activity, so the doctor could "study his pain" with him. He was to keep these charts private and not show his wife. He set himself a goal of walking certain distances each day and began walking to the Clinic to a carpentry group attended by a number of men with work injuries. This was a group where the men felt safe and unwatched, and did not feel incompetent. They could discuss their mutual difficulties and reduce their social isolation. With Mr. T. away from home Mrs. T. found more time to visit her sister and friends. In later sessions the children were included, with Mr. T. encouraged to talk with them about his boyhood in Greece and to play ping-pong with them. Mrs. T. was supported in not interfering.

The T. family was followed over a couple of years. Their course was up and down, with frequent crises and struggles. Mr. T. did not lose his symptoms, but his violent outbursts decreased. Mrs. T. showed some improvement in her health but did not return to work. The daughter stopped bedwetting and made a good transition to high school; the son started primary school without any great problems. Although Mr. T. kept his pains, he complained of them much less, bearing then with a reserved dignity, his form of silent protest at the world. Mr. and Mrs. T. were finally granted an Invalid Pension and Mr. T. was able to accept this as an entitlement rather than as a further blow to his self-respect. He still rails at the doctors and lawyers who he believes cheated him. The family is considering a return to Greece when Mrs. T's compensation case is settled. Mr. T. thinks that they would return to Australia "for the children." Mr. and Mrs. T. bear painful witness to the courageous struggle of post-war migrants to Australia, and to the great costs they have borne.

IMPLICATIONS FOR HEALTH CARE DELIVERY

The problems we have described are problems lying at the interface of the individual, family and larger social systems. It is erroneous to blame the individual or the family and overlook the key iatrogenic factors in the emergence of chronic disability. The plight of the end-stage accident victim and his family represents one extreme of a widespread phenomenon—the development of stress symptoms in individuals who have been victims of sudden traumatic events, often in the context of "front-line" occupational stress, who are then exposed to adversary legal proceedings. Chronic stress symptoms similar to the accident victim syndrome have been described in school teachers (Bloch, 1977), police (Maslach & Jackson, 1979), and victims of rape and assault (Burgess & Holmstrom, 1977). While it is relevant to examine individual factors here, we believe that an examination of the harmful ways that the health care and legal systems interact is of greater importance.

A health care system that treats somebody subjected to an attack, injury or emotional insult by fragmenting his care, ignoring his family and social network and implicitly laying blame on the victim by colluding with an adversary legal system is bound to have damaging rather than therapeutic effects. Re-ordering health care systems to overcome these problems poses a major challenge.

REFERENCES

Balla, J. & Moraitis, S. Knights in armour: A follow-up of injuries after legal settlement. *Medical Journal of Australia*, Aug. 1970.

Behan, R. & Hirschfeld, A. The accident process. I. Etiologic considerations. II. Rational treatment. III. Disability: Acceptable and unacceptable. *Journal of the American Medical Association*, 1963, *186*, (3) 4; and 1966, *197*, (7).

Bloch, A. Combat neurosis in inner-city schools. *American Journal of Psychiatry*, Nov. 1977, *134*, (11).

Burgess, A.W. & Holmstrom, L.L. Rape trauma syndrome. *American Journal of Psychiatry*, Nov. 1977, *134*, (11).

Casey, H. & Yaman, N. Slow down the line: Occupational health hazards amongst South American and Turkish workers in Flemington. *Flemington Community Health Centre*, 1980.

Centre for Urban Research and Action (C.U.R.A.). Migrants and Occupational Health: A Case Study of a Melbourne Industry. 1979.

C.U.R.A. But I Wouldn't Want My Wife to Work Here. . . A Study of Migrant Women in Melbourne Industry. 1975.

Cooper, W. Prevention, Rehabilitation Program at General Motors Holden-Melbourne. Presented at *Low Back Pain and Invalidity Seminar*, Australian & New Zealand Society of Occupational Medicine, 1980.

Grassby, A. Migrants, trade unions and racism. In G. Crough, T. Wheelwright, & T. Wilshire, (Eds.). *Australia and World Capitalism*. Harmondsworth: Penguin, 1980.

Grinker, R. & Spiegel, J. *Men Under Stress* (1945). New York: Mc-Graw Hill, 1963.

Hackett, B. Who gets an invalid pension?, *Australian Family Physician*. Nov. 1979, *8*.

Hudgens, A.J., Family-oriented treatment of chronic pain. *Journal of Marital & Family Therapy*, Oct. 1979, *5*, (4), 67-78.

Lloyd, J. & Stagoll, B. The accident victim syndrome: Compensation neurosis or iatrogenesis? *New Doctor: Journal of the Doctor's Reform Society*, 1979, *13*, 29-34.

Loh, M. & Lowenstein, W. *The Immigrants*. Harmondsworth: Penguin, 1978.

Loh, M. With courage in their cases: The experiences of thirty-five Italian immigrant workers and their families in Australia. *F.I.L.E.F.*, Coburg Vic., 1980.

Maslach, C. & Jackson, S.. Burned out cops and their families. *Psychology Today*, May 1979.

Minuchin, S. *Families and Family Therapy*. Cambridge: Harvard University Pess, 1974.

Modlin, H. The post-accident anxiety syndrome: Psychosocial aspects. *American Journal of Psychiatry* 1967, *123*, 8.

Morrissey, M. & Jakubowicz, A. Migrants and occupational health: A report. *Social Welfare Research Centre Report*, University of N.S.W. Nov. 1980, No. 3.

Rabkin, R. Conversion hysteria as social maladaptation. *Psychiatry*, 1964, 349-363.

Sluzki, C. Migration and family conflict. *Family Process*, 1979, *18*, (4)

Watson, J. Adding insult to injury. Paper presented at Australian Anthropological Society Conference, Aug. 1980.

Wikler, L. Folie à Famille: A family therapist's perspective. *Family Process*, 1980, *16* (3).

Wyett, J. The Industrial Injury Clinic at Port Adelaide, S.A. 1978, Unpublished.

Editor's Commentary: Relocation
Trials and Tribulations

Although Stagoll describes the "accident victim syndrome" as it appears specifically in Greek workers who have migrated to Australia, one can extrapolate the universality of the dilemmas posed. When families relocate, particularly across cultures, they are confronted with new life styles, folkways and mores, expectations, and modi operandi. All of this is conveyed in a strange language. Accommodating is stressful; unfamiliarity heightens ambiguity and the level of tension. In attempting to adjust, the adult members of the family often find their children begin to acculturate more rapidly. This may cause intrafamilial conflict as the youngsters become bilingual and more adept at negotiating in their new world. The parents may be proud of their youngsters and yet troubled about their departure from the family's traditions and the seeming rejection of their parents' values and attitudes. Role reversals may occur, as, for example, when children serve as interpreters for their parents when lawyers and doctors become involved in situations such as those Stagoll describes. This may be essential for coping with the demands of the external reality but it may threaten the internal family relationship system if it causes a flip-flop crossing of generation boundaries and responsibilities.

In reading this chapter, one can identify with the dilemma of the worker who, in trying to make good in his new country, works double shifts. He becomes over-tired and probably over-anxious. The family misses his presence at home—and may make covertly conflicting demands for more money and more attention. In the strange factory context, the worker becomes increasingly vulnerable to mishaps; Stagoll's designation of the possibility of "an accident waiting to happen" is a colorful, provocative depiction. Unconsciously one finds what he needs; the accident may beckon as a way to find relief from mounting tension.

As one reads Stagoll's moving chronicle of the worker's injury, the family's bewildered involvement and escalating anxiety, the confused journeys to a multitude of doctors, the unwanted and nebulous trips to attorneys to prepare them to stake claims, the conflicting messages from all sides, one gets some sense of the pathos and anguish these families must experience. They become irrevocably trapped between wanting to be healthy and productive again and needing to justify the illness for the purpose of being awarded a good financial settlement for the injury and ensuing disability.

This chapter causes us to contemplate the difficulties families encounter when their own ethical value system conflicts with the demands of the economic, medical or legal systems that circumscribe their lives. How can they survive in a strange country if: 1) they do not understand the society and its procedures; and/or 2) they do not conform to its expectations and dictates? It is perplexing and difficult!

Stagoll's material also has generalizable implications for all those involved in dealing with the impact of sudden and then chronic illness of one member on the rest of the family. This too is more severe with new residents in an area, especially when the relocation entails a move from one country to another.

To the extent that our own health care and legal systems perpetuate these problems, perhaps we all share a responsibility for trying to mitigate the implicit inhumanity and for building a more cohesive, rational, equitable system that contributes positively to individual and family readjustment and living patterns. This may mean taking action that results in changing legislation and influencing the ethos in which injury cases get processed, as well as being knowledgeable about the issues and accompanying feelings experienced by those seeking treatment and how best to intervene to enable them to cope effectively and rationally.

Chapter 19

From the Family Approach to the Sociopolitical Approach

By Mony Elkaim

This paper opens with a description of the thought process which prompted the author to switch from an essentially individual approach—that is, one geared to the person who is "mentally disturbed"—to a family approach in which one tries to understand a person's behavior in his or her family context. Next it discusses the limits of family therapy which apply equally to the more traditional psychotherapeutic techniques and are due mainly to general failure to appreciate the socioeconomic and political reality. Finally, it deals with new approaches which we have tried to outline in an attempt to break out of these limits. By "we" I mean a number of mental health workers, including myself, who happen to believe that one cannot separate work in the mental health field from politics without willy-nilly becoming social control agents for the Establishment.

FROM THE INDIVIDUAL TO THE FAMILY APPROACH

I was trained as a psychiatrist in Belgium along conventional lines. Here I was taught to listen to what was said by the delirious subject,

This chapter is a revised and updated version of an address delivered in March 1977 in Brussels during a debate on alternative mental health practices and published in French in *Cahiers Critiques de Thérapie Familiale et de Pratiques de Réseaux,* 1980, 2. It has also been published in German in *Psychologie und Gesellschaftspritik,* 1979, 9-10; in Spanish in *Antipsiquiatia y politica,* Sm. Marcos (Ed.), *Editorial Extemporaneos,* Mexico, 1980; and in Portuguese in *Terapia Familia e Comunitaria,* 1981, 2.

Mony Elkaim, M.D., is President of the Institute for Family and Human Systems Studies, Brussels, Belgium.

not in order to try to read a meaning into his apparently senseless words or actions, but rather to ask myself in which nosographic category the patient should be classified. Deliriousness, emotions, and behavior could only be understood in terms of a set of patterns which finally allowed the therapist to make a diagnosis, the treatment that followed more often than not being based on drugs.

During my first year of residency I recollect going through the ward in the mental hospital. I went through it accompanied by the teacher in charge of my training in order to get to a small room where patients were questioned. There was a general stampede by the patients who rushed up to my teacher: Some would ask him for a cigarette, some would ask when they would be able to get away from the institution, and others would ask for a pass for the weekend. To all of them came the invariable response "How are you today?" I recall being struck by this totally inadequate reply, which was the kind of sign of inappropriateness I was being taught to look for when questioning the people we called "patients." Throughout the early months of this period of practical training, it was striking to recognize that what was said by these people undergoing psychiatric treatment was extremely coherent as soon as it was integrated into a context. Their discourse was perhaps poetic and symbolic—but also how true!

I learned a great deal at the time from a young Greek who had been sent to the hospital because he took himself for Christ and called me "Sanhedrin" ;[1] however, it was during my practical training in the children's psychiatric department that I began to look upon the family as a system. In the first family I encountered there was a 10-year-old Italian child who was considered to be psychotic. The boy had a very intense bond with his mother. The father was "peripheral." I failed to realize at the time that I was confronted with a known structure which Haley calls the "perverse triangle" (1959). My efforts to produce a greater differentiation between mother and child led to what is called by Minuchin (1974) "restructuring the family." The father came closer to the child and a change took place in the parental relationship. The son improved; the symptoms disappeared. It was at that point that the 14-year-old brother began to wake up every night and compulsively sweep his room. I later learned that this was also a familiar structure that Jackson (1957) had described by the term "family homeostasis." As long as the family system was disturbed, if the so-called patient improved, another member of the family would take over and show signs of disturbance in his stead.

THE SOUTH BRONX

On completion of my formal studies in psychiatry, I left Belgium to take a fellowship in social and community psychiatry at the Albert Einstein College of Medicine in New York. While receiving training there in family therapy, I began to work in the South Bronx, first as a fellow and subsequently as the director of a mental health center.

In order to better explain how this neighborhood work helped me to become aware of a series of limitations of family therapy and to look for other approaches extending beyond the narrow framework of the family, I will first provide a thumbnail sketch of the South Bronx. According to an article published under the title of "Emancipation of Lincoln" (Reverby & Handelman, 1972), the South Bronx district contained 400,000 Puerto Ricans and Blacks, eight dwellings out of 10 were in an advanced state of disrepair, and infant mortality was running at a rate of 30 deaths per 1000 live births (twice the national average). The principal cause of death in adolescents and young adults was overdoses of heroin. According to Kaplan and Roman (1973), average earnings were a third below the mean recorded throughout the rest of the city of New York. The delinquency rate in 1966 was 320.5 per 1000 juveniles and the incidence of venereal disease was twice as high as in the rest of the city of New York. The rate of admissions to psychiatric hospitals was also higher than in the rest of the city. In 1970, the catchment population of the Lincoln Mental Health Center for which I was working was comprised of 57% Puerto Ricans, 33% Blacks, and 10% whites (1970 U.S. Census, second and fourth count).

The mental health workers of the Lincoln Community Mental Health Center (CMHC) had long been aware of the inadequacy of traditional mental health approaches in their day-to-day work. In a text dated October 1970, Ruth Grant, Director of the Careers Escalation and Training Department of the Lincoln CMHC wrote: "The Community mental health workers had been seeking practical help in serving their community and felt that an In-Service Training Program could and should offer them this. Over the years the workers had become acutely aware of the sociopolitical reasons for much of the mental illness and the poverty of the South Bronx and thus the original curricula of the early In-Service Training was rapidly becoming both irrelevant and obsolete." In the same text, Grant presented a new training program "which would focus on the worker and the patient in their class and cultural role within the context of the American system." By way of example here is a description of one of the courses she proposed to mental health workers: "Family Environmental Influence, Race and Culture: Consideration of the causes and relationship between individual mental illness and family environment, racial background, discrimination and other cultural factors with particular emphasis on Puerto Rican, West Indian and African customs and the role of the CMHW in the treatment process" (Grant, 1970).

When I arrived in the South Bronx in July 1971, the movement which had carried the revolt of the Lincoln Hospital mental health workers against the Albert Einstein School of Medicine to which the Lincoln Hospital was affiliated had fizzled out, but the spirit of struggle remained alive in the minds of many of the mental health workers with whom I was then working with daily.[2]

THE SYSTEMIC APPROACH

In addition to my work in the South Bronx, I continued my training in family therapy at Albert Einstein College of Medicine. It was there through my contact with Al Scheflen that I learned to think no longer in terms of "who catches whom" in a family but rather in terms of structures in which everybody participates. It was no longer a case of "who does what to whom?" but of "what is it they all do together?" (Ferber & Beels, 1970).

A quote from an article by Haley (1959) illustrates how in a double bind situation the question as to who started comes to have merely a theoretical interest:

Suppose that a mother said to her child, "Come and sit on my lap." Suppose also that she made this request in a tone of voice which indicated she wished the child would keep away from her. The child would be faced with the message, "Come near me," qualified incongruently by the message, "Get away from me." The child could not satisfy these incongruent demands by any congruent response. If he came near her, she would become uncomfortable because she had indicated by her tone of voice that he should keep away. If he kept away, she would become uncomfortable because after all she was inviting him to her. The only way the child could meet these incongruent demands would be to respond in an incongruent way; he would have to come near her and qualify that behavior with a statement that he was not coming near her. He might, for example, come toward her and sit on her lap while saying, "Oh, what a pretty button on your dress." In this way he would sit on her lap, but he would qualify this behavior with a statement that he was only coming to look at the button. Because human beings can communicate two levels of message, the child can come to his mother while simultaneously denying that he is coming to her . . . after all, it was the button he came to be near.

When faced with that sort of process governing the whole system of family communication, asking the question as to who started is rather like asking "Which came first, the chicken or the egg?"

Scheflen introduced me to general systems theory. With him I tried to learn to stop thinking in terms of linear causality. In an attempt to apply in my work in the South Bronx concepts to which I had been won over, I tried, together with a number of mental health workers,[3] including Richard Weeks, director of the Training and Careers Escalation Department of the Lincoln Community Mental Health Center, to train paraprofessionals in family therapy and to bring them to use this type of approach in their day-to-day work.

TECHNIQUES AND POLITICS

At the outset I was quite satisfied with the work we were doing. It seemed to me to be fundamental to take, together with the family, the qualitative leap forward which would consist of no longer putting the blame on the victim or designating a person, but bringing about a change in the "dance" in which everybody takes part, changing the system of transaction in which the whole family is caught up. However, I felt something was wrong. This system of disturbed communications had not emerged out of thin air. It was obvious that economic, sociocultural and political elements of reality played a part and that the tools at our disposal enabled us to understand and to intervene only on the basis of intrapsychic or communicational-relational grids. We were ourselves in fact possessed by the techniques we thought we had in our possession.

I realized that we were transmitting to the families who came to consult us the unspoken message that their problems were exclusively bound up with their past or with their present relations. Since, to cap it all, our action was relatively effective, we were in fact becoming strong agents of social control playing our part in the masking of a number of political contradictions, although we had no wish to do so.

FAMILY STRUCTURES AND SOCIAL STRUCTURES

Case 1—South Bronx

A family which had as the identified patient a boy of 10 years of age came to consult us at the Mental Health Center. He was enuretic, had tremendous problems at school and had one nightmare after another. We learned that a few years earlier the mother had gone shopping leaving the second child at home in the keeping of the first. When she returned home, she found the apartment on fire; the younger child had played with matches. He was badly burned and died shortly afterwards. The father came to reproach the mother for having left the children alone and the mother reproached the older child for having left his brother unguarded. She took drugs and became a prostitute in order to be able to afford to buy heroin and accused her husband of having forced her into that situation. For his part, the surviving child thought it was all his fault.

The family therapist could have attempted to act on the family communications, point out how the mother was rejecting her son as she had been rejected herself in her original family, but in so doing he would have been ignoring what one might call the "political" aspect of the situation.

This poor family from the South Bronx had been disintegrating like so many others living in that district. The mother was unable to afford a baby-sitter and since she had nobody to help her, she was practically compelled to take risks. This family had been nurtured on all the myths peculiar to Western democracies, most particularly by the one that everybody can succeed and that people who end up on welfare have only themselves to blame. The facts that their reality is at variance with this myth and that anybody born in the South Bronx stands a bigger chance of ending up in prison than at a university do not suffice to demolish it.

In this context, mystified by the values spread by the dominant ideology, confronted with a crisis situation, the family turned against itself and attributed to itself its own misfortune.

To what extent then did our "therapeutic" action, laying stress as it did on the internal elements peculiar to the family system, entail a risk of setting a seal of approval on the encompassing alienation?

Case 2—Brussels

Recently I treated a young couple in Brussels that reproduced within itself a series of structures characteristic of the surrounding sociocultural system.[4] The husband was formerly a left-wing militant. He complained that his wife never did what she would like but rather did what she thought he expected of her. At a given moment he would say: "I want you to be free." The couple was planning to leave the country a few days later and a decision was required: Would they leave together? During the conversation the man asked the woman whether she intended to leave with him. She hesitated. After a few moments' silence, during which he was getting more and more agitated, he said: "I see it's all decided!" I then asked him to let her formulate her own reply. A fresh silence was followed by further agitation and another intervention: "Do you want me to go out for a moment? Do you wish me to leave?" The girl then took her head in her hands and said: "Can't we stop a moment? I am utterly confused."

Confronted with this situation the technician in communication would put his finger on the paradoxical injunction: "I want you to be free," the contradictory verbal and nonverbal messages, what family therapists call the "double bind." He/she may content him/herself with that level of analysis and say: "A double message has been sent to that person; it is only logical that she should feel utterly confused. Let's change that disturbed communication and teach this couple how to communicate differently and she will get better." He/she may also try to understand how the conflicting rules inherent to the family system impose a double bind. What is forgotten is that this disturbed communication does not just happen in a vacuum or from the family system only and that it corresponds to other levels of reality.

A different approach would consist in saying that this young couple was reproducing the mystifying process which is a characteristic feature of the pseudo-democratic society which surrounds the couple and pervades it. The "official program" is that everybody is free to make decisions as he/she so chooses. In reality, we are left no choice and the structures by which we are trammeled and which restrict our freedom are denied and even wrapped up in a veneer of pseudo-benevolence. The two members of the couple thus reproduce the social control process inherent in a society that they otherwise challenge.

THE THERAPIST'S POLITICAL CHOICE

To all this one might retort: "You say that your action is relatively effective; therefore why look further than that?" The reason is that, for me, effectiveness is not the only criterion. It is admittedly important to relieve people's suffering, but not at any price, especially not by masking the socioeconomic contradictions which also play a part in the appearance of the "symptom." Over and above that, when in our work we tackle only the visible part of the iceberg we later often have to start all over again. As long as we refused to square up to housing problems, job problems and school problems of the people in the district, problems which play a direct part in the appearance of the symptom, our work was just laughable. Joel Feiner, who worked with me in the South Bronx, caricatured the situation by comparing it with that of somebody who, on the pretense that that was not his role, would prefer to heal the cracked bones of a whole number of people rather than stop the hand of those delivering the blows.

The actions undertaken by different community groups seemed much more important to me. One example was the action undertaken in November 1970 by militants belonging to various revolutionary groups who occupied a floor at the Lincoln Hospital in order to launch the "Lincoln Detox Program." This detoxification program was made up of 10-day periods during which the addicts received decreasing doses of methadone while taking part in "political education" seminars where stress was laid on political awareness as a therapy.

It was through coming into contact with such organizations and activities that I began to ask myself questions about my function as a mental health worker and about the techniques which I had been taught and which I was promulgating. What guided me then and what continues to guide me today in my interventions is the refusal to be a social control agent serving the establishment, defusing crises and psychiatrizing people. It is the will not to stifle any contradiction whatsoever, political contradictions included. It is the refusal to distort my work by masking the socioeconomic and political elements it contains.

THE REDUCING APPROACH OF FAMILY THERAPY

Like other more traditional therapeutic approaches, family therapy chooses to compartmentalize its field of activity, even though it is gradually beginning to integrate cultural elements, and to leave politics out of it, as if that in itself were not a political choice.

Minuchin aptly summarizes this position in a text entitled: "Some points in family therapy grammar" (Minuchin, 1974, pp. 25-26): "I would like to point out one thing I think family therapy is not. It is not a tool for humanistic revolution. It is often the opposite: one of the family's tasks is to provide continuity with a society which a family therapist, in his own value system, may consider restrictive. But the field for social change is not family therapy, but politics, and perhaps the society of family therapists acting in cooperation with their colleagues." This position helps explain why, even when certain themes which would make it possible to understand the link between the surrounding sociocultural values and the social control process in the family emerge, the family therapist masks them in order to conform to his explanatory grid.

Here is an example taken from an article by Wynne (1961):

> On one occasion, when the father had been haranguing Betty to sit down for her "own good," the therapist, noting the father's uneasiness when Betty was standing, wondered if the father also wanted to sit down in order to make himself more comfortable. Betty interrupted the exploration of this question:
>
> Betty: He's trying to do to other people what you're trying to do for your own self and other people. Constitutionalism. Written in the . . . in the land just for one person. It's written by the people, for the people, and of the people.
>
> Father: That's true, yeah.
>
> Betty: In the United States. States what you get, united.
>
> Father: That's why I say when she's sitting down, she's for the people by the people.
>
> Therapist: I gather that whatever Betty said, you would get it turned into something that you would agree with?
>
> Father: Well, she said it right! More than one person involved, more than one person . . . .

Wynne uses this example to illustrate what he calls "pseudo-mutuality": "a type of surface alignment that blurs and obscures from recognition and conscious experience both underlying splits and divergences, on the one hand, and deeper affection and alignment, on the other hand" (Wynne, 1961). Although no doubt true, this takes account only of one aspect of the reality that lends itself to the therapist's gaze.

Other family therapists make no attempt to conceal their function as agents in the service of the dominating ideology. Thus, MacGregor wrote at the end of an article entitled *Communicating Values in Family Therapy* (MacGregor, 1967, p. 185):

> We have proposed that at times it is a useful therapeutic procedure to attempt to change a family's system of values. We have illustrated the way in which this decision, like others in therapy, can follow from adequate family diagnosis. We have shown that the value system can be poorly communicated or can itself reflect pathology. We have defended the advocating of conventional middle-class values with a particular type of case, and have related it to the therapeutic maneuver of fostering the development of neurotic conflicts as a way of rendering the psychopath accessible to treatment.

Is it not therefore logical, although it might seem a caricature, that the police should ask that some of its members be trained so as to be better able to face up to family crises?[5] The social control agent has taken off his mask. We have turned full circle.

THE NEW TRENDS

We find the same reticence in relation to the socioeconomic or political elements of reality in the new trends emerging in family therapy: multiple family therapy, the ecological perspective and network therapy.

Laqueur, one of the pioneers of multiple family therapy, emphasizes the way in which participants at such a meeting should be selected (Laqueur, 1973, pp. 76-77):

> We try to make multiple family therapy groups as random as possible in their socioeconomic as well as their ethnic, religious, political and age characteristics. The more one selects families for any specific factor, such as psychiatric diagnosis, intelligence, economic status and special interests, the higher the probability of pseudo-intellectuality and of superficial discussions around so-called "common interests."

Auerswald, one of the founders of the ecological perspective, which stresses the interfaces between a person or a family and external systems such as the school, neighborhood or administration, has deliberately chosen to place himself outside politics (Auerswald, 1971, p. 266). He states, "There is a growing group of such people, coming from a large number of sociocultural and educational backgrounds, who have become convinced that political process will not produce change in the society of mankind with the rapidity necessary to prevent ecological disaster." Turning his back on political categories, Auerswald, using the terminology created by Gioscia (1970), calls radicals persons "who are meta-chronic in relation to a particular social system" (Auerswald, 1971, p. 268). This in no way detracts from the importance of his contribution for all those who refuse to be wedded to "familyism." The fact that he also rejects political categories does not cause the class society we live in—nor the alienation or oppression which are its characteristics—to disappear as if by magic.

Therapeutic action with the family network has been popularized in the United States in recent years by Speck and Attneave (1971; 1974). In this type of action, the therapeutic team works with the patient as well as his family and the latter's social network (40 to 50 people). Several three-to-four-hour sessions are organized in the evening every fortnight for two to three months. One of the aims of this type of intervention is to mobilize the potential resources of the family network so that its members can help one another.

Many have been influenced by the richness of this type of approach, which not only is directed to the identified patient or to his family but also recreates a micro-society around him. We feel that mutual assistance in the network is very important. But in meetings such as those organized by Speck it appears that the therapeutic activity which precedes the mobilization of the network is essentially centered on feelings. Nothing seems to be done to attempt to clarify the socioeconomic, cultural and political contradictions potentially present in the network.

ELABORATION OF A SOCIOPOLITICAL APPROACH

Having spent a little over three years in New York, I returned to Brussels, where I have been working since the end of 1974 with a group of mental health workers in a district of northern Brussels, Schaerbeek. This catchment area has a population of 50,000 people. It consists mainly of immigrant workers (Moroccans, Turks, Albanians, Yugoslavs and Spaniards) or Belgian senior citizens and sub-proletarians. We have tried to create new approaches to integrate socioeconomic, cultural, and political factors in the work performed with a family network or within the framework of a meeting with several families.

Using a network approach, we determine with the family, before inviting the network, the specific problems for which they would like assistance. In an economically underprivileged environment, such as the one in which I at present work, problems are almost always related to a series of socioeconomic or cultural pressures. Therefore, in our work with the network we try to create a setting so that the team's interventions of a psychological nature are reduced to a minimum. In the course of discussions, participants realize that such problems as the unemployed person who attempts to commit suicide, the delinquent youth, or the old lady who feels persecuted are the problems of a group caught up in the same contradictions. It is no longer just a question of the behavior of Mr. X or Mrs. Y but of the conditions common to the network. Subsequently, *mutual assistance* takes on a new meaning. It is born of the awareness that one is a member of a community subject to the same oppressions.

In an action bringing several families together, we attempt, unlike Laqueur, to group together families having the same socioeconomic and cultural backgrounds and experiencing the same type of problems. In the following section, extracts from a recording made in Brussels at a meeting of this type with Moroccan families are presented. Some of the children from 14 to 17 years of age had been expelled from the technical schools in the district and had been in trouble with the police.

Case 3—A Moroccan Family Group

At the first meeting there were members of five Moroccan families. Whole families had been invited but, for different reasons, not everybody could be present. Also present were two headmasters of technical schools from which some of the youngsters had been expelled, some of the latter's friends, and members of the team of "La Gerbe."

Phase 1

From the outset of the meeting, there was a clash between the children, their parents and their headmasters: One of the adolescents complained about the circumstances in which he had been expelled from school 1.

A: It had all been cleared up, during the week's absence. My father came and cleared up things with Mr. X. Two weeks later, I don't know why, he came to me . . . I hadn't done anything. When he doesn't like somebody's face, he shows them the door. Many people are thrown out for no reason. That lady's brother is wondering why he was thrown out, because he didn't do anything.

Headmaster of school 2: I think that apparently in their view there was no reason but there is the last straw that breaks the camel's back. We have a responsibility not only in relation to this or that boy who is on the point of being expelled; we have a responsibility to a large number of kids. In our school there are 800 of them and when you see disruptive elements who educationally speaking are of no interest, it's a little difficult to say to them: "Little Johnny, you did this" or "Little Johnny, you did that," but we know full well the sort of role they play in a class. I'm not talking about you, mind you, but we know very well that lurking in the background there is one element which is ruining the efforts of 25 pupils and the teacher and which means that a lot of children, 25 of them, 30 Belgians and perhaps foreigners as well, are condemned to a slowing-down of the effort and the results they achieve and it is then probably in this particular case or in others this last straw that breaks the camel's back. Maybe one seizes on a pretext. In any case, I can tell you that in my school whenever somebody is expelled I never decide anything alone. A lot of people are consulted because I distrust myself and am on my guard against an angry reaction. Very often we put off a decision until the next day, or the day after, and with the help of a number of people we make a decision. Contrary to what you would have us believe here, this decision is rarely motivated by one fact. Facts are excused time and time again. It isn't facts that are important; it's the mentality, the outlook that we judge. . . .

Headmaster of school 1: There's a lack of understanding, a lack of communication certainly. There are things that have taken place in certain cases between Mr. X and . . . don't say no, did anything ever happen between you and me?

A: No.

Headmaster 1: OK, something happened between Mr. X and him and it is in order to avoid this sort of thing recurring that I have come here tonight. Otherwise I've got work to do at school. I'd like to give the context. Undoubtedly, it is a barrack-like school with 620 pupils. You know the premises, you know the buildings. There is no room at the school and every year 30, 40, 60 more pupils than we can put into the school are registered. It will be the same next

September. If we have a beginning of the school year like the one
we had last year, there are already 50 pupils who can't be enrolled.
So what did we do this year? We took the pupils hoping that some
time later we would be able to occupy new premises, to have new
workshops. Now the year is coming to an end and we have nothing
new . . . so when the term starts in September there must be new
buildings, there must be new premises, otherwise we shall have
to do something.

We are thinking of organizing an entrance exam, inconceivable
as that may seem. In September we would have to have a competition to accept the best and turn down the less good. These are
not decisions taken at the level of the organizing authority or at
the level of the headmaster, but they were taken at the general
assembly of all the teachers. Because, I don't know whether you
know, but in the school we now have an association of the teachers
and all the school staff. Well, if all these things have to be applied,
on what criteria will it be? Should we accept pupils who speak
French and turn down those who don't speak French well? Stupid!
Absurd isn't it? Should we accept those who are good at math and
reject those who are bad at math? On what criteria? It's equally
absurd! I don't mind admitting that it is perhaps in that context of
overpopulation that there are injustices, but there is certainly a lack
of understanding between me and the pupils. What I intend if
there is the slightest problem next year is for me to be informed
of it as soon as it starts and to discuss the matter together.

Mr. B (*translated from the Arabic*): I have an eight-year-old son in a school.
The teacher grabbed him just like that and broke two of his front
teeth. . . . It existed, Belgium existed for a time in '66, but now if
you open your mouth you are told "Get out!"
Headmaster 2: But you're happy in Belgium, after all?
Mr. B (*in French*): Before, not the same as now.
Headmaster 1: There is a movement emerging which is more and more
hostile to foreigners.
Headmaster 2: It's always the same problem in a period of recession.
There are already many people in Belgium; in addition there are
foreigners to be fed in a certain way.
Headmaster 1: I have just seen in the street a poster calling for segre-
gationist measures in so many words . . . .
Headmaster 2 (*speaking of J, an Algerian friend of the young Moroccans who
has not had "either school, work, or dole" for four years*): Wouldn't he

really be happier in his own country? Maybe he won't go now of his own accord. Couldn't we help him with advice? It's a very sad problem after all.

Headmaster 1: The solution must be found here. Do you like it here?

J: Yes!

A: The police came to see me.

Headmaster 1: I didn't send them.

A: It was Mr. X who sent them to me at home. They came to fetch me at half past seven at home. The cops came to fetch me.

Headmaster 1: What had you done?

A: I did nothing, nothing at all. It was because I didn't go to school last week.

Headmaster 1: How old are you?

A: I wasn't yet 16 at the time.

Headmaster: How old were you?

A: I was 15 and a half.

Headmaster 1: I'm sorry, but it simply isn't done.

A: Since I'm telling you, they even accompanied me as far as the door.

Headmaster 1: I'm quite willing to discuss but on concrete matters. A pupil who is not 14 has to attend compulsory schooling and the absence of a 14-year-old pupil is in fact a matter for the youth protection service. When you are older than 14 it's another problem altogether.

P: (*a member of the "La Gerbe" team*): You say "It simply doesn't happen" but for me, loosely speaking, it happens very often. People don't openly talk about this sort of problem or write about it but the telephone was in fact working. Personally I can quote other cases I know of in which you can check all the passages where everything is left unsaid. You will never find any traces of things like that. Policemen who don't shrink from blackmailing without instructions and who say to somebody: "I shall call by in a month from now and if you're not at work or at school. . . ."

Headmaster 1: I entirely agree, that's the reason I never ever call in the police. There have been cases of complaints lodged by parents of pupils about questions of stealing and we discussed matters so that the complaint would not be filed or would be withdrawn because we know only too well the sort of trouble that that can give rise to. . . . But they have never wittingly been placed in the hands of the police.

P: It's more subtle than that. Quite a number of boys don't want to stay at school. They're fed up with it and it isn't always their fault either. But at that stage, the lack of information, the failure of the school and the teaching staff to appreciate the consequences of this worsening of the situation means that the boy is already caught up in the cogs of the judicial system even before the school has come to realize it. . . . Before you know where you are, the machine is on its way.

Phase 2

In the second phase concrete proposals of mutual assistance were put forward by the participants. One of the headmasters suggested that when there was a "problem" with a pupil at one of the schools, he should be able to go to the other and vice versa.

Headmaster 2: You were shouting earlier and he in chorus with you: stop going to school 1, come to school 2, when there is a problem at school 2 go to school 1.

However, the parents were not mollified by that administrative arrangement. They continued to press their claims concerning the unequal functioning of the school and to criticize the violence of certain teachers and the way in which headmasters cover them at the expense of the children:

Mr. B.: Me come with him down there, me explain, him begin to get up like that: "Go to door!" and me angry, me ill.
Mr. B's daughter: You say that we come here to pick up the family allowances. That's got nothing to do with it. A teacher doesn't pick up a pupil's satchel and throw it like that.
Headmaster 1: The teacher who did that has offered to repair the satchel. You were shouting, so it would appear. I've come here so that we can solve problems. If you don't understand that and if you continue as you have been doing to talk nonsense like that . . .
Mr. B's daughter: You said so yourself!
Headmaster 1: There were three of us. I'm sorry if you mix up the discussion of three people and put the onus on me; in that case do as you wish. But then let's stop discussing. I am ready to do whatever we can so that such things don't happen again. But you will have to consider me differently from the way you consider me now and as you did when you came to tackle me in the school corridor.

Mr. B's daughter: You shouldn't answer like that.

Headmaster 1: I agree. But I didn't say it. What you're doing here is summarizing the conversation among three people and putting the blame on me.

A: What do you expect?

Commentary

These extracts give an idea of what might arise out of what seem to be individual problems as soon as a number of people with the same type of problem are brought together. In the case of this meeting, for example, the parents and children gradually learn that "it is the mentality" that certain teachers judge; they begin to understand how the processes of exclusion operate on the basis of structural elements of which both children at school and parents at work are the victims; they discover the connection between the police and the school but also how the headmasters themselves are trapped by structures they are unable to control.

Over and above these elements we find ourselves confronted at this meeting with elements common to any action with a social network or a set of families:

1) The problem of an individual appears as that of a group caught up in the same contradictions: "Mrs. So and So has the same problem as the one facing me. The same thing." Mr. S says to Mrs. C at one time, "My son has the same problems."

2) We witness the appearance of a whole series of political situations: situations of exclusion, oppression and mystification that the family or the network reproduce within themselves. The framework of some of these situations is that of the family. For example, Mrs. C speaking of her son M: "I took him to Brussels to study, not to steal. I took you to get a diploma, not a thief's diploma. It's because children get enough to eat that they act like that. If there were poverty, it would be different. Here the police doesn't do anything to them. They give them papers to fill in, but they don't punish them severely, they don't take them into the cellar and give them six of the best as they do in Morocco. If they were properly punished they would think twice . . ." or "Don't make them ashamed of you, they have come here to help you and if you start stealing it will be pointless."

3) Other similar political situations arise between members of the network. For example, Headmaster 2 asks Mr. S how it came about that

his son should be in trouble with the police whereas he had never gotten into trouble in Morocco and what mistake had he committed. Mr. S replies: "I didn't commit any fault; it was the question of religion. There are Christians, Moslems, Protestants. This boy is neither Christian, nor Moslem, nor Protestant. He just grows without any rules, just like that." Other participants point out that one can only compare like with like and that you have to take account of the social context to understand why his son had never been in trouble in Morocco and seems to frequently run into trouble in Belgium.

4) Once the concrete solutions have been suggested, a discussion is initiated and the paternalist aspect of some of these proposals is often denounced.

5) On the basis of their awareness of forming a community of excluded people, the participants at this meeting created their own network of support and mutual assistance. The network set up has continued to operate in the daily lives both of adults and adolescents.

Such difficulties seem to arise directly as a "sociocultural" rather than a "psychopathological" problem. But the fact is that every day children are sent to mental health centers because of difficulties at school and problems of maladjustment without any attempt being made to look into the socioeconomic or cultural components of their situation.

It is not only because the population we are working with in this district of Brussels is made up essentially of immigrants and sub-proletarians that we should integrate these components into our approach. These components operate, although in a different way, in other situations. True, there are other things in addition to these components. Other explanatory grids could be applied to help these adolescents in an individual and/or family context. We have given priority to an action related to the social context without rejecting other types of action. The fact that we have chosen to place our action at the soicopolitical level does not mean that we are imposing a political interpretation.

When acting with several families or with a social network, we generally work in four stages:

1) We explain to the entire group who we are, why we have brought about the meeting and what our objectives are. We then propose a program to those assembled. During this stage we assume responsibility for our actions whereby we have delineated the frame of reference for this work and we try to explain clearly why we are doing it. We talk about *our* expectations.

2) We offer a framework which makes it possible to express certain problems. This is often the time when the participants begin to become aware of their common condition and their common problems.
3) We set up working groups to try to find concrete solutions to some of the problems expressed.
4) Returning to a general assembly, the participants finally confront the proposed solutions. We witness the recreation of a micro-society which often repeats the alienating structures of the surrounding world, but in a context in which these structures can be dismantled. Often, when a task of mutual assistance is initiated, it is on a clearer basis of the awareness of shared deprivation.

We are still in the process of taking our very first tentative steps. I have described this work in order to suggest a direction for those wishing to explore it. Those who do so undoubtedly will often find themselves faced with much more intricate and much less sharply contrasted situations than those presented here.

EPILOGUE

I still agree with what I wrote four years ago. But my practice has evolved in the meantime.

On the one hand, network interventions and multiple family therapies have made us aware of the fact that a symptom such as delinquency, for example, could, when it was a matter of a collective phenomenon, have a function within the community. This leads us to an intervention which is different from that depicted in the previous pages (Elkaim, 1980).

On the other hand, when rereading this article, I realize that the broadening of the scope of intervention, linked to my desire to include a maximum number of components that apparently are not directly linked to the person or the family aspect, involved the danger of cautioning against my wish for some sort of onion peel structure—to start from a center which is the individual and to add on new layers as the family context is extended to the institutions, the neighborhood, the society. However, it is clear that these different levels coexist and are interrelated at any moment irrespective of the situation. My attempts at extending the confines of intervention were linked to my difficulty in perceiving in individual, couple or family therapy this profusion of levels and their mutual interaction.

Today, I still consider that multiple family therapies and network interventions are necessary, but I try more and more, on the basis of my work with a person, a couple or a family, to understand the manner in which a set of cultural, social, and political processes are being mediated, internalized and reproduced, all the more so as traditional explanatory grids do not allow us to integrate these processes.

Moreover, it seems to me that an approach which aims at being as little reductionist as possible should take an interest not only in extra-family "singularities" such as the ones described in this article but also in infra-family "singularities." It is in this direction that I am currently orienting my research.

REFERENCE NOTES

[1]"Sanhedrin": assembly of doctors of law who made up the civil and religious court in ancient Palestine.

[2]One of the people who helped me most in my work in the South Bronx, Harris Peck, the former director of the Lincoln Mental Health Services, was one of the victims of the clash between the Lincoln Hospital Mental Health Workers and the Albert Einstein School of Medicine. His warm support was precious to me on many an occasion, not only with the Albert Einstein School of Medicine but also with mental health workers, formerly his opponents. Some people fell "foul" of the structures; I believe Peck was one.

[3]This group was made up of young psychiatrists who had come to attend a training course in social and community psychiatry at the Albert Einstein College of Medicine: Maurizio Andolfi, William MacFarlane and Kenneth Terkelsen. Two other psychiatrists completed the group, Joel Feiner and Michael Serieye, who had already been working in the South Bronx for many years.

[4]This example is taken from a debate on "techniques and the political alternative" in which I took part with Robert Castel, Felix Guattari and Giovanni Jervis. The report of the debate was published in the autumn 1977 in a joint work published in Paris in the "Collection 10/18."

[5]Cf., in the April 1976 issue of *"Delinquency and Rehabilitation Report"* the article headed "Police officers act out family crises to learn how to handle them" in connection with a program carried out by the Garden City Police Department.

REFERENCES

Auerswald, E.H. Families, change and the ecological perspective. *Family Process*, 1971, *10*, (3), 263-280.

Elkaim, M. Family system and social system: Some examples of intervention in an impoverished district of Brussels. In M. Andolfi & I. Zwerling, (Eds.), *Dimensions of Family Therapy*. New York: Guilford Press, 1980.

Ferber, A.S. & Beels, C.C. Changing family behaviour programs. *International Psychiatry Clinics*, 1970, *7*, (4).

Gioscia, V. On social time. In Osmund, Jaker and Cheek (Eds.), *The Future of Time*. New York: Doubleday, 1970.

Grant, R. In Service Training Program, summary of history, rationale, structure and future plans of in-service training program. Stencilled, October 1970.

Haley, J. An interactional description of schizophrenia. *Psychiatry*, 1959, 22, (4), 321-322.

Jackson, D. The question of family homeostasis. *Psychiatric Quarterly Supplement*, 1957, 31, 79.

Kaplan, S. & Roman, M. *The Organization and Delivery of Mental Health Services in the Ghetto.* New York: Praeger, 1973.

Laqueur, H.P. Multiple family therapy: Questions and answers. In D.A. Bloch (Ed.), *Techniques of Family Psychotherapy: A Primer.* New York: Grune and Stratton, 1973.

MacGregor, R. Communicating values in family therapy. In G.H. Zuk & I. Boszormenyi-Nagy (Eds.), *Family Therapy and Disturbed Families.* Palo Alto: Science and Behavior Books, 1967.

Minuchin, S. Some points in family therapy grammar. Stencilled, February 1974, pp. 25, 26.

Reverby, S. & Handelman, M. Emancipation of Lincoln. *Health Pac Bulletin*, January 1972, 37.

Speck, R.V. & Attneave, C.N. Social network intervention. In J. Haley (Ed.), *Changing Families.* New York: Grune and Stratton, 1971.

Speck, R.V. & Attneave, C.N. *Family Networks.* New York: Vintage Books, 1974.

Wynne, L.C. The study of intrafamilial alignments and splits in exploratory family therapy. In N.W. Ackerman, F. Beatman, & S. Sherman (Eds.), *Exploring the Base for Family Therapy.* New York: Family Service Association of America, 1961.

Editor's Commentary: A Broader
Therapeutic Universe

Elkaim stretches our horizons, going beyond the conjugal family system, the extended family network, and multifamily groups to encompass the cultural environment and sociopolitical milieu and institutions in which the families he treats reside. He writes from a perspective originally gleaned in Belgium, greatly modified and enlarged in New York, and further enriched by years of thoughtful front-line experience treating families in a lower socioeconomic sector of Brussels. He argues convincingly for his position—liberally sprinkling his chapter with highly illustrative case material. He thereby goads the reader not to be content with knowing and altering the intrapsychic and interpersonal dynamics underlying patholgocial behavior; he makes a case that it is imperative to group families with similar problems together so that they gain a new consciousness of the social causation of their plight and band together to provide mutual assistance and jointly engage in problem-solving efforts—gaining strength from one another and becoming more potent in waging their common battle. It is probably not coincidental that while Elkaim was in training at Bronx State Hospital, Israel Zwerling was Chairman of the Department of Psychiatry and was utilizing his incisive mind and clinical acumen to extend the foundations of family therapy and lay the groundwork for community psychiatry. Today both Elkaim and Zwerling (1981) speak in more radical terms than much of the field, are deeply concerned about alienation and the social context, and believe that treatment should not take place in a vacuum. It is a message that bears reiterating.

Stagoll, in Chapter 18, deals with the same kinds of issues in relation to injured immigrant workers in Australia who are mystified by the baffling messages and demands of the insurance and medico-legal professions who hold the worker and his family's future in their hands that Elkaim discusses here in regard to Moroccan immigrant children in Belgium schools where the expectations and administrative style are unfamiliar and confusing. Similar disorienting dilemmas confront Mexicans, Puerto Ricans, Cubans and others who have relocated in the United States. They find difficulty making the transition to those aspects of the society that are vastly different from in their homeland and seem to enter a period of cultural shock. Clearly such problems are not culturally specific; rather there is a universality in the predictable upheaval and disorganization caused by relocation. As Elkaim so persuasively points out, what ensues may seem like individual and family pathology and dysfunction, but *only* looking at and intervening at these levels is woefully inadequate.

I agree with Elkaim that the skilled therapist must also be mindful of the larger macro-system and the impact of its educational, socioeconomic and political institutions, utilizing this knowledge as part of his understanding of the problems presented. However—and this is a departure from Elkaim's stance—*if* the clinician does not believe it is his/her function to intervene at the macro-system level by doing multiple family therapy and encouraging the various patients to organize as a community group to take united action, then it is also valid to refer this to a community worker proficient in this kind of activity. The therapist can continue to handle the individual and family system adjustment reactions and work cooperatively, as needed, with the community organizer. We cannot all be all things to all people in our therapeutic endeavors and it is important to be cognizant of the parameters of what we can do effectively and to link our patients up to other resources for assistance in other areas. Nonetheless, it appears equally valid for those who can intervene at the micro- and macro-systems levels to do so. What is the overriding consideration is to formulate the picture so that help will be provided—perhaps thinking in terms of a professional network of services when one person cannot or chooses not to handle it all.

It is interesting to note that Elkaim, like Loader et al. and Pollack et al., has written in the first person—sharing his journey from the beginning point of his ideas to where he is now in his thinking—taking us step by step through his evolution and enabling us to gain fuller knowledge of the raison d'etre for his perspective. Such candor, which makes any author more vulnerable to the reader's criticism, blends surprisingly well with his strong clarion call to enter into a battle much more complex than the usual family wars we treat.

REFERENCE

Zwerling, I. Family therapy and the alienation syndrome. *Journal of Marital and Family Therapy*, July 1981, 7, (3), 331-338.

Chapter 20

The Extended Family in Transition: Clinical Implications

By Judith Landau-Stanton,
John Griffiths,
and Jean Mason

The sociological transition of the family follows a universal pattern. Specific family problems arising from the process of transition from extended to nuclear family are examined. The South African Indian extended family in transition is used as a universal model. The culture and traditions of the Indian family in the South African situation provide a clear view of this process and its clinical implications. This model facilitates an understanding of families in cultural and sociological transition throughout the world and provides a basis for therapeutic intervention.

This is a revised version of an article originally published in *Psychotherapeia*, South Africa, Oct. 1981, 7, (4), under the title of "Link Therapy as a Family Therapy Technique for Transitional Extended Families."

Judith Landau-Stanton, M.G., Ch. B., D.P.M., was a Consulting Psychiatrist and Family Therapist in private practice in Westville, Natal, South Africa; Honorary Senior Lecturer, Department of Psychiatry, University of Natal; and Senior Lecturer, Faculty of Health Sciences, University of Durban-Westville, when this was written. She is now living and working in Philadelphia. John Griffiths, M.Sc., is a Clinical Psychologist and Senior Lecturer, Department of Psychiatry, University of Zimbabwe, Salisbury, Zimbabwe. Jean Mason, M.Soc.Sc., is a Senior Lecturer, Department of Social Work and Department of Mental Health and Medical Social Work, University of Durban-Westville, Durban, South Africa.

It has been postulated that the sociological transition of the family follows a universal pattern (Landau & Griffiths, 1981). The first stage of this transition is from extended to nuclear family. The second stage is from the nuclear unit to new configurations of nuclear unit, including those arising from realignment of the relationships and, in extreme cases, fractionation of the nuclear unit family.

Until recently the clinical ramifications of this process of transition from one stage to another had not been explored. Guerin, for example, stated that:

> The best psychoanalytic thinkers, like Otto Kernberg, frequently speak of general systems applications to the larger social context both in order to understand human behavior and to mobilize forces to alter the context. On an interventional level, however, they move back to cause-and-effect individual theory and the corresponding techniques. Other general systems thinkers, like Scheflen, are heavily into the study of context determinants, sociology and anthropology. Since this type of general system abstraction has not as yet been translated into clinically relevant terms, these people assume a position of interventional nihilism (Guerin, 1976, p. 21).

The current authors, however, believe that specific problems arise that are not pathological per se but are precipitated by the transition from one stage to another (Landau & Griffiths, 1981). The clinical relevance of this statement and the implications for therapy can be demonstrated by examining particular family structures and case studies of this transition. The sociological transition of each individual family should be a major consideration of the family therapist.

The South African Indian (immigrant from India and Pakistan) has been selected for this examination because the group is predominantly in transition from extended to nuclear family structure. This nucleari-zation is found wherever there is a transition from a traditional rural hierarchical to a modern urbanized life-style. Other examples are to be found in certain immigrant groups from Europe and the Far East (Spanish, Portuguese, Italian, Irish, Chinese, Greek) and among rural farming communities exposed to the forces of urbanization and acculturation. The South African Indian group, because of its emphasis on tradition and culture, provides an almost exaggerated example of this universal process.

THE TRADITIONAL EXTENDED FAMILY

Although the Indian South Africans are well integrated into the urban organization, their pattern of social life tends to remain sociologically rural and therefore traditional, as does that of many immigrant families in cultural transition. This is seen particularly in the network of family relations, best described by the terms *kutum* (Gujerati, Hindustani and Urdu language groups), *kudumbom* (Tamil), and *kuduma* (Telegu). The kutum (or kudumbom or kuduma) is a complex kinship system of several nuclear families arranged in a hierarchical structure of male seniority. There are usually three generations involved. The structure is generally patriarchal with patrilineal and patrilocal relationship ties. It may also be matriarchal and matrilocal but even in these instances remains patrilineal. The power structure is therefore male dominated, with young brides becoming part of their husband's family in all aspects. These families are generally co-residential and commensal (that is, living in one house and sharing cooking and eating arrangements). Many share property and business interests according to coparcenary arrangement (Jithoo, 1978; Kuper, 1960; Kolenda, 1968; Meer, 1969; Maasdorp, 1968) which allows for equal partitioning. "The kutum is like an intimate collective conscience which socializes and controls; binds and integrates members into a closely watched system of social integration" (Meer, 1969, p. 66).

Therefore, in common with other forms of the extended family, such as those found among Spanish, Italian, Greek and Portuguese, the kutum is characterized by extensive involvement on the part of all its members in decisions affecting the group. Relationship and interpersonal problems are resolved within the group according to a set of extremely rigid prescriptions. Therapeutic intervention is neither invited nor indicated. Problems are resolved traditionally within the kutum. Maasdorp's view is that, "The joint family system has always contained within it the seeds of discord, but such feelings were usually repressed" (Maasdorp, 1968, p. 130). It would, however, appear that rather than repression, what occurs is a concealment of problems from anyone outside the intimate circle of the kutum. Interference from the outside is not brooked under any circumstances whatsoever. The therapist may be tempted to intervene, but will invariably be extruded and made impotent by the hierarchical structure which closes ranks and ultimately resolves its problems according to its traditional rules (Landau & Griffiths, 1981).

The following case is an illustration of the type of request an outside agency might receive from a member of the kutum, and the restrictive quality of the assistance that is acceptable in the case of such a request.

Mrs. S., a South African Indian grandmother, while attending hospital for treatment of a peptic ulcer, requested assistance from the medical social worker in drafting a will. She lived, with 14 other family members, in a two-room house. The kitchen was also used as a bedroom to provide sufficient sleeping place for the kutum. The social worker's assessment was that she was confronted with a multi-problem extended family. One son was in prison, a granddaughter was an uncontrolled mentally retarded epileptic, and two of the adult sons were financially dependent on Mrs. S. while making no attempt to contribute to the household in any way. In addition, Mrs. S.'s eldest daughter refused to work while her husband, an epileptic with a police record, was unemployed and awaiting a state disability grant. Mrs. S.'s second son had died and she had adopted his illegitimate child. It was with regard to this child that Mrs. S.'s difficulty with her will had arisen. She wished to ensure that in the event of her death, the child's biological mother would obtain custody. At the same time, however, she wanted to preserve the anonymity of this woman.

Mrs. S. was faced with a predicament. In the kutum, the provision of a will is traditionally open, the decisions pertaining to it are shared by the family members and its format conforms to traditional prescription. In this case, elements of secrecy and the desire for the legal sanction of a civil will forced her to seek advice outside the family.

The social worker, concerned about the multiple problems evident in the family, felt obliged to proffer help in areas beyond that of the drafting of the will. She suggested that Mrs. S. contact the agency concerned with youthful offenders about her son. She also wanted to refer the epileptic granddaughter for reassessment and to secure employment for the sons. She offered to persuade the eldest daughter that it was her obligation to go out to work in order to contribute to the family's income. Mrs. S. was also advised to contact the child welfare agency about the question of her granddaughter's custody. Furthermore, the worker embarked on a program of family sessions, with a view to improving interpersonal communication, and individual sessions with Mrs. S. to train her in assertive techniques.

Over a period of six months, the social worker became progressively more desperate because Mrs. S. and her family failed to contact the child welfare agency, the legal aid society, the agency for criminal offenders, the epilepsy clinic and employment agencies.

By the end of the first month, for example, the social worker had reported that, "Mrs. S. implied that her family wouldn't appreciate interference by worker. Worker had no option but to opt out. . . ." Mrs. S., however, continued to keep her appointments. Two weeks later the social worker had stated that "The patient is very resistant to counseling from child welfare society. . . . Patient shows much resistance to referral, thus plan of treatment will be to motivate patient to go to the child welfare society, i.e., to make her aware of the necessity of their services . . . and to work through her fears of referral."

After six months of interviews, both in the office and at Mrs. S.'s home, the social worker realized that Mrs. S. and her family, ". . . were not prepared to allow the worker entry . . . did not want to accept change from outside intervention . . . despite the sharing of many problems with the worker, only wanted help with the drafting of the will."

This social worker's experience is typical of the frustration that results from an attempt to intervene in areas which the extended family would traditionally negotiate within the kutum according to strict prescription. In this case, advice was sought for a problem requiring legal sanction, an area beyond the normal jurisdiction of the kutum. The social worker's error was in attempting intervention in other areas. Her motives for intervention are easily explicable, in that other unresolved problems were apparent. It was only in the course of her association with the family that she realized that the sharing of these problems did not imply a request for help in their solution. This would ultimately be achieved through the family's own enforcement of traditional prescription.

The importance of assessing whether an extended family is functioning traditionally or whether it is in the process of transition is clearly vital. In the former instance, intervention is neither indicated nor invited. Problems are generally concealed but their exposure to outside view, as in this case, must not be misinterpreted as pathological; instead, they must be seen in the light of the culture and tradition of the family as well as its position on the map of the sociological transition pathway. In the case of the transitional family, however, intervention becomes appropriate if invited.

THE TRANSITIONAL EXTENDED FAMILY

"The Indian family is being presently threatened by many factors which may change it. There is a drive to grow away from the folkways of the kutum, a desire for individual, rather than collective, expression" (Meer, 1969, p. 72). A transitional extended family may be defined as one in which one or more members have embarked on the transitional pathway towards nuclearization. There is invariably a loosening of the tight traditional relationship bonding in some part of the family system. If the transitional process is accepted by all members of the family, transitional problems do not arise. Not infrequently, however, one or more members of the extended family become transitional (generally second and third generation members), while others (generally the oldest and therefore those traditionally holding hierarchical power) remain resistant to the process of change and attempt to retain the structure. The resultant interpersonal conflict between transitional and resistant members typically leads to emotional and behavioral problems for which the family has no existing prescription. *Recognition of this transitional conflict is the key to treatment.*

This is likely to be the first time that the family has been confronted by these transitional conflicts which, by their very nature, have not been provided for in the traditional extended structure. Their only recourse is to an external agent. The mere fact that self-referral is made for emotional or interpersonal difficulties entitles one to conclude that transition is in progress.

Problems are presented to the clinician either by a transitional member or by an entrenched traditional member of the family. If presented by a traditional member, they are invariably directly related to the transitional conflict and represent a request for external support of the traditional system. Nontransitional problems would be resolved within the system. On the other hand, problems presented by a transitional member need not be transitional in nature. They may be difficulties for which a traditional prescription exists and which would previously have been contained and resolved within the extended family. Their presentation by the transitional member arises out of his questioning and rejection of these customary prescriptions.

The following case study is an example of referral by a transitional member of the extended family.

Mrs. M., a professional woman aged 39 years, asked her general practitioner to refer her for psychotherapy. The psychotherapist realized at the time of referral that there were marital problems and requested an initial interview with Mr. and Mrs. M. Mr. M., 41, a prominent member of the community, attended the interview "for the sake of my wife." During this session it became apparent that the marital problems were based on transitional conflict.

Mr. and Mrs. M. and their daughter lived with Mr. M.'s older brother and his family in the patriarchal home. Mr. M.'s father, 86, had lost his wife five years earlier. There was incessant conflict between Mrs. M.

and her senior sister-in-law who had assumed matriarchal power in the family. Mrs. M. also complained bitterly that her husband devoted excessive attention and financial consideration to the extended family. She felt that their nuclear unit was being deprived as a result. Mr. M.'s response to his wife's bitterness had been to remove himself from their bedroom. Their four-year-old daughter had taken his place.

Despite the fact that Mrs. M. was evidently more transitional than Mr. M., it was decided that Mr. M. would have more authority as transitional link co-therapist[1] responsible for liaison between the family therapist and the traditional extended family. Link therapy involves the training and coaching of a member of the family to function as a therapist to his own family system (Landau, 1981). The link therapist needs to be both acceptable to and effective with the family, as well as being available and amenable to the family therapist. Usually the most effective link will be a man of some seniority, such as an uncle or older son. It is very important that the therapist not be tempted to select the most acculturated member of the family whose life-style and values most closely approach the therapist's. Selection of either the most traditional or the most acculturated member would result in artificial momentum to the direction of resolution of the transitional conflict. The family member who initiates family therapy is most frequently either an acculturated member or an entrenched traditional member. In each case the motivation is clear and agreement to work with either would predetermine the transitional direction taken. We have found that the most effective link therapist is a family member whose position has not yet been resolved, one who is caught in the system's transitional conflict and is therefore in the process of cultural transition. He is generally not the complainant and may even be a peripheral member of the family. The most transitional member of the extended family is used as a link between the family therapist and the rigid family structure which would, under normal circumstances, deny the therapist adequate entry. The link co-therapist is coached to enable him to assist the family in resolving its transitional conflict in a direction of the link co-therapist's choice. After an initial family assessment, the link therapist is selected and goes back alone into the family and originates the intervention with the continued supervision and coaching of the family therapist.

Mr. M. agreed, as link therapist, to work towards realigning family relationships in order to facilitate his wife's integration into the family. Moderate success was achieved in this direction over a three-week period. Then Mr. M.'s father died and Mr. M. was able to express his desire to alter the direction of therapy and to move towards nuclearization of his own family unit: *"Everything changes now with Father dead. We both had to live the way he wanted because of all he did for us. . . . I want to keep the family finances together, but I feel that moving out with my wife and child will help us."*

Mr. M. proceeded to help his brother's family adjust to the new direction and, after three months, Mr. M. and his nuclear family moved out of the extended family home. Conventional marital therapy was initiated and systems techniques were employed in the restructuring of relationships within the nuclear unit.

In this example, the problems highlighted were clearly transitional in nature. Therapeutic intervention was both invited and indicated.

If one accepts the transitional nature of the family it becomes as unrealistic to assume or impose nuclear stability as it would be to hold a growing youngster in permanent puberty. The therapist is tempted to decide whether to move the family towards, or away from, one configuration or another (and there has been, among family therapists, a strong bias in favor of an acceptance of the nuclear family as the stable paradigm). If the therapist succumbs to this temptation his or her decision becomes critical. It becomes irrelevant once the transitional etiology of the problems is understood.

Therapists are well aware of the need to understand the transitional factors involved in treating, for example, adolescent problems, the mourning process, the empty nest and other individual and intrafamilial changes. The authors would like to underline the importance of assessing the relevance of the broader transitional issues as well. Mapping has become a relatively standard practice in both individual and family therapy and is extremely useful in the assessment of transition.

Sluzki, working with migrant families, states categorically that, "In the course of the first interview, the therapist should establish which phase of the process of migration the family is currently in and how they have dealt with the vicissitudes of previous phases" (Sluzki, 1979, p. 389). *A comprehensive map should extend beyond that of the position of the individual in his own and his family's life, and beyond that of the family in its life cycle to include the transitional position of the multigenerational family in society.* Appropriate therapy can only be instituted once the therapist is aware of the elements precipitating the problems that he wishes to treat.

Once the transitional etiology of certain family problems had been firmly established, it became evident to the authors that the therapy techniques in their armamentarium were insufficient for dealing with transitional conflict, and that it was necessary to develop modes of assisting such families that did not necessarily precipitate them into a value system and family constellation of the therapist's own preference. The following additional factors emerged as being significant to assess prior to the initiation of therapy:

When is it appropriate or inappropriate to treat?
How does one establish the goals of therapy?
Who should be involved in the treatment?

An understanding of the position of the family on the transitional map will provide the answer as to when it is appropriate to offer treatment. Traditional extended families (as discussed above), should only be given assistance in those areas in which they request it, which areas are invariably limited to problems for which there is no traditional prescription. From the point of commencement from the transitional extended family onwards, therapeutic intervention is appropriate.

As to establishing the goals of therapy, we have found that it is vital to assist the family in the formulation of their own goals and direction and to offer therapeutic aid in the achievement of this, rather than to determine the desired direction of transition for the family.

CONCLUSION

A comparison of interventions in rigid traditional and transitional extended families illustrates the need for careful assessment of the presence of transitional factors. The presence of these factors and the position of the family on the map of the sociological transition pathway should determine whether therapeutic intervention is appropriate and which therapeutic techniques should be employed. The conflicts arising from transitional factors must provide the initial focus for therapy.

REFERENCE NOTE

[1]Research into the use of link therapy was presented by J. Landau at the International A.A.M.F.T. Conference, Toronto, Nov. 1980.

REFERENCES

Guerin, P.M. (Ed.) *Family Therapy: Theory and Practice*. New York: Gardner Press, 1976.

Jithoo, S. Complex households and joint families amongst Indians in Durban. In J. Argyle & E. Preston-Whyte, (Eds.), *Social System and Tradition in Southern Africa*. Cape Town: Oxford University Press, 1978.

Kolenda, P.M. Region, caste and family structure: A comparative study of the Indian "joint" family. In M. Singer & B.S. Cohn, (Eds.), *Structure and Change in Indian Society*. Chicago: Aldine Publishing Co., 1968.

Kuper, H. *Indian People in Natal*. Pietermaritzburg: University of Natal Press, 1960.

Landau, J. *The Family in Transition: Theory and Practice*. New York: Guilford Press, in preparation.

Landau, J. Link therapy as a family therapy technique for transitional extended families. *Psychotherapeia*, Oct. 1981, 7, (4).

Landau, J. & Griffiths, J.A. The South African family in transition—Therapeutic and training implications. *Journal of Marital and Family Therapy*, July 1981, 7, (3).

Maasdorp, G.G. *A Natal Indian Community*. Durban: University of Natal Press, 1968.

Meer, F. *Portrait of Indian South Africans*. Durban: Avon House, 1969.

Sluzki, C.E. Migration and family conflict. *Family Process*, December 1979, *18*, 371-390.

Editor's Commentary: Families—
A Tradition of Transition

By framing the changes from extended family system to nuclear family system as a transitional process, Landau-Stanton, Griffiths and Mason provide an in-depth and dynamic perspective for understanding the sequence of events and modifications that has universal implications.

Because the transition is never complete, it is dynamic and often unsettling. Although we could posit a linear continuum from extended to nuclear family, it seems to me this would be an inadequate conceptualization to include what we see evolving in some parts of the world—beyond nuclearity—to alternate family forms. Sometimes this takes the form of an extremely fragmented family—individuals related by blood or marriage who live in the same domicile but in isolation—barely speaking or interacting on any other level. Other times what is purposely created is a communal type family: One variant is single individuals living together and sharing their financial and personal resources; another is married couples and their children living in the same or closely connected households and pooling assets and services, sharing their lives in many ways. The communal family resembles the tribal or extended family in many ways; it seeks to foster a network of mutual caring and responsibility to replace the anonymity and alienation often experienced in nuclear or fragmented-fractionated families. Thus, a more applicable model with greater explanatory power may well be a *curvilinear model*. When a society moves to the extreme of either the small, too isolated family or the large, possessive kinship family, some members become disgruntled enough to seek the assets inherent in another family form and the cycle of the change process is again activated. One form of family life is not inherently superior to another; each affords a different adaptive and emotional potential and is partially contingent on the nature of the economic, political, educational and religious ideologies and structures of the given society at that time in history.

For example, as with the South African Indian family described by Landau-Stanton, Griffiths and Mason, in other cultures too—in the past or present when the socioeconomic climate precipitated a shift from a predominantly agrarian culture to a more urbanized, industrial society, family life underwent major alterations. The large kinship network that had sufficient space for all members to dwell together on the farm and needed many pairs of hands to do the numerous tasks which abounded on the land and in the homestead became unwieldy and burdensome in a small urban home. Ascribed roles and predictability of life-style were replaced by newly fashioned assumed roles and greater flexibility of life-style. Security and stability were often traded for new experiences and instability. The tremendous potential beckoned with opportunities and challenges; it was even patriotic to join the urban work force. But as with all large-scale change, it was often fraught with traumatic up-heaval, anxiety, disorientation and much fear of the unknown. The natural tendency of the more conservative members of the family to cling to tradition and eschew the ramifications inherent in change are understandable; they wish to protect and preserve what they have worked hard to build and to feel safe with what is familiar. Conversely, the younger members are more eager to forge new pathways, think their own thoughts and build their own brave, new world. Conflict and hear-tache are inevitable; autonomy and self-actualization are worthy goals, but the pathway toward them can be lonely and the need for belonging is rarely stilled. Where does the precarious balance lie? Where does one find the golden mean between independence and belonging, and be-tween the merits of the conjugal family and the different merits of the consanguine family, and how does one bring about the rapprochement between the members of the family who apparently seek disparate life-styles?

The three authors of this novel chapter suggest that neither the most transitional nor the most entrenched member of the family serve as a "link" therapist. Instead, an undecided member should be designated and coached by the therapist. Herein seems to lie an excellent, ingenious route to mediating the breech and facilitating growth. Another possible way that I tried in a demonstration interview with a South African Indian family during a recent (1981) visit was to utilize a South African co-therapist who is steeped in tradition yet who has moved quite far on the transitional course toward a nuclear family structure in his own life as the link between the traditional and nontraditional members of the patient family. Whatever intervention is used, the caveat that Landau-Stanton, Griffiths and Mason prescribe, to not intrude in areas which the family considers its private, almost sacred purview, should be seriously respected. Too often, therapists who place a premium on open communication do not have the kind of multicultural perspective being advocated here, which suggests recognizing our patients' sense of their boundaries and not transgressing these inappropriately.

We look forward to seeing some outcome studies on the efficacy of "link" therapy.

Part IV

Treating Marital Conflict and Sexual Dysfunction

Chapter 21

How to be a Marriage Therapist
Without Knowing Practically
Anything

By Jay Haley

Therapists in training as marriage and family therapists often do not learn techniques for bringing about change. They also do not learn ways to conceal from colleagues and from clients the fact that they do not know how to solve the presenting problems of couples in distress. Both general and specific techniques are reviewed for concealing ignorance as well as ways to make correct excuses for failure. The presentation is designed for therapists who find themselves not knowing what to do with a couple in a particular case and for therapists who do not know what to do with any case.

During their professional training, therapists are taught psychodynamic and other theories of abnormal psychology, learning theory, personality development and the science of diagnosis. Some even learn what medications to give troubled people that will cause the least harm. Yet a surprising number of clinicians graduate from departments of psychology, social work and psychiatry without learning how to solve the presenting problem of a client. In addition, a new generation of

This article was originally published in the *Journal of Marital and Family Therapy*, October 1980, *6*, (4), 385-391. It has also been published in Haley, Jay. *Refections on Therapy*. Washington, D.C.: Family Therapy Institute of Washington, D.C., 1981.

Jay Haley, M.A., is Director of the Family Therapy Institute, Chevy Chase, Maryland.

marriage and family therapists is appearing who do not know how to solve marriage and family problems. Young marriage therapists by the thousands are in graduate schools for members of the "fourth profession" of marriage and family therapists. They not only learn psychological theories but also systems theory, family development, divorce statistics, and what to say to pass the state licensing examinations. Yet a surprising number have not beeen taught how to change a marital problem. Not knowing ways to change anyone, they have also not been taught how to conceal that fact. This paper is designed for therapists who find themselves not knowing what to do with a couple in a particular case, as happens to all of us. However, it is primarily for the therapist who is ignorant about how to change a marriage relationship in any case and who wishes to sound knowledgeable and appear to know what he, or she,[1] is doing.

The many varieties of marital problems brought to a therapist are all dilemmas to the therapist who does not know what to do to cause a change. The problem might be a husband who is insanely jealous of his wife, or a couple might be using a child to carry on a marital quarrel, or a spouse could have a symptom as part of the marriage contract. A symptomatic spouse could be one who drinks, or is depressed, or who has stomach aches, or is anxious, or has some other distressing problem that maintains the marriage and makes it unfortunate.

It does not matter what the marital problem might be when a therapist does not know how to solve any problem and can only diagnose, talk about defenses and anxiety, and discuss systems theory. It is incorrect for the therapist to say to a client in distress, "I don't know what on earth to do with a problem like yours." The therapist must pull up his or her socks and proceed as if competent enough to be worthy of a fee.

CONCEALING IGNORANCE FROM COLLEAGUES

There are two problems for the therapist who does not know how to change anyone: how to conceal that fact from colleagues, and how to conceal it from the customers. It is most simple to conceal incompetence from colleagues. Methods have been worked out by several generations of clinicians. To review a few common ones:

---

[1]The author uses the pronoun *he* for convenience and acknowledges the inequity of the traditional use of the masculine pronoun since ignorance about how to do therapy occurs in both sexes.

1. One should routinely insist on the importance of confidentiality in therapy. All doors and walls of offices should be soundproofed so that a colleague casually leaning against a door will not hear a therapist being ineffectual. If it is suggested that videotapes of interviews be made for training or research purposes, this idea should be banished with a contemptuous comment about unethical practices and a patient's right to privacy.
2. All supervision should be done without recordings or observation. If one takes notes to a supervisor, the notes can emphasize relationship issues. The fact that one floundered ineffectually in the therapy need not be known. Supervisors often prefer to discuss dynamics rather than interventions to cause change since that subject was usually neglected in their supervisory training.
3. Long-term therapy should be done so that colleagues who refer people will forget who they referred. In this way people continue to refer marital problems over the years to a therapist without ever discovering that he never changed anyone.
4. At professional meetings one should emphasize the scientific nature of diagnosis, research, systems theory, and family and child development. Therapy should be referred to as a mere "how to do it" matter. When clinical work is denigrated as practical, in contrast to scientific contributions, therapy is made to seem too unimportant for the revelations of incompetence that might be made by scientific research.
5. When accrediting therapists for licensing, and in academic training, one should emphasize the importance of having the correct degree and not skill in therapy. The accredited therapist is a person who has a Ph.D., an M.S.W., an M.D., an Ed.D., an R.N., or a Master's in Marital Therapy. Basing licensing on degrees protects a therapist who does not know how to do therapy. He, or she, only needs to know how to take classes in a university for a number of years. Should there be a public clamor to base licensing on more than an academic degree because of obvious incompetence, it is possible to insist that there must also be one hundred and two hours of supervised therapy experience. This is not a problem since the therapist can see customers alone in a room and later disclose to a supervisor only what he wishes to have known (see #2 above). Attempts to accredit therapists by tests of skill or measures of successful outcome should be ridiculed as impractical. One can say, "After all, who can really define a successful marriage in this complex and changing world? Therefore, how can we say that we succeeded in improving a marriage?"

CONCEALING IGNORANCE FROM THE CUSTOMERS

Colleagues need not know what actually happens in a therapy room but clients must. The procedures for concealing from customers the fact that one does not know how to change them can be classed as general and specific.

The general procedure used by most experienced therapists who don't know how to cause change is to encourage the client to talk and talk on the gamble that this will cause improvement. When interviewing a spouse alone, the therapist can use what he learned in academia and from watching television shows and say, "Tell me more about that," and "Have you wondered why that was so important to you?" When seeing the couple together, the therapist can say, "I want you to talk to each other so I can observe your communication." Then he can be quiet and need only encourage them occasionally if their argument sags.

While encouraging clients to talk, a therapist should say as little as possible to conceal the fact that he does not know what to say. This is called "active listening." Silent behavior also introduces an air of mystery, which makes specific skills less necessary, as high priests have known for centuries. Since the client inevitably attributes significant meanings to silence, the therapist is given a reputation for eloquence when the fact of the matter is he just does not know what to say. To further encourage the couple to talk, the therapist can make occasional interpretations, pointing out that the unfortunate things the couple are saying to each other are examples of their poor interpersonal relationship. It is helpful to say "Isn't that a sexist statement?" at random moments. The couple will begin to prefer the therapist be silent, and then he can be so comfortably without feeling he, or she, should do more.

Discussing past history is always welcomed by clients who would rather avoid present issues. The review of the past might have no relation to change, but it is expected by most people. A phrase to use is, "I see this problem is very distressing to you both. Now tell me what your marriage was like before, and when you first began to notice this problem developing." Unless the clients are mute or retarded, which calls for modifications of the approach, that inquiry will release a deluge of words that can last anywhere from one interview to a whole course of therapy. Married couples enjoy arguing about the past and about who said what and when since they have experience at that. How long the talk will last depends partly upon the loquaciousness of the customers and also on how skillfully the therapist encourages them by saying, "Can you tell me more about that?" Involved in arguing about the past, the customers do not notice that the therapist does not know what to do about their present problem.

An unfortunate happening can occur when the therapist encourages a couple to talk freely, express their feelings, and to argue about who caused what in the past. That type of discussion often leads to such anger and disruption in the marriage that the couple decides to separate. The therapist can feel sad about this. However, he soon finds compensation in the fact that a separation makes it possible to do "divorce therapy." The therapist can help the couple in the difficult task of separating. In the process, the therapist can be pleasantly surprised to discover that one customer has become two customers, each paying a separate fee.

Many therapists who are not able to help couples separate can double their fees by seeing them as a couple in interviews and also placing them in a group with other couples. The therapist does not need skill when doing a couples group because the couples take over the sessions and share and talk and interpret to each other. Everyone feels something important is happening even if they are not changing, and the therapist gains a double fee while needing to know only how to remain silent.

Exploring other problems is something to do either early or late in the therapy. For example, if a couple comes in with a husband who is angry and jealous of his wife who has had an affair, the therapist who does not know what to do should take the focus off the presenting problem as quickly as possible. He can say, "After all, jealousy is just a symptom and we must talk about other matters so we can get at the roots of the symptom in the marriage relationship." Another way to put it is to appear thorough and cautious by saying, "Well now, I would like to put this jealousy problem in perspective. Could you review for me all the different problems about your marriage that have ever distressed you?" Some clients need to be encouraged to bring up other problems, but most of them can think of enough to keep the conversation going. Examples to help bring out reminiscences and satisfy the curiosity of the therapist, such as, "After a group sexual orgy, do you have special marital conflicts?"

Examining the consequences of the problem will provide clients with the impression that the therapist appreciates how serious it is, even if nothing is being accomplished. One can ask how much time is wasted with the problem, what it prevents the couple from doing, how many inconveniences it causes, how embarrassing it is in relation to children or in-laws, and what would be done if the couple did not have the problem. Often the couple will say they had not realized how many consequences there were, and now they are determined to get over the problem. The therapist can say, "Well, you've taken the first step by coming to therapy; that is the important thing."

If the therapist likes to focus upon interpersonal relations, he can make insightful comments about the client-therapist relationship by saying, "Have you noticed that you treat me as if I am an authority figure who is supposed to solve your problem for you?" This kind of comment encourages the clients not to expect the therapist to be an expert and will also bring out reminiscences about bosses and other authorities. The therapist can also have the spouses not only talk about the ways they relate to each other but to all their relatives and friends.

Exploring what has been tried to get over the problem includes discussing previous therapy, if any. One should always explore what advice customers were given in the past. While appearing to explore history, the therapist is actually getting ideas of what he might do with a customer. Therapists communicate about therapy techniques to one another through their clients as they learn what colleagues have done to try to solve a problem.

Before proceeding to more specific tactics, the general ones can be summarized with a case example. Choosing an arbitrary problem, let us suppose that a woman comes to a therapist and says she is failing in her marriage and her career, as well as going out of her mind, because she cannot stop compulsively counting everything she does. When she does housework, walks, plays tennis, has sex, or chairs a board meeting, she must count the numbers of times that everything happens. She reports that a crisis came about when her husband discovered she was counting how many breaths he took when they were having sexual relations. The husband threatened divorce as they entered therapy and said he now looks longingly at women who count less.

What can a therapist do with this problem when he does not know how to change it. In general, he can follow the procedures outlined here. He can keep confidential what happens in the therapy from his colleagues, he can encourage the couple to talk while he actively listens. He can have them explore their past marriage relationship, their past individual histories, and their childhood with their extended families. He can talk about philosophical issues in marriage, including tolerance for weaknesses of mates. Out of the problem he can manage months, perhaps years, of marital therapy without having any idea how to change the couple and without anyone discovering that fact. He might even be able to include the case in a paper or book on the topic of interesting problems in marriage therapy. It should be noted in passing that when a therapist wishes to conceal his, or her, incompetence he should avoid any verbatim transcripts of therapy interviews in a publication. Instead, he should offer summaries of cases. For example, a clinician can say about a woman who has the problem of compulsive counting, "The patient was encouraged to explore the origins of the counting compulsion, and the roots of psychopathology were discovered in childhood experiences." This will sound better than a verbatim transcript which might read, "Therapist: When you were a child, did you refer to different ways of going to the bathroom as number one and number two?"

SPECIFIC TACTICS

Within the framework of general principles for concealing ignorance, the therapist can use specific procedures learned at workshops or in the literature. Some are passing fads while others remain classic maneuvers because they help give the customer the impression that the therapist is skillful.

Reflecting back to people whatever they say is a classic tactic which has stood the test of time and generations of inadequate therapists. The procedure conceals like a blanket the fact that the therapist does not know what to do to cause change. Most important, it impresses the customer with the idea that the therapist is empathetic and understanding. Reflecting back a person's words gives an illusion of intimacy. A spouse says, "I feel so ashamed of myself because we have this childish marital problem." The therapist replies, 'M hmm, you feel so ashamed of yourself because you have this childish marital problem." As far as the couple is concerned, two minds have met and understanding has been achieved. Even a socially withdrawn therapist appears to be warm, empathetic and understanding by just thoughtfully repeating back what people say. The chief merit of the procedure is that it is easy to learn even by people with limited intelligence. Research studies have shown that six-year-old children, both male and female, can master the technique with only one 40-minute training session.

Getting in touch with feelings is another classic procedure which can be done, and always is, by novice therapists. Whatever customers say, the therapist says, "How do you feel about that?" With experience, or with the help of a particularly inspiring professor in social work school, the therapist risks more complex phrases such as, "How do you really feel about that," or even "I wonder if you could communicate to your

husband the depths of your feelings about that." These statements encourage the expression, or the simulation, of feelings and distract the
emotionally aroused customer from noticing that nothing is being done
about his problem.

Interpretations which make connections between this and that are, of
course, the trusted tactic of a therapist who does not know how to cause
change. A customer with even a rudimentary education enjoys interpretations which connect one thing with another, and so they are easily
distracted from noticing that nothing is changing. One can find a similarity between a husband and a boss, or a mother and a wife. Since
people do not think randomly, there is always a connection between
what a person says about something at one time and what is said at
another time.

Relationship games and sensitivity procedures are a way to pass the
time and give the customers the illusion that change must be happening
because they get upset. One can easily learn confronting games from
the group therapy literature and popular self-help books. For example,
one can confront the couple with the way they are playing the game
"help me." The clients are impressed with the self-discovery and do not
notice that the therapist does not know how to help. One can point out
that the "adult" in one spouse is talking to the "child" in the other, and
discuss their games of teasing and rejection, or dependency. Talking
about one's own marital difficulties and divorces sometimes helps the
therapist and shows that he, or she, is human and that everyone's
problem is humanistic.

Another modern technique is "sculpting." One can bring action into
the room by having the couple sculpt their problem instead of just talking
about it. The husband can lean on his wife to show his dependence on
her, and she can hover over him as he leans on her to show how she
is burdened with protecting him. The therapist can say things like, "Now
we're getting to the basic kinesics and not merely intellectualizing."
Couples enjoy this kind of action, and the therapist can learn the technique in an afternoon workshop. Some experience in amateur theatricals
helps. With a dramatic type couple one can have them do genograms
of everyone in their family networks and then do simulations of their
relationships with all their relatives. They might not get over their marital
problem, but they benefit from therapy by having lots more to talk about
with their relatives and friends.

EXCUSING FAILURE

Therapists who do not know what to do will fail, but not in all cases, because of the high rate of spontaneous remission. It is spontaneous change which keeps referral sources providing clients and gives the therapist the illusion that perhaps, after all, he really knew what to do even if he did not realize it. Still, failures often occur and the therapist must be able to conceal the fact that failure happened because he did not know what to do.

There are two audiences to be concerned about when failing: fellow professionals and the customers. Colleagues are the least problem since one can avoid observation and not be involved with outcome studies. There are various ways to avoid outcome studies ranging from the concern with confidentiality through arguments about complexity; the emphasis upon growth as not a measurable issue. One can also use the class argument originated by Freud where he said that each case is unique and, therefore, cannot be classed with another in any percentage measurement.

Dealing with the disappointed customer is the main problem. Let us suppose that a couple says indignantly that no change has taken place. After months of therapy they are still miserable and their only marital agreement is that the therapist failed with them. There are several standard defenses to follow. (Showing one's state license, or listing one's degrees and naming the famous universities where one trained, might be useful early in therapy but not at this point. The customer will not be impressed, and the alma mater is given a poor reputation.) The correct procedures fall into two categories: blaming the customer, and saying that more change has taken place than was realized.

Blaming the client can be done in many ways. When the couple says they are disappointed at the failure by the therapist, they can be asked whether they have noticed that there might be a life pattern here of finding helpers disappointing. This topic becomes a subject to "work on." The therapist has turned an awkward moment into a reason for continuing therapy so they can discuss their past disappointments in people back through their lifetimes.

Another way to blame the customer is more subtle. One can imply that the couple has gone about as far as they can go right now, given the material they are made of. Even with the masterful skills of the therapist nothing more can be done. The implication is that the customers have reached a plateau, not the therapist. Sometimes this can be done by suggesting that a new stage of social development needs to be achieved, like getting older, before the couple can solve the problem. A good word to use is "integrate." One can say that the couple needs to "integrate" their insight into the meaning of the emotional experiences achieved in therapy before it is possible to go further with the problem.

If the customer has not done everything asked, the therapist can imply that more cooperation would have solved the problem, and perhaps the couple isn't quite ready yet to get over it.

An amiable way to end without admitting that one did not know what to do is to say that the customer does not really know how much change has taken place. "The way you talk about your marital problems now, and the way you talked about them when you first came in—well, the change is remarkable." In the case of the woman's counting, the therapist can say, "You might not remember it now, but when you first came in you counted every word I said and every breath your husband took. Now it's only occasional." This kind of statement prepares the way for the classic ending of the incompetent therapist—the customers say they still have the problem but do not mind it so much.

The therapist can also review all the gains made in self-expression, in insight and self-understanding, in resolving problems with distant relatives, and point out that after all these are more important than the trivial presenting problem the customer once thought was so important.

This list of ways to deal with failure is not meant to be all-inclusive, and each therapist has his own favorite way. One way becoming popular recently is to refer to someone in your own group of therapists when you have failed with a couple. That colleague supports whatever you said to the clients and also proceeds just as you did so it appears that all therapists do that and what you did was correct even if it failed. (Some therapy groups of colleagues of this kind are small, and some are quite large.)

In general, dealing gracefully with failure means offering an ending that is pleasing. Termination should leave the customers feeling a bit guilty about not having done all that they should, believing they have gone as far as they are capable of progressing in their marriage at this time and no therapist could have done more, and sorry to have put the therapist to so much trouble when more severe problems are undoubtedly waiting at the door. The customer should also be pleased that the problem, even if it is still there, is really more of an irritation than the misfortune it once was. With these simple techniques a therapist can do therapy for months, even years, with customers who fail to change and they never discover that the therapist knew no more than a plumber about how to get them over the problem they presented when they came in the door.

Editor's Commentary: Let the Consumer Beware!

Haley deftly wields his rapier wit to highlight the chicanery and superficiality which characterize the practice of some (many?) marital therapists. Behind the satiric humor is a serious critique and challenge. Implied are such questions as: How dare we as a field permit such shortchanging of our clientele under the rubric of a professional emblem? How dare training programs continue to grind out graduates who merely pretend to help people understand better—by active listening and reflecting back—but who are unskilled in making the kinds of strong, critical, strategic interventions that cause needed change to occur? How dare licensing and certifying boards credential such woefully inadequate clinicians just because they have a requisite degree and can pass a written examination which indicates they have good memories for facts? Apparently collusion reigns supreme between educational institutions, credentialing bodies and practitioners. Serious charges indeed and ones that we need to seriously attend to.

One could call upon Ralph Nader and his allies and put the consumer on guard. But this shifts the responsibility from the supposedly competent educators, legislators and therapists to the allegedly less competent "customers" who already are confused and distressed enough to seek our services. Surely, we can and must take responsibility for our own (professional) behavior; otherwise we can no longer present ourselves as superb role models of how to do this. At the least, graduate and medical schools, training institutions, and certifying boards could insist on competency based exams in which the individual presents a live, actual demonstration of his/her clinical acumen and skill!

One wonders at the use of the term "customer" instead of client, patient or consumer of service. Has the field, or a good portion of it, really shifted so far from a professional, caring, helping motivation to a big business stance, selling a commodity for the highest possible fee?

If yes, then the field needs to reassess where it is, in the "here and now," making the ideal and the real more congruent. If not, why would someone of Haley's stature pen such provocative remarks?

In decrying the use of such techniques as sculpting, perhaps the indictment is too extreme. When skillfully and appropriately used, the insights derived and feelings unleashed can be utilized as the dynamic energy to bring about behavioral and structural changes in the system. Just as there are many "wrong" ways to do therapy, I believe there are also many "right" ways and that no one therapist or school of thought has a monopoly (Kaslow, 1981).

REFERENCE

Kaslow, F.W. A diaclectic approach to family therapy and practice: Selectivity and synthesis. *Journal of Marital and Family Therapy,* July 1981, 7, (3), 345-351.

Chapter 22

The Agoraphobic Married Woman and Her Marriage Pattern: A Clinical Study

By Hans Jørgen Holm

Between 1973 and 1979, 228 patients, men and women, with agoraphobic symptoms were admitted to and treated in Ward A, Modum Bads Nervesanatorium, Norway. Data from this sample were analyzed by computer and tabulated. The present article reports on part of the research project concerned with the female patients. It describes the typical personality profile of both the patient and her husband and focuses on the marital interaction as one of the main precipitating causes of female agoraphobia. A multimodal treatment procedure consisting of individual psychotherapy, marital therapy, exposure treatment, and antidepressive medication is described.

Phobias are usually classified as situation phobias, phobias to objects, and phobias to animals. The typical reaction in all of these is avoidance. The patient tries not to expose himself or herself to the dreaded stimuli.

The research for this study took place in 1973-79. The article was first published in *Fokus på Familien*, (Norwegian Journal for Family Therapy), 1980, 3, 106-119. This translated English version has been revised by the author and the editor. I am grateful to Peter Broch, M.D., who worked together with me on the first part of the research project. I also wish to thank Ciba-Geigy A/S, Norway, for their free EDB service.

Hans Jørgen Holm, M.D. is a psychiatrist and clinical director at Modum Bads Nervesanatorium, Norway. He has been editor of *Fokus pa Familien* since 1973.

Instead, an attempt is made to avoid the situation, object, or type of animal that causes anxiety.

This article deals with the agoraphobic married woman and reports on part of a larger research project on agoraphobic patients. The research has been (and continues to be) conducted at Modum Bads Nervesanatorium, Ward A, Vikersund, Norway. The Nervesanitorium is a private, 106-bed psychiatric hospital located in a peaceful rural area some 80 kilometers west of Oslo. The hospital was built on the grounds of a luxurious spa dating from the nineteenth century. The bath (Bad) is retained in the name solely for historical reasons. The hospital admits patients from all of Norway. Since its opening in 1957 it has been known for its psychotherapeutic profile in the treatment of individuals, couples, and families. The majority of the patients are neurotics. Some are borderlines or character disorders, and a minority are psychotics. Addiction problems are quite frequent, either as a main complaint or as part of the diagnosis. Ward A has 54 beds and uses a therapeutic community approach combined with individual and group psychotherapy and psychopharmacological treatment. Most patients are treated individually, but spouses and family members are often drawn into treatment. The mean length of stay is 45 days. When marital therapy is indicated, the spouse of the index patient may come to the hospital for treatment once a week or he/she may be admitted together with the index patient for two to three weeks of intensive couple treatment.

METHODOLOGY

During the time period from January 1, 1973 to June 30, 1979, 228 patients with agoraphobic symptoms were admitted to and treated in Ward A. The patients had agoraphobia as either the major or a minor diagnosis. Many of them had multiple phobias. In addition to the agoraphobic symptom, they exhibited a great deal of social anxiety. Many of them feared and avoided heights, bridges, and elevators. They regularly avoided public means of transportation, cinemas, theaters, shops and queues. A typical agoraphobic symptom is the fear of leaving home or a safe, homely place. Open places or crowded public areas are usually avoided. Some agoraphobics even fear being alone at home. Typical is also the "fear of fear," the anticipation of spontaneous anxiety attacks or anxiety when exposed to the feared situation.

Some patients experienced little anxiety and complained more about dizziness, nausea, or palpitations. Many of the patients seldom left their houses, and daily activities had become increasingly limited. A typical manifestation is also the "anxious attachment" (Bowlby, 1973) or dependency upon a dominant other, most often the spouse. However, mothers may also be placed in this position.

This sample of patients was analyzed in two ways:

1. Data from the 228 patients' journals were registered on code sheets, analyzed by computer and tabulated. (See the code sheet, Appendix I.)
2. Individual patients and their marriages were clinically analyzed in depth to give a more dynamic assessment of typical personality and marriage pattern.

Little attention is given here to tables and statistics, since the main purpose is a clinical and dynamic description. The clinical cases presented near the end of the article were chosen because: 1) they represent fairly typical personality and marriage profiles, and 2) I personally treated them and am therefore quite familiar with them. As head of the department I had the opportunity to observe and to supervise the treatment of all the patients in the study sample. Many other cases might have been chosen for clinical illustration, but it is believed those that were selected should suffice for this purpose.

STATISTICAL DATA

The sample consisted of 156 women and 72 men. One hundred and twenty-seven of the women were or had been married. Of these, 102 were married for the first time, six were widows, two were separated or divorced, and eight were divorcees or widows who had married again.

The average age at first hospital stay (in our ward) for the whole sample was 37.1 years; for the women it was 37.2 years. The average length of time that the agoraphobic symptom had lasted at the time of the first admission was, for the married women, 9.6 years; for the unmarried women, 6.8 years. This indicates that the condition involves a chronic neurosis. Most patients had also been treated both in psychiatric hospitals and as outpatients before their first admittance to the Nervesanatorium.

Figure 1 provides some interesting data concerning the onset of symptoms related to the inception of the first marriage. The figure shows some quite significant differences between men and women. It indicates that the probability of a man becoming agoraphobic is not affected by getting married. Before marriage both men and women have about the same inclination to acquire agoraphobic symptoms. After marriage, women have about twice as high a probability as men of becoming agoraphobic. The figure also reveals that women have an especially high frequency of symptom onset during the first three years after marrying.

Altogether, 24 of the married female agoraphobic patients had their symptom onset before marriage and 103 after marriage. On the average, the phobic symptom occurred for the first time 7.8 years after the wedding. The average age at marriage was 22.9 for women. Thus it becomes evident that the average married agoraphobic woman has her symptom onset just after 30 years of age. (This concurs with earlier studies which have also shown that the majority of agoraphobic women have their symptom onset in their twenties or thirties.)

Of the 127 married women, 60 had agoraphobia as the major diagnosis, 67 as minor diagnosis. Of this latter 67, 28 were classified as anxiety neurosis, 24 as depressive neurosis, three as unspecified neurosis, seven as hysteria, one as character neurosis, two as addiction, and one as depersonalization syndrome. Among the 60 who had the main diagnosis of agoraphobia, there were six patients with minor diagnosis of anxiety neurosis, 19 had a secondary diagnosis of depression and 11 had hysteria. It is interesting to note that only two had a secondary diagnosis of obsessive-compulsive neurosis. It appears that agoraphobia is not nearly as associated with obsessive-compulsive illness as was earlier assumed (Strömgren, 1961, p. 213). Both our statistical data and our

Figure 1. Symptom Onset Related to the Establishment of the First Marriage

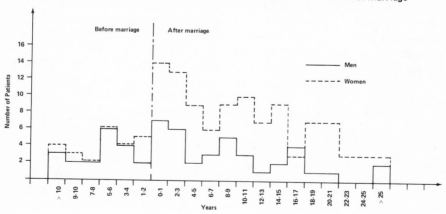

clinical impressions make a convincing case for the agoraphobias being much more closely related to depression than to obsession.

About 10.2% of the 127 women had problems with alcohol. The comparative figure for married agoraphobic men was 32.1% and for unmarried agoraphobic men it was 50%. One possible reason why women are so overrepresented with agoraphobia may therefore be that men's agoraphobic symptoms are masked by problems with alcohol. Another reason is undoubtedly that the men had jobs, which represented constant exposure training situations. Only 14.2% of the married agoraphobic women were employed full-time. The comparative figure for unmarried female patients was 55.2% (16 of 29). Motives for leaving the home and trying to master the symptom are strengthened by occupational activity. Possibly it is also more embarrassing for men than it is for women to give in to agoraphobia. This is intrinsically connected to the dependency aspect which is an element in most agoraphobias.

BRIEF LITERATURE REVIEW

There are an enormous number of publications about phobias in general. An overview would be impossible here, so only a brief summation has been done.

There is no general agreement about the causes and dynamics. Several psychotherapy researchers, among them Jerome Frank (1961), have shown that exposure treatment according to learning theory principles is more effective than insight-oriented psychotherapy for phobic conditions. Professor Isaac Marks and co-workers at Maudsley Hospital in London (1981) have done valuable research on phobias and their treatment, especially anti-phobic exposure training with groups of patients (Hand, Lamontagne, & Marks, 1974). At the Nervesanatorium, we use a modified version of the Maudsley group training procedures.

Much has been written about intrapsychic conditions and the influence of childhood relationships and experiences on later phobias from the psychoanalytic point of view. In March 1973 Thomstad gave a lecture to the Norwegian Psychiatric Association which offered a good summary of the psychoanalytic literature and aspects of individual psychology. Bowlby (1973) has associated the phobias to attachment problems and separation anxiety. Arieti (1979) is of the opinion that phobic patients have a healthy basic personality built up from a happy childhood. This is later followed by a fundamental disappointment, which occurs late in childhood or during puberty and suddenly tears them out of "a state of innocence." Roth (1959) examined phobic women's childhood relationships and found intense family ties, especially between mother and daughter. Webster (1953) found that 24 out of 25 patients had been raised by dominating and overprotective mothers.

Until the last few years there were few publications about the ago-raphobic woman's marital problems. After the initial Norwegian printing of this article, I found three significant contributions. Goodstein and Swift (1977) presented four cases, stressing the marital relationship as the source of symptoms and the focus of treatment. They claim that: "the pathologic situation leading to initial outpatient appointment seems to result from the current marriage relationship." Chambless and Gold-stein (1981) used a multimodal treatment, quite similar to the program described in this publication. They stressed the agoraphobic patient's fear of separation from important figures, and noted that "the most common stressor preceding the onset of panic attacks is marital malad-justment." Goldstein and Chambless (1981) also indicated that initially both spouses often *deny* marital conflict. Marital therapy becomes pos-sible and necessary when the agoraphobic woman grows more inde-pendent and the male spouse is threatened by her change.

ETIOLOGY AND PROBLEMS ASSOCIATED WITH PHOBIA

Several therapeutic schools have something to contribute when it comes to understanding the causes of phobias. Analytically oriented extended therapy with many phobic patients has convinced me that one here sees *predisposing* infantile neuroses founded both in the preoedipal and oedipal levels. Similarly, one finds *precipitating*, pathogenic factors in the concrete life situation, often associated with mourning or loss experiences, drive provocations, and marital conditions. When thinking of causes, it can be fruitful to distinguish between "here and now" reasons and more distant predisposing reasons, most often from child-hood. Some are common for both sexes, other factors are sex specific. One can also analyze phobic patients on four different dimensions: 1. problems with sexuality; 2. problems with self-assertion; 3. problems regarding dependency and attachment; and 4. problems with ideas of self-reference and guilt feelings. These dimensions are not independent of one another. Dimensions 1 and 3 seem to be especially prevalent in women. Self-assertion problems and difficulties with aggression are es-pecially important for men. Problems with ideas of self-reference and guilt are often found in borderline and subparanoid patients, and are also common in patients with alcohol problems.

Concerning the connection between obsession and phobias, it is interesting that in the data derived from agoraphobics, one sees relatively little obsession, even though considerable obsessive-compulsive character traits are manifested. A sample of obsessive-compulsive patients, however, will always contain marked phobic symptoms.

Our material shows a clear association between depression and agoraphobia. Many of the women phobic patients had fluctuations in mood. Similarly we have observed many cases of almost melancholic depression with, or as an alternative to, agoraphobic symptoms. For many years it has been recognized that many female agoraphobic patients also have hysterical traits.

CLASSIC PROFILE OF AN AGORAPHOBIC WOMAN

This woman's childhood seems to have been characterized by a distant, somewhat cool, obsessive mother who was more concerned about order and cleanliness than with emotional contact with her child. This cool mother seems to have left a preoedipal deprivation. The woman's father was often presented as warmer, more feeling, rather imaginative, or artistically gifted. He could more easily relate himself to his daughter on an emotional level. Sometimes this took a clearly oedipal form, which probably explains the hysterical traits found in many agoraphobic women. However, the father could not be trusted. A significant finding in our data on agoraphobic women was that about half of them had alcoholic fathers. This is the minimum incidence. In the material on 127 married women, we found clear indications of alcoholism in the fathers of 40.2% of the cases. For 42 patients, their journal entries gave no such information; however, their descriptions of their fathers gave strong indications that they had an alcohol problem which the patient was hiding from us. Only in 22 of the 127 cases (17%) had the agoraphobic married woman not had alcohol problems in her home. Fully 63 of the 127 gave reliable information about their fathers' or their father's siblings' problems with alcohol. This number, about 50%, is a minimum.

For long periods of her early childhood, this woman had a close relationship with her father. She was often the father's favorite. In some cases it seems as if he had taken on some of the traditional functions of the mother, and that the daughter looked to the father for some of the warmth and care that the mother found difficult to give. At some point in childhood, often before or during puberty, the father was experienced as intensely disappointing, inconsistent and sometimes also threatening. We found numerous instances of daughters, just before or during puberty, having experienced their fathers' having extramarital affairs. They deceived the mother or they treated her in a brutal and negligent manner.

This inconsistency in the fathers is experienced as something deeply painful and disappointing. It is as if the security of childhood was shattered by the experience of the father's unreliability. Arieti (1979) has paid special attention to these dynamics, which are confirmed in our study. The father was close, but he could also turn his daughter away with his behavior. At the same time, some fathers were strongly bound to their daughters and tried to monopolize them and defend them from dangers in the outside world. Their mothers also contributed to give these young women a picture of men as dangerous—people to watch out for and not come too close to.

Our data indicate that the young girl who later becomes agoraphobic is endowed with rather strong drives; she has been active, lively, and open to her surroundings. She has sexual experiences early and enjoys them. Many are somewhat impulsive. At the same time, they tend to have a strict superego, which causes strong tensions in the personality. The agoraphobic usually has a greater ability for affection and sexual enjoyment than the hysterical married woman.

After the appearance of agoraphobic symptoms, it is as if this vitality becomes frozen or put away. Instead, the phobic woman appears with a correct, middle-class façade, outwardly well-adjusted, well dressed, tasteful and stiff, and inwardly characterized by a great degree of self-doubt and lack of self-respect. Some of these women then dress shabbily. Three of the married agoraphobic women in the study population had cut their hair very short. In the course of psychotherapy, it was discovered that the motive for this was to deny themselves a threatening feminine power of attraction. These women adjusted easily in the first phase of marriage, but gradually became more and more frustrated. This frustration came from both the husband's and the wife's personality makeup.

Apparently the potentially phobic woman chooses a sombre, solid, reliable man who often makes a success of his career and who is skillful in his profession. He is seldom aggressive, and often lacks the ability to give close emotional contact, something this woman seeks most of all. He is kind and protective, but stays somewhat distant. His kind, weak, mild attitude provides a sense of security, yet at the same time it is irritating. The agoraphobic woman is often much more active and has stronger drives than her husband. However, she cannot permit herself to explode because her husband is so kind and considerate. When she gets angry, he gets hurt and withdraws. She cannot show her frustration and disappointment without at the same time feeling guilty because she is being unreasonable.

Many of the husbands exhibit considerable masculine insecurity, including regarding sexual activity. Many have premature ejaculation, but whether or not the frequency is greater than in the normal population is difficult to determine. Their wives often experience frustration regarding their sexual drives because the husbands are not expressive enough. This regularly results in their putting "on ice" some of their own vitality, in order to not put their husband's insecurity in focus and to protect him from the fears and doubts experienced by both partners.

Just what the agoraphobic woman is longing for in her husband is exactly what he finds difficult to give her. Among other things, she is seeking a somewhat motherly security and closeness as a result of a preoedipal deprivation. Her husband offers her protection, a good material standard of living, and a willingness to lead her around the different phobic situations. However, he is not very affectionate and keeps a kind of emotional distance, even though he is protective and safe.

These women also have a great need for excitement. Typically, they manage the first child well. After the birth of the second child, they feel more and more confined and bound within the framework of the "Doll's House," which, consciously or not, they have contributed to establishing. As the years of marriage pass, it is also probable that home and children fill less of these women's lives than they did earlier in marriage. In this period, many women begin to look outward. They have a great need for self-realization and would like to relate to more people. Some men who are married to agoraphobic women are skeptical about such fulfillment outside the home. They react with bad moods and jealousy, and try to keep the wife within the four safe walls of home. Even if few of these men are tyrannical and angry, many of them have dominating traits. They hold their wives down and fear their vitality. This happens in the kind of subtle way that can create guilt. Primarily, it is the husbands' willingness to serve which is a striking characteristic. Secondly, they look upon their wives in a condescending, somewhat underestimating manner, which the wives may not recognize until they have been married for several years.

Undoubtedly, many of these men feel most secure and satisfied when they have a dependent, somewhat helpless wife, who stays at home and does not demand too much of them in the form of either closeness or masculine sexual performance. Over the years, the male spouses will provoke the helplessness and dependence which these women bring with them as a potential possibility from childhood. However, these women typically have a great deal of vitality and independence at the time the relationship begins. The marital interaction reduces their autonomy and increases their helplessness. Although these are general characteristics of many marriages, the agoraphobic women are special because of their symptom formation and because they become fixated in their helplessness and their dependence on their husbands. Open defiance is rare; more often indentification with the husband and what he stands for evolves.

Most often phobic women describe their marriage as happy and successful, and they describe their husband in idealized terms. Their affect, however, is flat and without enthusiasm, revealing hidden frustration and dissatisfaction. The sexual relationship can function satisfactorily for both partners, but often the woman expresses a decreasing sense of attachment and sexual enjoyment. Many of these women have, however, a rich emotional life and some are more endowed than usual with the ability to give and receive erotic enjoyment. Several say they have multiple orgasms. In this way, they clearly stand apart from the hysterical woman who, as a rule, is sexually unresponsive and has been so throughout most of her life. However, some agoraphobic women have had problems with vaginismus and sexual dysfunction throughout marriage. This is most pronounced in the hysteriform (woman with hysterical traits) women and those with the most marked infantile personality traits.

One can speculate about whether these women choose their spouses on the basis of disappointing experiences with their fathers. Often their spouses are in fact the fathers' exact opposite. While the fathers were warm, emotional, full of excitement, but also inconsistent and unreliable, the spouses are often boring but dependable. They provide security, but not emotional closeness. They protect their wives, but do not take them on exciting journeys, either in emotional life or around the world. This builds up an increasing degree of frustration, which is repressed. Sometimes, this discontent is displaced onto external factors, for example, onto the house in which the couple lives. This displacement of the discontent and frustration is a typical aspect of the agoraphobic patient's reaction. Repression of libidinous and aggressive forces happens largely with the help of guilt. The thought sequence is, "I cannot possibly be angry at my husband; he is so kind."

In this situation, the woman encounters one or several kinds of difficulties or provocations which make the conflict acute. Problems with the children, physical illnesses, deaths in the family and many other stress factors can be noted. However, there are often extramarital erotic provocations. Typically, the agoraphobic woman does not dare recognize her own fantasies about extramarital relationships. She treats her daydreams and erotic fantasies as if they had been real actions. While most women can permit themselves fantasies and accept their longing to sometimes escape from the children and a boring husband and experience something exciting outside of marriage, for the potentially phobic woman this results in just as much guilt as if she had actually left her home and family and committed the worst sexual sins. She treats her fantasies as if they were actions. In this way the agoraphobic woman resembles the obsessive neurotic who also confuses fantasies and reality in symbolic ritualizing and washing. Going out, going into open spaces and taking part in social life all become symbols of a freedom which is both tempting and threatening. The symbol results in both anxiety and guilt. The reply from such a frustrated agoraphobic woman to my question of what she would most wish to do if she were totally free was "to go to a carnival in the Rhine valley."

These women often act inferior to their husbands. If they are dominant to any degree, they do this through their helplessness. They bind their husbands to themselves as protection. In this way they are different from the obsessive neurotic woman, who to a larger degree develops power and control over her spouse. The agoraphobic women are closer to a depressive helplessness than they are to the power orientation of the obsessive.

What happens when these women go through therapy or otherwise become more able to admit their own inner lives to themselves? Very often a break in the homeostasis of marriage occurs, a change which can seem very threatening to their reliable, but insecure husbands.

Serious crises can occur for the husband while his wife is being treated in the hospital. We find depressions, anxiety states and strong jealousy reactions occurring. One doctor called the agoraphobic syndrome in married women "the fear-of-flying syndrome," in reference to Erica Jong's book (1973). Paradoxically, these women are more able to fly than most women, but they have either had their wings clipped or put themselves in a kind of voluntary cloister to avoid the joys and dangers of flying.

When these women get rid of their phobias and dare to live to their full potential vitality, in almost all cases the marriage benefits by it. However, this demands a concomitant change in the husbands' attitude. They must be helped to achieve a greater degree of self-assurance and to enjoy their wife's new vitality. In the period of transition, there are many examples of extramarital sexual relationships between these women and other men. It is as if the dam bursts and the women act out their newly won freedom. This can create crises in the marriage, shocking and alarming the husbands, but leading to deeper attachment and communication.

Sometimes, the male spouse tries to sabotage the therapy. However, most men are tired of the babysitting job they have had for many years in relation to their wives. The majority will therefore both want and not want the wives to change.

Typical examples of this appear in the following cases:

Case 1. Lilly and Petter

A woman about 45 years old, from an upper-middle-class suburban family, married to a professor, with three grown or adolescent children, was admitted to the Nervesanatorium for swings in mood, both manic and depressive. In the preliminary conversation with her and her husband, it was agreed to try lithium treatment.

After admission to the hospital, it was revealed that this woman had massive phobic symptoms which had confined her completely to the home for the past six years. She also had a long history of illness going back to 14 years of age. Her relationship to her alcoholic brother, the family outcast, seems to have been especially important.

This woman had an uncompromising vitality which she exploded onto her husband, sometimes in a destructive manner, especially in her hypomanic phases. During the first conversation at the hospital, the husband let himself be "run over" and was not capable of setting limits or stopping her. However, he was kind, considerate, and protective. For several years, he had driven her from place to place when she went to shop, to have her hair done, or to visit friends. It seemed that he accepted this without too much protest.

This woman was offered exposure treatment in addition to her drug treatment. Her husband protested loudly, both on the telephone and in letters, demanding that the hospital stay not be extended and that the original agreement of only drug treatment be maintained. During marital therapy in the hospital, he was on the verge of depression and accused both the therapist and his wife of breaking the contract. Despite his objections, the therapist and patient agreed to continue treatment.

Two weeks after discharge, the patient's husband wished to talk to me. In the course of a five-minute conversation he presented me with a rather large check to the order of the Nervesanatorium. He was sorry that he had been unreasonable and "totally irrational" during his wife's treatment. He understood now that his wife and he himself had benefited greatly from the extension of the treatment agreement which he at first had protested against. He also expressed a deep gratitude because his wife was now more capable of expanding her range of activities.

The lithium treatment was later discontinued without any recurrence of either the phobias or the changes in mood. The antiphobic exposure treatment was very successful. Eight to nine years of posttreatment observation have shown that the cure is lasting.

Case 2. Tove and Erik

Tove came for treatment for the first time as an individual patient at 36 years of age. She had a chronic, crippling agoraphobic neurosis. This appeared after she gave birth to her first child 11 years earlier. The patient's personality was characterized by strong hysteriform elements, and she wanted very much to find a somatic explanation for her chronic anxiety, somatic complaints, dizziness, and varying symptoms.

Before admission, the patient had been treated by several psychiatrists, who had "given up on her," and had been a patient for 2½ months at the local psychiatric clinic ward. Her symptoms included significant experiences of depersonalization, mostly in connection with panicky, violent anxiety. She dared not be alone at home and dared not go out.

Tove had grown up in the eastern part of Oslo, in a crowded two-room apartment. Her father was a security guard and an artist. He was the warmer and more emotional of the parents, but at the same time he was volatile and excitable, with a tendency to drink too much. The mother was a housewife, cheerful and servile, who covered up any conflicts; she was somewhat distant, without the same ability for emotional contact as the father. (The four-year-younger sister was later treated for agoraphobic neurosis by the author. It turned out that she had a marriage situation very much like Tove's.)

The patient was her father's favorite daughter. She remembers being scared and disappointed when in prepuberty she discovered that her father had had an affair. The parents had many conflicts, and divorce was discussed. The patient was bright at school, passed her examinations, and worked for five years in a laboratory.

At 25 she was married to Erik, 34, who was employed in a leading business position. Her mother-in-law was a strong personality, stately, self-assured, and authoritative. Erik was a tall, rather handsome man. He always acted calm, controlled and considerate, but at the same time gave little emotional contact, both to his wife and in the therapeutic situations. Faced with enormous needs for contact from his wife, he often retreated into professional work or solitary hobbies. The patient felt that she had a lot more emotionality than her husband, but she seldom dared to express this. However, when she did, she was left with a paralyzing feeling of guilt because her husband never answered back, but rather overlooked her and was tolerant. In his quiet way the husband was rather dominating. Tove also felt herself to be in the shadow of her husband's dynamic and strong family, which came from a higher social class than her own.

Three sons of preschool and school age gave her enough to do as a housewife and mother. The boys irritated her greatly at times. In addition, the second son was brain-damaged and had epileptic attacks. In spite of considerable tension between the spouses, they had a good sexual adjustment with full mutual satisfaction. The emotional climate between them was characterized by her impulsive, hysteriform and easier manner, her enormous longing for contact, and his somewhat distant, sometimes humorous attitude toward her.

Before the advent of illness she was attractive, lively, outgoing, impulsive, charming, and made contact with other people easily. She also was somewhat volatile and explosive, never held a grudge, liked to read poetry and perform.

On admission this 36-year-old woman seemed tense, anxious, and depressed. In spite of her hysterical traits, she did not have the typical unaffected, smooth smile of a hysteric. The symptoms were dominated by agoraphobia, but otherwise were generally neurotic. Sometimes she experienced depersonalization. For the first 1½ months of hospitalization, she was treated as an individual patient with antiphobic exposure training, dynamically oriented individual therapy, and antidepressive medications in combination with diazepam. Individual therapy was rather dramatic, marked by aggressive outbursts when she was frustrated regarding contact and in connection with the therapist's vacation.

She felt herself to be extremely insecure and inadequate. She felt that she stood in the shadow of a dominating husband and a mother-in-law to whom she compared herself and to whom she felt small in comparison. She made good use of the exposure training, and mastered more and more situations which she had avoided earlier. Her symptoms were significantly better when Erik and the three children were brought into family therapy.

On the ward she received a considerable amount of confirmation of herself as a woman in that the male patients confided in her and appreciated her. She came in contact with more and more disappointment and frustration in relation to her husband, whom she experienced as "square," emotionally flat, and business-oriented. The patient had a relapse when the family was brought in. She readily fell back on an infantile, regressive pattern as a defense against libidinous and aggressive forces. This kept her from using her resources, her independence, and her mature womanliness. It became clear that her husband's attitudes stimulated the little dependent girl in her more than the adult, mature woman. He fought hard to be self-assured, secure, dominating—the one who stood over her. His way of dominating was difficult to attack because it was so friendly. This brought her to a tense emotional state, strongly characterized by guilt feelings. She often felt aggressive toward him, but showing this gave her a feeling of "hitting a feather pillow."

The patient's initial dream will illustrate some of the dynamics: She is at home and takes the trolley car to a party with some other women. She is glad that she can manage the journey. At the party, she starts to talk about her illness and her symptoms, but feels that no one is listening. This makes her furious and she leaves the party. As she is leaving, she meets a male friend, a warm and sensitive, "mild" man, the exact opposite of her husband. This friend from her high school days had now become a doctor. It turned out that this previous high school friend had turned up in her thoughts throughout her marriage "as an alternative to my husband."

The dream can be interpreted in the following way. When the patient can no longer seek refuge in illness and regression, in an infantile pattern, two things happen: Anger is mobilized, and she meets the adult woman in herself with all the anxiety and regret that is a consequence of an extramarital relationship.

While still an individual patient, she fell in love with a fellow patient. When the fellow patient suggested that they take a walk together, the patient said "no" and explained that she did not dare. She was afraid of her own erotic impulses and chose therefore to stay inside. This shows in a nutshell some of the central dynamics in her agoraphobia.

It turned out that this woman fell in love easily. She had lively, strong drives which gave her considerable enjoyment in marriage. At the same time they threatened her because her fantasies were often directed toward other men. She tried to push such thoughts away because they gave her a feeling of guilt and anxiety. The patient also had fantasies of leaving both husband and children, and being separated. To defend herself against all this, she confined herself to a voluntary cloister at home, or she dressed sloppily to avoid seeming attractive.

As this woman gradually dared to make use of her inner powers, her husband became depressed and got dyspepsia and gastritis.

The couple continued in outpatient marital therapy for a long while after discharge. A nurse was with the patient the first few days after discharge. She was to stimulate the patient's exposure training, support her and make sure that the patient did not have occasion to regress in the course of the early difficult time at home. After discharge the patient still had a moderate amount of anxiety and phobic reactions. However, she completed a six-month technical school program and mastered her anxiety symptoms rather well.

Because the patient often daydreamed about her earlier male friend (the medical doctor), and could not give up her fantasies about him, a therapeutic experiment was attempted in which she was confronted with her friend in the course of a therapy session. The confrontation was planned in agreement with her. The situation was explained to the friend by telephone before the session, and he agreed to act as the therapists's ally. When the patient suggested that the doctor and his wife could be friends with Erik and herself, the doctor turned this down in a friendly, but firm manner. The confrontation with the "forbidden object" had a good effect on the patient's further development.

However, a relapse occurred four years after discharge from the hospital. This time the depressive symptoms were more prominent. The patient began to have many somatic complaints as well. She started treatment with a professor of surgery, who was of the opinion that the patient's complaints were not emotional, but due to a blood sugar disease. The patient eagerly grasped this explanation. In this way she could escape from her increasing erotic and sexual impulses toward men other than her husband. She felt herself to be more and more like a teenager, and had an episode of crying when she discovered that a man she was in love with was more fascinated by other women than herself.

The professor of surgery referred her to a convalescent home. There she took the initiative in a sexual relationship with the director, who was quite a bit younger than she. Her first extramarital affair unfortunately resulted in her contracting venereal disease, which she transmitted to her husband. This led to a serious crisis. Erik reacted, characteristically enough, more wounded than angry. The patient regressed seriously and became depressed to the point of melancholy. Thus a new hospital stay of about 1½ months was necessary. During this period she never gave up hope of a somatic explanation, was extremely infantile and regressed, and demanded much contact from others. She described the relationship to her spouse as harmonic, supposedly because he, as a result of marital therapy, had developed into a more open and emotional man.

The dynamics are again revealed in a dream: She is at a party where a woman vomits. The vomit comes on to the patient. Her husband, Erik, is right beside her, and the patient tries to shield him so that the vomit will not reach him.

In the working-through, it became clear that the vomit was associated with despising, disgust, and negative feelings. The patient turned these inward against herself, in that she shielded her husband by idealizing the relationship with him. She had been successful in repressing her frustration, disappointment, and aggression after therapy was concluded the first time. She had strong feelings of guilt regarding her spouse, who was so kind, good, and friendly. This guilt kept her from recognizing her negative feelings toward him.

She was also afraid of making herself independent of Erik. Employment outside of the home was threatening. Her childishness and regression were defenses against leaving him. In addition, for her, being an independent, mature adult was much too closely connected with admitting the hostile, negative feelings she had against her husband. At the same time, she was afraid of losing him. She admitted that she was looking for something like a mother's nurturance from him. One time she said: "Do you think I will end up divorced if I admit my negative feelings?"

When this central conflict became clear, the patient made real progress. Antidepressant drugs helped. Several times she had contact with the professor of surgery, as she waited for the results of the blood tests which he had sent abroad. Once she told the nurses that Erik had sent her word that the test showed low blood sugar. But later this turned out to be false; the message from Erik had indicated that the tests were normal. She had desperately hoped that she was suffering from a somatic illness.

At discharge, she was in a good mood, optimistic and practically without anxiety. Since then she has managed well. As a result of emotional problems with the children, she has had some contact with a child psychiatrist, but she has mastered her phobias and depression for four years since the last discharge. During the second stay at the hospital, the exposure training was strongly encouraged and, as previously, she was treated in a group with patients all having the same symptoms.

Comments: This patient's life history, personality structure, marriage relationship, and dynamics show most of the traits which are characteristic of agoraphobic married women. One finds a somewhat cool, obsessive mother, a warm father who, however, has problems with alcohol, and who is not to be trusted. She has a lively, warm, impulsive temperament in adolescence, falls in love easily, is popular with boys, and has a much larger capacity for affection than the usual hysterical woman. She marries a sombre, reliable and solid man—in many ways her (and her father's) opposite. As children and the marital relationship become more of a strain, she reacts with anxiety, mild depression, and the formation of agoraphobic symptoms. For a long time she defends herself against admitting that these symptoms have something to do with her marriage, and instead idealizes her husband, who also has many worthwhile attributes. She becomes increasingly infantile and helpless, goes to many doctors, is committed to a psychiatric ward, and receives much outpatient psychotherapy, all without result.

Her treatment plan while at Modum Bad was typical of those usually designed there for agoraphobic patients. They receive dynamic, individual therapy and marital therapy and are strongly encouraged to train individually or in groups to master their agoraphobic symptoms. The treatment is supported by antidepressive drugs, as well as diazepam, which, however, has been less and less used for this purpose.

In this case the dynamics were clearly analyzed. Much could be traced to the preoedipal stage, probably as a deprivation problem arising from early contact with the mother. In addition, the oedipal situation had been a factor. It seems as though the father had taken over providing some of the warmth which mothers often give. Tove chose a spouse who was the father's opposite, but who also could be trusted. This led to disappointment, longing, and aggression. As the frustrations of the marriage built up, she became more and more threatened by the impulse to escape from it all, find a lover, and experience more adventure than she had a possibility for in her marriage. These fantasies resulted in feelings of anxiety and guilt, which were just as strong as if she had acted this way. The marital dynamics also show that there was collusion present. The husband was reliable but boring, characterized by masculine insecurity of the type which easily leads to a subtle dominance and infantilizing of the wife. When the wife recovered from her regressive and infantile state, he had problems with depression and psychosomatic symptoms.

Case 3. Beate and Hans

Beate was initially admitted to the hospital when she was 31 years old for a crippling phobic neurosis which had lasted for 13 years. Her mother had been critical, showing her very little interest, and had been an alcoholic. She had experienced her father as a supporter and good friend. At 18 years of age, at about the same time her father and a friend of hers died, she became agoraphobic. The symptom disappeared when she moved back home to her mother three months after her father's death. She lived with her mother until she married, when already pregnant, at age 21. Her husband was a transportation worker. She was of average intelligence, and worked as a secretary and mostly as a housewife after marriage. In connection with moving from her mother's to her own house, she experienced increasing anxiety attacks with agoraphobic symptoms, as well as periods of depression. Her personality could be described as dependent, immature, unsure of herself and with a poor self-image. She had a tendency to repress her own feelings and lacked ability for introspection. Her sexual adjustment was reported as good, with full ability for orgasm, except during a period of depression 10 years before admission to the hospital.

During her first admission the patient was treated with a combination of behavior-oriented exposure training in a group setting of fellow patients, individual sessions with one of the staff, and occupational therapy. She was weakly motivated for treatment and was hesitant to go into the training program. She was discharged after three weeks. She had fallen in love with a male fellow patient. This caused complications. She was readmitted about one month later. She had made contact with the male patient, but discovered that he was an alcoholic and wished to break off the relationship, something which she could not manage to do.

During her first stay in hospital she had hidden much of her frustration and disappointment about her marriage. During her second stay she brought this up. She expressed not having any desire to continue with her husband. She tried to break off with her friend, but became sadder and felt very lonely. She bound herself up in a mother-like transference relationship to a female fellow patient. After she broke off with her friend, her husband was brought into marital therapy. He was nervous, unsure of himself, and extremely dependent on his wife. Their relationship was characterized by the fact that increasing independence on Beate's part was understood as a threat to Hans. Beate made herself dependent on him. Both were dissatisfied with the other's way of being, but both induced it in the other. He was dissatisfied because Beate criticized him and communicated that he was not good enough for her. On the other hand, under the influence of alcohol he reacted with episodes of extreme jealousy in which he was very angry, broke windows, and threatened to kill them both. Usually he was kind and meek.

The marital therapy ended abruptly when her husband opened a letter from Beate's friend. He demanded that she come home from the hospital at once; otherwise she would find the door locked. We succeeded in getting him to come in and talk it over. These conversations made the crisis less dramatic and brought the couple closer together. During her last hospital stay she was more motivated to participate in exposure training and had made progress in mastering the phobic symptoms. She wished to begin working, and was discharged much improved.

Comments: This woman had anxiety and agoraphobia before marriage. Her agoraphobia seemed to be connected to separation anxiety and dependence, probably stemming from a distant and difficult relationship to her mother in the early, formative stages. She had not mourned when she had lost people close to her. She bound herself dependently to a man who himself was dependent and anxious and tried to dominate her and hold her down. She gradually developed a strong readiness for extramarital relationships, daydreamed about leaving her husband and two children, and protected herself against this by intensifying the agoraphobia. During her stay in the hospital, she established uncritically a relationship to a male alcoholic, fellow patient. This resulted in a major marital crisis which, however, led to the couple's communicating better and coming closer to each other. Even before her affair, her husband had reacted to her absence with an increasing degree of symptom formation. Undoubtedly, many of the precipitating, intensifying factors in this woman's agoraphobia could be found in the relationship to her spouse.

TREATMENT PRINCIPLES

Treatment of agoraphobic married women is difficult, as is treatment of agoraphobics in general. Our present research indicates that it is important to use a multimodal treatment program, of which marital therapy is part. Although the main focus of this article does not permit me to delve into therapeutic questions, I will briefly describe the treatment interventions we use.

Most patients have a preparatory psychiatric session before admittance. We especially try to establish a contract on exposure treatment. After admission we use four treatment modalities: 1) individual, dynamically oriented psychotherapy; 2) exposure treatment; 3) psychoan-aleptic, antidepressive medication; and 4) marital therapy. This therapeutic "cocktail" has to be blended in accordance with each patient's person-ality, ego strength, motivation and symptoms. An evaluation of the patient's marriage is also important. Some marriages are so flexible to dynamic changes that marital therapy is unnecessary. That most often happens when the index patient is a man.

Seldom do we use only one modality; if we do, the choice is usually exposure treatment. Often individual psychotherapy is used together with exposure treatment. When necessary, three or four approaches are utilized. Exposure treatment is the modality that in one or another form should never be omitted.

Individual Psychotherapy

Eighty-seven percent of the agoraphobic patients in the total sample have received psychoanalytically oriented psychotherapy. For some this is rather supportive; others receive more anxiety-provoking therapy. If possible, we try to use a focal, short-term technique with early inter-pretation of the main motives and rather forceful confrontation with marital frustrations. The female patients themselves regularly bring into focus their marital problems after a short time of exposure treatment and individual psychotherapy. The exposure treatment facilitates the surfacing of hidden motives, emotions, and frustrations. Some patients are offered long-term outpatient psychotherapy, often combined with marital sessions and continued exposure treatment.

Exposure Treatment

Seventy percent of the agoraphobic patients in the whole sample are offered exposure treatment in a group of fellow agoraphobic patients. The rest take part in individual exposure treatment. We prefer group treatment, but sometimes there are not enough agoraphobic patients admitted to form a group. The patients in the group also do a lot of individual training, during the hospital stay, on visits to their home, and after discharge.

The groups have four to six patients. Preferably both sexes should be included. The first day the group is given an introductory lecture on anxiety, the connection between anxiety and breathing, the somatic equivalents to anxiety, and the training principles. The lecture is given in a rather emotional style, and often anxiety reactions during the lecture are used to illustrate what is being put forward. The main therapeutic principle in this lecture might be termed "cognitive restructuring." In addition, patients are instructed on how to cope with anxiety attacks. Then the group is handed over to two psychiatric nurses who lead the exposure training. The patients tell each other about their phobias. Often humor enters the process. The group trains together four or five days a week for three weeks. The daily exposure should be of long duration, at least two hours. The nurses plan each day's treatment together with the group; they sometimes follow the patients through the feared situation, and then meet with the group at the end of the treatment tasks. It is of special importance for the nurses and for the individual therapist to discover and to be able to handle *resistance* against the exposure treatment.

Individual and group exposure can both use either systematic *desensitization* (Wolpe, 1958) or *flooding in vivo* (implosion therapy) (Stampfl & Levis, 1967). During treatment in groups *modeling* acts as a working principle. Paradoxical intention (Frankl, 1959) is sometimes used during individual exposure treatment. This treatment is almost the same as imaginal flooding.

Psychopharmacological Treatment

Twenty-eight percent of the patients receive a full trial of antidepressant medication. It has been known for some years that psychoanaleptics sometimes have a salutary effect on agoraphobic symptoms. It is not yet clear which of the tricyclic agents are best, but clomipramine is often used. The length of treatment must often be three or four weeks before any effect is registered. Many agoraphobic patients are reluctant to continue medication because of amphetamine-like side effects. These remind them of anxiety. Sometimes the side effects are greatly influenced by the patients' habitual fear of vital and aggressive emotions, emotions that partly are facilitated by the drug effect. Encouraging the patients to stay with the medication, eventually on a reduced dosage, might be indicated. There is strong evidence that these drugs mostly affect the anxiety attacks and not the anticipatory fear (fear of fear).

Marital Therapy

One hundred and two of the 158 (60%) agoraphobic patients living in an existing marital relationship have received marriage therapy. This treatment was more frequently used when the index patient was female.

Because an agoraphobic woman's symptoms are strongly connected to a specific homeostatic collusion pattern between her and her husband, it is essential to include the husband in the treatment. It is important to stimulate his feeling of individuality and bring him to regard his wife's newly won freedom positively. The individuation process is important for both of them; it also helps keep the marriage from being destroyed. Many of the patients who relapse do so because the husband has a difficult time accepting a symptom-free, mature, independent, active and lively woman.

After having treated or supervised the treatment of over 150 agoraphobic married women, I am struck by how much frozen passion these women usually possess. In fact, they are more afraid of their resources than most other patients. At the same time, one finds that they are prepared to regress into immaturity and dependence. They seek a large degree of security from their husbands. This security comes in conflict with the adult woman's wishes for freedom and life experiences which are associated with sexuality, self-assertion, and adulthood. They find it difficult to experience these aspects of themselves within the frame of a conventional and often somewhat boring marital relationship. Thus, they turn their fantasies outward, become paralyzed by guilt feelings, and protect themselves by regression, helplessness, dependency and phobic symptoms.

In treatment it seems important to help them achieve emotional insight. Also essential is that the symptoms be put under pressure by individual or group-oriented exposure training. A good result is often totally contingent upon the marital pattern being worked through and modified.

It is our impression that this form of treatment, along the several dimensions discussed, gives very good results. Thus far there has been no follow-up study of the material, but among the group which has continued in outpatient therapy for a long period of observation after discharge there seem to be good or excellent results in 80-90% of the cases. A detailed and systematic follow-up study is planned.

APPENDIX I
CODE SHEET, AGORAPHOBIC SAMPLE

Name: .... Born. ....
Journal no.: ....
Address ....
Identification: 001-003 ....☐☐☐

Variables	*Code sheet, agoraphobic sample*	*Categories*

001-003.   *Identification* ....
1   2   3
☐ ☐ ☐

004.   *Sex:*   1. Man.   2. Woman ....
4
☐

005.   *Marital status* ....
1. Unmarried. 2. Married. 3. Widow/er.
4. Divorced/separated. 5. Divorced, remarried.
6. Widow/er, remarried.
5
☐

006-007.   *Year of birth* ....
6   7
☐ ☐

008-009.   *Year of first admittance* ....
8   9
☐ ☐

010-011.   *Year of symptom-debut (agoraphobia)* ....
10 11
☐ ☐

012-013.   *Major diagnoses* ....
01. Phobia. 02. Anxiety. 03. Depression. 04. Unspecified neurosis. 05. Hysteria. 06. Character neurosis. 07. Character disorder/psychopathia. 08. Alcohol problem. 09. Drug addiction. 10. Anorexia nervosa. 11. Heart neurosis. 12. Neurasthenia 13. Obsessive-compulsive neurosis. 14. Depersonalization syndrome. 15. Other.
12 13
☐ ☐

014-015.   *Minor diagnoses* ....
(same categories as under major diagnosis)
Besides: 16. No minor diagnosis.
14 15
☐ ☐

016.   *Alcohol problem in 1. or later minor diagnosis* ....
1. Present. 2. Not present.
16
☐

017.   *Alcohol problem in the family* ....
1. Not present. 2. Father. 3. Spouse. 4. Spouse and father. 5. Father and others. 6. Siblings. 7. No information.
17
☐

018.   *Social class (4 categories)* ....
18
☐

19
☐

019.   *Occupational activity* ....
             1. Full-time work. 2. Part-time work. 3. No job.
             4. Disability insurance. 5. Pensioner. 6. Pupil/student.
             7.Housewife/housefather with formerly insignificant
             occupational activity. 8. Housewife/housefather with
             formerly significant occupational activity. 9. Rehabil-
             itation insurance/other economical support. 10. Other.

20   21
☐   ☐

020-021.   *Year of first wedding* ....
22
☐

022.   *Exposure treatment in group* ....
             1. Once. 2. Twice. 3. Three times or more. 4. Group
             treatment interrupted. 5. No group treatment.

23
☐

023.   *Exposure treatment, individually* ....
             1. None. 2. Little. 3. Much. 4. No information.

24
☐

024.   *Dynamic individual psychotherapy* ....
             1. Insignificant or none. 2. Active therapy.

25
☐

025.   *Antidepressant pharmacological treatment* ....
             1. Fully tried. 2. Not fully tried.

26
☐

026.   *Other pharmacological treatment* ....
             1. Minor tranquillizer. 2. Major tranquillizer. 3. Com-
             bination 1 and 2. 4. Combination 1+2+ insufficient
             doses antidepressants. 5. No pharmacological treat-
             ment.

27
☐

027.   *Marriage therapy* ....
             1. None. 2. Outpatient. 3. Spouse admitted.

28
☐

028.   *Outpatient treatment* ....
             1. Insignificant or none. 2. Some. 3. Active. 4. No
             information.

29
☐

029.   *Earlier psychiatric treatment* ....
             1. Never. 2. Outpatient. 3. Admitted psychiatric in-
             stitution.

30
☐

030.   *Numbers of stay in Modum Bads Nervesanatorium* ....
             1. Once. 2. Twice. 3. Three times. 4. Four times.
             5. Five or more.

31
☐

031.   *Therapeutic result at time of first discharge* ....
             1. Good or very good. 2. Some. 3. None or worse.

32
☐

032.   *Therapeutic result finally* ....
             Same categories as 031.

REFERENCES

Arieti, S. New views on the psychodynamics of phobias. *American Journal of Psychotherapy*, 1979, *13*, 82-95.

Bowlby, J. *Attachment and Loss, Vol 2*. New York: Basic Books, 1973.

Chambless, D.L. & Goldstein, A.J. Clinical treatment of agoraphobia. In M. Mavissakalian & D. Barlow (Eds.), *Phobia: Psychological and Pharmacological Treatment*. New York: Guilford, 1981.

Frank, J. *Persuasion and Healing: A Comparative Study of Psychotherapy*. Baltimore: John Hopkins Press, 1961.

Frankl, V.E. *Handbuch der Neurosenlehre und Psychotherapie unter Einschluss wichtiger Grenzgebiete*. Munchen: Urban & Schwarzenberg, 1959.

Goldstein, A.J. & Chambless, D.L. Denial of marital conflict in agoraphobia. In A.S. Gurman (Ed.), *Questions and Answers in the Practice of Family Therapy*. New York: Brunner/Mazel, 1981.

Goodstein, R.K. & Swift, K. Psychotherapy with phobic patients: The marriage relationship as source of symptoms and focus of treatment. *American Journal of Psychotherapy*, 1977, *31*, 284-293.

Hand, I., Lamontagne, Y., & Marks, I.M. Group exposure (flooding) in vivo for agoraphobics. *British Journal of Psychiatry*, 1974, *13*, 82-95.

Jong, E. *Jeg tør ikke fly*. Oslo: H. Aschehoug & Co, 1975. (*Fear of Flying*, printed first time in 1973).

Marks, I.M. New developments in the psychological treatment of phobias. In M. Mavissakalian & D. Barlow (Eds.), *Phobia: Psychological and Pharmacological Treatment*. New York: Guilford, 1981.

Roth, M. The phobic anxiety-depersonalization syndrome. *Proceedings of the Royal Society of Medicine*, 1959, *52*, 587-595.

Stampfl, T.G. & Levis, D.J. Essentials of implosion therapy: A learning theory based psychodynamic behavioral therapy. *Journal of Abnormal Psychology*, 1967, *72*, 496-503.

Strömgren, E. *Psykiatri*. Copenhagen: Munksgaard forlag, 1961.

Thomstad, J. Om agorafobi. Lecture at Norwegian Psychiatric Association, March, 1973 (unpublished manuscript).

Webster, A.S. The development of phobias in married women. *Psychological Monographs*, 1953, *67*, 1-18.

Wolpe, J. *Psychotherapy by Reciprocal Inhibition*. Stanford: Stanford University Press, 1958.

Editor's Commentary: Agoraphobia— A Symptom in Many Countries

Holm has traveled extensively and has read the writings of leading theoreticians and clinicians from numerous countries. In this chapter he culls from a diversity of sources and indicates how he and his colleagues at Modum Bads Nervesanatorium have adapted a modified version of the group model of anti-phobic exposure training developed at Maudsley Hospital in England, how they incorporate desensitization techniques derived in part from Wolpe's work in the United States, and how they utilize a widely held psychoanalytic framework for understanding the oedipal attachments and other unconscious components of the multi-determined symptom, agoraphobia, drawing on the work of Frank and Frankl. He provides a good review of both the intrapsychic and inter-personal theories of etiology of agoraphobia and comprehensively dis-cusses the relationship of agoraphobia to anxiety, depression, alcoholism, inhibited assertiveness, obsessive-compulsive traits, and ambivalence about independence. His descriptive powers are rich—so much so that the reader begins to feel he/she has met the patients discussed—Lilly, Tove, and Beate. They also seem so familiar because apparently the face of agoraphobia is similar in many countries; it is not culturally specific!

Perhaps the major contribution of this chapter is the important ma-terial it presents, derived from a solid, research-based study, on the kind of dyadic relationship the agoraphobic woman establishes. The spousal interaction may or may not precipitate the original eruption of the symp-tom; it certainly seems to help maintain and exacerbate it once it is evidenced. Holm portrays the agoraphobic woman as craving freedom, excitement, and stimulation, as having an abundant supply of sexual energy and as being potentially highly expressive. At the same time, she longs for an anchor point to protect her from her strong sexual and aggressive impulses, and to offer her stability and security. She gravi-tates toward a solid, mild and gentle, non-expressive and emotionally

414

distant man who seems to promise that he is trustworthy and will make her safe. (He is also boring and minimally interested in sex.) In appreciation, the dependent, helpless part of her personality gains ascendence so as not to threaten his weak sense of self. She inhibits her vitality, imprisons herself in her house as a voluntarily built cloister to protect her from the beckoning temptations of the outside world. He then is the vital link to the external reality, chauffering her when she must go out and feeling essential and important. This pattern of interaction can become fixed and continue for a long time—until one partner is no longer content with this way of life. If the woman enters treatment and mobilizes her resources to become increasingly self-sufficient and less frightened of her thirst for life and living, she endangers the precarious marital balance.

Thus, Holm urges that the therapist consider a multi-model treatment approach which includes 1) individual, dynamically oriented psychotherapy, 2) exposure training, 3) antidepressant medication, and 4) marital therapy. It is the inclusion of the marital relationship as a factor in the conceptualization of the symptomatology and of marital therapy in the treatment approach, as well as the analysis of the focus and process of the couple's therapy, that makes this chapter significant.

Chapter 23

Clinical Hypnosis in
Treating Sexual Abulia

By Daniel L. Araoz

Sexual abulia is described as a pathological condition where sexual desire is depressed or absent. Reasons for preferring the current descriptive label are proposed. The clinical use of hypnosis in its treatment is outlined with emphasis on careful diagnosis and constructive imagery production. Results of hypnotic treatment with 10 abulic patients are given. A detailed clinical case illustrates the procedure of hypnotherapy in treating an extreme case of sexual abulia. General conclusions are drawn and two hypotheses are suggested to explain the cure of this sexual dysfunction. The need for further research is stressed.

Sexual abulia refers to the pathological condition which Kaplan, in 1977, called hypoactive sexual desire, identifying it as a separate sexual dysfunction belonging to the desire phase of human sexual response (the other two phases being excitement and orgasm). Her new book (1979) deals comprehensively with the sexual disorders of the desire phase, describing them as inhibition of sexual desire (ISD) or sexual anorexia.

The article was originally published in *The American Journal of Family Therapy*, 1980, *8*, (1), 48-57.

An earlier version of this paper was presented at the American Psychological Association 86th Annual Convention, Toronto, Canada, August 1978.

The author wishes to thank Drs. Michael Jay Diamond, Barbara Hariton and Dorothy Strauss for their comments and suggestions on the first draft of this manuscript.

Daniel L. Araoz, Ed.D., is Professor of Community Mental Health Counseling, C. W. Post Center of Long Island University, New York, New York.

416

Before Kaplan, authors had mentioned this pathology only in an un-differentiated way. Thus, Kroger and Fezler (1976) offered special "standard structured images" to produce sexual arousal. Caird and Wincze (1977), Lazarus and Karlin (1978) and, before them, Fisher (1973) seemed to refer to desire and arousal without distinguishing between the two. The LoPiccolos (1978) mentioned it in passing, though later Leslie LoPiccolo (1979) identified "low sexual desire" and attributed it, in part, to faulty cognitions and expectations. Schwartz (1979) studied the correlation between testosterone levels and sexual desire. Finally, Levine (1979) requested a clear definition of sexual desire, raising the possibility of important distinctions at the desire level of sexuality, such as desire and "horniness."

On the other hand, another group of authors seemed to imply that sex therapy presupposes sexual desire (Kass and Strauss, 1975). Older authors especially imply that everybody desires sex (Hastings, 1963). Even Hite (1976) ignored sexual abulia as such. In 1977 Kaplan admitted that the sex therapy literature had neglected this dysfunction. She also claimed that the current methodology for the treatment of sexual dys-functions (Hartman and Fithian, 1972; Kaplan, 1974; Masters and John-son, 1966; 1970) did not seem to be effective with disorders of the desire phase of human sexual response. Her conclusion was that "there is an urgent need to develop more effective treatment techniques for this condition" . . . because "the least favorable (prognosis) is for disorders of the desire phase" (pp. 4 and 9).

This assessment did not consider hypnotherapy for sexual abulia; however, hypnosis seems to offer the needed treatment technique. Ac-cordingly, this paper will first cover the diversities of this sexual dys-function and, second, attempt to elucidate the clinical application of hypnotic techniques for its treatment, reporting on the author's suc-cessful brief, active therapy using hypnosis with 10 patients diagnosed as sexually abulic. Finally, some conclusions and hypotheses will be presented.

Instead of using the term *clinical hypnosis,* it would be more exact (Araoz, 1979) to modify the noun hypnosis with the adjective psycho-educational in order to emphasize the skill-learning nature of hypnosis (Barber, 1978). Hypnosis, used by a trained clinician is, indeed, a psy-choeducational tool, which the patient will learn to use for his/her benefit in the future (Diamond, 1977a), increasing that skill with practice.

In 1975 I became especially concerned with this phenomenon when several patients could not "get with" the sexual exercises prescribed as part of sex therapy. Possible dynamics intervening in the depressed or absent sexual desire were carefully explored with negative results. Such dynamics are 1) anger towards the partner, the opposite sex in general or towards self; 2) guilt about pleasure, bodily enjoyment or other realities, such as extramarital involvements; 3) resistance to change when motivation came mainly from the partner's dissatisfaction; and 4) secondary gains derived from the symptomatology. The negative outcome of this diagnostic analysis forced me to recognize a lack of sexual desire on the part of the patients, despite their protestations to the contrary. After attempting more traditional forms of sex therapy, hypnosis proved to be the treatment of choice for this condition.

Seven males and three females were studied in a two year period. Of these, five males and two females were treated exclusively with hypnosis. However, two males and one female had nonhypnotic therapy of a psychodynamic, insight-directed nature for 5-10 sessions before hypnotherapy was employed. The reason for the change to hypnotic sex therapy in these three cases was that the presenting marital problem was redefined and diagnosed as sexual abulia on the part of one spouse only after several sessions. These three patients can be considered as a quasi-control group. In summary, the 10 patients were distributed as follows: one female and two males were given nonhypnotic therapy for 5-10 sessions before hypnotherapy was used, and two females and five males were treated exclusively with hypnotherapy.

CLINICAL DISTINCTIONS

Before proceeding, a brief review of concepts is in order. Sexual desire is difficult to quantify, as Levine (1979) has pointed out.* To establish a diagnosis of sexual abulia, the therapist must be sure that other dynamics are ruled out—at least as serious variables in the etiology of the symptom. Recent studies (e.g., Schwartz, 1979) seem to point to the advisability of an endocrinological analysis before assuming a purely psychogenic case of sexual abulia; however, no endocrinological variables were considered in the 10 cases studied here. Another important factor in this dysfunction is that the motivation for treatment is vicarious. The patient is interested in his/her depressed or absent sexual desire because of a partner's dissatisfaction with the condition. This motivation does not have to be questioned if there is evidence that the patient wants to improve his/her sexual desire because of caring and concern for the

---

*Following Dr. Diamond's (1979) suggestion, I am now using a 100-point subjective rating scale for sexual desire, about which I hope to report in the future.

partner. In this case, the vicarious motivation is sufficient to establish a positive prognosis, all other things being equal.

Though the expression *sexual abulia* is not perfect, there are three reasons for preferring it. First, hypoactive (Kaplan, 1977) or low (Lo-Piccolo, 1979) desire can become a contradiction in terms, because *desire*, by definition, is always *active*, and in severe cases, desire proper is simply nonexistent. Second, sexual abulia is less cumbersome an expression than hypoactive sexual desire. Finally, abulia is an accepted, though rather outdated, psychiatric term used to denote a special pathology of desire, intention or will. Sex therapists frequently deal with a lack or diminution of sexual desire which has become pathological in context (Levine, 1979; LoPiccolo, 1979; Schwartz, 1979). Kaplan's (1979) phrase *inhibition of sexual desire* (ISD) refers to the same conditions covered by my term *sexual abulia*. Eventually her nomenclature may prevail due to its simple, descriptive nature.

Sexual abulia may be primary or secondary, situational or global, moderate or severe. *Primary* sexual abulia occurs when the individual has never experienced sexual desire; *secondary* sexual abulia manifests itself as one of the outcomes of another primary pathology; *global* sexual abulia is found when no stimuli of any kind arouse sexual desire; and *situational* sexual abulia is encountered in individuals who experience no desire in some normally arousing situations but feel sexual desire in other situations. As Kaplan (1977) pointed out, sexual variations are examples of situational abulia. where statistically normal preferences elicit no desire. *Moderate* sexual abulia is low sexual desire, whereas *severe* refers to its complete absence.

Because our culture assumes that every normal, healthy adult — especially male — wants sex frequently, sexually abulic persons deny their condition. They focus instead on difficulties of the second and third phases of the sexual response which, in truth occur as a consequence of the inhibited sexual desire. Thus, the presenting complaints may relate to erectile/orgasmic problems, ignoring the causative trouble at the first phase.

IMAGINATION AND SEX

Hypnosis may be partly described as the systematic use of imagination (Barber et al., 1974; Barber, 1978) for therapeutic purposes. This is the concept of imagery conditioning as Kroger and Fezler (1976) presented it. Moreover, in hypnotherapy for sexual dysfunctions, imagery conditioning is particularly useful. Hariton (1973; Hariton and Singer, 1974) emphasized the role of imagination in women during sexual intercourse and its therapeutic importance in increasing orgasmic response, making it feasible for the clinician to apply concepts in sex therapy.

The extensive literature on the clinical application of hypnosis in treating sexual arousal and resolution problems (dysfunctions at the second and third phases of human sexual response) stresses hypnotic imagery. To give a few examples: Cox and Araoz (1977) reported on three women who were able to experience sexual excitement and orgasm during hypnosis by means of mere imagery production. Cheek (1961; 1979) and Wijesinghe (1977) dealt with orgasmic dysfunction, while Wollman (1964) reported on successful use of hypnosis in erectile and orgasmic dysfunctions. Beigel (1972) succeeded in treating female sexual anesthesia. Deabler (1976) used hypnosis in erectile problems and Erickson (1935; 1973) used it in treating premature ejaculation. Nims (1975) also employed imagery in orgasm, whereas Weitz (1977) made use of age regression and mental rehearsal for the same purpose.

This is only a small sampling of the many reports in the professional literature on the use of hypnosis in treating dysfunction relating to the second and third phases of sexual behavior. However, nothing has been spelled out about the use of hypnosis with sexual abulia, perhaps because the literature of sex therapy itself had ignored this pathology until Kaplan's (1979) recent major contribution to its understanding, treatment and cure. At the other end of the spectrum, Conn (1968) mentioned the effectiveness of hypnosis in treating the hyperactive sexual desire and activity of criminal offenders.

A CLINICAL CASE

Due to space limitations, the case of one male patient, which has many similarities with the other nine treated, will be reported.

Jim was a 37-year-old professor in a business school, married 12 years, with three children, a boy 11 and twin girls nine years old. He was in excellent physical health and at the peak of his career, involved in university affairs, recognized as an authority in his field. He had published two successful textbooks and several articles. His wife, 34, had insisted on marital therapy because of his disinterest in sex. For the two years previous to therapy, they had engaged in sexual activities on an average of once every two months and only at her prompting. He had declared that he could "take sex or leave it." The presenting clinical picture was that he had experienced premature ejaculation and, later, erectile dysfunction. There was no evidence of serious intrapsychic or relationship problems. Lack of sexual desire was not mentioned initially, but it soon became clear that the correct diagnosis was sexual abulia.

Hypnotherapy was used to attain three goals:

1) revivification,
2) uncovering, and
3) mental rehearsal.

The first goal was to relive a period of his life when sexual functioning was exciting and desired. In working on this first goal, it became clear that Jim had never had an exciting sexual experience of any kind, as will be explained presently. When this is the case (sexual abulia of the global, primary, severe type), hypnosis is used to imagine possible sexual situations and scenes. Admittedly, it is easier to relive past, pleasant experiences than to imagine situations never experienced (Barber et al., 1974), but with training in imagery production, the latter can be accomplished, as Diamond (1977a and b) has forcefully pointed out.

The second therapeutic goal was to uncover at what point and why there had been an attitudinal change or to discover the developmental reasons for the sexual abulia. The discussion below points out the reasons why the psychodynamic goal is important in understanding the patient's resistances.

The third goal was to rehearse in imagination a life of greater sexual interest and enjoyment. Only then could the more traditional type of sex therapy begin. These three goals seem to be essential, generally, in treating sexual abulia by means of hypnosis.

In the first visit, Jim and his wife were seen together initially, then were interviewed individually: conjointly/wife alone/husband alone/conjointly. In the last segment of the first session, it was decided, with the couple, that Jim would be hypnotized without his wife being present. He was ambivalent about her witnessing his hypnosis and she preferred it that way, "at least this first time." The hypnotic session followed immediately.

The prehypnotic interview made it clear that Jim had never been particularly interested in sex. He had always been an *enfant prodige*, advanced in his intellectual development. His family had reinforced all his intellectual interests, both emotionally and materially, considering him the smartest of 18 cousins. Puberty occurred normally but he had not masturbated nor experienced any sexual exploration until the age of 17, when other boys involved him in heavy petting with a few hired girls. Jim had considered this experience "boring," though "interesting," and added that he was not sorry to have had this "opportunity to know what prostitutes are really like."

He had known his wife since the age of two, both families being neighbors and friends. When he became interested in her during his first college year, he was affectionate and attentive, but not sexual. They had intercourse for the first time after the wedding. His wife was overly inhibited at the time and did not experience any sexual pleasure. In fact, she had never masturbated until about two years before therapy and could not remember having had orgasm through intercourse. In the last two years, however, she had become more aware of herself, "more alive," as she put it, and had awakened sexually, proudly admitting her sexual needs and expecting sexual satisfaction as a personal right in her relationship with Jim. Her caring for and commitment to Jim were genuine, her anger was not neurotic and the relationship was gratifying in all other areas.

The therapist obtained from Jim an expression of willingness to try to learn a new means of enjoying sex for himself, not just to please his wife. Hypnotherapy was then described and a pleasure hierarchy was established, consisting of a list of any items in his sexual experience with his wife which he found even slightly more attractive, appealing or pleasurable than others. Jim reported some pleasant feelings in the following order:

1) When his wife held him in an embrace.
2) When he rubbed accidentally against his wife's naked body in bed.
3) When his wife showed "urgency of desire" while making love.
4) When she massaged his chest and abdomen.
5) When he massaged her thighs and buttocks.

In hypnosis, the patient was invited to imagine his wife and him in bed. On the basis of the above pleasure hierarchy, the therapist built up an elaborate sexual scene in Jim's mind's eye. The setting of a sexual encounter with his wife was described in great detail; the activities were also spelled out in a progressive fashion; and sounds, aromas or tastes pertinent to the situation were pointed out and incorporated into the imaginary sexual scene. All along suggestions of relaxation, well-being and happiness were intermingled so as to pair these good feelings with the sexual images. Verbal interaction was encouraged throughout, thus getting constant feedback from the patient so that the hypnotic suggestions could be accommodated to his ongoing experience.

Two posthypnotic suggestions were given. First, that the good feelings experienced in hypnosis would return when he and his wife were in the bedroom, ready to retire for the night. The rationale for suggesting these feelings before being in bed was that Jim needed a sense of control of these new feelings. To experience them before being in bed would give him some time to decide rationally whether to act on them or not.

The second posthypnotic suggestion was that the whole chain of reactions, which would culminate in a clear, enjoyable desire for sex, would be elicited by his wife's embrace. Consequently, he could ask his wife for an embrace when he wanted to act on his sexual desire. In other words, the new sexual desire would not control him unless he wanted this to happen. The wife was advised not to initiate sex until the next therapy meeting.

An audio tape to be used exclusively by Jim was made during the first session while he was experiencing hypnosis. He was told to practice self-hypnosis with the aid of the tape, at least once a day.

The second session was a week later. Jim reported that he had followed instructions and had definitely experienced sexual desire for the first time in his life, but that he and his wife felt too self-conscious about it, after 12 years of routine and infrequent sex. He was surprised at having recaptured, while using the tape on his own, the positive feelings experienced during the first session. He had purposely practiced three times when he was completely indifferent to sex as a way of "testing" his hypnotic experience of the first session. He and his wife had engaged in sexual activities twice during that first week.

At the second session Jim asked to have his wife in the office while he was hypnotized. By using single hypnosis (Araoz, 1978), the therapist invited the wife to get as much as she wanted out of the experience, while Jim achieved hypnosis speedily and with very little direction from the therapist. In hypnosis, he was asked to describe, once more, his mental images of enjoyable sex with his wife. She spontaneously joined him in this experience, contributing to it. A third posthypnotic suggestion was added to the previous two, namely, that he would be able to experience sexual desire at other times and to enjoy this experience as a regular aspect of his life.

The third appointment was planned for four weeks later due to oncoming vacations. However, a telephone minisession was arranged for the following week. Jim's telephone report was enthusiastic. He had wanted sex and enjoyed it thoroughly. He and his wife no longer felt self-conscious about his "new interest." Over the telephone the previous posthypnotic suggestions were repeated.

The scheduled third interview never took place due to circumstances of weather and transportation problems, but a second minisession was employed to reinforce the gains obtained. Follow-up telephone calls, six and 12 weeks after the last minisession, indicated that sexual desire had been maintained and sexual activity had peaked to a mean of three times a week. Jim indicated both times that he was extremely happy with the developments and that he and his wife were enjoying their whole relationship more than ever before. A final telephone call was made eight months later, with the same positive results reported by the patient.

DISCUSSION

The 10 cases of sexual abulia mentioned in this article responded successfully to hypnotherapeutic techniques. Jim's case was presented at length to illustrate the procedure, but there were enough similarities in the 10 cases to warrant classifying them as one sample, despite the fact that each case was individually different and that only four of them were of primary sexual abulia. Thus, in each of the 10 cases, sex had never been, or had completely ceased to be, a matter of strong personal interest, desire or concern. The last point is important, because none of these people were dissatisfied with their condition. What motivated them to seek sex therapy was, in each case, a spouse or partner. In three cases, the patients had recently started a new relationship and the partner was dissatisfied with their lack of interest in sex. In six cases, a sexually unhappy spouse prompted the patient to seek help, as in the case of Jim. In one case, the patient was in an open relationship where other sexual partners were accepted individually and in groups, but his lack of interest and participation in sex made him "feel different."

The second trait common to the 10 patients was that all were able to experience hypnosis as a natural, though different, way of using their own minds. Hypnotic treatment started in the first session (except for the three quasi controls, as explained earlier).

Third, in all 10 cases the same three goals described in the case of Jim were established and obtained, and the same posthypnotic suggestions were given, though modifications were used to fit the individual needs of each patient. The second therapeutic goal—to uncover the reasons and circumstances for sexual abulia—needs further elucidation. Since intimate relationships between adults can easily suffer distortions of developmental or of perceptual origin (Araoz, 1978), the therapist must ascertain that the libidinal dysfunction is not a secondary manifestation. Developmental conflicts, such as negative beliefs about sex subconsciously accepted without questioning in the early years of life, can be deeply repressed but must be dealt with when they do exist, if sexual abulia is to be overcome. A common perceptual conflict, on the other hand, is that of reification (Caruso, 1953), where the partner or the relationship itself is perceived as a thing which is supposed to provide happiness. In this case, reification must be solved before sexual abulia disappears. Finally, traumatic circumstances usually explain the onset of secondary sexual abulia. These may range from stern repression of normal childhood sexual curiosity to violent rape. Consequently, the therapist must consider these possible hidden dynamics in order to establish an accurate diagnosis.

It should be added, incidentally, that hypnosis provides a flexible and effective tool for the diagnosis of sexual dysfunctions (Araoz, 1977). Bell (1976) put it succinctly: "As one fully explores the possibilities of hypnotic behavior therapy techniques, one is also likely to increasingly involve himself with the intrapsychic factors of pyschodynamics, as well as to become more sensitive to the therapist-patient relationship" (p. 274). The work of other authors who do not subscribe to psychodynamic theories, such as Haley (1973), confirms the above observation.

Fourth, except for the quasi controls, no patient was seen for more than four sessions, and only two had four sessions (Jim is considered as having had four sessions). Finally, in all cases follow-up telephone calls were made four months and again eight months after the last session. In nine cases, the gains had remained, as measured by the frequency of enjoyable sexual activity. In one case, injury had ensued as a result of a car accident and sexual activity had come to a temporary stop; however, the patient reported that he still had sexual fantasies and desires.

HYPOTHESES

To explain the resurgence of or the original arousal of sexual desire, there are two hypotheses that suggest themselves. The first is that there is an element of choice, albeit subconscious, in the experience of any desire. Most advertisement is based on this principle. By artificially introducing a product into the person's perception, the advertisement can trigger a desire for that product, which may not be directly related to any natural need of the person exposed to the advertisement. If this process works with artificial desires, it can be expected to work also in a natural desire such as sex. It has long been known that, in hypnosis, a person who is sated can be made to feel hungry.

In the case of the sex drive, hypnotic imagery seems to produce or reawaken the natural "neural circuitry" responsible for sexual interest, desire and stimulation. The question of neural circuitry and of the brain's role in the neurological production of sexual desire warrants careful physiological study, as Schwartz (1979), among others, has emphatically pointed out. The hypothesis, therefore, is that by reaching the subcortical brain activity responsible for sexual desire, hypnosis can become the means of either arousing this desire for the first time in a person's life or of reawakening it.

The second hypothetical formulation is related to the defense mechanisms in general and to repression in particular. The evidence (Levine, 1979; LoPiccolo, 1979; Rosen et al., 1979) seems to indicate unequivocally that sexual abulia inevitably goes back to negative messages decoded in earlier periods of the patient's life and not reinterpreted by him/her later in life. The repressive mechanism has been massive. The individual acts as if he/she were asexual. This phenomenon has to be researched further, especially with populations who voluntarily renounce sexual activity but lead otherwise normal lives, such as Catholic priests.

Somewhat differently when a later, traumatic event has intervened and is not fully consciously known by the patient, it seems that its anxiety-producing nature has inhibited sexual desire. In both cases (early-alone and early-plus-later anxiety-producing events related to sex), hypnosis can free sexual desire from the inhibiting circumstances which were repressing it, either by helping the person to reinterpret early negative scripts (Rosen et al., 1979) or by separating the traumatic events from the normal sex drive (LoPiccolo, 1979). It should be stressed that possible dynamic issues, like guilt or anger, may have to be worked through before direct sex therapy is employed.

CONCLUSIONS

The clinical fact is that hypnosis does, indeed, offer an effective treatment technique for sexual abulia. The small sample mentioned in this paper presents enough clinical realities of successful intervention to warrant further attention to the utilization of hypnotherapeutic techniques in treating sexual abulia. However, no general or simplistic solution is implied. The cogent treatment of the limitations of hypnobehavioral methods by Kroger and Fezler (1976, p. 408) comes to mind. Suffice it to emphasize that two conditions are essential for hypnotherapeutic success, namely, a correct diagnosis of sexual abulia and the therapist's skill and imagination, rooted in well-established knowledge of the cognitive-based skill approach to hypnosis (Barber, 1978; Diamond, 1977b; Katz, 1979). This report presents therapeutic realities that reasonably justify cautious optimism in the utilization of the hypnotherapeutic approach. Sex and marital therapists would do well to acquaint themselves with this therapeutic modality.

REFERENCES

Araoz, D. L. Hypnosis in the Treatment of Sexual Dysfunction. Paper presented at the 20th scientific meeting of the American Society of Clinical Hypnosis, Atlanta, October, 1977.

Araoz, D. L. Clinical hypnosis in couple therapy. *Journal of the American Society of Psychosomatic Dentistry and Medicine,* 1978, *25,* 58-67.

Araoz, D. L. Psychoeducational hypnosis. *Newsletter of the American Association of Psychoeducational Therapists,* 1979, *5,* 3-5.

Barber, T. X. *Hypnosis and Psychosomatics.* San Francisco: Proseminar Institute, 1978.

Barber, T. X., Spanos, N., & Chaves, J. F. *Hypnotism, Imagination and Human Potentialities.* New York: Pergamon, 1974.

Beigel, H. The use of hypnosis in female sexual anesthesia. *Journal of the American Society of Psychosomatic Dentistry and Medicine,* 1972, *19,* 4-14.

Bell, G. K. Clinical hypnosis: Warp and woof of psychotherapies. In E. Dengrove (Ed.), *Hypnosis and Behavior Therapy.* Springfield, IL: C. C. Thomas, 1976.

Caird, W. & Wincze, J. P. *Sex Therapy: A Behavioral Approach.* New York: Harper & Row, 1977.

Caruso, I. A. Le sourmoi et le buc emissaire. *Psyche,* 1953, *8,* 262-271.

Cheek, D. Gynecological uses of hypnotism. In L. M. LeCron (Ed.), *Techniques of Hypnotherapy.* New York: Julian, 1961.

Cheek, D. Hypnotherapy for secondary frigidity after radical surgery for gynecological cancer. *American Journal of Clinical Hypnosis,* 1979, *19,* 13-19.

Conn, J. H. Hypnosynthesis: Dynamic psychotherapy of the sex offender using hypnotic techniques. *Journal of the American Society of Psychosomatic Dentistry and Medicine,* 1968, *15,* 18-27.

Cox, T. H. & Araoz, D. L. Sexual excitement and response by imagery production. *Journal of the American Society of Psychosomatic Dentistry and Medicine,* 1977, *24,* 82-93.

Deabler, H. L. Hypnotherapy for impotence. *American Journal of Clinical Hypnosis,* 1976, *19,* 9-13.

Diamond, M. J. Hypnotizability is modifiable. *International Journal of Clinical and Experimental Hypnosis,* 1977, *25,* 147-166 (a).

Diamond, M. J. Issues and methods for modifying responsivity to hypnosis. In W. E. Edmonson (Ed.), *Conceptual and Investigative Approaches to Hypnosis (Annals of the New York Academy of Sciences,* Vol. 296). New York: New York Academy of Sciences, 1977 (b).

Diamond, M. J. Personal communication, January 18, 1979.

Erickson, M. H. A study of an experimental neurosis hypnotically induced in a case of ejaculatio precox. *British Journal of Medical Psychology*, 1935, *15*, 34-50.

Erickson, M. H. Psychotherapy achieved by a reversal of the neurotic process in a case of ejaculatio precox. *American Journal of Clinical Hypnosis*, 1973, *15*, 217-222.

Fisher, S. *The Female Orgasm*. New York: Basic Books, 1973.

Haley, J. *Uncommon Therapy: The Psychiatric Techniques of M. H. Erickson*. New York: Norton, 1973.

Hariton, E. B. The sexual fantasies of women. *Psychology Today*, March 1973, 39-44.

Hariton, E. B. and Singer, J. L. Women's fantasies during sexual intercourse. *Journal of Consulting and Clinical Psychology*, 1974, *43*, 313-322.

Hartman, W. E. & Fithian, M. *The Treatment of Sexual Dysfunctions*. Long Beach, CA: Center for Marital and Sexual Studies, 1972.

Hastings, D. W. *Impotence and Frigidity*. Boston: Little, Brown, 1963.

Hite, S. *The Hite Report*. New York: Macmillan, 1976.

Kaplan, H. S. *The New Sex Therapy*. New York: Brunner/Mazel, 1974.

Kaplan, H. S. Hypoactive sexual desire. *Journal of Sex and Marital Therapy*, 1977, *3*, 3-9.

Kaplan, H. S. *Disorders of Sexual Desire and Other New Concepts and Techniques in Sex Therapy*. New York. Brunner/Mazel, 1979.

Kass, D. J. & Strauss, F. F. *Sex Therapy at Home*. New York: Simon & Schuster, 1975.

Katz, N. W. Increasing hypnotic responsiveness: Behavioral training vs. trance induction. *Journal of Consulting and Clinical Psychology*, 1979, *47*, 119-127.

Kroger, W. S. & Fezler, W. D. *Hypnosis and Behavior Modification: Imagery Conditioning*. Philadelphia: Lippincott, 1976.

Lazarus, A. A. & Karlin, R. A. Hypnosis in the context of behavior therapy. In F. H. Frankel & H. S. Zamansky (Eds.), *Hypnosis at its Bicentennial*. New York: Plenum, 1978.

Levine, S. B. Conceptual Suggestions for Outcome Research in Sex Therapy. Paper presented at the 5th annual meeting of the Society for Sex Therapy and Research, Philadelphia, March 1979.

LoPiccolo, J. & LoPiccolo, L. (Eds.). *Handbook of Sex Therapy*. New York: Plenum, 1978.

LoPiccolo, L. An examination of the phenomenon of low sexual desire. Paper presented at the 5th annual meeting of the Society for Sex Therapy and Research, Philadelphia, March 1979.

Masters, W. & Johnson, V. *Human Sexual Response*. Boston: Little, Brown, 1966.

Masters, W. & Johnson, V. *Human Sexual Inadequacy*. Boston: Little, Brown, 1970.

Nims, J. Imagery, shaping and orgasm. *Journal of Sex and Marital Therapy*, 1975, *1*, 198-203.

Rosen, R. C., Leiblum, S. R., & Gagnon, J. H. Sexual scripts, assessment and modification in sex therapy. Paper presented at the 5th annual meeting of the Society for Sex Therapy and Research, Philadelphia, March 1979.

Schwartz, M. F. Plasma testosterone in sexually dysfunctional men. Paper presented at the 5th annual meeting of the Society for Sex Therapy and Research, Philadelphia, March 1979.

Weitz, R. D. Hypnotherapeutic techniques in the treatment of sexual disorders and counterparts in the new therapies. Paper presented at the Winter meeting of the Division of Psychotherapy of the American Psychological Association, Orlando, FL, March, 1977.

Wijesinghe, B. A. A case of frigidity treated by short term hypnotherapy. *International Journal of Clinical and Experimental Hypnosis*, 1977, *25*, 63-67.

Wollman, L. Sexual disorders managed by hypnotherapy. Paper presented at the meeting of the Society for the Scientific Study of Sex, New York, January 1964.

Editor's Commentary: Disorders of the
Sexual Desire Phase

As Araoz points out, a widely held belief is that sexual desire is something everyone has. Frequently the concern is that the desire and drive may be too profuse. Conversely, little attention has been paid to the lack of a strong wish for sexual activity. Probably this "dysfunction" has been slow to surface because patients and others characterized by lack of sensuous feelings have either been unconcerned, pleased by their triumph over bodily dictates which they relegate to a lower level of animalistic craving, or reluctant to admit this difference for fear of seeming strange and "not with it" in an era of heightened sexuality.

In this chapter, Araoz deals primarily with treatment of the first group—those who are basically unconcerned but whose mates would like a more active and passionate sexual relationship. His work also has implications for the third group—those who may be reluctant to admit their low sexual desire but who nevertheless are troubled by it. They probably would not present for sexual dysfunction; their discontent is more likely to be expressed in the course of individual, marital or family therapy as they begin to focus on poor body image, low self-esteem issues, or the budding sexuality of an adolescent child that distresses them. The second group, those who elevate their lack of desire to a virtue, in accord with those orthodox religious beliefs systems which hold the life of the mind and spirit to be far superior to the life of the body, are unlikely to be seen in therapy. If they are, this would not initially constitute a therapeutic issue.

Recently, as treatment of sexual dysfunction has become both more research based and clinically validated, thanks to pioneers like Masters and Johnson, Kaplan, and the LoPiccolos, the lack of sexual desire has been recognized and discussed more. Various labels seem to be used interchangeably. Kaplan subsumes hypoactive sexual desire under disorders of the sexual desire phase, labeling them inhibition of sexual desire (ISD) or sexual anorexia. LoPiccolo speaks of low sexual desire and Araoz discusses the condition under the term sexual abulia. Whichever label one utilizes to convey absent or minimal sexual desire, it seems to be a condition resistant to standard verbal psychotherapeutic procedures.

Since a poor sexual relationship, in which the partner with a more "normal" level of sexual desire is apt to feel confused, rejected, and increasingly hostile toward the disinterested party, is likely to lead to marital discontent and friction and spill over into family conflict, the treatment of this sexual disorder fits within the purview of this book. Araoz's approach of replacing of negative affirmations, defeatist sexual imagery, and "negative self talk" with positive affirmations and sensuous visual images invoked through hypnosis should be useful to clinicians in many corners of the world. His discussion of the efficacy of this approach, though predicated on only ten patients, marks a persuasive beginning.

Although much of the flavor of this chapter reflects a behaviorist orientation, coupling task assignments and structured exercises with hypnosis, the underlying diagnostic stance is a psychodynamic one. Caution must be exercised regarding handling transference and countertransference issues since the therapist's attitudes toward sexuality should not be superimposed or allowed to interfere in less subtle ways. Suggestions made during hypnosis must be ego-syntonic for the patient (as well as therapeutically ego-syntonic for the therapist).

And, of course, as Araoz points out, if a therapist decides that clinical hypnosis is the treatment of choice for sexual abulia, he/she should be well trained in this technique before attempting to practice it. Otherwise, a referral to a skilled hypnotherapist is in order. It is hoped we will see this approach utilized with a larger sample and the results reported in keeping with the latest rigorous standards for psychotherapy outcome research.

Chapter 24

Marital Homeostasis and Spouse-aided Therapy in Persisting Psychological Disorders

By R. Julian Hafner

The concept of marital homeostasis is introduced to help explain the persistence of psychological disability in many married people. The symptoms of the designated patient are seen as often having a protective effect on the psychological adjustment of the ostensibly healthy marriage partner. Spouse-aided Therapy is introduced as a goal-oriented, time-limited outpatient approach designed to enable the patient's spouse to acknowledge and relinquish his contribution to the patient's continuing disability. This is followed by changes in marital interaction which facilitate the patient's symptomatic improvement.

The concept of family homeostasis, introduced over 20 years ago by Jackson (1957), is now well-established in family therapy. Jackson and Yalom (1965) described the concept as arising in part from the observation that: "The patient's improvement was accompanied by the appearance of severe mental illness in some other family member . . . It would seem that, despite the family's natural concern for the ill member, there are strong forces operating in the family to keep the patient sick."

This is a slightly revised version of the article which was originally published in the *Australian Journal of Family Therapy*, 1980, 2, (1), 2-8.

R. Julian Hafner, M.D., is a Senior Lecturer in Psychiatry, Flinders Medical Centre, Bedford Park, South Australia.

It was the introduction of family therapy, and the application within a family setting of powerful and sophisticated psychological interventions, which allowed the concept of family homeostasis to emerge, but which also restricted its application mainly to the families of severely disturbed adolescents. In a more general context, the recent introduction of powerful behavioral and drug therapies for persisting psychological disorders has revealed that the concept of family homeostasis may have a far wider application than originally believed. This paper utilizes the concept of marital homeostasis as a widespread sub-type of family homeostasis. Marital homeostasis is proposed as an explanation for persisting psychological disorder in a significant proportion of married people, and provides the rationale for Spouse-aided Therapy.

THE SPOUSE'S CONTRIBUTION TO PERSISTING PSYCHOLOGICAL DISABILITY

A traditional notion in psychiatry is that of the long-suffering, almost superhumanly patient spouse married in martyrdom to a difficult, troublesome and demanding chronic psychiatric patient. Although such an idea is naïve, it is often hard to relinquish, particularly where an illness model of psychiatric disorder prevails. However, a number of recent studies have exposed, unequivocally and on empirical grounds, such notions as simplistic and misleading in many instances.

Goodstein and Swift (1977) report the treatment of three agoraphobic women in a marital context. In the first case they state: "Couple therapy proved unfeasible as the husband stated that he felt he could only be content with a completely submissive wife." After individual supportive psychotherapy the patient initiated divorce proceedings and moved to a new home, during the course of which her agoraphobic symptoms resolved. In the second case, when the patient responded well to phenelzine, her husband became depressed and rapidly lost nine kilograms in weight. However, after twice-weekly conjoint marital therapy for six months, the husband's depression, the wife's agoraphobia, and the marriage were all greatly improved. In the third case, the couple feared that improvement in the wife's agoraphobia might lead to the dissolution of the marriage, which neither wanted. Conjoint marital therapy focused on helping the patient to become more independent and assertive towards her husband, and on helping him to accommodate this, which he became able to do once he realized that dominating and controlling his wife in an overbearing manner was not the best way of minimizing the risk of her leaving him. Once these basic marital issues were resolved, the wife's agoraphobia disappeared.

Hand and Lamontagne (1976) found an unexpectedly high rate of acute interpersonal crises after the successful treatment of agoraphobics by group exposure in real life. Fourteen of 21 married patients reported chronic marital problems before treatment, but all regarded the phobia as the necessary focus of therapeutic intervention, and viewed marital therapy as inappropriate. However, six of the 14 couples with unsatisfactory marriages, and one other couple, reported acute marital crises after successful phobia removal. Nonetheless, only three couples agreed to conjoint marital therapy.

Hafner (1977) systematically studied 30 married agoraphobic women and their husbands before, during and after intensive, mainly behavioral, group and individual therapy for the patients. Patients were divided into two equal groups based on questionnaire levels of hostility: the most hostile group was also the most disabled, with severe general neurotic disability in addition to agoraphobia. In the most hostile group, patients' mean hostility scores decreased and self-esteem increased throughout 12 months' follow-up. Their husbands' mean symptom scores increased and their self-esteem significantly decreased at the three month follow-up, and several husbands developed serious psychological problems of their own. Patients' dissatisfaction with their husbands increased throughout follow-up, and the husbands' self-esteem remained lower at the 12 month follow-up than before treatment. These and other findings suggested strongly that a proportion of husbands reacted adversely to their wives' symptomatic improvement.

Milton and Hafner (1979) measured psychological symptoms and marital adjustment in 15 agoraphobic patients and their spouses before, during and after intensive group and individual exposure in real life for the patients. After the patients' symptomatic improvement, marital dissatisfaction increased in nine couples, and an increase in marital dissatisfaction was strongly associated with a greater likelihood of relapse. An increase in marital disharmony was reported more often by patients who rated their marriages as poor before treatment than by those who rated their marriages as satisfactory.

In a 12 month follow-up study of general neurotic patients, Sims (1975) found that marital and sexual factors were highly predictive of outcome, with poor marriages strongly associated with poor outcome, irrespective of psychiatric diagnosis. Weissman and Klerman (1977) followed up 150 acutely ill depressed female patients for 20 months. They found that moderate symptoms remained in 60 percent, with no change or worsening in 12 percent. Thirty-eight of the original 150 women were randomly assigned to eight months of individual psychotherapy focusing on interpersonal and marital factors (Rounsaville et al., 1979). Of these, 35 were married, and 22 of the married patients had marital disputes. In only six did the marital disputes improve during therapy. That majority of women whose marital disputes did not improve remained depressed, or worsened. In spite of the manifest failure of individual psychotherapy to help the majority of these depressed women, the authors reject conjoint marital therapy as generally impracticable, and instead argue for the further refinement of individual psychotherapy.

Mayo (1979) examined the impact of successful treatment with lithium carbonate on the marriages of 12 patients with manic-depressive psychosis. She suggested: "Some therapists have assumed that if the illness can be cured, the marriage will be fine. Frequently the opposite is true . . . revealing in bas-relief a marriage that is faulty in its own right. More importantly it becomes clear that the marriage was 'sick' from its inception." She goes on to point out that individual psychotherapy with such patients yields poor long-term results. Conjoint marital therapy, while difficult, is often more effective, enabling the spouse to ". . . assume more responsibility for his/her own behavior that may unwittingly trigger a chain of events, which leads to exacerbation of symptoms in the patient."

Bastani and Kentsmith (1980) described the spouses and marital interaction in three cases of sexual deviance in males. They suggest that ". . . these women derived some psychological gain through the deviant acts of their husbands . . . The wife is recognized as an integral part of the dynamic systems involving the man, and as such, the necessity for her participation in the treatment is recognized. By encouraging change in the wives, a measure of change would be induced in their husbands."

In a two year follow-up of treatment outcome in 58 married male alcoholics, Rae (1972) found that only 20 percent of patients with poor marriages remained free of alcoholism, whereas 75 percent of patients with good marriages remained predominantly sober. Schaffer and Tyler (1979) found that wives' coping styles were significantly related to their alcoholic husbands' drinking behavior. Wives who directly confronted their husbands' drinking within a relatively safe marital atmosphere appeared to enhance treatment outcome; wives who withdrew or disengaged from their husbands or who took action against their husbands per se, rather than against their drinking, appeared to minimize the likelihood of successful treatment outcome for their husbands.

Much anticipated marital discord has occurred after intestinal bypass surgery for massive obesity. Marshall and Neill (1977) found that nine out of 10 female patients regarded their marriages as unsatisfactory before bypass surgery, and uniformly described their husbands as inadequate, weak, docile and clinging. Nine patients reported increased sexual interest after weight loss, and anxiety and jealously were prominent in their spouses' reactions to this. Spouses often attempted to stop the patients from going out and meeting other people, and this resulted in increased marital strife. Two spouses became actively homosexual and two impotent in the face of their wives' increased sexual demands. The authors conclude that the obesity had a marked stabilizing effect on the marriage, protecting against fears of abandonment in particular. This in turn stabilized the obesity.

MARITAL HOMEOSTASIS: THE RATIONALE FOR SPOUSE-AIDED THERAPY

Haley (1963) has suggested that ". . . most patients with symptoms tend to minimize their marital difficulties, in fact the symptom is apparently used to deny marital problems." While this may be true in some of the studies outlined above, it is clear that many patients with persistent psychological disorders openly admit to high levels of marital dissatisfaction. Often, however, the patient's symptoms are blamed for this, particularly by the spouse. This helps explain why it may often be difficult to engage spouses in a conjoint marital approach to the therapy of persisting psychological disorders, although few clinicians can have had as little success as Forrest (1969), discussing phobic patients: "Insight derived from family therapy ought to be helpful in changing these patterns, but in only one case out of 18 . . . has it been possible to get the husband and wife to come together regularly."

The concept of marital homeostasis implies that the spouse of a person with persisting psychological disability will often resist improvement in that disability because it is likely to result in a deterioration in their own psychological adjustment. This helps to explain both the persistence of disabling psychological disorder in many married psychiatric patients, and the observed reluctance of their spouses to become involved in the patient's therapy. The following are some themes, based mainly on personal observation, in support of this viewpoint:

1. Protection Against Fears of Abandonment

In agoraphobia, it is not uncommon for female patients to say "If my agoraphobia allowed it, I would leave my husband." Perhaps less commonly, husbands state they would leave the patient if their conscience allowed it, but instead they feel compelled to remain and look after the patient. In such instances, the symptoms clearly have a stabilizing effect on the marriage, protecting both partners against fears of abandonment. However, the patient is the most "trapped" in the marriage since both she and her husband believe that she could not manage alone. The husband believes that it is only his sense of duty which keeps him in the marriage, and that he would otherwise be able to find a more suitable partner. However, he is free to behave towards his wife in ways which might not be acceptable to her if she did not feel "trapped" in the marriage. Hence, the husband may have the most to lose through successful therapy for his agoraphobic wife, whose improvement may reveal that, should the marriage end, it is the husband who would have the greatest problems of readjustment. Similar themes have been observed in the marriages of massively obese people, in manic-depressive patients, and in patients with severe chronic obsessive-compulsive disorders.

2. Spouse's Denial of Personal Problems

Marriage to a person with a severe persisting psychological disorder may protect the spouse from examining his or her own personal problems. For example, chronically depressed, agoraphobic, or massively obese patients often avoid social activities. If the spouse has social anxieties or phobias, these are obscured by the patient's psychological disorder, which is blamed entirely for the couple's failure to socialize. Similarly, a spouse's sexual problems may be obscured by the disinclination to shared sexual activity generated by chronic psychological symptoms and related marital conflict. One's dependency problems, in particular, may be disguised by marriage to someone with equal or greater problems of dependency.

3. Spouse's Projection and Denial of Unwanted Feelings and Impulses

Persisting psychological symptoms often provide a focus for the spouse's projection of hostility. Unwanted aggressive impulses and feelings, instead of being projected directly onto the patient, are displaced onto the symptoms. This lessens overt marital conflict, but consolidates the symptoms as the main focus of marital dissatisfaction. Such a mechanism may be unusually prominent where the spouse has had an unresolved or abnormal response to bereavement. Here, feelings of anger, frustration, guilt and anxiety are displaced from the original loss onto the patient's symptoms. While this may help protect the spouse from the pain of loss, it prevents grief resolution. Unwanted sexual feelings may be projected onto the spouse, as in morbid jealousy. The author has reported (Hafner, 1979) several cases of agoraphobic women married to morbidly jealous men. The wives' agoraphobia, which kept them virtually housebound, protected their husbands from an irrational belief in their wives' unfaithfulness. On the wives' recovery, greatly increased marital conflict occurred in relation to their husbands' accusations and suspicions of the wives' infidelity. Increased marital conflict led to partial relapse of the agoraphobia in some wives, and one wife said "you can't have an affair if you're agoraphobic."

4. Direct Enhancement of Spouse's Self-esteem

The idea of helping or caring for a weak or disabled person allows the spouse of a chronically psychologically disabled patient to feel valued, wanted, worthwhile and good. Marriage to a dependent, passive person may generate feelings of relative strength and competence. In contrast to the patient's symptom-related indecisiveness, weakness, and inadequacy, the spouse often feels strong, assertive, masterful and capable. Where spouses are dissatisfied with their work or domestic roles, the patient's illness may allow a measure of role-reversal. For example, the husband of an agoraphobic woman may enhance his self-esteem by fulfilling all domestic requirements outside the home; the wife of an unemployed chronic alcoholic may welcome the opportunity of being the family's breadwinner.

5. Iatrogenic Contributions

Many patients with persisting psychological disorders have had contact with a range of mental health workers. It is common for such patients to misrepresent aspects of therapy. For example, a patient who is resentful of his or her spouse may misrepresent the therapist as having criticized the spouse, or as having recommended a course of action to which the spouse is opposed. Since the spouse is generally excluded from individual therapy, the therapist cannot identify or counter such manipulations, but instead creates a framework for them.

Patients not uncommonly idealize their therapists. If this is communicated to the spouse, then the spouse may despair of ever matching the therapist's capacity to meet the patient's needs. This may result in a protective withdrawal from any attempt to help the patient. Where patients experience idealized or sexual fantasies about the therapist, they may themselves be ambivalent about conjoint therapy, particularly if it seems likely to expose any of their previous misrepresentations of the therapist. They may therefore deter their spouses from conjoint therapy, but without mentioning this to the therapist.

Marital homeostasis is a term which attempts to capture the essence of some of the rich, subtle and complex interpersonal processes outlined above. Just as Jackson and Yalom (1965) described ". . . strong forces operating in the family to keep the patient sick" as part of their concept of family homeostasis, so does the concept of marital homeostasis rely on similar events occurring within the marital dyad.

THE PROCESS OF SPOUSE-AIDED THERAPY

The process of Spouse-aided Therapy is designed to facilitate the constructive involvement of the patient's spouse in goal-orientated, time-limited, out-patient therapy. It is outlined as follows.

1. The Preliminary Invitation

A direct, personal invitation to the spouse by letter or telephone is essential, outlining reasons for the invitation and the aims of therapy. It is helpful to point out that Spouse-aided Therapy is not a marriage therapy but an opportunity for the spouse to become constructively involved in the patient's therapy as an agent of change or co-therapist. This emphasis on the spouse's active role in partnership with the therapist allows the patient's symptoms to be preserved initially as the main focus of therapy, and protects the spouse from fears of criticism and exposure.

2. The Interview with the Spouse

It is essential to interview the patient's spouse alone. The objects of the interview are: to enable the spouse to freely give his or her account of the patient's disorder, to make suggestions, and to ask questions; to give the spouse an opportunity to discuss any personal problems and what help, if any, is required in relation to these; to assess the spouse in terms of psychological development, general adjustment and psychopathology; to elucidate any obstacles to Spouse-aided Therapy such as a lack of commitment to the marriage or extramarital liaisons which are not to be revealed to the patient; and to initiate a relationship between therapist and spouse based on mutual honesty and trust, and within which the therapist demonstrates a personal commitment to the spouse as well as to the patient.

3. Establishing Therapy Goals and Duration

This is carried out in a conjoint setting. Therapy goals may pertain to the spouse, the patient, or to their marriage. The therapist and the couple must arrive at a concensus concerning the major treatment goals, and this will usually require compromise. Once treatment goals are agreed upon, the duration of therapy is discussed. Time-limited therapy to a maximum of 15 one hour sessions at weekly intervals seems appropriate to the great majority of disorders. It may occasionally be necessary for further therapy to be conducted on an individual basis with either or both partners. If therapy goals cannot be established, then Spouse-aided Therapy cannot proceed.

4. Achieving Treatment Goals

Problems and obstacles in the achievement of treatment goals are inevitable. Dealing with these is central to Spouse-aided Therapy, since it creates the opportunity for the focus of therapy to shift from the patient's symptoms to the marriage relationship. Examination of the couple's attempts at joint problem-solving activities invariably exposes any non-constructive or undermining behavior and attitudes in the spouse. However, any related discussion or confrontation can be safely undertaken by the therapist within the context of his or her developing relationship with the spouse. Similarly, any examination of previously denied marital problems can be addressed within the therapy triad. The spouse is more likely to be able to acknowledge his or her own contribution to the patient's persisting psychological disability within a supportive, warm, non-threatening relationship with the therapist. Even more important, the spouse will feel relatively secure about examining and resolving any personal inadequacies or psychological problems which underlie his or her contribution to the patient's continuing disability.

CONCLUSION

Spouse-aided Therapy as outlined above has been used successfully in the treatment of chronic anxiety disorders (Hafner, 1981) but remains to be systematically evaluated across a range of psychiatric disorders. A pilot study has shown that it is an acceptable and effective mode of intervention in recurrent depression, manic-depressive psychosis and anxiety disorders, whether therapy is conducted by psychiatrists, social workers or psychiatric nurses. Indeed, there is evidence that Spouse-aided Therapy may be a particularly appropriate framework within which to allow psychiatric nurses to make a skilled psychotherapeutic contribution to overall treatment in many cases. A full-scale project is now underway at Flinders Medical Centre, South Australia, comparing individual psychotherapy with Spouse-aided Therapy in persisting psychological disorders. Whatever the outcome of current evaluations of Spouse-aided Therapy, there is clearly a need for the development of better therapy techniques to help the many married people in our society with chronic psychological disorders. It is likely that Spouse-aided Therapy will emerge as just one of many possible strategies which aim to mobilize and make full use of therapeutic resources within marriage. Family therapy has such an aim in the context of entire families, and family therapists naturally believe in the efficacy of their approach. However, systematic controlled evaluations of family therapy are methodologically of enormous complexity, which helps explain why so few methodologically adequate studies have been conducted (Humphreys, 1980). Spouse-aided Therapy, by focusing on marital interaction rather than on more complex interactions within whole families, allows controlled evaluation more readily. This may yield sufficiently unequivocal evidence for its success or failure in specific instances to persuade more mental health workers to adopt a marital approach to therapy where appropriate. This should generalize to a greater awareness of the value of understanding and treating psychological disorders in a marital or family context.

SUMMARY

The concept of marital homeostasis is introduced to help explain the persistence of a psychological disability in many married psychiatric patients. A main feature of marital homeostasis is the need of the ostensibly healthy marriage partner to preserve psychological disability in the designated patient in order to protect his or her own psychological adjustment. Spouse-aided Therapy is a goal-oriented, time-limited approach designed to influence marital homeostasis in a way which allows the ostensibly healthy marriage partner to acknowledge and modify his or her contribution to the patient's persisting disability. This facilitates changes in marital interaction which allow symptomatic improvement in the patient. Spouse-aided Therapy can be effectively conducted by a range of mental health workers, including psychiatric nurses, but its efficacy across a range of persisting psychological disorders remains to be evaluated.

REFERENCES

Bastani, J.B. & Kentsmith, D.K. Psychotherapy with wives of sexual deviants. *American Journal of Psychotherapy*, 1980,*34*, 20-25.

Forrest, A.D. Manifestations of "hysteria": Phobic patients and hospital recidivists. *British Journal of Medical Psychology*, 1969, *42*, 263-270.

Goodstein, R.K. & Swift, K. Psychotherapy with phobic patients: The marriage relationship as the source of symptoms and focus of treatment. *American Journal of Psychotherapy*, 1977, *31*, 285-292.

Hafner, R.J. The husbands of agoraphobic women and their influence on treatment outcome. *British Journal of Psychiatry*, 1977, *131*, 289-294.

Hafner, R.J. Agoraphobic women married to abnormally jealous men. *British Journal of Medical Psychology*, 1979, *52*, 99-104.

Hafner, R.J. The marital context of the agoraphobic syndrome. In D. Chambless & A. Goldstein (Eds.), *The Agoraphobic Syndrome*. New York: Wiley, 1981.

Haley, J. Marriage therapy. *Archives of General Psychiatry*, 1963, *8*, 213-234.

Hand, I. & Lamontagne, Y. The exacerbation of interpersonal problems after rapid phobia removal. *Psychotherapy: Theory, Research and Practice*, 1976, *13*, 405-411.

Humphreys, J. Family therapy—Review of outcome research. *Australian Journal of Family Therapy*, 1980, *1*, 116-120.

Jackson, D.D. The question of family homeostasis. *Psychiatric Quarterly Supplement*, 1957, *31*, 379-390.

Jackson, D.D. & Yalom, I. Conjoint family therapy as an aid to intensive psychotherapy. In A. Burton (Ed.), *Modern Psychotherapeutic Practice: Innovations in Technique*. California: Science and Behavior Books, 1965.

Marshall, J.R. & Neill, J. The removal of a psychosomatic symptom: Effects on the marriage. *Family Process*, 1977, *16*, 273-280.

Mayo, J.A. Marital therapy with manic depressive patients treated with lithium. *Comprehensive Psychiatry*, 1979, *20*, 419-426.

Milton, F. & Hafner, R.J. The outcome of behavior therapy for agoraphobia in relation to marital adjustment. *Archives of General Psychiatry*, 1979, *36*, 807-811.

Rae, J.B. The influence of wives on the treatment outcome of alcoholics. *British Journal of Psychiatry*, 1972, *120*, 601-613.

Rounsaville, B.J., Weisman, M.M., Prusoff, B.A., et al. Process of psychotherapy among depressed women with marital disputes. *American Journal of Orthopsychiatry*, 1979, *49*, 505-510.

Schaffer, J.B. & Tyler, J.D., Degree of sobriety in male alcoholics and coping styles used by their wives. *British Journal of Psychiatry*, 1979, *135*, 431-437.

Sims, A. Factors predictive of outcome in neurosis. *British Journal of Psychiatry*, 1975, *127*, 54-62.

Weissman, M.H. & Klerman, G.L. The chronic depressive in the community: Unrecognized and poorly treated. *Comprehensive Psychiatry*, 1977, *18*, 523-532.

Editor's Commentary: Frequent Couple Interaction Patterns

This short chapter by Hafner makes an excellent companion piece to Chapter 22 by Holm. His description of couples in Australia in which the wife is agoraphobic is extremely similar to that given by Holm of such couples in Norway. It is exactly these universal aspects of syndrome and symptom that make it possible for us to now speak in terms of an international family of family therapists and to conduct workshops which are pertinent in countries other than our own.

Hafner here adds to the growing body of frequently encountered dyadic pairings—like the rejection-intrusion couple described by Napier (1978) and the depressive dyad discussed by Rubinstein and Timmins (1978). He looks at such factors as dominance and submission and such reciprocal roles as caretaker and patient.

Spouse-aided Therapy is an innovative approach to engaging the seemingly healthier spouse as an ally and quasi-co-therapist, thereby harnessing his/her strength in the service of the couple, rather than alienating him/her by appearing in a more adversarial or pedantic role. It certainly appears a viable way to enlist the participation of the peripheral spouse and to move toward improvement in the identified patient's functioning, as well as in the marital relationship.

REFERENCES

Napier, A.Y. The rejection-intrusion pattern: A central family dynamic. *Journal of Marriage and Family Counseling*, January 1978, *4*, (1), 5-12.

Rubinstein, D. & Timmins, J.F. Depression dyadic and triadic relationship. *Journal of Marriage and Family Counseling*, January 1978, *4*, (1), 13-24.

Part V

Training and a Glimpse at the Future

Chapter 25

Bad Therapy—
A Way of Learning

By Moshe Lang

This paper describes a new training technique. The therapist, with a role-playing family, is instructed to do "bad therapy"—to make the family worse. Usually the "patients" and observers regard the "bad therapy" as beneficial—in fact, better than before. Several examples are given and a short discussion follows.

> *"When I am good I am very very good,*
> *But when I am bad I am better."*
>
> Mae West

A well-known Israeli poet sat in a popular cafe on a Tel-Aviv boulevard talking of this and that. The conversation turned to writing poetry and the ability of the public to discriminate the good from the bad. As a result, a bet was made that the poet could write a nonsensical and valueless poem that would become very popular. To everyone's surprise he was a winner. Not only was the poem extremely popular and its

This article was originally published in the *Australian Journal of Family Therapy, 1,* (3), 102-109. This chapter is a revised and updated version.

Moshe Lang, M.A., is Director, Williams Road Family Therapy Centre, Windosr, Victoria, Australia.

The author would like to thank the following people for their contributions and advice—Barbara Burge, Peter McCallum, Shirley Shiff, Ian Thomas, Fay Yule, Aija Wilson. Special thanks to Brian Stagoll for his careful editing and scholarly suggestions.

nonsensical quality unchallenged, but it was regarded as high quality poetry.

Something very similar happened in Australia in the 1940s when two young poets, in setting out to prove the local critics incompetent, wrote poems attributed to an unknown (and nonexistent) poet named "Ern Malley." The poems, to the writers' delight, were enthusiastically praised by the critics. The poets then proceeded to disclose that they had written these poems as a poetical hoax. In their own words "the writings of Ern Malley are utterly devoid of literary merit as poetry." However, the critics and most of the interested public still insisted the poetry was of high quality and so it was acclaimed. In one critic's view "they wrote poetry in spite of themselves." The poems provoked a great Australian debate on the value of poetry in general, these poems in particular, and the role of the critic (Harris, 1961; Jeffares, 1964). Apart from these being good stories to tell, they are worth quoting as they demonstrate the major theme of this paper.

The license to be bad, provocative or devious may release some unsuspected creative processes. Further, such permission has great potential for stimulating new ideas and challenging some of the customary assumptions and habitual ways of thinking and working.

While supervising a therapist whose treatment with a family seemed to be stuck, I suggested that she set up a role-play with her colleagues in the supervision group. Soon after the role-play started it became apparent that the therapist was stuck in just the same way that she had described herself with the real family. She seemed repetitive and overcautious. I stopped the role-play and consulted with her and the rest of the group as to how to improve her therapy. A series of suggestions was made and she returned to the role-play family. Some improvement was noticed, but clearly not enough to bring about a positive outcome. I was still struck by how careful she was and how hard she was trying to be a good therapist.

Spontaneously, I decided to perform a crazy experiment. I stopped the role-play, invited her back to the observing group and proposed that she was trying too hard to do good therapy. I proceeded to ask her, "What would you do if you wanted to do bad therapy, that is, try to make the family worse rather than better?" Her first response was "I'd go back and tell mother she's a terrible pain, a bitch and a nag." So I asked, "Why haven't you done so?" She replied, "She couldn't take it." I asked, "Will she get worse?" "Yes," she said. I said, "This is the kind of intervention we are looking for." With the help of the group we continued to build a list of "bad" interventions that could be guaranteed to produce "harmful" results.

I then asked the therapist to go back and do "bad therapy" on her unknowing and unsuspecting family. A lively and gripping human drama then proceeded to unfold.

The mother, to the therapist's great astonishment, was delighted to give back as good as she got, revealing a punch hitherto unsuspected. Father, who had been told by the therapist that she felt utter contempt for his passivity and withdrawal, responded by revealing his own distress and feeling of exclusion from his family, and pointed out that he experienced his passivity not as a choice, but as a role forced on him, one which he found very distressing.

During the deroling[1] (Churven, 1977) and subsequent discussion, the group members all agreed that when the therapist was "bad" she was very, very good—in fact, she was better. The discussion in the group was most energetic and lively and some fundamental questions about the basic assumptions governing therapy were raised. The issue of what constituted good or bad therapy, both for this particular family and in general, was brought into focus with heightened urgency and vividness and from a new perspective.

I am reminded of a story of a famous general who received a communique from headquarters which said "you are outnumbered, outgunned and outflanked and no help will be forthcoming. What will you do?" He replied "Attack of course." The major thesis is not that "attack" is always better than "defense" or that "bad" is better than "good" therapy, or that "opposite" behavior for a stuck therapist is better than his "current" behavior, but rather that a good general should always be aware of his position and of the various possibilities of attack as well as defense. In order to properly appreciate the strategic issues involved in defense, he would be well advised to consider ways of attack. To appreciate where one is, it may be valuable to shift position and look back at where you were as the therapist. In order to evaluate your behavior, you may well be advised to behave differently and to closely monitor the responses your new behavior elicits and the nature of the feedback you get.

The story of the famous general reminds me of the infamous one. He was taken prisoner along with his brigade without putting up any resistance. When asked why he surrendered without firing a shot, he replied, "I did not want to give away my position!"

Watching a number of therapists at work I am often struck by their fear of giving away their position; they appear to be seriously inhibited by the importance they attach to gaining acceptance by the family, apparently at all costs. Others appear too deeply preoccupied with the scientific reliability and validity of their observations and inferences, while some seem more concerned with the maintenance of their superior professional role (cf. Haley, 1979; Whitaker, 1976).

Experimenting with "bad therapy" as a teaching technique for a few years has proven very useful in demonstrating to trainees that such superficial considerations must give way to much more important and fundamental issues. If you find that what you believe to be good and what you have been doing for years is found by both "role-playing patients" and colleagues to be inferior in its effectiveness to that which you believe to be "bad," then you are inevitably forced into some fundamental questioning of the nature of therapy and your own therapeutic endeavors. Furthermore, if in fact your serious attempts to be harmful and to make people worse fail, then you can no longer assume that you really know the score.

On a number of occasions I have used the "bad therapy" technique in ongoing training and/or supervision groups. This technique seems to have had long-term effects on how a particular therapist conducts therapy. This is illustrated in the following case.

CASE 1

Flo, a very experienced social worker, sent the following report of her work with a family before and then after the experience of "bad therapy."

The family consisted of the mother, a nurse and perfectionist, who came from a disturbed family background. She was seen as "mad" or borderline by herself and the many helping professionals who had been in continuous contact with the family over a number of years. I was afraid of "pushing her over the edge" if I went too far. Father was a barman who worked long hours and in the evenings. The oldest child, Bill, was aged 15, followed by Fred, aged 13—the identified patient. Fred had suffered head injuries following a motor car accident and was epileptic. He lived in a hostel during the week and came home on weekends. A younger boy, John, aged 11, had been before the court for shoplifting and was ordered to see a psychiatrist. Two younger girls completed the family. My contact had been restricted to long telephone calls with the mother in which she ventilated her negative feelings about the hostel. I responded by patient listening. When the mother decided to discontinue treatment with the psychiatrist who had been seeing her and her two younger sons for six months, I was at a loss to know what to do. I had been counting on this psychiatrist to sort out the family problems.

I decided to present the problem of what to do next to the supervision group. A role-play of the family was set up and, as instructed, I tried hard to make the role-playing mother worse, but was a dismal failure. I was totally unable to produce the negative response I had confidently expected of this "fragile" mother. This left me confused and unable to understand what had happened, and I rationalized the situation by saying to myself that "the role-playing mother didn't respond as the real one would have." After this "bad therapy" experience came the recognition that I was terrified of triggering a response in mother that I couldn't handle, followed by the realization that I wasn't handling the situation anyway.

Finally, I determined to adopt a different role. When the mother next contacted me I refused to talk on the telphone, said I doubted the seriousness of her desire to bring about some change in her situation, and refused further contact unless both she and her husband were involved. This resulted in the father telephoning to ask that I visit them to discuss their difficulties in coping with Fred. Subsequently there were three joint interviews. My perception is that I said and did little. Mother and father talked to each other as if they had never discussed their difficulties before. They maintained that Fred was a handicap to the whole family and that permanent full-time placement was the only solution. I gave the parents the responsibility for finding such a place. They went together to see an institution which they found "quite excellent but not for Fred." They talked about the implications for the whole family if Fred was placed, and then involved the other children in the discussion of what was best for Fred. The decision was made for him to return to live at home. The family then discussed what would have to happen for his return to be a success. It was decided, for example, that his father would need to spend more time at home and with his sons, and become more explicit in his support of his wife. The mother would need to be more explicit in making her needs known, as well as recognizing that Fred's return home could substantially reduce the settlement he would receive in a pending court case. The parents were given the responsibility for planning his return home and arranging the school transfer. They were able to follow through and Fred returned home without difficulty.

I agree with Flo that the change in her therapeutic style from a passive and accepting listener to an active and effective change agent, who successfully handed back responsibility to the family, can be seen as being triggered by the "bad therapy" experience.

One recent variation of the "bad therapy" exercise has been based on splitting the group into two. While the therapist and some observers are plotting (planning) "bad therapy" in one room, the role-playing family and other observers are (in another room) discussing what have been the shortcomings of the therapy to date and how it can be improved.

The fascinating outcome which occurs almost universally is that when the therapist comes back and does the "bad" therapy, both the role-play family and the observers see him/her as carrying out the plan they had proposed for "good" therapy.

CASE 2

A therapist had been seeing a 15-year-old girl for depression for a couple of months in individual therapy. In the course of treatment she discovered that her patient was using (abusing) sedatives and tranquilizers which had been prescribed for her parents without their knowledge. The danger was that she also talked at times of feeling trapped and of the hopelessness of her current life, and how sometimes she felt suicidal. The therapist struggled with whether or not to tell the parents this, knowing that if she did she would probably lose the girl from therapy. When instructed to plan "bad therapy" in supervision, in conjunction with some of the observers, she decided to prescribe the drugs to the "patient" with the firm expectation that with a free supply of medication she would surely take an overdose. In the meantime the role-playing "patient" and her observers in the other room decided that in order to improve therapy and arrive at a positive outcome, the therapist should do exactly the same, that is, to prescribe medication for the girl, because this would put the therapist in charge of the situation and make the "patient" responsible for her own life, legitimating her independence from her parents.

CASE 3

A very experienced and competent therapist reported to the supervision group about her work with a family which consisted of a woman, her peripheral alcoholic husband and her two uncontrollable children.

The group thought the mother was overprotective and that mother and son were caught up in a vicious circle in which her inappropriate and ineffectual attempts at controlling him led to more unmanageable behavior on his part.

The therapist was sucked into this system and her attitude and behavior towards the mother paralleled mother's attitude towards her own children, that is, the therapist was overprotective and overcontrolling, specifically protecting mother from her own feeling of possibly being a bad mother.

The group was divided into two and the therapist and some observers were asked to decide on ways of making the family worse and how this could be achieved. They decided that as the mother was very concerned about the possibility that she was a "bad mother," this could be worked on to a point where she could be totally devastated by her badness. To achieve this it was decided that the therapist was to confront mother with a barrage of her shortcomings, failings, and inadequacies regarding her husband, her children, and her homemaking until she could take it no longer.

Simultaneously, in the other room the role-play family and their observers agreed that in order for therapy to improve the therapist needed to become firmer, clearer, and more confronting.

After the therapy exercise, the role-play patients were asked who they thought was the better therapist—the one before or the one after the break. They all agreed that the latter was a much better therapist, and in fact they saw her carrying out their plan for improving therapy. They were amazed and could not believe that in fact she was instructed to make the mother worse.

The person who role played the mother reported later:

> The first experience left me fairly unmoved. I began to feel there was no solution to my problem, and that I was somehow alone and responsible for a child I could not control.
>
> The "bad" therapy was at least challenging. She (the therapist) seemed "quite crazy"—she didn't seem to think it mattered that the child was out of control—and then suggested that "perhaps I

was too keen on controlling him anyway, instead of helping him to establish his own limits." She called me a "bad mother"—that surprised me but it was a challenge. I began to see that I could look at being a bad mother; it was suddenly "out there" and not inside me. "Bad mother" was also beginning to be all the things that I had thought of as being a "good mother"—like controlling the children and keeping them clean. I would not go as far as she seemed to think I should, but she was giving me permission to let go a bit. She shocked me into thinking I could leave my anxiety and self-pity behind and be myself, and allow my children to be themselves.

The therapist made it clear she hated my cringing self-pity and said so. She was straightforward and honest, and that both shocked and impressed me. She issued a challenge—I had a choice of rising to meet it or to run away from it. This made me express the anger I had felt for a long time. I saw that my obsession for control was unnecessary and producing bad results. In this I was a "bad" mother. She gave me permission to hand some of my responsibility over to her (cf. Weakland, 1977).

The therapist reported that she was unable to fully carry out the agreed plan. She experienced strong inhibition against attacking the mother as viciously as was decided. This is a very common theme reported by most therapists, that is, a failure to be as confronting and destructive as intended. However, from her perspective she attacked the mother more than ever before and she was totally amazed that the mother did not collapse, and in fact had found this experience helpful.

CASES 4 AND 5

My own first experience of "bad therapy" occurred many years ago. I was working with Tom, a 15-year-old who was referred to the clinic because of delinquent behavior. At that stage in my professional life I was a committed but misinformed Rogerian (e.g. Rogers, 1951; 1961). One day Tom confessed to me that the night before he broke into a school and stole some tape recorders. Without thinking, and to my total horror, I heard myself say, "You stupid idiot—what did you do that for?" Then I was taken aback, feeling I had forever destroyed my chances of doing any good. I had violated the most important principle in therapy—I had broken the spell of acceptance, and in my mind's eye I saw Rogers looking down at me with strong disapproval. However, while I was feeling totally devastated by my mistake, I was surprised to hear Tom say, "You know what—you are damn right." I was amazed to hear him approving of my "bad intervention." This led to a total change in our relationship and considerable change in my ideas of therapy.

Years later, when I was already a family therapist, I had another experience which I believe is worth reporting. A professional colleague phoned and asked if I would agree to see her and her family in therapy. I worked with them for a while and helped them to resolve a number of issues, primarily those to do with her sister. I then terminated with the family. Months later she called me one morning very distressed and told me that her mother had just attempted suicide. Having established that mother was physically OK, I arranged for them to come and see me the following day.

When I arrived at the waiting room I saw Mrs. Blackman. She looked better than I had ever seen her before and I was about to say to her "suicide becomes you." Taken aback by the absolute inappropriateness and the lack of tact of this comment, I naturally refrained.

Months later when many of the family issues were resolved I told the family and Mrs. Blackman what I had been tempted to say. She said, "I wish you had. It has been many years now that I have wanted people to be much more open with me, and maybe that would have been just the sort of thing I needed."

For me one of the important benefits of the "bad therapy" technique has been the increased interest with which I listen to my own urges to make "bad interventions," and also the greater care with which I observe my patients' responses to my "mistakes." I believe this is a common experience among therapists who have participated in "bad therapy" role-play.

There seems to be a general consensus among patients and observers that the therapist doing "bad therapy":

1. Is in control of the therapy, but at the same time hands back responsibility to the patients for their own lives.
2. Communicates more directly and clearly.
3. Relates to the patient as if the latter is strong and capable rather than weak and ineffectual.

In return the patients report that they:

1. Experience an increase in their own strength and assertiveness.
2. Feel freer to express their feelings.
3. Feel more hopeful.

"Bad therapy" doesn't occur only in role-play. I believe it happens daily, as a very important event in the work of most therapists. Unfortunately, this importance often is not recognized.

One of the most interesting experiences that I have in meeting and discussing work with therapists is that of encouraging them to tell me about the "bad interventions" they make from time to time that work for them, interventions which they are usually too embarrassed or ashamed to admit publicly. Once they begin, a wealth of stories gush out.

DISCUSSION

The purpose of this paper has been to describe an interesting and challenging experience, and to recommend the use of this technique to other therapists so that they may hopefully have similar experiences.

Further, it is written with the hope of encouraging the freer use of different supervisory and teaching methods. Role-playing is particularly useful here. To take full advantage of it we can be, and perhaps should be, much more daring and risk-taking than can possibly be allowed in a real life situation, as the risks are being taken with each other rather than with our patients. By now, the imaginative reader will be able to grasp the possibilities and extensions inherent in "bad therapy." Role-playing is a human situation which allows a unique opportunity for experimentation. Therefore, after trying "straight" therapy in role-play, therapists can be instructed to try a number of different approaches, including:

1. The exact opposite of what they have been doing to date.
2. Restricting themselves to "I" statements.
3. Positive relabeling.

My experience is that the practice of therapy with such constraints is highly instructive.

One of the reasons that I am attracted to family therapy/systems theory is that I see it as the most humane, kind and positive way of conceptualizing human suffering and individual symptomatology. Thus, it would be distressing to me if this paper were to be misconstrued as a recommendation for increased toughness or aggression towards patients. Rather, it provides an opportunity to examine the therapist's work without advocating any specific direction and helps the therapist to become aware of alternative approaches.

This paper does not intend to enter into a detailed theoretical explanation about why "bad therapy" seems to work, apart from raising a few possibilities. It may be that the benefit to therapists of this experience is in its "permission giving" quality. In "bad therapy" therapists are given instructions and opportunities to say and do things that they wish to, but never dare. The "bad therapy" role-play experience is often deeply reassuring to therapists who find that most of their worst fears are not realized. In fact, they find that both their patients and their relationships with them are much more resilient than they thought, and this gives them more courage in similar situations.

Perhaps it is useful on those occasions where the stuck therapist's previous behaviors have become part of the problem rather than its solution. In such a case the instruction for total reversal, that is, to do "bad therapy," clearly brings out how the therapist has contributed to the maintenance of the very problem he was trying to change. This theme is often highlighted and discussed at length after "bad therapy." It leads to much freer and more open discussion of the needs in the therapist that are met by the "maintenance of the problem," such as his need for approval and love by the patients and his need to keep the patients coming.

It may be that the specific message given to the therapist—to do "bad," to harm his patients, to make them worse—stands in direct contrast to the social context in which the therapist and his patient find themselves. Thus, the therapist is placed in a double-bind situation and the only way out of this predicament is through a second order solution—a creative leap forward to a new level of conceptual organization (Goding, 1979; Hoffman, 1979; Watzlawick, Beavin, & Jackson, 1967; Watzlawick, Weakland, & Fisch, 1974). Perhaps it is this new way of thinking and organizing the material that may account for the lasting beneficial effect reported by some therapists.

The discovery that "bad" therapy may be better than "good" forces therapists to look much more closely at outcome and effectiveness rather than method, and thus they may become more like experienced than beginning therapists (Haley, 1972).

It is important to note that, since Watzlawick et al. (1967) developed a coherent theory to explain the use of paradoxes, there have been an ever increasing number of publications describing a kind of therapy which appears irrational, noncommonsensical, or uncommon (e.g. Haley, 1973; Whitaker, 1975; Watzlawick et al., 1974). This has culminated in a new paradigm of family therapy (Selvini Palazzoli, Boscolo, Cecchin, & Prata, 1978). However, in spite of the centrality of this approach, to date it has been taught only by didactic, linear, direct, rational, and commonsensical methods (Haley, 1976; Weeks & L'Abate, 1979).

In a recent paper, my colleagues and I (Stagoll, Lang, & Goding, 1979) argued for the importance of the parallel process between training and therapy. The "bad therapy" technique can be seen as extending the principles and the flavor of this other type of therapy to training. Thus, the learning itself becomes indirect, crazy, unusual, as well as, and perhaps more importantly, experiential.

Paradoxical techniques in therapy should be used on resistive families and only when commonsensical and direct methods have failed (Haley, 1976, Rabkin, 1977, Selvini Palazzoli et al., 1978, Weeks & L'Abate, 1978, 1979). This again parallels my own position regarding "bad therapy"; it is potentially a very powerful teaching technique and as such should be used sparingly and only when a free and comfortable relationship exists between group leader and trainees. Further, my experience to date suggests it is clearly more beneficial for experienced therapists who are familiar with the direct approach than for beginning therapists.

Haley writes "to use the paradoxical approach, a therapist must develop skill and must practice. He also needs to be able to think about problems in a game-like or playful way even though he realizes that he is dealing with grim problems and real distress" (Haley, 1976, p. 71).

Others, like Whitaker (1975, 1976), emphasize the use of humor. Again "bad therapy" parallels this. It is a game, it is play, it is fun, at times unbelievably funny, but it is also very, very serious.

SUMMARY

My old uncle told me about this character who complained, "I've been boiling this egg for hours and it's still hard!" This is often a central issue in therapy. Therapists continue with an approach that fails to produce results. This paper describes a specific role-playing technique to help the therapist bring about changes in his way of thinking and working with the specific family in question, as well as in his general philosophy and practice of psychotherapy.

So, when next in a stuck siutation, try this "crazy" technique and you never know, you may, in the words of Mae West:

"Find yourself climbing the ladder of success
wrong by wrong"
or
"You may lose your reputation and never miss it."

REFERENCE NOTE

[1]Deroling is a procedure I always use at the end of a role-play to reduce the mental health risk to the role players, and also to enhance the didactic value to all the participants. The procedure I usually follow is:

a. Each role player is asked to stay in role and tell all other role players including the therapist everything that he has not been able to say before.
b. Each role player is asked to come out of role and as him/herself to tell all others anything they have not been able to say until this point.
c. The role players are then asked to join the larger group, making sure they sit away from each other. They are then asked how each felt playing his/her particular role and how the role-play character compared to him/herself.

The deroling procedure is conducted by someone other than the therapist.

REFERENCES

Churven, P. Role playing, deroling and reality. *Australian Journal of Social Work*, 1977, *30*, (4), 23-27.

Goding, G. Change and paradox in family therapy. *Australian Journal of Family Therapy*, 1979, *1*, (1), 9-15.

Haley, J. Beginning and experienced family therapists. In A. Ferber, M. Mendelsohn, & A. Napier (Eds), *The Book of Family Therapy*. New York: Science House, 1972.

Haley, J. *Uncommon Therapy*. New York: Ballantine Books, 1973.

Haley, J. *Problem-Solving Therapy*, San Francisco: Jossey-Bass, 1976.

Haley, J. Ideas that handicap therapy with young people. *International Journal of Family Therapy*, 1979, *1*, (1), 29-45.

Harris, M. *Ern Malley's Poems*. Melbourne: Lansdowne Press, 1961.

Hoffman, L. The simple bind and discontinuous change. *Australian Journal of Family Therapy*, 1979, *1*, (1), 16-25.

Jeffares, N. Ern Malley's poems. In G. Dutton (Ed.), *The Literature of Australia*. Melbourne: Pelican Press, 1964.

Rabkin, R. *Strategic Psychotherapy*, New York: Basic Books, 1977.

Rogers, C.R. *Client-Centered Therapy*. Boston: Houghton Mifflin, 1951.

Rogers, C.R. *On Becoming a Person*. Boston: Houghton Mifflin, 1961.

Selvini Palazzoli, M., Boscolo, L., Cecchin, G. & Prata, G. *Paradox and Counterparadox*, New York: Aronson, 1978.

Stagoll, B., Lang, M., & Goding, G.A., A model for family therapy training. *Australian Journal of Family Therapy*, 1979, *1*, (1), 35-42.

Watzlawick, P., Beavin, J.H., & Jackson, D.D. *Pragmatics of Human Communication*, New York: W.W. Norton, 1967.

Watzlawick, P., Weakland, J., & Fisch R. *Change: Principles of Problem Formation and Problem Resolution*. New York: W.W. Norton, 1974.

Weakland, J. OK—You've been a bad mother. In P. Papp, (Ed.), *Family Therapy: Full Length Case Studies*. New York: Gardner Press, 1977.

Weeks, G. & L'Abate, L. A bibliography of paradoxical methods in the psychotherapy of family systems. *Family Process*, 1978, *17*, (1), 95-98.

Weeks, G. & L'Abate, L. A compilation of paradoxical methods. *The American Journal of Family Therapy*, 1979, 7, (4), 61-76.

Whitaker, C. Psychotherapy of the absurd: With a special emphasis on the psychotherapy of aggression. *Family Process*, 1975, 14, (1), 1-16.

Whitaker, C., The hindrance of theory in clinical work. In P. Guerin, (Ed.), *Family Therapy: Theory and Practice*. New York: Gardner Press, 1976.

Editor's Commentary: When Being
Bad Is Really Being Good!

In this chapter Moshe Lang, an Australian, joins American therapists like Haley, Whitaker and Erickson, and Italian therapists like Selvini Palazzoli and her colleagues and Andolfi in the skillful use of paradox. However, apparently he also fashioned much that is innovative in using paradoxical injunctions in training and supervision, evolving this technique by trial and error experimentation quite independently.

As is usual in the history of ideas and inventions, several people in differents parts of the world, quite separately, seem to create a new way to solve a problem or fill a need. The current of scientific or professional thinking may be leading in a particular direction which is conducive to a discovery whose time has come. Innovative pioneers have the courage to risk departing from tradition to introduce something radically different in response to an externally apparent or internally felt gap.

In reading Lang's account of how he began training therapists to do "bad therapy," one can sense his frustration, born of finding that in some situations orthodox strategies did not work. Like Keith and Whitaker (1978), who imply they only resort to acting crazy and other absurd behaviors when the normal interventions are not fruitful, Lang also reaches toward the novel to circumvent getting stuck and jolts trainees and patients.

Lang's note on deroling or debriefing illuminates a process I also utilize. However, I have attended programs where leaders did not and participants were left in a state of acute anxiety. This caveat to derole by Lang merits attention.

I for one am greatful to Lang for sharing with this wider readership his delightfully engaging article and for his unusually clear explication of what he does, when, why and how he thinks it operates. Such clarity is a rarity in the ingenious sphere of the intuitive wizardry of paradox.

REFERENCE

Keith, D. & Whitaker, C. Struggling with the impotence impasse: Absurdity and acting. *Journal of Marriage and Family Counseling*, 1978, 4, (1), 69-78.

Chapter 26

Epilogue—
Crystal Ball Gazing

By Florence W. Kaslow

Chapter 1, *History of Family Therapy*, written in 1979, concludes with a section entitled The Fourth Decade: A Forward Look. Now, four years later, I believe the trends predicted there are still the most significant ones. Some bear further elucidation. Concern about licensure and/or certification of marital and family therapists is increasing, since third-party insurance payments and freedom of choice legislation usually only provide for reimbursement to licensed practitioners. During the current economic recession, competition for the therapeutic dollar is tightening and the battle lines between various disciplines are sharpening as that professional identification becomes increasingly tied to economic considerations. Efforts to influence legislators to enact laws favorable to the practice of marital and family therapy have also accelerated.

Organizationally there has been somewhat of a rapprochement between AAMFT and AFTA, with much duplication of membership —particularly at the leadership level. AFTA provides much more of a scientific forum; its membership remains small by design—still under 500. AAMFT continues to view itself as a professional organization geared to serving a large membership through its journal, newsletter, conferences and legislative activities. The Academy of Psychologists in Marital, Family and Sex Therapy has become more active and was instrumental in creating the American Board of Family Psychology which

463

awards a Diplomate in Family Psychology—the equivalent of board certification. This further attests to the concern for credentialing and the
likelihood that many will continue to press for acceptance of marriage
and family therapy as a distinct mental health specialty.

Additional evidence of this is the continued growth of family institutes
for training and treatment in many parts of this country and abroad. For
example, the past few years have witnessed the birth of the Southwest
Family Institute in Dallas, the Florida Couples and Family Institute in
West Palm Beach, the Wisconsin Family Institute in Madison, and the
Family Therapy Institute in Washington, D.C., among others. Each is
directed by one or several prominent people in the field and all appear
to be burgeoning. The "oldies and goodies" like The Ackerman Institute,
Philadelphia Child Guidance Clinic, Mental Research Institute, Boston
Family Institute and Chicago Family Institute continue to flourish and
to be led by outstanding individuals. Many clinicians are still seeking
training at the beginning, intermediate and advanced levels through
intern and extern programs operated by these institutes. The current
and future status of university and medical school based training programs seems less clear; in these larger institutions it is difficult to justify
funding for small programs and to tailor programs for seasoned practitioners seeking additional knowledge and skill.

Theoretically, the crystal ball suggests that the high priests and priest-
esses of paradox and epistemology will continue to be the darlings of
the cognizenti for a while longer and that their ideas will be rapidly
absorbed into most theoretical schemata. Ironically, it also reveals that
the garden variety of inpatient and outpatient families do not care about
the therapist's philosophic orientation but only about whether he or she
is skilled in reducing pain and conflict and helping the couple or family
cope and feel better and happier.

Increasingly we will deal more and more with one-parent families,
divorcing and divorced families and remarried families—in all their per-
mutations. Training programs will be including sessions on divorce and
remarriage therapy.

The internationalization reflected in this volume is multidetermined
and its spread inevitable and wondrous. Our international family of
family therapists will continue to grow, to feud, to exchange ideas and
visits, and to feel part of a hands-across-the-universe kinship, a tribal
network.

NAME INDEX

Lidz, T., 20, 232, 242n.
Liebman, R., 213, 225n., 246, 256n.
Lief, H.I., 188, 194n.
Lincoln, G., 18, 37n.
Linsenberg, M., 22, 36n.
Lloyd, J., 315, 317, 333n.
Loader, P., 148-69, 168, 169, 359
Loh, M., 315, 333n.
LoPiccolo, J., 417, 428n., 429
LoPiccolo, L., 417, 419, 426, 428n., 429,
    430
Luckman, T., 99, 100, 115n.
Luthman, S., 14, 36n.

Maasdorp, G.G., 362, 369n.
MacGregor, R., 346, 357n.
Madanes, C., 176, 183n., 184
Mahler, M., 8, 36n.
Malley, E., 448
Malone, T.P., 16, 37n.
Marks, I.M., 392, 413n.
Marshall, J.R., 434, 441n.
Maruyama, M., 81, 90n.
Maslach, C., 333, 333n.
Maslow, A.H., 197, 197n.
Mason, J., 117, 360-72, 370, 371
Masters, W., 417, 428n., 429
Maturana, H.R., 56, 60-65, 66n., 67, 68,
    175, 183n.
Mayo, J.A., 434, 441n.
McCubbin, H.I., 114, 115n.
McDermott, J.F., Jr., 259, 269n.
McElrath, D., 189, 194, 195n.
McFarland, D.J., 76, 90n.
Meer, F., 362, 364, 369n.
Mendelsohn, M., 17, 43, 47, 52n., 55,
    55n., 168, 169n.
Menghi, P., 122, 132n.
Menninger, K., 45, 53n.
Milman, L., 213, 225n., 246, 256n.
Milton, F., 433, 441n.
Minuchin, S., 18, 19, 27, 28, 36n., 37n.,
    71, 73, 90n., 156, 167n., 193, 194n.,
    213, 223, 224, 225n., 228, 243, 244n.,
    246, 248, 256n., 257, 330, 333n., 338,
    345, 357n.
Mitchell, P., 189, 194, 195n.
Modlin, H., 326, 333n.
Montalvo, B.G., Jr., 18, 27, 246, 256n.
Moraitis, S., 326, 333n.
Morrissey, M., 314, 334n.

Nader, R., 386
Nagy, I., 47

Napier, A.Y., 16, 37n., 43, 47, 52n., 55,
    55n., 168, 169n., 443, 443n.
Neill, J., 434, 441n.
Nichols, W.C., 33
Nicolo, A.M., 122, 132n.
Nims, J., 420, 428n.

Oliveri, M.E., 95-118, 97, 103-105, 115n.,
    117, 118
Olson, D.D., 104, 115n.
Olson, D.H., 28, 33, 37n., 187, 194, 195n.
Orfanidis, M., 17, 22
O'Shea, A.T., 271, 272n.
Osherson, S., 51, 53n.
Ostergaard, L., 233, 242n.

Papp, P., 17, 22
Parsons, T., 9, 10, 37n.
Patterson, G.R., 246, 247, 256n.
Paul, N., 20, 35n.
Phillips, V.A., 187, 194n.
Piperno, R., 121, 132n.
Pirandello, L., 119, 122, 123, 132n., 133
Pollack, S.L., 68, 168, 170-85, 184, 309,
    359
Prata, G., 58, 66n., 135-47, 172, 183n.,
    244, 244n., 458, 459n.
Proverbio, N., 299, 301, 307n.

Rabkin, R., 329, 334n., 458, 459n.
Rae, J.B., 434, 441n.
Rahe, R.H., 107, 115n.
Rakoff, V., 225, 225n.
Raskovsky, A., 233, 242n.
Raush, H.L., 89, 90n.
Ravnsborg, I.S., 275-92, 291, 310
Reddon, J.R., 187, 195n.
Reek, T., 211, 211n.
Reich, W., 133, 134n.
Reid, J.B., 246, 256n.
Reiss, D., 95-118, 96, 97, 99, 100, 102-105,
    115n., 116n., 117, 118
Reverby, S., 339, 357n.
Richmond, M., 10, 37n.
Riskin, J., 153, 167n.
Ritterman, M.K., 28, 37n.
Rogers, C.R., 299, 454, 459n.
Roman, M., 339, 357n.
Rosen, J., 17
Rosen, R.C., 426, 427n.
Rosenthal, R., 98, 116n.
Rosman, B.L., 18, 213, 225n., 244, 244n.,
    246, 256n.
Ross, J.J., 213, 225n.

SUBJECT INDEX